Football For Dumm...

BUSINESS AND
GENERAL
REFERENCE
BOOK SERIES
FROM IDG

W9-ACH-370

Sheet

A Common Player Lineup

The following figure shows the 4-3 defense (see Chapter 11) lined up against a strong-side-right offense (see Chapter 5). These lineups are common in the NFL as well as at other levels.

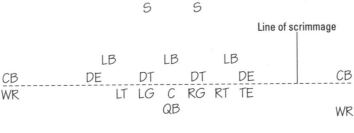

The offense:

- **QB = quarterback:** The leader of the team. He calls the plays in the huddle, yells the signals at the line of scrimmage, and then receives the ball from the center. Then he either hands off the ball to a running back, throws it to a receiver, or runs with the ball.

- **C = center:** The player who snaps the ball to the quarterback. He handles the ball on every play.

- **RB = running back:** A player who runs with the football. Running backs also are referred to as *tailbacks, halfbacks,* and *wingbacks.*

- **FB = fullback:** A player who is responsible for blocking for the running back and also for pass-blocking to protect the quarterback. Fullbacks are generally bigger than running backs, and are short-yardage runners.

- **WR = wide receiver:** A player who uses his speed and quickness to elude defenders and catch the football. Teams use as many as two to four wide receivers on every play.

- **TE = tight end:** A player who serves as a receiver and also a blocker. This player lines up beside the offensive tackle to the right or the left of the quarterback.

- **LG and RG = left guard and right guard:** The inner two members of the offensive line, whose job is to block for and protect the quarterback and ball carriers.

- **LT and RT = left tackle and right tackle:** The outer two members of the offensive line.

The defense:

- **DT = defensive tackle:** The inner two members of the defensive line, whose job is to maintain their position in order to stop a running play or to run through a gap in the offensive line to pressure the quarterback or disrupt the backfield formation.

- **DE = defensive end:** The outer two members of the defensive line. Generally, their job is to overcome offensive blocking and meet in the backfield, where they combine to tackle the quarterback or ball carrier. On running plays to the outside, their job is to force the ball carrier either out-of-bounds or toward (into) the pursuit of their defensive teammates.

- **LB = linebacker:** The players who line up behind the defensive linemen and generally are regarded as the team's best tacklers. Depending on the formation, most teams employ either three or four linebackers on every play. Linebackers often have the dual role of defending the run and the pass.

- **S = safety:** The players who line up the deepest in the secondary — the last line of defense. There are free safeties and strong safeties, and they must defend the deep pass and also the run.

- **C = cornerback:** The players who line up on the wide parts of the field, generally opposite the offensive receivers.

Football For Dummies®

Cheat Sheet

Football Lingo to Remember

down: A period of action that starts when the ball is put into play and ends when the ball is ruled dead (meaning that the play is completed). The offense gets four downs to advance the ball 10 yards. If it fails to do so, it must surrender the ball to the opponent, usually by punting on the fourth down.

end zone: A 10-yard-long area at both ends of the field — the promised land for a football player. You score a *touchdown* when you enter the end zone in control of the football. If you're tackled in your own end zone while in possession of the football, the other team gets a *safety*.

extra point: A kick, worth one point, that's typically attempted after every touchdown. The ball is placed on either the 2-yard line (NFL) or the 3-yard line (college and high school) and generally is kicked from inside the 10-yard line after being snapped to the holder. It must sail between the uprights and above the crossbar of the goalpost to be considered good. Also known as a *point after touchdown,* or *PAT.*

field goal: A kick, worth three points, that can be attempted from anywhere on the field but usually is attempted within 40 yards of the goalpost. Like an extra point, a kick must sail above the crossbar and between the uprights of the goalpost to be ruled good.

fumble: The act of losing possession of the ball while running with it or being tackled. Members of the offense and defense can recover a fumble. If the defense recovers the fumble, the fumble is called a *turnover.*

hash marks: The lines in the center of the field that signify 1 yard on the field. Before every play, the ball is spotted between the hash marks or on the hash marks, depending on where the ball carrier was tackled on the preceding play.

interception: A pass that's caught by a defensive player, ending the offense's possession of the ball.

kickoff: A free kick (the receiving team cannot make an attempt to block it) that puts the ball into play. A kickoff is used at the start of the first and third periods and after every touchdown and successful field goal.

punt: A kick made when a player drops the ball and kicks it while it falls toward his foot. A punt is usually made on fourth down when the offense must surrender possession of the ball to the defense because it could not advance 10 yards.

return: The act of receiving a kick or punt and running toward the opponent's goal line with the intent of scoring or gaining significant yardage.

sack: When a defensive player tackles the quarterback behind the line of scrimmage for a loss of yardage.

safety: A score, worth two points, that the defense earns by tackling an offensive player in possession of the ball in his own end zone.

snap: The action in which the ball is *hiked* (tossed between the legs) by the center to the quarterback, to the holder on a kick attempt, or to the punter. When the snap occurs, the ball is officially in play and action begins.

touchdown: A score, worth six points, that occurs when a player in possession of the ball crosses the plane of the opponent's goal line, or when a player catches the ball while in the opponent's end zone, or when a defensive player recovers a loose ball in the opponent's end zone.

...For Dummies: Bestselling Book Series for Beginners

Praise for Football For Dummies

"*Football For Dummies* is necessary reading for every fan — full of insights, strategies, and *me*. Howie put me on his all-time offensive team. Remember that this season when watching *FOX NFL Sunday*."
> — Terry Bradshaw, FOX NFL Commentator and
> Former NFL Quarterback

"Howie's book has got it all! He provides expert advice not just on the game but on how to keep both your body and mind trained on and off the field."
> — Jimmy Johnson, Head Coach and General
> Manager, Miami Dolphins

"Ever wondered why a gridiron is called a gridiron? Or why you get six points for a touchdown but only three for a field goal? Well, *Football For Dummies* has all the answers and more, so you'll never have to feel like a dummy for asking again."
> — Bill Cowher, Head Coach, Pittsburgh Steelers

"I had the fortune, or misfortune, of playing against Howie Long in 22 games during my career . . . and he was one of the most agile, hard-hitting linemen to play the game. Howie's passion and enthusiasm for football comes through on every page!"
> — John Elway, Quarterback, Denver Broncos

"Whether you're an armchair quarterback or a youth league coach or just someone who wants to learn more about the game, Howie Long has written the book for you! If you're going to buy one football book this year, it should be *Football For Dummies*!"
> — Norv Turner, Head Coach, Washington Redskins

"As a former NFL quarterback, I thought all linemen were dummies. But Howie Long proved me wrong time after time. His knowledge and insight into the game of football ring through loud and clear — just like the hits he delivered on the football field!"
> — Boomer Esiason, NFL Commentator and
> Former All-Star Quarterback

"With *Football For Dummies,* Howie once again demonstrates his impressive skill and knowledge of the game in a book that really breaks through the gridiron. A terrific reference for lifelong fans as well as for anyone looking for an easy and informative introduction to the game. Howie has assured me that the title is in no way a reference to his colleagues on the FOX pregame show."
> — Cris Collinsworth, FOX NFL Commentator

 ™

References for the Rest of Us!™

BESTSELLING BOOK SERIES FROM IDG

Do you find that traditional reference books are overloaded with technical details and advice you'll never use? Do you postpone important life decisions because you just don't want to deal with them? Then our *...For Dummies®* business and general reference book series is for you.

...For Dummies business and general reference books are written for those frustrated and hard-working souls who know they aren't dumb, but find that the myriad of personal and business issues and the accompanying horror stories make them feel helpless. *...For Dummies* books use a lighthearted approach, a down-to-earth style, and even cartoons and humorous icons to diffuse fears and build confidence. Lighthearted but not lightweight, these books are perfect survival guides to solve your everyday personal and business problems.

Already, millions of satisfied readers agree. They have made *...For Dummies* **the #1 introductory level computer book series and a best-selling business book series. They have written asking for more. So, if you're looking for the best and easiest way to learn about business and other general reference topics, look to** *...For Dummies* **to give you a helping hand.**

4/98

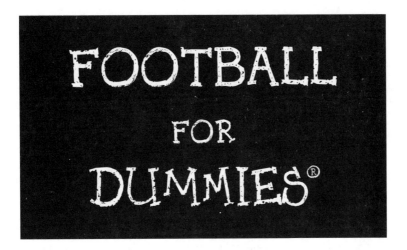

FOOTBALL
FOR
DUMMIES®

by Howie Long
with John Czarnecki

IDG Books Worldwide, Inc.
An International Data Group Company

Foster City, CA ♦ Chicago, IL ♦ Indianapolis, IN ♦ New York, NY

Football For Dummies®

Published by
IDG Books Worldwide, Inc.
An International Data Group Company
919 E. Hillsdale Blvd.
Suite 400
Foster City, CA 94404
www.idgbooks.com (IDG Books Worldwide Web site)
www.dummies.com (Dummies Press Web site)

Library of Congress Catalog Card No.: 98-85847

ISBN: 0-7645-5054-3

Printed in the United States of America

10 9 8 7 6 5 4 3 2 1

1O/SQ/QX/ZY/IN

Distributed in the United States by IDG Books Worldwide, Inc.

Distributed by Macmillan Canada for Canada; by Transworld Publishers Limited in the United Kingdom; by IDG Norge Books for Norway; by IDG Sweden Books for Sweden; by Woodslane Pty. Ltd. for Australia; by Woodslane (NZ) Ltd. for New Zealand; by Addison Wesley Longman Singapore Pte Ltd. for Singapore, Malaysia, Thailand, Indonesia and Korea; by Norma Comunicaciones S.A. for Colombia; by Intersoft for South Africa; by International Thomson Publishing for Germany, Austria and Switzerland; by Toppan Company Ltd. for Japan; by Distribuidora Cuspide for Argentina; by Livraria Cultura for Brazil; by Ediciencia S.A. for Ecuador; by Ediciones ZETA S.C.R. Ltda. for Peru; by WS Computer Publishing Corporation, Inc., for the Philippines; by Unalis Corporation for Taiwan; by Contemporanea de Ediciones for Venezuela; by Computer Book & Magazine Store for Puerto Rico; by Express Computer Distributors for the Caribbean and West Indies. Authorized Sales Agent: Anthony Rudkin Associates for the Middle East and North Africa.

For general information on IDG Books Worldwide's books in the U.S., please call our Consumer Customer Service department at 800-762-2974. For reseller information, including discounts and premium sales, please call our Reseller Customer Service department at 800-434-3422.

For information on where to purchase IDG Books Worldwide's books outside the U.S., please contact our International Sales department at 650-655-3200 or fax 650-655-3297.

For information on foreign language translations, please contact our Foreign & Subsidiary Rights department at 650-655-3021 or fax 650-655-3281.

For sales inquiries and special prices for bulk quantities, please contact our Sales department at 650-655-3200 or write to the address above.

For information on using IDG Books Worldwide's books in the classroom or for ordering examination copies, please contact our Educational Sales department at 800-434-2086 or fax 317-596-5499.

For press review copies, author interviews, or other publicity information, please contact our Public Relations department at 650-655-3000 or fax 650-655-3299.

For authorization to photocopy items for corporate, personal, or educational use, please contact Copyright Clearance Center, 222 Rosewood Drive, Danvers, MA 01923, or fax 978-750-4470.

is a trademark under exclusive license to IDG Books Worldwide, Inc., from International Data Group, Inc.

About the Authors

Howie Long is a former Oakland/Los Angeles Raider defensive end with eight Pro Bowl appearances, a Super Bowl XVIII victory over the Washington Redskins, and many other accolades to his credit. His size (6'5", 275 pounds), combined with his speed, strength, intensity, durability, and explosive quickness, set him apart. Long retired from the NFL after the 1993 season.

Long currently is a commentator on the Emmy Award–winning *FOX NFL Sunday* program, which is the most-watched NFL pregame show in America. His previous television broadcasting credits include ESPN's *Up Close,* on which he had a regular segment discussing current sports issues; HBO's *Inside the NFL;* the weekly *NFL Diary;* NBC's *NFL Live* as a guest studio analyst; and *Costas Coast to Coast.* He also wrote the opening chapter to Bo Jackson's book, *Bo Knows Bo.*

Long is no stranger to the limelight, as he's been involved in many commercials and campaigns for Nike, Hanes, Coca-Cola, and Pizza Hut. He also made his big-screen debut in the action-adventure film *Broken Arrow* with John Travolta and Christian Slater and was featured in the 1998 film *Firestorm.*

At Villanova University, Long was a four-year letterman in football as a defensive lineman. He was All-East and honorable mention All-America as a senior, and was tabbed the Most Valuable Player in the 1980 Blue-Gray Game. He was also a champion boxer as an undergraduate, and graduated with a degree in communications in 1981.

John Czarnecki has reported on the last 19 Super Bowls and has consulted for the *NFL Today* and currently for *FOX NFL Sunday.* A former newspaperman with such dailies as the *Los Angeles Herald Examiner* and the *Dallas Morning News,* Czarnecki is a frequent pro football contributor to *Sport* and *Inside Sports* magazines.

ABOUT IDG BOOKS WORLDWIDE

Welcome to the world of IDG Books Worldwide.

IDG Books Worldwide, Inc., is a subsidiary of International Data Group, the world's largest publisher of computer-related information and the leading global provider of information services on information technology. IDG was founded more than 25 years ago and now employs more than 8,500 people worldwide. IDG publishes more than 275 computer publications in over 75 countries (see listing below). More than 90 million people read one or more IDG publications each month.

Launched in 1990, IDG Books Worldwide is today the #1 publisher of best-selling computer books in the United States. We are proud to have received eight awards from the Computer Press Association in recognition of editorial excellence and three from *Computer Currents'* First Annual Readers' Choice Awards. Our best-selling *...For Dummies®* series has more than 50 million copies in print with translations in 38 languages. IDG Books Worldwide, through a joint venture with IDG's Hi-Tech Beijing, became the first U.S. publisher to publish a computer book in the People's Republic of China. In record time, IDG Books Worldwide has become the first choice for millions of readers around the world who want to learn how to better manage their businesses.

Our mission is simple: Every one of our books is designed to bring extra value and skill-building instructions to the reader. Our books are written by experts who understand and care about our readers. The knowledge base of our editorial staff comes from years of experience in publishing, education, and journalism — experience we use to produce books for the '90s. In short, we care about books, so we attract the best people. We devote special attention to details such as audience, interior design, use of icons, and illustrations. And because we use an efficient process of authoring, editing, and desktop publishing our books electronically, we can spend more time ensuring superior content and spend less time on the technicalities of making books.

You can count on our commitment to deliver high-quality books at competitive prices on topics you want to read about. At IDG Books Worldwide, we continue in the IDG tradition of delivering quality for more than 25 years. You'll find no better book on a subject than one from IDG Books Worldwide.

IDG BOOKS WORLDWIDE

John Kilcullen
CEO
IDG Books Worldwide, Inc.

Steven Berkowitz
President and Publisher
IDG Books Worldwide, Inc.

Eighth Annual Computer Press Awards ≥1992

Ninth Annual Computer Press Awards ≥1993

Tenth Annual Computer Press Awards ≥1994

Eleventh Annual Computer Press Awards ≥1995

IDG Books Worldwide, Inc., is a subsidiary of International Data Group, the world's largest publisher of computer-related information and the leading global provider of information services on information technology. International Data Group publishes over 275 computer publications in over 75 countries. More than 90 million people read one or more International Data Group publications each month. International Data Group's publications include: **ARGENTINA:** Buyer's Guide, Computerworld Argentina, PC World Argentina; **AUSTRALIA:** Australian Macworld, Australian PC World, Australian Reseller News, Computerworld, IT Casebook, Network World, Publish, Webmaster; **AUSTRIA:** Computerwelt Osterreich, Networks Austria, PC Tip Austria; **BANGLADESH:** PC World Bangladesh; **BELARUS:** PC World Belarus; **BELGIUM:** Data News; **BRAZIL:** Annuário de Informática, Computerworld, Connections, Macworld, PC Player, PC World, Publish, Reseller News, Supergamepower; **BULGARIA:** Computerworld Bulgaria, Network World Bulgaria, PC & MacWorld Bulgaria; **CANADA:** CIO Canada, Client/Server World, ComputerWorld Canada, InfoWorld Canada, NetworkWorld Canada, WebWorld; **CHILE:** Computerworld Chile, PC World Chile; **COLOMBIA:** Computerworld Colombia, PC World Colombia; **COSTA RICA:** PC World Centro America; **THE CZECH AND SLOVAK REPUBLICS:** Computerworld Czechoslovakia, Macworld Czech Republic, PC World Czechoslovakia; **DENMARK:** Communications World Danmark, Computerworld Danmark, Macworld Danmark, PC World Danmark, Techworld Denmark; **DOMINICAN REPUBLIC:** PC World Republica Dominicana; **ECUADOR:** PC World Ecuador; **EGYPT:** Computerworld Middle East, PC World Middle East; **EL SALVADOR:** PC World Centro America; **FINLAND:** MikroPC, Tietoverkko, Tietoviikko; **FRANCE:** Distributique, Hebdo, Info PC, Le Monde Informatique, Macworld, Reseaux & Telecoms, WebMaster France; **GERMANY:** Computer Partner, Computerwoche, Computerwoche Extra, Computerwoche FOCUS, Global Online, Macwelt, PC Welt; **GREECE:** Amiga Computing, GamePro Greece, Multimedia World; **GUATEMALA:** PC World Centro America; **HONDURAS:** PC World Centro America; **HONG KONG:** Computerworld Hong Kong, PC World Hong Kong, Publish in Asia; **HUNGARY:** ABCD CD-ROM, Computerworld Szamitastechnika, Internetto online Magazine, PC World Hungary, PC-X Magazin Hungary; **ICELAND:** Tolvuheimur PC World Island; **INDIA:** Information Communications World, Information Systems Computerworld, PC World India, Publish in Asia; **INDONESIA:** InfoKomputer PC World, Komputek Computerworld, Publish in Asia; **IRELAND:** ComputerScope, PC Live!; **ISRAEL:** Macworld Israel, People & Computers/Computerworld; **ITALY:** Computerworld Italia, Macworld Italia, Networking Italia, PC World Italia; **JAPAN:** DTP World, Macworld Japan, Nikkei Personal Computing, OS/2 World Japan, SunWorld Japan, Windows NT World, Windows World Japan; **KENYA:** PC World East African; **KOREA:** Hi-Tech Information, Macworld Korea, PC World Korea; **MACEDONIA:** PC World Macedonia; **MALAYSIA:** Computerworld Malaysia, PC World Malaysia, Publish in Asia; **MALTA:** PC World Malta; **MEXICO:** Computerworld Mexico, PC World Mexico; **MYANMAR:** PC World Myanmar; **NETHERLANDS:** Computer! Totaal, LAN Internetworking Magazine, LAN World Buyers Guide, Macworld Netherlands, Net, WebWereld; **NEW ZEALAND:** Absolute Beginners Guide and Plain & Simple Series, Computer Buyer, Computer Industry Directory, Computerworld New Zealand, MTB, Network World, PC World New Zealand; **NICARAGUA:** PC World Centro America; **NORWAY:** Computerworld Norge, CW Rapport, Datamagasinet, Financial Rapport, Kursguide Norge, Macworld Norge, Multimediaworld Norge, PC World Ekspress Norge, PC World Nettverk, PC World Norge, PC World ProduktGuide Norge; **PAKISTAN:** Computerworld Pakistan; **PANAMA:** PC World Panama; **PEOPLE'S REPUBLIC OF CHINA:** China Computer Users, China Computerworld, China InfoWorld, China Telecom World Weekly, Computer & Communication, Electronic Design China, Electronics Today, Electronics Weekly, Game Software, PC World China, Popular Computer Week, Software Weekly, Software World, Telecom World; **PERU:** Computerworld Peru, PC World Profesional Peru, PC World SoHo Peru; **PHILIPPINES:** Click!, Computerworld Philippines, PC World Philippines, Publish in Asia; **POLAND:** Computerworld Poland, Computerworld Special Report Poland, Cyber, Macworld Poland, Networld Poland, PC World Komputer; **PORTUGAL:** Cerebro/PC World, Computerworld/Correio Informático, Dealer World Portugal, Mac*In/PC*In Portugal, Multimedia World; **PUERTO RICO:** PC World Puerto Rico, ROMANIA: Computerworld Romania, PC World Romania, Telecom Romania; **RUSSIA:** Computerworld Russia, Mir PK, Publish, Seti; **SINGAPORE:** Computerworld Singapore, PC World Singapore, Publish in Asia; **SLOVENIA:** Monitor; **SOUTH AFRICA:** Computing SA, Network World SA, Software World SA; **SPAIN:** Communicaciones World España, Computerworld España, Dealer World España, Macworld España, PC World España; **SRI LANKA:** Infolink PC World; **SWEDEN:** CAP&Design, Computer Sweden, Corporate Computing Sweden, Internetworld Sweden, it.branschen, Macworld Sweden, MaxiData Sweden, MikroDatorn, Nätverk & Kommunikation, PC World Sweden, PCaktiv, Windows World Sweden; **SWITZERLAND:** Computerworld Schweiz, Macworld Schweiz, PCtip; **TAIWAN:** Computerworld Taiwan, Macworld Taiwan, NEW ViSiON/Publish, PC World Taiwan, Windows World Taiwan; **THAILAND:** Publish in Asia, Thai Computerworld; **TURKEY:** Computerworld Turkiye, Macworld Turkiye, Network World Turkiye, PC World Turkiye; **UKRAINE:** Computerworld Kiev, Multimedia World Ukraine, PC World Ukraine; **UNITED KINGDOM:** Acorn User UK, Amiga Action UK, Amiga Computing UK, Apple Talk UK, Computing Macworld, Parents and Computers UK, PC Advisor, PC Home, PSX Pro, The WEB; **UNITED STATES:** Cable in the Classroom, CIO Magazine, Computerworld, DOS World, Federal Computer Week, GamePro Magazine, InfoWorld, I-Way, Macworld, Network World, PC Games, PC World, Publish, Video Event, THE WEB Magazine, and WebMaster; online webzines: JavaWorld, NetscapeWorld, and SunWorld Online; **URUGUAY:** InfoWorld Uruguay; **VENEZUELA:** Computerworld Venezuela, PC World Venezuela; and **VIETNAM:** PC World Vietnam.   5/7/98

Authors' Acknowledgments

From Howie Long:

First, I'd like to thank my wife, Diane, and my three sons for all their support. I'd also like to thank my former coach at the Los Angeles Raiders, Earl Leggett, who taught me not only how to be a great football player but also how to be a man. And I can't forget my co-author, John Czarnecki, for all his hard work and dedication to this project. Thanks also go to my friends from around the NFL, Terry Robiskie, Hudson Houck, and Artie Gigantino, who contributed to this book. Finally, I'd like to thank all the people at IDG Books Worldwide who participated in this project.

From John Czarnecki:

Thanks go to my proofreading wife, Vicki, and to my daughters for staying clear of me on my bad days. To my mom, who knew I would do a book one day. To Ben, my computer expert, and Kathy, my transcriber, and John and Mike at Clone Copy. To the coaches, Earl Leggett, Terry Robiskie, Fritz Shurmur, Hudson Houck, and Ernie Zampese. To Barry Meier, my neighborly coaching expert. To Artie Gigantino, a special teams/television expert. To Garrett Giemont, a very special strength trainer. To two helpful workers, Don Seeholzer and Bryan Broaddhus. To Ron Wolf, for all his insightful football knowledge these past 15 years, and to my good friend, Peter King, for all his advice. And to my best friend, Pat, for not calling me for three months. Finally, to Pam Mourouzis, our fine editor, who never raised her voice when I was yelling (arguing) about anything. The calm in the storm!

Publisher's Acknowledgments

We're proud of this book; please register your comments through our IDG Books Worldwide Online Registration Form located at http://my2cents.dummies.com.

Some of the people who helped bring this book to market include the following:

Acquisitions, Editorial, and Media Development

Senior Project Editor: Pamela Mourouzis

Acquisitions Editor: Stacy S. Collins

Copy Editor: Kim Darosett

General Reviewer: Nick Mourouzis

Fact Checker: John Walters

Editorial Manager: Colleen Rainsberger

Editorial Assistant: Darren Meiss

Production

Project Coordinator: E. Shawn Aylsworth

Layout and Graphics: Lou Boudreau, Maridee V. Ennis, Angela F. Hunckler, Drew R. Moore, Brent Savage, Kate Snell

Special Art: Precision Graphics

Proofreaders: Christine Berman, Kelli Botta, Arielle Carole Mennelle, Rachel Garvey, Nancy Price, Rebecca Senninger, Janet M. Withers

Indexer: Joan Griffitts

Special Help

Ted Cains, Associate Project Editor; Kelly Ewing, Senior Project Editor

---

General and Administrative

IDG Books Worldwide, Inc.: John Kilcullen, CEO; Steven Berkowitz, President and Publisher

IDG Books Technology Publishing: Brenda McLaughlin, Senior Vice President and Group Publisher

Dummies Technology Press and Dummies Editorial: Diane Graves Steele, Vice President and Associate Publisher; Mary Bednarek, Director of Acquisitions and Product Development; Kristin A. Cocks, Editorial Director

Dummies Trade Press: Kathleen A. Welton, Vice President and Publisher; Kevin Thornton, Acquisitions Manager

IDG Books Production for Dummies Press: Michael R. Britton, Vice President of Production and Creative Services; Beth Jenkins Roberts, Production Director; Cindy L. Phipps, Manager of Project Coordination, Production Proofreading, and Indexing; Kathie S. Schutte, Supervisor of Page Layout; Shelley Lea, Supervisor of Graphics and Design; Debbie J. Gates, Production Systems Specialist; Robert Springer, Supervisor of Proofreading; Debbie Stailey, Special Projects Coordinator; Tony Augsburger, Supervisor of Reprints and Bluelines

Dummies Packaging and Book Design: Robin Seaman, Creative Director; Jocelyn Kelaita, Product Packaging Coordinator; Kavish + Kavish, Cover Design

◆

The publisher would like to give special thanks to Patrick J. McGovern, without whom this book would not have been possible.

◆

Contents at a Glance

Cartoons at a Glance

By Rich Tennant

page 147

page 233

page 333

page 7

page 197

page 57

page 305

Fax: 978-546-7747 • **E-mail:** the5wave@tiac.net

Table of Contents

Introduction

· ·

I think that millions of people across America are intrigued by professional football. Really, all types and levels of football. They may have a friend or a number of friends who have made the football season a ritual, from the last weekend in August until Super Bowl Sunday at the end of January. To be a part of that experience, you need to have a working knowledge of the game.

In my mind, this book only serves to realize that goal and better facilitate interaction with your friends, with your boyfriend, with your husband, with your fiancée, or whoever it may be. To many people, on the surface, football seems to be a very complicated game. There are 22 players on the field at one time, plus a number of officials. The intricacies of first down, second down, and third down, and everything from how many offensive linemen there are to what the quarterback really does or doesn't do — all of that needs to be explained and simplified. This book will help immensely; that's why I decided to write it.

I think the game itself is far less intimidating if you get a basic working knowledge of football. Once you break through that initial fear of being overwhelmed by football and what you don't understand, I know everything else about the game, like dominoes, will fall into place. After that starts happening, you'll see the game clearly, like when you wipe the early morning dew off your windshield. You can see! And once you've wiped the fog off, suddenly the game will become crystal clear.

I know a lot more about the game today as a whole than I did when I played. I was a high school and college player, plus I played for 13 seasons in the National Football League. But being a television analyst — 1998 will be my fifth season for FOX Sports — has forced me to learn even more about this game that I love.

I had a working knowledge of the passing game, how a secondary works in coverages, the offensive and defensive line formations. I had a working knowledge of general managers, scouts, and head coaches. But working as an analyst, you're forced to cover the entire game. I no longer view football from a defensive lineman's perspective, but from an overall perspective. And I'm still learning every day. That never changes. I don't think you will ever stop learning. It is the same for the players, the fans, the coaches, and the television experts. So don't feel alone out there.

About This Book

I wrote this book to help you find out what you want to know about football. Therefore, I'm not going to force you to read every single page, in order. Sure, you can read the book from front to back if you want, but if you'd rather skip around and just read about the topics that interest you, that's fine, too.

Neither do I make you remember obscure facts from earlier chapters to make sense of later chapters. If you need to know something that I discuss in an earlier chapter, I either define that thing again or refer you to the chapter that contains the information. What could be simpler?

Conventions Used in This Book

To help you follow along, this book uses certain conventions. For example, every time I use a new term, I put it in italics and then define it. (You can also find definitions of terms listed in the glossary at the back of the book.)

I also use diagrams — you know, those X and O things — to show you what I'm talking about when I describe lineups, formations, and plays. So that you're not left wondering what all those little symbols mean, here's a key to the diagrams used in this book:

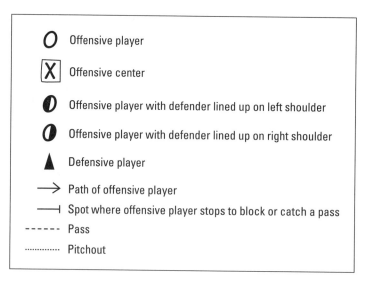

What You're Not to Read

You may want to know everything there is to know about football. Or you may want to know only what you need to know to get by, so you don't make yourself look dumb in front of your significant other by yelling "Touchback!" when you really mean "Touchdown!" Because I can't be sure what *you* want to know, I've set things up so that you can tell what to skip if you want only the basics. Throughout the book, I include things called *sidebars* — gray boxes that give background information, tell stories about famous players of yesterday and today, explain more technical concepts, and so on. Skip these if you just want to get through it and get back to the more important things in life.

Foolish Assumptions

You may not know much about football, but I know that you're no dummy, either. For whatever reason, you want or need to know more about football than you do now. You may be asking questions such as

- Why do they call it the "gridiron," anyway?
- Is the ball really made of pigskin, or is that an inside joke?
- Why do you get six points for a touchdown but only three points for a field goal?
- Does it really matter how all those guys line up on the field?
- Does it really mean something when the officials do those funny signals with their arms, or are they just bored out there?

This book answers all these questions and more.

Because I can't tell how much or how little you already know, I assume that you know nothing and explain everything clearly. But because you bought this book rather than *The Illustrated and Alphabetized Guide to Everything There Is to Know about Football, from the Day Football Began to Today,* I assume that you want to know what you *need* to know and not much more. I do keep it interesting for those readers who may have slightly more advanced knowledge, though, by throwing in tips and inside stories.

How This Book Is Organized

This book is organized into seven parts. Each part focuses on a major aspect of football.

Part I: Football 101

If you're a total newcomer to the game of football, this part of the book is a good place to start. In this part, I talk about why football is the best game there is. I also explain what all those marks on the field mean; tell you, in general, how the game is played; and list the rules that govern the game and keep all those big guys from maiming each other out there.

Part II: Go Offense

Offense is the exciting part of football; unless you witness a very unusual game, neither team will score if the offense doesn't make it happen. In this part of the book, I talk about the offense — the passing game, the running game, the offensive line, and the strategies that players and coaches use to achieve various goals on offense. You can also find out about all the offensive positions and what each player does (or at least is supposed to do).

Part III: The Big D

Without defense, offense wouldn't be all that exciting — who would stop the offense from scoring a touchdown on every play? This part talks about all the things the defense does to keep the contest a little more evenly balanced, score-wise. It explains player positions, from the defensive line to the secondary, and lists some strategies that defenses use against various offenses and in particularly sticky situations.

Part IV: Meet the Rest of the Team

No team is complete without its kickers, punters, coaches, managers, trainers, and so on. This part of the book talks about all the folks who don't fit neatly into the category of offense or defense. Not only does it give you insight into the techniques of highly skilled kickers, but it also explains the difference between the owner, the general manager, and all those other folks who seem to be in some way in charge of things.

Part V: Football for Everyone

Sure, I'm a little biased since I played in the NFL and now work as an analyst for NFL games. But that doesn't mean that I don't appreciate football at all levels. After all, I've been a high school player and a college player, too, and I'm certainly a fan. This part talks about all the ways you can get involved with football: as an "armchair quarterback," in youth leagues and on high school teams, by watching or playing in college or the NFL, or by participating in fantasy football leagues.

Part VI: Staying in the Game

If you're a player or a coach, this is the part for you. Here, I talk about two of the most important parts of football: motivation and physical fitness. You can find out how to psych yourself or your team up for a big game, what to say during a critical halftime break, how to make your body as strong as it can be, and much more.

Part VII: The Part of Tens

No ...*For Dummies* book would be complete without a Part of Tens — short chapters that contain lists of ten things. In this book, I include chapters about all-time greats: defensive players, offensive players, coaches, and teams. You may not agree with every one of my selections, but top ten lists are made to be contested!

Icons Used in This Book

To help you navigate your way through this book a little more easily, I place icons in the margins — little pictures that point you to a particular type of information. Here's a list of the icons in this book and what they mean.

This icon points out that a term is being defined. Add these terms to your vocabulary, and you'll sound like a veteran in no time!

When you see this icon, you know that you're reading a piece of information that's especially important to remember.

This icon highlights tips that can help make you a better player.

Look for this icon if you want information about becoming a more informed viewer, either on TV or in person.

This icons points out tips and techniques that are particularly helpful for coaches.

If you're a parent or coach of a younger player, these tips can help you either be a better fan or be a better coach.

A sports book wouldn't be the same without tales of the sport's greats. This icon flags stories about the game's greatest players, from the birth of the sport through today.

Being a commentator, I can't help but want to throw in my two cents once in a while. When I have my own tale to tell on a subject, I mark it with this icon.

Where to Go from Here

So you're geared up and ready to play, metaphorically speaking. Where to go from here depends on what type of information you're looking for. If you want a primer on football starting at square one, head to Chapter 1. If you want to know about how a particular phase of the game — say, the offensive line or the kicking game — works, head to that specific chapter. If you want to read about some of the greatest players in football history, head to The Part of Tens. Wherever you start, enjoy the game!

Part I
Football 101

The 5th Wave   By Rich Tennant

©RICHTENNANT

"IT'S A FOOTBALL/MATH PROGRAM. WE'RE
TACKLING MULTIPLICATION, GOING LONG
FOR DIVISION, AND PUNTING FRACTIONS."

In this part . . .

1 f you don't know a touchdown from a touchback or an interference penalty from an interception, then this part is for you. Here, I tell you why I think that football is the greatest game on earth, and then I get into the nitty-gritty of how the game works: who the players are, how the field is set up, and what happens when in a game.

Chapter 1

America's Greatest Game

*W*hen I was 14, a sophomore in high school, I moved out of Boston to live with my uncle. During my first weekend in Milford, Massachusetts, I saw my first high school football game. I had never seen anything like it. Before the game, an antique fire engine led a parade on the track around the football field while the crowd clapped and cheered. The players then thundered across a wooden bridge over a pond and burst through a banner to enter the stadium. I said to myself, "Wow, this game is for me."

I wasn't necessarily drawn to the game itself; I simply loved what came with the sport: *respect.* For me, football was an opportunity to belong to something, giving me confidence for the first time in my life. It was more of a personal thing than it was about playing football. It wasn't so much the football, but what football did for me. Football gave me a sense of self-worth, which I've carried with me throughout my life.

Sure, I experienced down periods when I first started playing, but I never thought about quitting. My first high school coach, Dick Corbin, was great to me and encouraged me to continue playing the game. Believe me, coaches are important. I've always had the support of football coaches, both on *and* off the field.

Football is responsible for everything that I've accomplished in my life. The discipline and hard work that made me a successful athlete has helped me in other areas of my life, allowing me to venture into new careers in movies and television.

Why Football Is the Best

Baseball may be America's pastime, but football is America's passion. Football is the only team sport in America that conjures up visions of Roman gladiators, pitting city versus city, state versus state — sometimes with a Civil War feel, like when the Jets play the Giants in New York or the Bucs play the Dolphins in Florida.

Football is played in all weather conditions — snow, rain, and sleet — with temperatures on the playing field ranging from −30 to 120 degrees. Whatever the conditions may be, the game goes on. And unlike other major sports, the football playoff system is a single-elimination tournament: no playoff series, do-or-die. It culminates in what has become the single biggest one-day sporting event in America: the Super Bowl.

Or, in simpler terms, anytime you stick 22 men in fiberglass helmets on a football field and have them continually run great distances at incredible speeds and slam into each other, people will watch.

Football has wedged itself into the American culture. In fact, in many small towns across America, the centerpiece is the Friday night high school football game. The National Football League (NFL) doesn't play on Fridays simply to protect this great part of Americana, in which football often gives schools and even towns a certain identity. For example, hard-core fans know that tiny Massillon, Ohio, is where the late, great Paul Brown of the Cleveland Browns began his coaching career. To this day, Massillon's high school has maintained a tremendous high school football tradition. With so many factions of a student body involved, plus their families, a strong core of fans is built. For many, this enthusiasm for football continues in college.

You may not think it now, but millions of people are familiar with the strategy of the game, and most of them pass it down through their families. A lot of fathers coach their sons. Mothers encourage their daughters to be cheerleaders or majorettes. Although the focus may have changed in today's society, there was a time when the only team that mattered at a high school was the football team. The pace of the game — stoppage after every play with a huddle — is perfect for most people because it allows them time to guess what the team will try next.

On two particular holidays, football has become an American tradition. Thanksgiving Day is reserved for a turkey dinner, a family sit-down, followed by a pro football game. The Detroit Lions started the tradition in 1934, and in 1998 they play in their 59th Thanksgiving Day game. For the past 25 seasons, the NFL has scheduled two games on this day, both of them nationally televised. New Year's Day has long been the day for the Rose Bowl and several other college football bowl games. These bowl games generally match up some of the nation's finest teams and help decide the mythical national champion.

The NFL is *it* in the U.S.

Over the past three years, Americans have consistently chosen the NFL as their favorite sport to watch at a rate higher than the next two sports combined, according to a 1997 ESPN/Chilton Sports Poll. In a survey of 2,000 people 12 years or older, 24.7 percent chose the NFL as their favorite spectator sport. That 1997 Harris Poll also showed that 51 percent of adults follow pro football, up from 46 percent in 1993. Pro football compared favorably to pro baseball, which was followed by 32 percent of fans polled in August 1997. Only 28 percent of adults selected professional basketball.

Paid attendance for the 1997 NFL regular season was the second highest in the history of the league. Fans purchased 14,966,294 tickets to the NFL's 240 regular-season games in 1997, representing paid attendance at 90 percent of stadium capacity. The NFL's best paid attendance occurred in 1995, when 15,043,562 tickets were sold. All of the top five regular-season paid attendance marks have occurred in the 1990s, which corresponds to pro football's outstanding growth.

Why Anyone Would Play Football

Of all the team sports, football is the most violent and dangerous, with hockey a distant second. I played football for respect, and I believe that it builds character. Considering some of the problems in society today, football can give a youngster's life some structure and also teach him discipline. All the players who belong to a football team are in the struggle together, sharing in the joy and the pain of the sport. Every play can be such an adrenaline rush.

Football is suited to all sizes of athletes. Larger athletes generally play on the offensive and defensive lines — what are called the *trenches*. Leaner athletes who are faster and quicker generally play the skill positions, such as quarterback, running back, and receiver. But no matter how big or how talented you are, you must have inner courage in order to play football. This game requires strength and perseverance. If you don't believe that you're tough enough to play, then you probably shouldn't try.

And if you're not up to the full-force-hitting variety of football, you can still enjoy the sport as a player. Touch football is totally different from tackle football. All you need are a ball and maybe six players, three per team. Both girls and boys can play this game, and they decide the rules and the size of the field at the start of the game. I've seen people playing touch football on the streets of New York City and in parks and front lawns all across America — the beauty of the game is that you can play anywhere.

How Television Has Helped to Increase Football's Popularity

Millions of kids learn the game from their fathers and through high school football, like I did. But today, most football fans are introduced to the game through television, which brings the game right into everyone's home. The action in a football game translates well to television. The field and all the action that takes place upon it fit just as nicely on a big screen as they do on a smaller model. Because television networks use 12 cameras for most games, viewers rarely miss out on plays. And with taped replay machines — which are housed in those big trailers outside every NFL stadium — the networks can show critical plays from several different angles, including a viewer-friendly angle for fans watching at home or at the neighborhood tavern.

Television shows like *FOX NFL Sunday* also help to make the game more personal by promoting the personalities under the helmets. Fans can watch and listen to a Brett Favre interview and feel that they know the Green Bay quarterback as a person.

Why the Super Bowl Is Number One

Each year, the highest-rated show in network television is the Super Bowl, with whatever the number-two show is running a distant second. Of the ten most-watched shows in the history of television, eight of them are Super Bowl games. The game has become an event that all of America focuses on; many people have parties on Super Bowl Sunday to watch the game. This game attracts both casual as well as hard-core football fans. For some people, the Super Bowl is the only game they watch all season.

The Super Bowl also has become an international event. More than 180 countries and territories televised 1998's Super Bowl XXXII, and in the U.S. 138.48 million fans watched. The game was broadcast in ten different languages, and for the third consecutive season it was broadcast live by BBC Radio to the United Kingdom. People all over the world saw the Denver Broncos' upset victory over the Green Bay Packers on that Super Bowl Sunday.

The main reason why the Super Bowl is so popular is that pro football is the only major professional men's team sport with a single-elimination playoff system. The other major sports declare their champions after a team wins four games in a best-of-seven series. The Super Bowl is do-or-die; that's what makes the game so special.

And it's not just the game itself that attracts viewers. Companies pay Madison Avenue advertising firms lots of money to create commercials, and some people watch the Super Bowl just to see those commercials. All the commercials are judged and summarized because hundreds of millions of potential customers are watching. The stakes are almost as high as those on the field.

The Super Bowl has even gone high-tech! Every Super Bowl has its own Web site and offers its own cybercast of the game. Generally, several experts provide instant analysis of the game. The National Football League created the site `www.nfl.com`, which fans can visit on Super Bowl Sunday to access live play-by-play of the game, *drive charts* (how many and what plays a team used during a scoring drive), and statistics, in addition to live audio of the press box and public address announcer. Nothing gives you a better feel of the stadium atmosphere. The site also provides audio and video clips from the game telecast, including a clip from the overhead blimp.

And the Super Bowl's audience continues to grow. Based on what the networks recently paid to maintain their television rights fees, they believe that America's appetite for the game remains strong.

The road to the Super Bowl

I played in my only Super Bowl after my third season in the NFL, and I thought I'd make it back at least two or three mores times during my career. Unfortunately, that never happened.

The media attention back in 1984 wasn't nearly as expansive as it is today. In fact, tracing the growth of the media from 1984 to today is like comparing the size of Rhode Island to the size of Montana. I remember taking a cab to Tampa Stadium to play in the Super Bowl. The traffic was so bad that I ended up walking the last three-quarters of a mile to the stadium. Today, the NFL provides police escorts for the players. The fanfare surrounding a team's arrival is as if the president is coming to town.

How Football Began

Just as many fans get caught up in the hype and hoopla of today's NFL, many others love the game for its sense of tradition. The game itself has endured for more than 125 years.

Games that involve kicking a ball into a goal on a lined field have existed for more than 2,000 years. American football evolved from two particular games that were popular in other parts of the world: soccer (as it's known in the United States) and rugby. Both the Romans and the Spartans (Remember that movie *Spartacus?* Now those guys were tough!) played some version of soccer. Soccer and rugby came to North America in the 19th century, and historians have noted that the first form of American football emerged on November 6, 1869, when teams from Princeton and Rutgers, two New Jersey universities, competed in a game of what was closer to rugby than football. Rutgers won the game 6-4.

The rules get defined

Walter Camp, a sensational player at Yale University and a driving force behind many new rules, is known as the father of American football. Camp helped write the first rules for football — which was already being played in universities on the East Coast and in Canada — at a convention in Springfield, Massachusetts, in 1876. In 1880, he authored rules that reduced the number of players per team from 15 to 11 (today's total) and replaced the rugby scrum with the center snap to put the ball in play. (In a scrum, players from both sides close up tightly together, the two teams butting heads while the ball is thrown between them. The players then try to gain possession of the ball with their feet. Using your hands to gain possession is uniquely American — both rugby and soccer forbid it.)

Camp also championed the rule that a team needed to gain 5 yards in three plays in order to maintain possession. Today, teams must gain 10 yards in three plays or decide to punt on fourth down. (See Chapter 3 for more information about these and other rules.)

Camp devised plays and formations and instituted referees. However, his biggest proposal was tackling, which was introduced in 1888. Tackling — which allowed players to hit below the waist for the first time that year — made the game more violent. It also popularized an offensive strategy known as the *flying wedge,* where an entire team (ten players) would mass in front of one ball carrier in the form of a wedge. Football was almost banned in 1906 after 18 deaths and 159 serious injuries were reported in the preceding season, but President Theodore Roosevelt saved the game by convincing college representatives to initiate stricter rules to make the game less brutal and dangerous.

The game has been cleaned up a great deal over the years. It's come a long way from close-line shots and quarterbacks taking late hits and direct blows to the head. But let's not kid one another: Football is a high-impact collision sport, and with collision comes pain and injury. Even with the rules being adjusted to protect today's quarterback, it's rare to look in the paper on a Monday morning and not see that at least one quarterback sustained a concussion. Players are bigger, faster, and stronger. Let me put it this way: You're driving down the road traveling at 35 miles per hour. Would you rather be met head-on by a car of similar size or by a truck? Well, that's the difference between 20 years ago and now. Only thing is, the truck's now going 45 miles per hour rather than 35.

Grange helps to spread the popularity of pro ball

Americans started playing football in colleges and on club teams in the 1870s. Football became a source of identity for collegians and a regular Saturday afternoon activity by the turn of the century.

In the first 90 years of football, college football was more popular than pro football; it was (and still is, at many schools) all about tradition and the many rivalries between colleges. Eighty years ago, having more than 50,000 fans attend a great college game was not unusual. During that same period, games in the NFL — which officially began in 1920 — were fortunate to draw 5,000 fans.

Two days after the 1925 college season ended, Illinois All-American halfback Harold "Red" Grange signed a contract to play with the struggling Chicago Bears. On Thanksgiving Day of that year, 36,000 fans — the largest crowd in pro football history at that time — watched Grange and the Bears play the league's top team, the Chicago Cardinals, to a scoreless tie in Cubs Park (now called Wrigley Field, the home of the Chicago Cubs baseball team). The Bears went on to play a barnstorming tour, and in New York's Polo Grounds, more than 73,000 fans watched Grange — nicknamed the "Galloping Ghost" — compete against the New York Giants. Although Grange did attract new fans to the pro game, fewer than 30,000 fans attended championship games in the early 1930s.

Pro football emerged as an equal to college football after its games began being televised nationally in the 1960s, but it took decades for the NFL to supplant college football. And to this day, many colleges have as much fan support as some NFL franchises. Universities like Nebraska and Notre Dame can claim more fans than, say, the Atlanta Falcons.

Football immortals

With every sport comes a list of immortals — those great players who nurtured the game and made it what it is today. Following are some of the legends of American football:

- **Walter Camp:** Known as the father of American football, Camp was a player and coach at Yale and was the first to snap the ball from center, form a line of scrimmage, design plays, and use numbers and words as a form of signal-calling.

- **John W. Heisman:** The annual award given to the nation's best college player — the John W. Heisman Trophy Award — is named after this Brown University (and later University of Pennsylvania) player. Heisman was also a member of New York's Downtown Athletic Club, where the award is presented every December. He was the first to recommend the use of the forward pass.

- **Fritz Pollard:** Pollard starred for Brown University from 1914 to 1916 and was the first African-American player to be selected to the college All-American team. He is also considered the first African-American football player to turn professional and the first African-American pro head coach (of the Hammond Pros in 1923). He was also the first African-American inducted into the College Football Hall of Fame in 1954.

- **Amos Alonzo Stagg:** Stagg was a famous University of Chicago coach who developed the "Statue of Liberty" play, in which a halfback takes the ball from the quarterback who has his hands raised as if to throw a forward pass. He was the first coach to put numbers on players' uniforms.

- **Jim Thorpe:** A Native American who won the decathlon and pentathlon in the 1912 Stockholm Olympics, Thorpe was an All-American at Carlisle (Pennsylvania) Indian School and was the first big-time American athlete to play pro football. He was paid the princely sum of $250 a game to play for the Canton Bulldogs in 1915. Today, Canton, Ohio is the home of the Pro Football Hall of Fame.

- **Pop Warner:** The national tackle youth league is named after this famous coach, who developed the single-wing formation, which snaps the ball directly to the running back and has four linemen to one side of the center and two to the other side. Warner was the first to use the hidden ball trick, in which an offensive lineman slipped the ball under his jersey. The first "hunchback play" went for a touchdown against Harvard in 1903.

How the Football Season Is Set Up Today

Football as an organized sport has come a long way since those early years. Teams at every level play during a standard season and are governed by various football leagues, such as the NFL and NCAA (National Collegiate Athletic Association).

The heart of the football season is during the fall months, although training camps, practices, and preseason games often begin in the summer, and playoffs and bowl games are staged after Christmas and into January. Here's how the season breaks down for each level of play:

✔ **High school football teams** usually play between eight and ten games in a season, starting after Labor Day. If teams have successful league seasons, they advance to regional or state playoff tournaments. Some schools in Texas play as many as 15 games if they advance to the state championship game. Most high school teams play in a regional league, although some travel 50 to 100 miles to play opponents. You can find out more about high school football in Chapter 15.

✔ **College football teams** play between 10 and 12 games, the majority in a specific conference — Pac-10, Big Ten, SEC, ACC, and so on. The top teams from Division I-A (generally the largest schools that offer the most money for athletic scholarships) advance via invitation to post-season bowl games, which take place at more than 25 sites across the country. At the top level, college football doesn't have a national tournament structure, though, like in college basketball. The smaller colleges and universities have a football playoff system, like every other men's and women's sport under the NCAA's influence. Read more about college football in Chapter 16.

✔ **NFL teams** play 16 regular-season games, preceded by a minimum of 4 preseason games that are played in August. The 30 NFL teams are divided into two conferences, the NFC (National Football Conference) and the AFC (American Football Conference), and the top ten teams from each conference advance to the playoffs with hopes of reaching the Super Bowl, which is played in late January. Chapter 17 gives you all the details about the NFL.

Football is pretty much a weekend sport, although the NFL began Monday Night Football in 1970, offering a marquee matchup between two of the league's better teams. (The Monday night game is almost always ranked in the top ten television shows for the week, and Monday Night Football is the longest running prime-time television series.) A few Thursday games are broadcast during the college and pro season. However, in general, the football season, which begins in earnest right around Labor Day, follows an orderly pattern:

✔ High school games are generally played on Friday nights.

✔ College games are played on Saturdays, mostly during the day, although a few are held at night and showcased on prime-time television.

✔ The NFL plays on Sundays. For television purposes, games start at 1 p.m. EDT and 4:15 p.m. EDT. One Sunday night game is played, which is a national game televised on ESPN, the largest cable-sports network.

No matter where you live, your daily newspaper probably publishes a schedule of all local and national football games. You can find such a listing in the sports section, usually on a back page under a "Scoreboard" heading. The sports section also should have a television section, telling you which college and NFL games are being broadcast that weekend. Games are televised on both a regional and a national basis, so you can choose from a broad selection of matchups. Serious fans and hard-core football junkies often hook up their own satellite dishes so that they can catch an even wider variety of games.

Predicting a season

The allure of football is that most teams open on equal footing. But predicting the winner of a football season is difficult because so many intangibles are involved. Injuries, coaching decisions, the weather, and overall performance can affect the outcome of any game.

Football is also a sport in which the champion, the team that won in the preceding season, generally gets more respect from opposing teams and becomes the team everyone wants to beat. Football is all about being King of the Hill. The players and coaches want to duke it out; competition is very much a macho thing.

Every NFL team uses the world champion as a measuring stick in the draft; free agent pick-ups are all geared toward beating the champ. Add to that the fact that everyone is trying to sign the champ's free agents, and you have arguably the most difficult championship in sports to repeat.

Commentators are paid good money to predict who may win certain games. Making predictions is difficult, and for me, it's often personal because I know most of the NFL coaches and players that I'm talking about. I have a tough time saying a coach or player that I respect won't win — or can't win.

Lots of people bet on college and NFL games. If you go to Las Vegas, every major hotel has a sports book room where odds are posted on every major game. Gambling is one big reason for the interest in football. All I know is that it's tough to pick winners. Before the 1997 season, I picked most of the right playoff teams, and both Terry Bradshaw and I predicted that Green Bay wouldn't repeat as NFL champions. James Brown, the only non-football player on the *FOX NFL Sunday* pregame show, predicted that Denver would win the Super Bowl, and the Broncos did. So you can see how tough this predicting business can be.

Chapter 2

Meet Me on the Gridiron

I spent a lot of time on football fields. Although the dimensions are the same, from high school to the NFL, every field seems different. That's because all across America, the atmosphere inside each stadium, or the architectural character of the stadium itself, tends to be unique to that region. But every field shares some common characteristics.

In this chapter, I explain the basics of a football field, and why teams don't always play on my favorite surface, good old green grass. I also talk about the number of players on the field, what they wear, and that odd-shaped ball they play with.

The Big Picture: Stadiums

As you probably know, a stadium is the whole structure or area in which football and other games are played: the field, the stands, and so on. Stadiums come in all shapes and sizes — the important thing is that they allow room for the 100-yard-long football field, which is, of course, obligatory. (For more on the football field, see the next section "Getting Down to Business: The Field.")

NFL stadiums come in two main varieties: dome stadiums and outdoor stadiums. Dome stadiums are designed so that the players and the fans don't have to deal with the weather; they always have a roof over them, and they're always on artificial turf. When you're talking about big-time football, both types of stadiums generally seat between 60,000 and 105,000 screaming fans.

The best stadium in pro football

There's no better setting in pro football than Lambeau Field in Green Bay, Wisconsin. With its circular seating and lack of an upper deck, Lambeau is a fan-friendly stadium. Every seat offers a good view of the action.

For a potentially cold arena, Lambeau is also a player-friendly stadium. To improve their field in freezing conditions, the Packers installed SportGrass in 1997. The new surface consists of natural grass planted on a recyclable, synthetic surface below field level. This setup creates a stable base that can't be destroyed by the physical wear and tear on the field, coupled with soggy, wet conditions. There's also a heating system under the surface for those frigid December games. Over 89,000 square feet of SportGrass sod was shipped by refrigerated trucks from Baskerville, Virginia, to Green Bay for the 1997 NFC Championship game.

New stadiums, many financed through public support and tax dollars, have become one of the NFL's top priorities. In the 1990s, 18 NFL stadiums have been either built, renovated, or targeted for such development by 2002. One of those stadiums — Jack Kent Cooke Stadium in Raljon, Maryland — was completed in under 18 months (the fastest stadium construction ever) and seats 80,116 fans. The Washington Redskins started playing in their new home, named in honor of the late Redskins owner, in 1997.

Getting Down to Business: The Field

There's nothing like a football field. If I could wish something for everyone, it would be the ability to stand on the sideline at an NFL game and hear, sense, and feel the impact of the collisions and see the speed of the game up close. There are selected areas around the sidelines for photographers and television cameramen, and that's where I love to watch the game. The following sections tell you what you'll see no matter whether you're on the field or in the stands.

Field dimensions

The dimensions of a football field haven't changed much through the years. The field has been 100 yards long and 53$\frac{1}{3}$ yards wide since 1881. In 1912, the two end zones were established to be 10 yards deep and have remained so ever since. Consequently, all football games are played upon a rectangular field, 360 feet long and 160 feet wide.

The marks on the field: Yard lines, hash marks, and more

All over the field, you see a bunch of white lines. Every line has a special meaning, as shown in Figure 2-1:

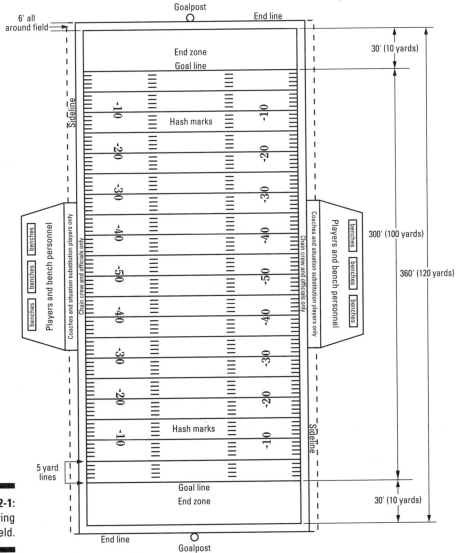

Figure 2-1:
The playing field.

✔ The lines at each end of the field are called the *end lines*.

✔ The lines along each side of the field are called the *sidelines*.

✔ The *goal lines* are 10 yards inside and parallel to each end line.

✔ The area bounded by the goal lines and sidelines is known as the *field of play*.

✔ The field is divided in half by the *50-yard line*, located in the middle of the field.

✔ The two areas bounded by the goal lines, end lines, and sidelines are known as the *end zones*.

The field also contains yard lines, hash marks, and lines marking the player benches, which I describe in detail in the following sections.

To make all these white lines, teams use paint or marking chalk. They're even painting grass fields these days. The end lines and sidelines are 4 inches wide and rimmed by a solid white border a minimum of 6 feet wide. All boundary lines, goal lines, and marked yard lines are continuous lines until they intersect with one another.

When players are in possession of the ball inside these white lines, they're considered to be in play, and the ball is live. For more on being out-of-bounds, see the sidebar "When you've gone too far."

Yard lines

Yard lines, at intervals of 5 yards, run parallel to the goal lines and are marked across the field from sideline to sideline. These lines stop 8 inches short of the 6-foot solid border in the NFL.

Yard lines are necessary to give players and fans an idea of how far a team must advance the ball in order to record a first down. As Chapter 3 explains in detail, an offensive team must gain 10 yards in order to post a first down. Consequently, every 10 yards, starting from the goal lines, the field is numbered in multiples of 10. In the NFL, the bottoms of these numbers are placed 12 yards from each sideline. The numbers 10, 20, 30, 40, and one 50-yard line are 2 yards in length. All these lines and numbers are white.

Hash marks

Hash marks mark each yard line 70 feet, 9 inches from the sidelines in the NFL. In high school and college football, the hash marks are only 60 feet from the sidelines. Two sets of hash marks (each hash is 1 yard in length) run parallel to each other down the length of the field and are approximately $18\frac{1}{2}$ feet apart. When the ball carrier is either tackled or pushed out-of-bounds, the officials return the ball in-bounds to the closest hash mark to where it's spotted. Punted balls that go out-of-bounds are also marked on the nearest hash mark.

When you've gone too far

A player is out-of-bounds whenever he steps from the field of play and touches (or flies over) the white sidelines or end lines. To remain in-bounds for a catch, an NFL player must have both feet (including the toes of his football shoes) touching the ground inside the end lines and sidelines and be in possession of the football. Like a receiver, a ball carrier is considered out-of-bounds when any part of his body touches the sidelines or end lines.

In college and high school football, a player needs to have only one foot inside the end lines and sidelines to be considered in-bounds while in possession of the football. Yes, technically, a receiver can have one foot out-of-bounds and still have his sideline catch ruled complete in high school and college football.

The hash marks are used for ball placement prior to most offensive plays so that more of the game can be played in the middle of the field, which makes the game more wide open. If the ball was placed 20 feet from where it went out-of-bounds rather than on the closest hash mark, offenses would be restricted to one open side of the field for many of their run and pass plays (in other words, they would have to run or pass to the right or the left, and wouldn't have the option to do both). But when teams run the football and the ball carrier is tackled between the hash marks, the ball is declared dead at that spot and generally is placed where the ball carrier was tackled and stopped.

REMEMBER

An important thing to remember is that an incomplete pass is returned to the spot of the preceding play, not where it actually goes out-of-bounds or where the quarterback was standing when he threw it.

Player benches

Six feet outside the border of the field, or 6 feet from the sidelines, is an additional broken white line that defines an area in which only coaches and substitute players may stand. Six feet farther behind this broken white line is where the *bench area* begins. The team congregates in the bench area during a game, watching their teammates play or resting on benches (refer to Figure 2-1). Within this area, team doctors and trainers examine injured players. All NFL bench areas are a minimum of 30 feet deep, and they extend to each 32-yard line. Many high school and college fields aren't as restrictive as NFL fields, although many adhere to the same dimensions, particularly the 32-yard line limit at both ends.

In the bench area, which is off-limits to fans and media walking the sideline area, quarterbacks and other players can use telephones on a communications table to talk with coaches located high above the stadium in rooms reserved for members of the coaching staff. Also, team officials use telephones from this area to inform the team's public relations staff of player injuries. This information is then relayed to members of the media (newspaper reporters, magazine writers, and radio broadcasters) in the *press box* area and to the television trucks so that their announcers can inform the viewing audience.

Field surfaces

Two types of surfaces are used in football — natural grass and artificial turf:

✔ Many natural grass surfaces exist, depending on the region's temperature and the stadium's drainage system. But natural grass is similar to your backyard lawn or any baseball outfield: It's green, soft, and beautiful. Many companies have invested a lot of time and effort into perfecting a combination of natural grasses that can withstand the heavy and destructive wear (cleats can rip up turf) that football presents.

✔ The artificial surface was developed for Houston's Astrodome, the first indoor stadium, which housed both professional baseball and football teams at one time. Without natural sunlight, no grass would grow. Because of the dome, the first surface was dubbed Astroturf. Artificial surfaces are made from synthetic nylon fibers that in some stadiums resemble very short blades of grass. On other surfaces, the fibers are very tightly woven, giving them the feel of a cushioned carpet. Not many football players like playing on artificial surfaces, believing that on some of them their shoes stick or get caught, which can lead to serious knee injuries.

After Astroturf was developed, companies improved the product, and many outdoor stadiums began to install artificial surfaces because they are cheaper to maintain than natural grass, which needs to be watered, mowed, and replaced. Plus, many football stadiums are multipurpose facilities that are used for outdoor concerts, political and religious rallies, and other sports such as baseball and soccer. When such events are held, some areas of the grass can become trampled and destroyed by the thousands of fans sitting or walking on it, so having artificial surface is advantageous.

Most players prefer to play on natural grass rather than on artificial turf. Playing on an artificial surface is much like playing on green-colored wall-to-wall carpeting. I used to get rug burns on my arms and legs from the stuff.

Grass beats artificial surfaces

I never liked playing on artificial surfaces. The problem with these surfaces, in my opinion, is that your shoes get stuck, which makes you more susceptible to injury. The game is faster on this surface, but when players make quick cuts or attempt to move too quickly, they seem to twist their knees and feet because their shoes stick to the surface.

I never could find the right shoe. I'd try basketball sneakers. I think I tried on maybe a thousand different styles of nub-tipped shoes. I tried everything on turf and retired never being satisfied with any of the shoes.

Players also suffer what I call *turf burns* when they dive to make a tackle or when a ball carrier skids across the surface. I've had the skin on my elbows and knees rip right off me.

Some teams use what doctors actually give burn victims, called "Second Skin." It's a jelly-like material that's flat, a little thicker than two or three pieces of paper stuck together. They cut a piece of second skin about the size of your turf burn and stick it in there. The problem with any turf burn is that it can last for two to three weeks, and even if you don't play on turf again, the scab gets ripped off every day in practice.

To prevent these types of injuries, a lot of players wear elastic sleeves over their elbows, forearms, and knees. I tried playing with them, but they kept slipping down after I started sweating. I didn't like having to pull them up or back on every play — it was an unnessessary, useless activity.

In many stadiums, the artificial surface is also harder than natural grass because it often is laid over cement, blacktop, or dirt. And on extremely hot days, artificial surfaces retain the heat, making a 95-degree day feel like a 100-degree day.

In the NFL, 16 teams currently play on natural grass for home games, while 14 play on artificial surfaces.

The things that sit on the field

The *goalpost* serves as the guideline for every kicker: A kicker's goal is to sail the ball high between the goalpost's two vertical bars, which is known as *splitting the uprights*. The goalpost rises from the back of the end zone. When a ball carrier reaches the end zone, he has scored a touchdown, worth six points. The *goal line* is 8 inches wide (twice as wide as the typical yard line) in the NFL, and 4 inches wide at the high school and college levels. The goalposts used to be located on the goal line, and then inside the goal line, and finally they were moved permanently from the goal line to the end zone's end line (refer to Figure 2-1) in 1974.

NFL goalposts are a single standard type, known as the *sling-shot* design; on some high school and youth fields, you may still find goalposts in the shape of an H. A sling-shot goalpost has one post in the ground and a curved extension that sweeps the crossbar into place (see Figure 2-2). This post is fully padded to protect players who might collide with it in the back of the end zone. The *crossbar* is 10 feet above the ground and 18 feet, 6 inches long in the NFL. In high school and college football, the crossbar is 23 feet, 4 inches long. The *uprights,* the two poles extending up from both ends of the crossbar, should rise about 30 feet (20 feet in college and high school) and be 3 to 4 inches in diameter.

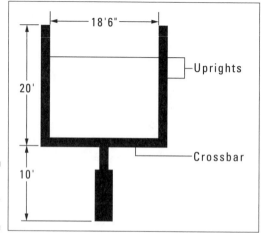

Figure 2-2:
The NFL
goalpost.

The goalposts generally are painted yellow or white. A 4-x-42-inch ribbon is attached to the top of each goalpost to aid the officials in determining the exact top of the upright when judging whether a kick has passed through the uprights. The ribbons also give kickers an idea of the wind conditions.

Goalposts aren't the only things you see sitting on the field; you also see the chains and down marker along one sideline, marking the spot of the ball and other important information. For more information about the chains and the people who work them, see Chapter 3.

Looking at That Funny-Shaped Ball

The ball is a very important component of a football game — you couldn't very well play *football* without the *ball* part. But you can't use just any ball; strict rules govern the ball's size, weight, and even brand.

In the NFL, the ball must be a Wilson brand, bearing the signature of the commissioner of the league, Paul Tagliabue. The ball can be inflated to between $12\frac{1}{2}$ to $13\frac{1}{2}$ pounds of air pressure. It's made of an inflated rubber bladder enclosed in a pebble-grained, leather case of natural tan color without grooves or ridges of any kind. The ball is the form of a prolate spheroid (basically an oblong shape with pointed ends). You may have heard a football called a *pigskin*. But footballs just *resemble* a toughened pig's skin, and at the turn of the century they were swollen like a chubby little piggy.

To make it easier to grip and throw, the ball has eight raised white laces in its center. A quarterback can wrap his pinkie, fourth finger, and middle finger between these laces for a perfect grip. Size and weight of the ball must conform to these specifications:

- ✔ **Long axis:** 11 to $11\frac{1}{2}$ inches
- ✔ **Long circumference:** 28 to $28\frac{1}{2}$ inches
- ✔ **Short circumference:** $20\frac{3}{4}$ to $21\frac{1}{4}$ inches
- ✔ **Weight:** 14 to 15 ounces

College balls are the same size as NFL balls, although you may find a white stripe encircling the tip area at both ends of the college and high school ball. The white stripe supposedly helps receivers see the ball better, which may be helpful for some of those night games in college and high school football.

In the NFL, the home club supplies 36 footballs in an open-air stadium or 24 footballs in a domed stadium. More balls are required for outdoors in case of inclement weather, such as rain, sleet, or snow. The referee is the sole judge as to whether all balls comply with league specifications. The referee tests each football with a pressure gauge approximately 90 minutes prior to kickoff.

Meeting the Cast of Characters

Each football team has 11 players per side, 11 on offense and 11 on defense. Teams are allowed to play with fewer than 11 players (why would they want to do that?), but they are penalized for having more than 11 players on the field during play, or what is known as live action. In high school, three or more talented players may play both offense and defense. And a few rare athletes may play both offense and defense in major college football and the NFL.

The nonstarting players (that is, those who aren't among the 22 or so players who are listed in the starting lineup) are considered reserves, and many of them are specialists. For example, defenses may play multiple schemes employing a nickel back (a fifth defensive back) or two pass rushers (linebackers or defensive ends who are used strictly on passing downs to rush the quarterback). Also, an extra player is often used as the long snapper who snaps (hikes) the ball for punts, field goal attempts, and extra point attempts. Some of the reserves make the team because they are excellent special teams players who are great on punt and kick coverages because they are fearless tacklers in the open field. (See Chapter 12 for more on special teams.)

The roster sizes in high school and college football tend to be unlimited, especially for home games. However, the NFL limits active, uniformed players to 45 per team. An additional player can be in uniform, but he must be a quarterback and enter the game only after the other quarterbacks have been removed from the game because of injury. When this extra quarterback, or 46th player, enters the game, the other quarterbacks are deemed ineligible and cannot return to that game even if they are healthy.

A typical NFL game-day roster includes three quarterbacks, a punter, a placekicker, a kick return specialist, eight offensive linemen, four running backs, five receivers, two tight ends, seven defensive linemen, seven linebackers, and six defensive backs. (For much more on the different positions, see Parts II and III.)

What Football Uniforms Are All About

In youth football (see Chapter 15), there are weight and size limitations, but as boys advance in football from high school to college to the pros, the uniform is the one common denominator. If you can play (and play well), a uniform will always be waiting for you in some team's locker room.

It isn't the uniform that separates one player from the others; it's his heart. But the uniform and its protective pads are a necessary part of the game, something any player would be foolhardy to take the field without. But think of this: Only 50 years ago, many men wore helmets without face masks, meaning that they had to have some pretty rugged noses.

Why the need for all the protection? Well, the NFL is made up of players ranging in weight from 170 pounds to 360 pounds and in height from 5'8" to 6'9". Some of these assorted sizes are able to bench press 550 pounds and run the 40-yard dash in as fast as 4.2 seconds. Because of the varied weights, sizes, strengths, and speeds of NFL players, the best protection possible is necessary. Smaller players want to be able to play without worrying about being crushed by all those large bodies.

Figure 2-3 shows a typical football uniform. The following sections talk about the various components of the uniform and the pads that go underneath it.

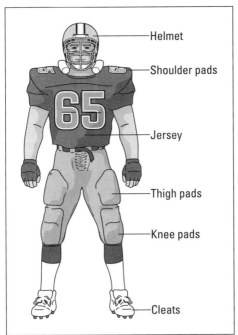

Helmet

Shoulder pads

Jersey

Thigh pads

Knee pads

Cleats

Figure 2-3:
The football
uniform.

The jersey

The *jersey* is the uniform's shirt. The jersey is basically each player's identity and marks his allegiance to a specific team. The jersey must be large enough to cover the shoulder pads.

Every NFL team jersey comes with a different numeral to differentiate one player from another. The numerals, which appear on the front and back of the jersey, are 8 inches high and 4 inches wide. Most high school and college teams have the same specifications, and some of them also place the number on the jersey's sleeve.

In the NFL, specific positions wear certain numerals. For example:

✔ Linebackers wear from 50 to 59.

✔ Offensive linemen wear from 50 to 79.

✔ Defensive linemen must select from between 60 and 79.

✔ Receivers wear from 80 to 89.

On the back of each NFL jersey is the player's surname in letters that are $2^1/_2$ inches high. His name appears across the upper back just above the numerals.

Team jerseys' colors and designs further separate one team from another. And most team colors have been with particular teams since their inception. In Green Bay, the jerseys are green with gold trim. In Oakland, the Raiders always wear black. The New York Giants wear blue. The Chicago Bears wear navy blue with a touch of orange. In Nebraska, the color is bright red. The different colors add to the spectacle of the game. In the NFL, the visiting team usually wears a white jersey. The colors for visiting teams vary on the high school and college levels.

Helmets and face masks

The helmet and face mask are designed to protect a player's face and head from serious injury. Many players also wear a mouth guard to protect their teeth and prevent themselves from biting their tongues. A few players even wear another protective cap on the outside of the helmet for added protection.

Helmets are equipped with chin straps to keep them snugly in place. To prevent serious concussions, many helmets have air-filled pockets inside them. A player tests his helmet by sticking his head inside it and then shaking it for comfort, also making sure that it's snug. If it's too tight, he simply lets some air out of the helmet.

All helmets are equipped with face masks. The rounded metal material that comprises all face masks cannot be more than $5/8$ inch in diameter. Most linemen wear a face mask called a *cage* that has a bar extending down from the middle and top of the helmet to below the nose area. There, this bar joins two or three bars that extend from both sides that completely prevent an opponent's hands from reaching inside the face area and under the chin. However, few quarterbacks and receivers have a face mask with a bar coming between their eyes, because they want to ensure that they can see clearly; many also leave the chin exposed. Twenty years ago, some quarterbacks wore a helmet with a single bar across the face. Today, you might see a punter or kicker with a helmet that has a single bar, but players who encounter more contact during games want more protection.

Pads

Next to the helmet, the shoulder pads are probably the number-one protective gear that players wear. These pads protect a player's shoulders, plus his sternum region, from injury. Some of these pads fall down and cover the top of the arm and the rotator cuff. Pads are necessary to protect every part of the body.

There are thigh pads, elbow pads, hip pads, and knee pads, too. A player needs the pads to absorb the many physical blows he takes during a game, thus protecting his body from major harm. Some quarterbacks even wear flak jackets to protect their rib cages, which are vulnerable when they lift their arms to throw the ball.

Shoes and cleats

Football cleats come in $1/2$-inch, $5/8$-inch, $3/4$-inch, and 1-inch lengths. Wearing the right cleat is definitely important for traction. If a player doesn't have the proper traction indoors or outside on a muddy surface, he simply can't do his job and perform at the highest level. The shorter cleat, which makes a player less prone to injury, is worn on dry, firm fields like the ones in Florida and San Diego. For such fast, dry fields, the $1/2$-inch cleat provides the ideal traction. The $5/8$-inch cleat is for average fields like Green Bay's Lambeau Field and Chicago's Soldier Field. On a slippery grass field, a player — especially a big lineman across the line of scrimmage — needs to dig deep to gain traction. In that situation, the player switches to a $3/4$-inch cleat or a 1-inch cleat, depending on how he is maneuvering (stopping and going) during warm-ups. Receivers and running backs often wear shoes with fewer cleats than the larger, more physical players do.

For artificial surfaces, most players wear a shoe that has a sole of dozens of rubber-nubbed $1/2$-inch cleats. Some linemen prefer a basketball-type shoe, especially on indoor turf, where there's no chance of rain and the surface isn't as slick. Because artificial surfaces tend to be slippery and sticky, players want to be able to glide over the surface. They don't want to "stop on a dime" and change directions. Many players believe that instant stop and restart can be hazardous to their knees and ankles.

Most teams are equipped with all sizes and types of shoes in case the weather changes during the course of a game. You often see players changing their shoes on the sidelines. On mushy days, you see them cleaning their cleats on a long rubber-stemmed mat to maintain the amount of traction they need. In the NFL, players test the playing surface an hour prior to the game and then go into the locker room and, if necessary, have an equipment manager change their cleats with a power drill, like a pit crew changing tires.

NFL uniform codes

In a high school or college game, you might see a player wearing a torn jersey, exposing his midriff area, or see 5 different styles or brands of shoes on 11 different players. None of this occurs in the NFL, where strictly enforced uniform codes can lead to players being fined. Here are some of the rules that NFL players must follow:

- The NFL shield or logo must be visible on pants, jerseys, and helmets.

- Tear-away jerseys are prohibited.

- All jerseys must remain tucked into the uniform pants.

- Stockings must cover the entire leg area from the shoe to the bottom of the pants and meet the pants below the knee. Uniform stockings may not be altered, and they must be white from the top of the shoe to about mid-calf.

- Size and locations of shoe logos must be approved by NFL Properties. Players are not allowed to wear shoes from companies not approved by the league.

- Sleeves cannot be torn or cut.

- All tape used on shoes or socks or pants must be transparent or of a matching color to the team uniform.

- Towels can be only 8 inches long and 6 inches wide and must be tucked into the front waist of the pants.

Dressing for a game

For each game, I would get a stock jersey from Wilson, and my team would bring in two or three tailors. The tailors would taper my jersey so tight that putting it on and taking it off was nearly impossible. The jersey being so tight prevented offensive linemen from being able to grab me. I tell you, the arms on my jersey were so tight that it would take an entire pre-game warm-up just to get the jersey loose enough to where I didn't look like Robocop out there.

My biggest problem wasn't getting the jersey on, but taking it off. I always needed a team-mate or two to help me get it off; at times, I had two guys pulling as hard as they could.

I liked to wear everything super tight and light, with as few pads as possible. I was the first defensive player for whom Nike made a shoe,

so I probably had some of the lightest cleats in football. A lot of cleats that you see now were modeled after the shoe I helped design for Nike around 1985 — the kind of shoes you see Reggie White wearing, I helped design.

I never wore pads on my arms, and I never wore pads on my hands. I taped my wrists and thumbs, and that was it. I wanted to feel light out on the field. I wore minimal thigh pads and knee pads because I always felt like they slowed me down. I wasn't worried about the lack of protection on my knees and legs because few linemen ever got to them. If I got hit in the legs, it was from the side. And there was nothing I really could do about that. I couldn't wear knee braces like you see some linemen today because my calves were simply too big. I wouldn't have worn them anyway.

Chapter 3

Rules and Regulations

. . . .

In This Chapter

▶ Keeping time in a game

▶ Tossing the coin

▶ Understanding the down system

▶ Scoring via touchdowns, field goals, and other methods

▶ Defining the roles of all the officials

▶ Interpreting all those referee signals

▶ Calling penalties, from offside to personal fouls

. . . .

Granted, football is a pretty complicated game. There are 22 players on the field at all times, plus a host of officials — not to mention all those people running around on the sidelines. But once you figure out who's supposed to be where, and what they're supposed to be doing there, a football game is pretty easy to follow.

This chapter walks you through all the phases of a game, from the coin toss to the opening kickoff to halftime to the time when the fat lady sings. It also explains how the clock works, how you score points, what the officials do, what every penalty means, and much more.

The Clock Is Ticking

To keep things in small, easily digestible chunks, every football game is divided into *quarters*. In college and pro football, each quarter lasts 15 minutes; high schools use 12-minute quarters. After the second quarter comes halftime, generally a 15-minute break that gives players time to rest and allows bands and cheerleaders time to perform, and gives fans time to go get a hot dog. There are often halftime ceremonies in which coaches, players, or alumni are honored.

The game clock doesn't run continuously throughout those 15- or 12-minute quarters, though. (If it did, when would they show the TV commercials?) The clock stops for the following reasons:

- Either team calls a time-out. Teams are allowed three time-outs per half. Consecutive team time-outs can be taken, but the second time-out is reduced from a full minute to 40 seconds.

- A quarter ends. The stoppage in time enables teams to change which goal they will defend (they change sides at the ends of the first and third quarters).

- The quarterback throws an incomplete pass.

- The ball carrier goes out-of-bounds.

- A player from either team is injured during a play.

- An official signals a penalty by throwing a flag.

- The officials need to measure whether the offense has gained a first down or need to take time to spot the ball correctly.

- Either team scores a touchdown, field goal, or safety.

- The ball changes possession via a punt, a turnover, or a team failing to have advanced the ball 10 yards in four downs.

- A punt or kick returner catches the ball after a fair catch signal.

- The offense gains a first down (college and high school only).

- Two minutes remain in the period (NFL only).

Unlike in basketball, where a shot clock determines how long the offense can keep possession of the ball, in football the offense can keep the ball as long as it keeps making first downs (which I explain a little later in this chapter). However, the offense has 40 seconds from the end of a given play, or a 25-second interval after official stoppages, such as replacing a wet ball with a dry one or allowing the chain crew, who mark the downs, to get in the proper position after an extremely long pass gain. If the offense doesn't snap the ball in that allotted time, it is penalized 5 yards and must repeat the down. (You can find detailed information about how penalties work in the section "Penalties and other violations," later in this chapter.)

With the exception of the last two minutes of the first half and the last five minutes of the second half of an NFL game, the game clock is restarted following a kickoff return, a player going out-of-bounds on a play, or after a declined penalty.

Getting a Game Started

Every football contest starts with a *coin toss*. Selected members of each team (called *captains*) come to the center of the field, where the referee holds a coin. In the NFL, the coin toss is restricted to three captains from each team. In college football, four players may participate. However, only one player from the visiting team calls heads or tails as the official tosses the coin into the air (hence the name *coin toss*). If that player calls the toss correctly, his team gets to choose one of two privileges:

- ✔ **Which team receives the kickoff:** Generally, teams want to start off the game on offense and have the opportunity to score as early as possible, so the team who wins the toss usually opts to receive. They are known as the receiving team. The referee, by swinging his leg in a kicking motion, then points to the other team's captains as the kicking team.

- ✔ **Which goal his team will defend:** The captain may select this option because his team wants to kick off, believing that weather will be a factor. By choosing the goal, the player wants his team to have the wind at its back for the second and the final quarters of the game.

The team that loses the toss is stuck with the other option. Of course, if the winning captain chooses the ball, the losing captain does have the choice of which goal to defend.

The team that earns the right to receive the ball gets the ball via a *kickoff*. The kicking team's *placekicker* places the ball in a holder (called a *tee*) on his team's 30-yard line (NFL), 35-yard line (college), or 40-yard line (high school). The tee is 1 inch tall in the NFL and 2 inches high in high school and college. The kicker then runs toward the ball and kicks it toward the other team. Figure 3-1 shows how teams typically line up for a kickoff.

At the far end of the field from the kicker, one or more *returners* awaits the kickoff. The returner's goal is to catch the ball and run it as far back toward the opponents' goal line as he can. After the return is complete, the first set of *downs* begins.

Downs, Yardage, and Stuff

Watching a game in which the offense kept running plays but never went anywhere would be really boring. To prevent that, the fathers of football created the *down* system. The offense has four downs (essentially four plays) to go 10 yards. If the offensive team advances the ball at least 10 yards in four tries or fewer, it receives another set of four downs. If the

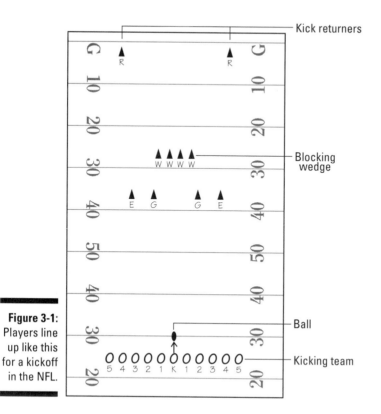

Kick returners

Blocking wedge

Ball

Kicking team

Figure 3-1:
Players line up like this for a kickoff in the NFL.

offense has failed to advance 10 yards after three tries, the team usually *punts* the ball on fourth down, or kicks it to the opponent without the use of a tee. The other team then begins with its own set of four downs, traveling in the opposite direction.

You may hear TV commentators use the phrase "three and out." What they mean is that a team has failed to advance the ball 10 yards (probably on more than one *possession,* or turn on offense) and has to punt the ball. You don't want your team to go three and out very often. But you do want to earn lots of *first downs,* which you get after your team advances the ball 10 yards or more. Getting lots of first downs usually translates to more scoring opportunities, which are definitely Good Things. This was proven true in the 1997 NFL season, when the Denver Broncos led the league with 340 first downs and also led in scoring with 472 points.

Football has its own lingo to explain the offense's progress toward a first down. A first down situation is also known as a "first and 10," because the offense has 10 yards to go to gain a first down. If your offense ran a play on first down in which you advanced the ball 3 yards, your status would be "second and 7"; you're ready to play the second down, and you now have 7 yards to go to gain a first down. Unless something really bad happens, the numbers here stay under ten, so the math is pretty simple.

As a viewer, you aren't expected to just remember what down it is and how many yards the offense needs to advance to gain a first down. Football makes it easy by providing people and signs to help you keep track. On the home sideline opposite the press box is a group of three people, known as the *chain gang* or *crew,* who hold three 8-foot-high poles.

✔ Two people called *rodmen* hold metal rods, with Xs at the top, connected by a thin metal chain that stretches exactly 10 yards when the two rods are thoroughly extended. One rod marks where the possession begins, and the other extends to where the offensive team must go in order to make another first down.

✔ The third person, known as the *boxman,* holds a marker that signifies where the ball is and what down it is. Atop this rod is the number 1, 2, 3, or 4, designating whether it is first, second, third, or fourth down.

✔ In all NFL stadiums, a person also marks where the *drive* began (that is, where the offensive team assumed possession of the ball). Many high school and college fields don't have these markers. An offensive team's possession lasts for as many plays as it has control of the football until it either relinquishes possession by scoring a touchdown or field goal or by punting to the other team.

Whenever there's critical measurement for a first down, the chain crew is brought to the hash marks nearest where the ball is positioned, and the officials use the rods to determine whether the offense has obtained a first down. The home team supplies the chain crew and also the ball boys, who are responsible for keeping the balls clean and free of excessive moisture.

How You Score Points

When a team has possession of the football, it can score points in several ways — and scoring points, after all, is the object of the game (more importantly, to score more points than the other team!). This section explains each method of scoring.

Touchdowns

A touchdown is worth six points — the ultimate goal. A team scores a touchdown, plus the loudest cheers from fans, when an offensive player carrying the ball advances from anywhere on the field and breaks the plane of his opponents' goal line with the ball. ("Breaking the plane" means that a ball carrier can soar over the goal line in midair and have his efforts count for a touchdown, even if he's hit in midair and lands back on the 1-yard line, as long as the ball crosses the plane.) A team is also awarded a touchdown when any player who is in-bounds catches or recovers a loose ball behind his opponents' goal line. This sort of touchdown can occur on a kickoff, a punt, or a fumble.

Extra points and two-point conversions

A try for an *extra point,* also known as a *point after a touchdown* (or *PAT*), is attempted during the scrimmage down that's awarded after a touchdown. The extra point is successful when the kicker kicks the ball between the uprights of the goalpost and above the crossbar (see Chapter 2 for more information about the goalposts), provided that the ball was snapped 2 yards away (or 3 yards away in high school or college) from the opponents' goal line. Teams should almost always make their extra point attempts — especially above the high school level — because the kick is a fairly easy one.

When a team is feeling particularly confident — or desperate — it might attempt a *two-point conversion* after scoring a touchdown. (Chapter 8 talks about situations in which a coach might decide to have his team "go for two.") Two-point conversions, which were added to the NFL for the 1994 season, have always been a part of high school and college football. The offense gets the ball on the 2-yard line and must advance the ball across the goal line, or break the plane, as if scoring a touchdown. The try (called a *conversion attempt*) is over when the officials rule the ball dead or if a change of possession occurs (the defense intercepts a pass or recovers a fumble).

Field goals

A *field goal,* often the consolation prize for an offense that tries to score a touchdown and then stalls within its opponents' 30-yard line, is worth three points. A team scores a field goal when a kicker boots the ball entirely through the uprights of the goalpost without touching either the ground or any of his teammates on the offensive team. The kicked ball must travel between the uprights and above the crossbar of the goalpost.

You get the distance of a field goal by adding 10 yards (the distance from the goal line to where the goalposts are placed) to the spot (yard line) from which the ball is kicked. Or simply add 17 to the number of yards that the offense would have to advance to cross the goal line. For example, if the offense is on its opponents' 23-yard line, a field goal attempt would be 40 yards.

Safeties

A *safety* is worth two points. The important factor in a safety is *impetus,* the action of an offensive player that gives the ball momentum. For example, if a ball carrier retreats from the field of play into his own end zone and is downed there, the ball carrier provided the impetus. A defensive player can never push a ball carrier a yard back into the end zone and then be awarded a safety. Only the ball carrier can provide the impetus.

A safety is awarded to the opposing team if the defending team sends the ball into its own end zone and the ball becomes dead in its possession. This occurs when a quarterback, running back, or receiver is tackled with the ball in his own end zone or goes out-of-bounds behind the goal line. A safety also is awarded when the offensive team commits a penalty (say, holding a defensive player who is preparing to tackle the ball carrier in the end zone) that would otherwise require it to have the ball marked in its own end zone.

A safety is also awarded when a blocked punt goes out of the kicking team's end zone. And when the receiver of a punt muffs the ball and then, when trying to retrieve the ball, forces or illegally kicks it into the end zone (creating new impetus) and it goes out of the end zone, the defensive team is given a safety, worth two points. If a muffed ball is kicked or forced into the end zone and then recovered there by a member of the receiving team, the defensive team is awarded a safety.

The Roles of the Officials

Officials play many important roles in a football game — they basically have control of every game. For example:

- ✔ They're responsible for any decision involving the application of a rule, its interpretation, or its enforcement.
- ✔ They keep players from really hurting each other and doing other illegal actions.
- ✔ They enforce and record all fouls and monitor the clock (the stadium clock, operated by a timekeeper in the press box, is the official time-keeper) and all time-outs charged.

All officials carry a whistle and a weighted, bright yellow flag, which they throw to signal that a penalty has been called on a particular play.

Officials are part-time workers for the NFL, college, and high school football. They're paid for working the game and are given travel expenses. In the NFL and college football, the work can be financially rewarding; depending on seniority and experience, officials earn between $20,000 and $80,000 a season.

The officials' lineup

If you want, you can just call them the officials, or — if you're in a particularly belligerent mood — you can call them the idiots who aren't even qualified to officiate a peewee football game. But true diehards know that each of the seven officials (five or six at some levels) has a different title and task. The following sections explain who they are and what they do.

Referee

This official has general oversight and control of the game. He's the final authority for the score, for the number of a down in case of a disagreement, and for all rule interpretations when a debate arises among the other officials. Although some players and coaches consider the referee a bad guy, he's the only official who wears a white hat. (All the other officials wear black hats.)

The referee announces all penalties and confers with the offending team's captain, explaining the penalty. Before the snap of the ball, he positions himself in the offensive backfield, 10 to 12 yards behind the line of scrimmage, and favors the right side if the quarterback is right-handed. The referee also monitors any illegal hits on the quarterback, such as roughing the passer. He follows the quarterback throughout the game and watches for the legality of blocks made near him.

At the end of any down, the referee can request the linesman and his assistants to bring the yardage chains onto the field to determine whether the ball has reached the necessary line for a new first down. This official also notifies the head coach when any player is disqualified for unnecessary roughness or unsportsmanlike conduct and tells the coach on whom each penalty is called.

Umpire

This official is responsible for the legality of the players' equipment and for watching all play along the line of scrimmage. He makes sure that the offensive team has no more than 11 players on the field prior to the snap of the ball. At the start of a play, he positions himself 4 to 5 yards off the line of scrimmage on the defensive side of the ball. Consequently, if he's not quick on his feet, the umpire is the official most likely to be trampled by oncoming players, especially ball carriers running up the middle.

Because he's responsible for monitoring the legality of all contact between the offensive and defensive linemen, this official calls most of the holding penalties. He also assists the referee on decisions involving possession of the ball in close proximity to the line of scrimmage. He records all time-outs, the winner of the coin toss, and all scores, and makes sure that the offensive linemen don't move downfield illegally on pass plays. Finally, when it's raining, the umpire wipes the wet ball dry prior to the snap.

Head linesman

This official sets up on the side of the field designated by the referee. He straddles the line of scrimmage and watches for encroachment, offside, illegal men downfield, and all the other line-of-scrimmage violations. He's also responsible for ruling on all out-of-bounds plays to his side of the field.

The linesman is responsible for the chain crew and grabs the chain when measuring for a first down. He's usually the official who runs in after a play is whistled dead and places his foot to show where forward progress was made by the ball carrier at the end of the play. He assists the line judge (who stands opposite the head linesman) with illegal motion calls and any illegal shifts or movement by running backs and receivers to his side. Also, during kicks or passes, he checks for illegal use of hands, and he must know who the eligible receivers are prior to every play. (For more information about these violations, see "Penalties and other violations" later in this chapter.)

Line judge

This official lines up on the opposite side of the field from the head linesman and serves as an overall helper while being responsible for illegal motion and illegal shifts. He assists the head linesman with offside and encroachment calls. He assists the umpire with holding calls and watching for illegal use of hands on the end of the line, especially during kicks and pass plays. He assists the referee with calls regarding false starts and forward laterals behind the line of scrimmage. He also makes sure that the quarterback hasn't crossed the line of scrimmage prior to throwing a forward pass. On punts, he remains on the line of scrimmage to make sure that none of the ends move downfield prior to the ball being kicked.

One of the line judge's most important jobs is supervising the timing of the game. If the game clock becomes inoperative, he assumes the official timing on the field. He advises the referee when time has expired at the end of a period. In the NFL, he signals the referee when two minutes remain in a half, stopping the clock for the two-minute warning. The *two-minute warning* was devised to essentially give the team in possession of the ball another time-out. In the NFL, the referee has more jurisdiction over stopping the clock, thus allowing more time for the offensive team to run its plays. The line judge also supervises substitutions made by the team seated on his side of the field. During halftime, he notifies the home team's head coach that five minutes remain before the start of the second half.

Back judge

This official has similar duties to the field judge (see the following section) and sets up 20 yards deep on the defensive side to the wide receiver side of the field. He makes sure that the defensive team has no more than 11 players on the field and is responsible for all eligible receivers to his side.

After the receivers have cleared the line of scrimmage, the back judge concentrates on action in the area between the umpire and the field judge; it's vital that he's aware of any passes that are trapped by receivers. He makes decisions involving catching, recovery, or illegal touching of loose balls beyond the line of scrimmage. He rules on the legality of catches or pass interference. He also rules on whether a receiver is interfered with, or whether a receiver has possession of the ball before going out-of-bounds.

The back judge calls clipping when it occurs on punt returns. During field goal and extra point attempts, he and the field judge stand under the goalpost and rule on whether the kicks are good.

Field judge

This official lines up 25 yards down the field on the defensive side of the ball and on the same side as the offensive tight end. In the NFL, he's responsible for the 40/25 second clock. (When a play ends, the team with the ball has 40 seconds in which to begin another play or is penalized for delay of game. If stoppage occurs due to a change of possession, a time-out, an injury, a measurement, or any unusual delay that interferes with the normal flow of play, a 25-second interval exists between plays.)

The field judge also counts the number of defensive players and is responsible for watching that players at the line of scrimmage to make sure that everyone is onside. He is responsible for forward passes that cross the defensive goal line and any fumbled ball in his area. He also watches for pass interference on the strong side of the field, monitoring the tight end's pass patterns, calling interference, making decisions involving catching, recovery, out-of-bounds spots, or illegal touching of a fumbled ball after it crosses the line of scrimmage. He also watches for illegal use of hands by the offensive players, especially the ends and wide receivers, on defensive players to his side of the field.

Side judge

With teams passing the ball more often, the side judge was added in 1978 as the seventh official for NFL games. Some high school games are played without a side judge, but college teams have adopted the use of the seventh judge as well. The side judge is essentially another back judge who positions himself 20 yards down the field from the line of scrimmage. He's another set of eyes monitoring the legalities downfield, especially during long pass attempts. On field goal and extra point attempts, he lines up next to the umpire under the goalpost and decides whether the kicks are good.

Penalties and other violations

A *penalty* is an infraction of the rules. Without rules, a football game would evolve into total chaos because the game is so physically demanding and the collisions are so intense. A dirty deed or a simple mistake (like a player moving across the line of scrimmage prior to the ball being snapped) is a penalty. There are over 100 kinds of penalties or rule violations.

Because it's awfully hard to yell loud enough that a stadium full of people can hear you, the referee uses a set of signals to inform everyone of penalties and other bad things that have transpired on the field. Referees give signals for all scoring plays, penalties, and play stoppages in order to communicate with the game's timekeepers. Table 3-1 shows what these signals look like and explains what they mean.

Table 3-1	Penalties and Violations
Signal	*What It Means*
	Touchdown. The referee extends his arms straight above his head to signify that a touchdown was scored. He also uses this signal to tell the offensive team that it successfully converted a field goal, extra point, or two-point conversion.
	Safety. The referee puts his palms together above his head to show that the defensive team scored a safety. Look for this signal whenever the offense is operating near its own goal line with the quarterback and running backs actually lined up in the end zone.
	First down. When the offensive team gains enough yardage for a first down, the referee points with his right arm at shoulder length toward the defensive team's goal.
	Stop the clock. The referee raises one arm above his head with an open palm to signify that there is excessive crowd noise in the stadium, telling the timekeeper to stop the clock. This signal also means that the ball is dead (the play is over) and that the neutral zone has been established along the line of the scrimmage.
	Fourth down. The referee raises one arm above his head with his hand in a closed fist to show that the offense is facing fourth down.

(continued)

Table 3-1 *(continued)*

Signal	What It Means
	Illegally touched ball. The referee uses the fingertips of both hands and touches his shoulders to signal that the ball was illegally touched, kicked, or batted.
	Time-out. The referee signals a time-out by waving his arms and hands above his head. The same signal, followed by the referee placing one hand on top his head, means that it's an official time-out, or a referee-called time-out. The referee makes the same signal when a ball is kicked into the end zone and not returned, declaring it a touchback. He waves his arms, followed by swinging one arm out from his side.
	Clock doesn't stop. When the referee moves an arm clockwise in a full circle in front of himself, he's informing the offensive team that it has no time-outs, or that the ball is in play and that the timekeeper should keep the clock moving.
	Delay of game. The referee signals a delay of game by folding his arms in front of his chest. This signal also means that a team called a time-out when it had already used all its allocated time-outs.
	False start/illegal formation. The referee rotates his forearms over and over in front of his body to signify a false start, an illegal formation, or that the kickoff or the kick following a safety is ruled out-of-bounds. (A *false start* is when any offensive lineman takes or simulates a three-point stance and then moves after taking that stance prior to the snap of the ball. The offensive team is penalized 5 yards and repeats the down. Also, any quick, abrupt movement by a single offensive player who is set prior to the snap of the ball is called a false start. The quarterback can be called for a false start if he makes an obvious attempt with his body or voice inflection to try to draw the opponent offside.)
	Personal foul. The referee raises his arms above his head and strikes one wrist with the edge of his other hand to signify a personal foul. If the personal foul signal is followed by the referee swinging one of his legs in a kicking motion, it means roughing the kicker. If the signal is followed by the referee simulating a throwing motion, it means roughing the passer. Finally, if the signal is followed by the referee pretending to grab an imaginary face mask, it's a major face mask penalty, worth 15 yards.

Signal	What It Means
	Holding. The referee signals a holding penalty by grabbing one wrist with the clenched fist of his other hand and pulling his arm down in front of his chest.
	Illegal use of hands. The referee grabs one wrist and extends the open hand of that arm forward in front of his chest to signal illegal use of the hands, arms, or body.
	Incomplete pass. The referee shifts his arms in a horizontal fashion in front of his body to signal that the pass is incomplete, a penalty is declined, a play is over, or a field goal or extra point attempt is no good.
	Juggled pass. The referee gestures with his open hands in an up-and-down fashion in front of his body to show that the pass was juggled in-bounds and caught out-of-bounds. This signal follows the incomplete pass signal.
	Illegal forward pass. The referee puts one hand behind his back waist-high to signal an illegal forward pass. The referee then makes the loss of down signal.
	Intentional grounding. The referee waves both his arms in a diagonal plane across his body to signal intentional grounding of a forward pass. This signal is followed by the loss of down signal.
	Interference. The referee, with open hands vertical to the ground, extends his arms forward from his shoulders to signify pass interference or interference of a fair catch of a punted ball.
	Invalid fair catch. The referee waves one hand above his head to signal an invalid fair catch of a kicked ball.

(continued)

Table 3-1 *(continued)*

Signal	What It Means
	Ineligible player downfield. The referee places his right hand on top of his head or cap to show that an ineligible receiver on a pass play was downfield early or that an ineligible member of the kicking team was downfield too early.
	Illegal contact. The referee extends his arm and an open hand forward to signal that illegal contact was made.
	Encroachment. The referee places his hands on his hips to signal that an offside, encroachment, or neutral zone infraction occurred.
	Illegal motion. The referee flattens out his hand and makes a horizontal arc with it to show that the offensive team made an illegal motion at the snap or prior to the snap of the ball.
	Loss of down. The referee places both hands behind his head to signal a loss of down.
	Illegal push. The referee uses his hands in a pushing movement with his arms below his waist to show that someone on the offensive team pushed or illegally helped a ball carrier.
	Illegally touched pass. The referee is sideways and uses a diagonal motion of one hand across another to signal an illegal touch of a forward pass or a kicked ball from scrimmage.
	Unsportsmanlike conduct. The referee puts his arms outstretched with palms down to signal an unsportsmanlike conduct penalty.

Signal	What It Means
	**Illegal cut block.** From the side, the referee uses both hands to strike the front of his thighs to signal that a player made an illegal cut block. When he uses one hand to strike the front of his thigh, preceded by a personal foul signal, he means that an illegal block below the waist occurred. When he uses both hands to strike the sides of his thighs, preceded by a personal foul signal, he means that an illegal chop block occurred. Finally, when he uses one hand to strike the back of his calf, preceded by a personal foul signal, he means that an illegal clipping penalty occurred.
	**Illegal crackback block.** The referee strikes with an open right hand around the middle of his right thigh, preceded by a personal foul signal, to signal an illegal crackback block.
	Player ejected. The referee clenches his fist with the thumb extended, a gesture also used in hitchhiking, to signal that a player has been ejected from the game.
	**Tripping.** The referee repeats the action of placing the right foot behind the heel of his left foot to signal a tripping penalty.
	Uncatchable pass. The referee holds the palm of his right hand parallel to the ground and moves it back and forth above his head to signal that a forward pass was uncatchable and that no penalty should be called.
	Illegal substitution. The referee places both hands on top of his head to signal that a team made an illegal substitution or used too many men on the field on the preceding play.

(continued)

Table 3-1 (continued)

Signal	What It Means
	Face mask. The referee gestures with his hand in front of his face and makes a downward pulling motion to signal that a player illegally grabbed the face mask of another player.
	Illegal shift. The referee uses both arms and hands in a horizontal arc in front of his body to signal that the offense used an illegal shift prior to the snap of the ball.
	Reset 25-second clock. The referee makes an open palm with his right hand and pumps that arm vertically into the air to instruct the timekeeper to reset the 25-second play clock.
	Reset 40-second clock. With the palms of both hands open, the referee pumps both arms vertically into the air to instruct the timekeeper to reset the 40-second play clock.

The rest of this chapter walks you through the specific penalties and their ramifications. I warn you, though: This stuff can get pretty complicated. You may want to read through Parts II and III to get a handle on the offense and defense first if you're a beginner and really want to understand this stuff. If you have trouble with a particular term, turn to the glossary at the back of the book.

Five-yard penalties

The following common penalties give the offended team an additional 5 yards. Some of these penalties, when noted, are accompanied by an automatic first down.

- ✔ **Defensive holding or illegal use of the hands:** When a defensive player tackles or holds an offensive player other than the ball carrier. Otherwise, the defensive player may use his hands, arms, or body only to protect himself from an opponent trying to block him in an attempt to reach a ball carrier. The penalty is 5 yards and an automatic first down.

- ✔ **Delay of game:** When the offense fails to snap the ball within the required 40 or 25 seconds, depending on the clock. If the defense repeatedly charges into the neutral zone prior to the snap, the referee can call a delay of game penalty, which brings an automatic first down. The ref can also call this penalty when a team fails to play when ordered (because, for example, the players are unsure of the play called in the huddle), a runner repeatedly attempts to advance the ball after his forward progress is stopped, or a team takes too much time assembling after a time-out.

✔ **Delay of kickoff:** Failure of the kicking team to kick the ball after being ordered to do so by the referee.

✔ **Encroachment:** When a player enters the neutral zone and makes contact with an opponent before the ball is snapped.

✔ **Excessive time-outs:** When a team calls for a time-out when it has already used its three time-outs allotted for the half.

✔ **Failure to pause for one second after the shift or huddle:** When any offensive player doesn't pause for at least one second after going into a set position. The offensive team also is penalized when it's operating from a no-huddle offense and immediately snaps the ball without waiting a full second after assuming an offensive set before snapping the ball.

✔ **Failure to report change of eligibility:** When a player fails to inform an official that he has entered the game and will be aligned at a position he normally doesn't play, like an offensive tackle lined up as a tight end. In the NFL, all players' jersey numbers relate to the offensive positions they play; consequently, the officials and opposing team know when it's illegal for a player wearing a number 60 through 79 (offensive linemen generally wear these numbers) to catch a pass.

✔ **False start:** When an interior lineman of the offensive team takes or simulates a three-point stance and then moves prior to the snap of the ball. The official must blow his whistle immediately. A false start is also whistled when any offensive player makes a quick, abrupt movement prior to the snap of the ball.

✔ **Kickoff goes out-of-bounds between the goal lines and is not touched:** When the kicking team fails to keep its kick in-bounds, it is penalized 5 yards and must rekick.

✔ **Forward pass is first touched by an eligible receiver who has gone out-of-bounds and returned:** Offensive players are not allowed to leave the field of play (even if shoved out), return in-bounds, and still be an eligible receiver.

✔ **Forward pass is thrown from behind the line of scrimmage after the ball crosses the line of scrimmage:** Players are not allowed to catch a pass, run past the line of scrimmage, and then retreat behind the line of scrimmage and attempt another pass. However, they are permitted to lateral the ball to another player, provided that the ball is not thrown forward.

✔ **Forward pass touches or is caught by an ineligible receiver on or behind the line of scrimmage:** When an offensive lineman catches a pass that is not first tipped by a defensive player.

✔ **Grasping the face mask of the ball carrier or quarterback:** When the face mask is grabbed unintentionally and the player immediately lets go of his hold, not twisting the ball carrier's neck at all.

✔ **Illegal formation:** When the offense doesn't have seven players on the line of scrimmage. Also, running backs and receivers who are not on the line of scrimmage must line up at least 1 yard off the line of scrimmage and no closer, or the formation is considered illegal.

✔ **Illegal motion:** When an offensive player, such as a quarterback, running back, or receiver, moves forward toward the line of scrimmage moments prior to the snap of the ball. Illegal motion is also called when a running back is on the line of scrimmage and then goes in motion prior to the snap. It's a penalty because the running back wasn't aligned in a backfield position.

✔ **Illegal return:** When a player returns to the field after he has been disqualified. He must leave the bench area and go to the locker room within a reasonable time.

✔ **Illegal substitution:** When a player enters the field during a play. Players must enter only when the ball is dead. If a substituted player remains on the field at the snap of the ball, his team is slapped with an unsportsmanlike penalty. If the substituted player runs to the opposing team's bench area in order to clear the field prior to the snap of the ball, his team incurs a delay of game penalty.

✔ **Ineligible member(s) of kicking team going beyond line of scrimmage before the ball is kicked:** In the NFL, only the two players aligned at least 1 yard outside the end men are allowed to go downfield when the ball is snapped to the kicker. All the other players must remain at the line of scrimmage until the ball is kicked.

✔ **Ineligible player downfield during a pass down:** When any offensive linemen are more than 2 yards beyond the line of scrimmage when a pass is thrown downfield.

✔ **Invalid fair catch signal:** When the receiver simply extends his arm straight up. To be a valid fair catch signal, the receiver must fully extend his arm and wave it from side to side.

✔ **Less than seven men on the offensive line when the ball is snapped:** This formation is illegal.

✔ **Loss of team time-out(s) or 5-yard penalty on the defense for excessive crowd noise:** This penalty is called when the quarterback informs the referee that the offense cannot hear his signals because of crowd noise. If the referee deems it reasonable to conclude that the quarterback is right, he signals a referee's time-out and asks the defensive captain to use his best influence to quiet the crowd. If the noise persists, the referee uses his wireless microphone to inform the crowd that continued noise will result in either the loss of an existing time-out or, if the defensive team has no time-outs remaining, a 5-yard penalty.

✓ **More than one man in motion at the snap of the ball:** In the Canadian Football League, two offensive players are allowed to be in motion at the same time, but having two men in motion at the same time is illegal on all levels of football in the U.S. However, two players can go in motion prior to the snap of the ball. But before the second player moves, the first player must be set for a full second.

✓ **More than 11 players on the field at the snap:** Teams are penalized for having more than 11 players on the field at any time when the ball is live. The offense receives an automatic first down if the penalty is committed by the defensive team.

✓ **Neutral zone infraction:** When a defensive player moves beyond the neutral zone prior to the snap and continues unabated toward the quarterback or kicker even though no contact is made by a blocker. If a defensive player enters the neutral zone prior to the snap and causes an offensive player to react immediately and prior to the snap, he has committed a neutral zone infraction.

✓ **Offside:** A player is offside when any part of his body is beyond the line of scrimmage or free kick line when the ball is put into play.

✓ **Player out-of-bounds at the snap:** When one of the 11 players expected to be on the field runs onto the field of play after the ball is snapped.

✓ **Running into the kicker or punter:** This is a 5-yard penalty only if the defender's action does not seem flagrant. A defender is not penalized for running into the kicker if the contact is incidental and occurs after he has touched the ball in flight. It also is not a penalty if the kicker's own motions cause the contact, or if the defender is blocked into the kicker, or if the kicker muffs the ball, retrieves it, and then kicks it.

✓ **Second forward pass behind the line of scrimmage:** The offensive team is allowed to attempt only one forward pass during each play from scrimmage.

✓ **Shift:** This is movement by an offensive player from one position on the field to another. After a team huddles, the offensive players must come to a stop and remain stationary for at least one second. If an offensive player who didn't huddle is in motion backwards at the snap of the ball, it is an illegal shift.

Ten-yard penalties

These penalties cost the offending team 10 yards:

- **Deliberately batting or punching a loose ball:** When a player bats or punches a loose ball toward an opponent's goal line, or in any direction if the loose ball is in either end zone. An offensive player cannot bat forward a ball in a player's possession or a backward pass in flight.

- **Deliberately kicking a loose ball:** When a player kicks a loose ball in the field of play or tries to kick a ball from a player's possession. The ball is not dead when an illegal kick is recovered, however.

- **Helping the runner:** When a member of the offensive team pushes or pulls a runner forward when the defense has already stopped his momentum.

- **Holding, illegal use of the hands, arms, or body by the offense:** When an offensive player uses his hands, arms, or other parts of his body to hold a defensive player from tackling the ball carrier. The penalty is most common when linemen are attempting to protect the quarterback from being tackled for a loss (sacked) behind the line of scrimmage. The defense is also guilty of holding when it tackles or prevents an offensive player, other than the ball carrier, from moving downfield after the ball is snapped. On a punt, field goal attempt, or extra point try, the defense cannot grab or pull an offensive blocker in order to clear a path for a teammate to block the kick or punt attempt.

- **Offensive pass interference:** When a forward pass is thrown and an offensive player physically restricts or impedes a defender in a manner that is visually evident and materially affects the opponent's opportunity to gain position to catch the ball. This penalty usually occurs when a pass is badly underthrown and the intended receiver must come back to the ball and interfere rather than watch the pass be intercepted.

- **Tripping a member of either team:** This penalty usually occurs close to the line of scrimmage when a lineman sees someone running past him and sticks out his leg, tripping the player.

Fifteen-yard penalties

These are the penalties that make coaches yell at their players because they cost the team 15 yards — the stiffest penalties (other than ejection or pass interference) in football:

- **Any player using the top of the helmet unnecessarily (known as *spearing*):** When a player dives onto a defenseless opponent, using the top of helmet to tackle him violently.

✔ **A tackler using his helmet to butt, spear, or ram an opponent:** This action involves using the top or crown and forehead of the helmet, plus the face mask, to unnecessarily butt, spear, or ram an opponent. The officials monitor particular situations, such as

- When a passer is in the act of throwing or has just released a pass

- When a receiver is catching or attempting to catch a pass

- When a runner is already in the grasp of a tackler

- When a kick or punt returner is attempting to field a kick in the air

- When a player is on the ground at the end of a play

✔ **A punter, placekicker, or holder who simulates being roughed by a defensive player:** When these players pretend to be hurt or injured or act like a defensive player caused them actual harm when the contact is considered incidental.

✔ **A defender who takes a running start from beyond the line of scrimmage in an attempt to block a field goal or point after touchdown and lands on players at the line of scrimmage:** This penalty prevents defensive players from hurting unprotected players who are attempting to block for their kicker.

✔ **Chop block:** When an offensive player blocks a defensive player at the thigh or lower while another offensive player occupies that same defensive player by attempting to block him or even simulating a blocking attempt.

✔ **Clipping below the waist:** When a player throws his body across the back of the leg(s) of an opponent or charges or falls into the back of an opponent below the waist after approaching him from behind, provided that the opponent is not a ball carrier or positioned close to the line of scrimmage. However, within 3 yards on either side of the line of scrimmage and within an area extended laterally to the original position of the offensive tackle, offensive linemen can block defensive linemen from behind.

✔ **Delay of game at the start of either half:** If the captains for either team (and they must be in uniform) fail to show up in the center of the field for the coin toss three minutes prior to the start of the game or the start of the second half, they lose the coin toss option and are penalized from the spot of the kickoff. The other team automatically gets the coin-toss choice.

✔ **Fair catch interference:** Except when a kick fails to cross the line of scrimmage, no player from the kicking team can impede the punt or kick returner or his path to the ball, or even touch the ball prior to it hitting the ground.

✔ **Illegal crackback block by the offense:** An offensive player who lines up more than 2 yards laterally outside an offensive tackle, or a player who is in a backfield position at the snap and then moves to a position more than 2 yards laterally outside the tackle, may not clip an opponent anywhere. Nor may he contact an opponent below the waist if the blocker is moving toward the position from which the ball was snapped and the contact occurs within a 5-yard area on either side of the line of scrimmage.

✔ **Illegal low block:** Players on the receiving team are prohibited from blocking below the waist during a down in which a kickoff, safety kick, punt, field goal attempt, or extra point try occurs.

✔ **Piling on (automatic first down):** When a ball carrier is helpless or prostrate, defenders must refrain from jumping onto his body with excessive force with the possible intention of causing injury.

✔ **Roughing the kicker (automatic first down):** A defensive player may not make any contact with the kicker if he hasn't touched the kicked ball. Sometimes this penalty is committed by more than one defensive player as they attempt to block a kick or punt.

✔ **Roughing the passer (automatic first down):** The NFL wants to protect its star players, so this penalty is watched closely. Once the quarterback has released the ball, a defensive player may make direct contact with the quarterback only up through the rusher's first step after his release. Thereafter, the rusher must attempt to avoid contact and must not continue to "drive through" or forcibly contact the passer. The defensive player is called for roughing if he commits intimidating acts such as picking up the passer and stuffing him into the ground, wrestling with him, or driving him down after he has released the ball. Also, the defender must not use his helmet or face mask to hit the passer.

✔ **Twisting, turning, or pulling an opponent by the face mask:** Simply grasping an opponent's face mask is a 5-yard penalty. However, if the opponent grasps the face mask and then twists, turns, or pulls it, thus recklessly turning that player's head or neck, he's charged with a 15-yard penalty. If the referee considers the action flagrant, that player may be disqualified from the game.

✔ **Unnecessary roughness:** This penalty has different variations:

- Striking an opponent above the knee with the foot, or striking any part of the leg below the knee with a whipping motion

- Tackling the ball carrier when he's clearly out-of-bounds

- A member of the receiving team going out-of-bounds and contacting a player on the kicking team

- Diving or throwing one's body on the ball carrier when he is defenseless on the ground and is making no attempt to get up

- Throwing the ball carrier to the ground after the play is ruled dead [official(s) have blown the whistle]

✔ **Unsportsmanlike conduct:** This penalty applies to any act that is contrary to the generally understood principles of sportsmanship, including the use of abusive, threatening, or insulting language or gestures to opponents, officials, or representatives of the league; the use of baiting or taunting acts or words that engender ill will between teams; and unnecessary contact with any game official.

Specific pass-play penalties

These penalties occur only when the offensive team has attempted a forward pass. Here are three of the most common penalties you see on pass plays:

✔ **Illegal contact:** A defensive player is penalized 5 yards for blocking a wide receiver who is at least 2 yards outside his own tackle unless the quarterback hands off the ball or is tackled. Also, once the receiver is 5 yards beyond the line of scrimmage, the defensive player cannot grab, hold, or shove the receiver, thus knocking him off his intended pass route.

✔ **Intentional grounding:** This penalty, which is a loss of down and 10 yards from the preceding spot, is called when a passer, facing an imminent loss of yardage due to pressure from the defense, throws a forward pass without a realistic chance of completing it. If he throws such a pass in his own end zone, a safety (two points) is awarded to the defense. It is *not* intentional grounding when a passer, while out of the *pocket* (the protected area within the area of two offensive tackles), throws a pass that lands at or beyond the line of scrimmage with an offensive player having a realistic chance of catching the ball. When out of the pocket, the passer is allowed to throw the ball out-of-bounds.

✔ **Pass interference:** When a defensive player physically restricts or impedes a receiver in a visually evident manner and materially affects the receiver's opportunity to gain position or retain his position to catch the ball. This penalty is an automatic first down, and the ball is placed at the spot of the foul. If interference occurs in the end zone, the offense gets a first down on the 1-yard line. However, when both players are competing for position to make a play on the ball, the defensive player has a right to attempt to intercept the ball.

Part II
Go Offense

The 5th Wave   By Rich Tennant

"Sure you can call your own plays, as long as they fire *you* when we lose."

In this part . . .

*E*ven though I played defense throughout my football career, I admit that offense can be the more exciting half of the game, especially for fans who are new to the game. In this part, I talk about the "general" of the offense: the quarterback. If you're ready to look a little deeper into the offense, this part also explains the two phases of offense: the passing game and the running game. Finally, I explain some common offensive plays and strategies that you see in football games at all levels.

Chapter 4

The Quarterback

*B*eing a former defensive player, I hate to admit that the quarterback is the most important player on a football team. My only consolation is that although quarterbacks command the highest salaries in the NFL, my fellow defensive linemen are number two on the list. That's because their job is to make the quarterback's life miserable. Quarterbacks get all the press during the week, and defensive guys knock the stuffing out of them on weekends.

I like my quarterback to be the John Wayne of the football team. He should be a courageous leader, one who puts winning and his teammates ahead of his personal glory. Joe Montana, who won four Super Bowls with the San Francisco 49ers, and John Elway, who won his first Super Bowl in 1998 with the Denver Broncos, quickly come to mind. Both of them played with toughness, although they also had plenty of talent, skill, and flair to somehow escape the worst situations and throw the touchdown pass that won the game.

In this chapter, I talk about the fundamental skills that you need to play quarterback. I also discuss stance, vision, and arm strength and solve the puzzle of that mysterious quarterback rating system.

The Quarterback's Job

With the exception of kicking plays (see Chapter 12), quarterbacks touch the ball on every offensive play. A quarterback's job is to operate and guide the offense efficiently. In a typical NFL game during the 1997 season, each team possessed the ball only 11 times during a game. (When I talk about a *possession,* I'm not talking about a single play, but a series of plays in which the offense either scores or is forced to punt the ball away.) The quarterback's goal is to direct his team toward the end zone and score as many points as possible. During the 1997 season, the typical team scored on one-third of those offensive possessions, resulting in either a touchdown or a field goal. So you can see that there is enormous pressure on the quarterback to generate points every time the offense takes the field.

The quarterback (QB) is the player directly behind the center receiving the ball, as shown in Figure 4-1. He is the player who announces the plays in the huddle. The quarterback may receive adulation for a fine performance, but coaches on all levels of football (peewee, high school, college, and the NFL) decide what plays the offense will use. I know that my partner at FOX, Terry Bradshaw, called his own plays, but that's another story for another time.

Figure 4-1:
The quarterback lines up directly behind the center at the beginning of each play.

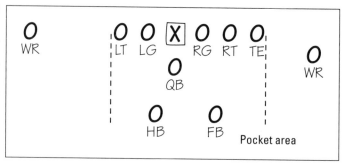

In the NFL, a quarterback receives plays from a coach on the sidelines via a hearing device placed in his helmet. In high school and college football, an assistant coach generally signals in the plays from the sidelines after conferring with the head coach or offensive coordinator. In critical situations, a player may bring in the play when being substituted for an offensive player already on the field.

When Bradshaw played in the 1970s, many coaches allowed their veteran quarterbacks to call their own plays after practicing and studying all week. But eventually the coaches wrested control of the play-calling away from the quarterbacks, believing that the responsibility was too much of a mental burden for those players. When the game became more specialized (with multiple substitutions on both offense and defense) in the 1980s, coaches decided that they wanted the pressure of making the play calls. They didn't think a quarterback needed the additional responsibility of facing the media after a game and explaining why he called certain plays in a losing game. Head coaches wanted to be the ones to answer those tough questions.

Although NFL coaches don't allow quarterbacks to call their own offensive plays (except in no-huddle situations when little time remains on the clock), a player must be prepared to change the play at the line of scrimmage if it doesn't appear that the play will succeed. Changing the play at the line of scrimmage in this fashion is called *audiblizing*.

After the quarterback is in possession of the ball, he turns and, depending on which play was called, hands the ball to a running back, runs with the ball himself, or moves farther back and sets up to attempt a pass. Depending on the design of the offense, the quarterback takes a three-step, five-step, or seven-step *drop* before throwing the ball (see the section "Dropping back," later in this chapter, for more information).

The area in which the quarterback operates, most likely with a running back and the offensive line protecting him from the defense, is called the *pocket*. It is as wide as the positioning of the quarterback's offensive tackles. The quarterback is instructed to stay within this so-called protective area; if he ventures out of the pocket, he's likely to suffer a bone-crushing tackle. And the last thing a coach wants is for his quarterback, the leader of his team, to get injured.

The quarterback rarely runs with the ball unless he's being chased out of the pocket or instructed to run a *quarterback sneak* when the offense needs a yard or less for a first down. In a quarterback sneak, the quarterback takes a direct snap from the center and either leaps behind his center or guard or dives between his guard and center, hoping to gain a first down. However, the quarterback's main job is to throw the football and encourage his teammates to play well.

While the quarterback is setting up a play, he also must be aware of what the defense is attempting to do. In Chapter 5, I discuss how quarterbacks "read" a defense.

The Qualities of a Quarterback

When scouts or coaches examine a quarterback's potential to play in the National Football League, they run down a checklist of physical, mental, and personality traits that impact a quarterback's success on the field. These qualities are required for success at all levels of football; however, in this chapter, I discuss them in terms that relate to a professional athlete.

Some scouts and coaches break down a quarterback's talent and abilities further, but for this book's purposes, the following are the main criteria necessary to excel in the NFL. If a quarterback has five of these seven traits, he undoubtedly ranks among the top 15 players at his position.

Arm strength

Unlike baseball, football doesn't use a radar gun to gauge the speed of the ball after the quarterback releases it. But velocity is important when throwing a football because it allows a quarterback to complete a pass before a single defensive player can *recover* (react to the pass) and possibly deflect or intercept the ball. Consequently, the more arm strength a quarterback has, the more able he is to throw the ball at a high speed.

Many good quarterbacks, with practice, could throw a baseball between 75 and 90 mph, comparable to a Major League Baseball pitcher. Because of its shape, a football is harder to throw than a baseball, but NFL quarterbacks like the Oakland Raiders' Jeff George and the Green Bay Packers' Brett Favre throw the fastest passes at over 40 mph.

Competitiveness

A player's competitiveness is made up of many subjective and intangible qualities. A quarterback should have the desire to be the team's offensive leader and, ideally, overall leader. No one should work harder in practice than he does.

Quarterbacks are fan favorites

Every football fan has a favorite quarterback. Because quarterbacks touch the ball on virtually every play, except for punts and kicks, fans usually focus on a team's quarterback. It's the glamour position — and believe me, most defensive players are jealous of these guys.

In a 1998 Harris Poll, seven NFL players placed in the fans' top ten list for all sports. Five of those seven NFL players were quarterbacks. Dallas Cowboys quarterback Troy Aikman and Green Bay Packers quarterback Brett Favre finished second and third, respectively, on the fans' ballot behind the NBA's Michael Jordan. The Denver Broncos' John Elway, who won his first Super Bowl in 1998 after four attempts, finished fourth, and Joe Montana, who played his last NFL game in 1994, ranked fifth. Montana and my TV partner, Terry Bradshaw, are the only quarterbacks to have won four Super Bowl championships. Miami Dolphins quarterback Dan Marino, who owns every major NFL passing record, ranked ninth with the fans.

The quarterback's performance affects the entire offensive team. If he doesn't throw accurately, the receivers will never catch a pass. If he doesn't move quickly, the linemen won't be able to protect him. He also should have the courage to take a hard hit from a defensive player. During games, quarterbacks must cope with constant harassment from the defense. They must stand in the pocket and hold onto the ball until the last split second, knowing that they're going to be tackled the instant they release the ball.

To be a competitive player, a quarterback must have an inner desire to win. The quarterback's competitive fire often inspires his teammates to play harder. Competitiveness is a quality that every coach (and teammate) wants in his quarterback.

Intelligence

The quarterback doesn't have to have the highest IQ on the team, but intelligence does come in handy. Many NFL teams have a 3-inch-thick playbook that includes at least 50 running plays and as many as 200 passing plays. The quarterback has to know all of them. Not only does he have to know what he's supposed to do in every one of those plays, but he also needs to know what the other *skilled players* (running backs, receivers, and tight ends) are required to do. Why? Because he may have to explain a specific play in the huddle or during a time-out. On some teams, the quarterback is also responsible for informing the offensive linemen of their blocking schemes.

Prior to the NFL draft, the league administers an intelligence and personality test called the Wonderlic Test. Most quarterbacks score above 30 (out of a possible perfect 50 score). Conversely, more than 50 percent of all players score below 20. Many quarterbacks are what coaches call "football-smart." They know the intricacies of the game, the formations, and the defenses. They play on instinct and play well. Former San Francisco 49ers quarterback Joe Montana had football smarts; he may have been the best of all time in that category. The New York Jets' great, Joe Namath, was also very instinctive on the field.

Current San Francisco quarterback Steve Young is both football-smart and book-smart. Young is a lot like former great quarterbacks Otto Graham of the Cleveland Browns and Roger Staubach of the Dallas Cowboys. Being book-smart and football-smart can be an unbeatable combination on game days.

Mobility

A quarterback's mobility is as important as his intelligence and his arm. He must move quickly to avoid being tackled by defensive players. Therefore, he must move backward (called *retreating*) from the center as quickly as possible in order to set himself up to throw the ball. When a quarterback has excellent mobility, you hear him described as having *quick feet*. This term means that he moves quickly and effortlessly behind the line of scrimmage with the football. A quarterback doesn't have to be speedy to do this. He simply must be able to maneuver quickly and gracefully. In one simple step away from the line of scrimmage, a good quarterback covers $4^1/_2$ feet to almost 2 yards. While taking these huge steps, the quarterback's upper body should not dip or lean to one side or the other. He must be balanced.

Mobility is also critical when a quarterback doesn't have adequate pass protection and has to move out of the pocket and pass while under pressure and on the run. Coaches call this type of mobility *escapability*. Both Steve Young and Brett Favre are great at escaping defensive pressure. Maybe the best of the old-timers was Fran Tarkenton, who played with the New York Giants and the Minnesota Vikings. Roger Staubach of the Cowboys was nicknamed "Roger the Dodger" because he was tough to trap.

Release

If a quarterback doesn't have exceptional arm strength, he'd better have a quick *release*. After the quarterback raises the ball in his hand, usually near his head or slightly above and behind it, he *releases*, or rapidly brings his arm forward and lets loose of the ball. Miami Dolphins quarterback Dan Marino, who holds virtually every NFL passing record, probably has the game's quickest release. His arm and hand remain a blur when filmed and replayed in slow motion. For you Western-movie fans, the release is comparable to the quick draw that Alan Ladd had in *Shane*.

Quarterbacks with great releases generally are born with the ability. Average quarterbacks can improve and refine their releases, but their releases will never be great. A quarterback either has this coordinated motion between his arm, elbow, and wrist, or he doesn't. Throwing a football is not a natural arm movement like slinging your arm to roll a bowling ball.

Size

Players of all different heights and weights have played the quarterback position, but NFL quarterbacks are preferably over 6'1" and 210 pounds. A quarterback who is 6'5" and 225 pounds is considered ideal. A quarterback wants to be tall enough to see over his linemen — whose average height in the NFL is 6'5" to 6'7" — and look down the field, beyond the line of scrimmage, to find his receivers and see where the defensive backs are positioned.

Weight is imperative to injury prevention because of the physical wear and tear that the position requires. A quarterback can expect a lot of physical contact, especially when attempting to pass. Defenders relentlessly pursue the quarterback to hit him, tackling him for a *sack* (a loss of yards behind the line of scrimmage) before he can get off a pass or making contact after he releases the pass. These hits are sometimes legal and sometimes illegal. If the defensive player takes more than one step when hitting the quarterback after he releases the ball, the hit is considered illegal. Regardless, defensive linemen and linebackers are taught to inflict as much punishment as possible on the quarterback. They want to either knock him out of the game or cause him enough pain that he'll be less willing to hold onto the ball while waiting for his receivers to get open. When a quarterback releases a pass prematurely, it's called *bailing out of the play.*

Vision

A quarterback doesn't necessarily need the keen peripheral vision that basketball greats Earvin "Magic" Johnson and Larry Bird possessed, but it doesn't hurt. A quarterback must quickly scan the field when he comes to the line of scrimmage prior to the snap of the ball. He must survey the defense, checking its alignments and in particular the depth of the defensive backs — how far they are off the receivers, off the line of scrimmage, and so on. After the ball is snapped, the quarterback must continue to scan the field as he moves backward. Granted, he may focus on a particular area because the play is designed in a certain direction, but vision is critical if he wants to discover whether another receiver — other than his first choice — is open on a particular play. Most pass plays have a variety of options, what are known as *passing progressions*. One pass play may have as many as five players running pass routes, so the quarterback needs to be able to check whether any of them is open so that he has an option if he is unable to throw to his intended (first choice) receiver.

A quarterback needs to have a sense of where to look and how to scan and then quickly react. Often, a quarterback has to make a decision in a split second, or the play may fail. Vision doesn't necessarily mean that the quarterback has to jerk his head from side to side; often, his *passing reads* (how a quarterback deciphers what the defense is attempting to accomplish against the offense on a particular play) follow an orderly progression as he looks across the field of play. A quarterback must have an understanding of what the defensive secondary's tendencies are — how they like to defend a particular play or a certain style of receiver. Sometimes, after sneaking a quick glance at his intended target, he looks in another direction in order to fool the defense. Many defensive players tend to follow a quarterback's eyes, believing that his eyes will tell where he intends to throw the pass.

Quarterbacking Fundamentals

Playing quarterback requires a lot of technical skills. Although a coach can make a player better in many areas of the game, I don't believe that any coach can teach a player how to throw the football. Otherwise, every quarterback in the NFL would be a great passer. And if such a coach existed, every father would be taking his son to that coach, considering the millions of dollars that NFL quarterbacks earn every season.

You *can* teach a quarterback how to deal with pressure, how to make good decisions, and how to make good connections with his receivers and predict where they will be. But quarterbacks either have the innate talent to throw the football — that natural arm motion and quick release— or they don't. Think of how many good college quarterbacks fail to survive in the NFL. Plus, NFL scouts, coaches, general managers, and so on will tell you that the league has only 10 to 15 really good quarterbacks. If throwing could be taught, they all would be great.

Quarterbacks *can* improve and refine their skills in the following areas with a lot of practice and hard work.

Stance

To play the most important position in football, a quarterback must begin with his stance under center. The quarterback takes his stance behind the center to receive the ball; the center snaps it back to him (see Figure 4-2). The quarterback's stance under center starts with both feet about shoulder width apart. He bends his knees, flexes down, and bends forward at the waist until he's directly behind the center's rear end. The quarterback then places his hands, with the thumbs touching each other and the fingers spread as far apart as possible, under the center's rear end. Because some centers don't bring the ball all the way to the quarterback's hands (often the quarterback is blamed for fumbled snaps), the quarterback will lower his hands below the center's rear end in order to receive the ball cleanly. The quarterback needs to avoid pulling out early, a common mistake when the quarterback and the center have not played together very much.

A good way to tell whether a quarterback has bent down far enough and has his hands down far enough is to make sure that his chest is no more than 10 inches above the center's rear end.

The quarterback starts his stance with a little more of his weight on the ball of his left foot if he's a right-handed passer, and on the ball of his right foot if he's left-handed. This foot is the push-off foot, the one that he uses to move quickly away from the center after the ball is snapped. He pushes back on

Figure 4-2:
A quarterback lines up behind the center, who snaps the ball to him to start the play.

Quarterback   Center

that foot while slightly turning the trunk of his body to the side in which he holds the football. He must work on this technique by repeating it as many times as he can until it becomes one fluid motion.

Dropping back

After he masters the stance, a quarterback learns how to *drop back* and set up to pass. Dropping back is what a quarterback does after he receives the ball from the center. Before he passes the ball, he must move away from the line of scrimmage (and the opposing defense) and put himself in a position to be able to throw the football.

I believe that the fastest way to drop back from the line of scrimmage is to have a right-handed quarterback slightly turn his body sideways, open up his right hip (by turning or pivoting his left foot), and then run out from under center rather than backing out. A left-handed quarterback would do the opposite.

You see quarterbacks backing up from center, or *backpedaling,* when the offensive formation is aligned to the left of a right-handed quarterback. Backpedaling is essential in those alignments so that the quarterback can see whether the linebacker on that side is *blitzing* (rushing across the line of scrimmage in an attempt to tackle the quarterback). The quarterback must be alert to a possible blitz; consequently, he can't afford to half-turn his back to that side.

The depth in which a quarterback drops in the pocket generally is determined by how far from the line of scrimmage the receiver is running. If the receiver is running 5 to 6 yards down the field and then turning to catch the ball, for example, the quarterback takes a drop of no more than three steps. The quarterback generally moves farther away from the line of scrimmage as the pass routes (the paths that receivers take when going out for a pass) of his receivers get longer. If the receiver is running 10 to 12 yards down the field, the quarterback takes five steps to put himself about 7 yards deep from the line of scrimmage. When a wide receiver is going 15 to 17 yards down the field, the quarterback must take a seven-step drop, which puts him about 9 or 10 yards deep from the line of scrimmage.

All these drops are critical to the timing of the receiver's run, move, and turn and the quarterback's delivery and release. In practice, the quarterback works on the depth of his steps according to the pass route.

On a *post route* (a deep pass in which the receiver angles in to the goalpost) or a *streak route* (a deep pass straight downfield), the quarterback takes a seven-step drop. Taking a longer drop when a shorter one is required enables the defense to recover and may lead to an interception or an incompletion.

The best drill that I know of to improve a quarterback's footwork while dropping back is to play a game of tag. Have the quarterback stand at the line of scrimmage, ready to take the snap. Put two players opposite him, about 2 or 3 yards away, in three-point stances like defensive linemen. Then follow these steps:

1. **The quarterback pretends that he takes the snap and drops back.**

2. **The two players take off after him, trying to tag him before he reaches the 5-yard mark or the 7-yard mark.**

   I suggest placing a cone 5 or 7 yards deep, depending on the desired distance.

This drill teaches a quarterback how to set up quickly on pass drops.

Handing off

One of the most important things for a quarterback to learn is the running game and how it affects his steps from center. (See Chapter 6 for more on the running game.) Some running plays call for the quarterback to open his right hip (if he's right-handed) and step straight back. This technique is called the *six o'clock step*. The best way to imagine these steps is to picture a clock. The center is at twelve o'clock, and directly behind the quarterback is six o'clock. Three o'clock is to his right, and nine o'clock is to his left.

For example, a right-handed quarterback hands off the ball to a runner heading on a run around the left side of his offensive line (it's called a *sweep*) at the five o'clock mark. When handing the ball to a runner heading on a sweep across the backfield to the right, the quarterback should hand off at the seven o'clock mark. When practicing, a quarterback can make these marks on the field, visualizing a big clock. The six o'clock mark is about 3 yards behind the line of scrimmage.

Grip

Because different quarterbacks have different-sized hands, one passing grip does not suit everyone. Some coaches say that a quarterback should hold the ball with his middle finger going across the ball's white laces or trademark. Other coaches will tell you that both the middle and ring finger should grip the laces.

Many great quarterbacks have huge hands, allowing them to place their index finger on the tip of the ball while wrapping their middle, ring, and small fingers around the middle of the ball. However, the ball slips from many quarterbacks' hands when they attempt to grip the ball this way. As a quarterback, you simply need to find the grip that works for you.

Calling Plays and "Audibilizing"

The quarterback relays to his teammates in the huddle what play has been called. The play is a mental blueprint or diagram for every player on the field. And everything that he says refers specifically to the assignments of his receivers, running backs, offensive linemen, and center. For example, the quarterback may say "686 Pump F-Stop on two."

The first three numbers (686) are the passing routes that the receivers — known as X, Y, and Z — should take. Every team numbers its pass routes and patterns (look for them in "Passing Patterns" in Chapter 5), giving receivers an immediate signal of what routes to run. On this play, the X receiver runs a 6 route, the Y receiver an 8 route, and the Z receiver another 6 route.

"F-Stop" in this case refers to the fullback's pass route. And "two" refers to the *count* on which the quarterback wants the ball snapped to him; the center will snap the ball on the second sound. Most teams snap the ball on the first, second, or third count unless they are purposely attempting to draw the opposition offside by using an extra-long count. For example, if the quarterback has been asking for the ball on the count of two throughout the game, he may ask for the ball on the count of three, hoping that someone on the defense will move prematurely.

After the quarterback reaches the line of scrimmage and puts his hands under center, he says "Set" (at which point the linemen drop into their stances) and then something like "Green 80, Green 80, Hut-Hut." The center snaps the ball on the second "Hut." "Green 80" means absolutely nothing in this case. However, sometimes the quarterback's remarks at the line of scrimmage prior to the snap count inform his offensive teammates of how the play will be changed. The offensive linemen also know that the play is a pass because of the numbering system mentioned at the beginning of the called play.

Teams give their plays all sorts of odd monikers, such as Quick Ace, Scat, Zoom, and Buzz. These names refer to specific actions within the play; they are meant for the ears of the running backs and receivers. Each name (and every team has its own terms) means something, depending on the play that is called.

Quarterbacks are allowed to change the play at the line of scrimmage. They usually alter the play when they discover that the defense has guessed correctly and is properly aligned to stop the play, which in this example is Green 80. When he barks his signals, the quarterback simply has to say Green 85, and the play is altered to the 85 pass play. Usually, the quarterback elects to inform his offensive teammates in the huddle what his audible change may be.

A quarterback also may use an offensive strategy known as *check with me*, in which he instructs his teammates to listen carefully at the line of scrimmage because he may call another play, or his call at the line of scrimmage (check with me) will be the play. To help his teammates easily understand, the play may simply change colors — from Green to Red, for example.

Quarterback Math

Quarterbacks are judged statistically on all levels of football by their passing accuracy, which is called *completion percentage,* and by the number of touchdowns they throw, the number of interceptions they throw, and the number of yards they gain by passing. This last statistic — passing yards — can be deceiving. For example, if a quarterback throws the ball 8 yards beyond the line of scrimmage and the receiver runs for another 42 yards after catching the ball, the quarterback is awarded 50 yards for the completion. (You may hear television commentators use the term *yards after the catch* to describe the yards that the receiver gains after catching the ball.) Quarterbacks also receive positive passing yards when they complete a pass behind the line of scrimmage — for example, a pass to a running back who goes on to run 15 yards. Those 15 yards are considered passing yards.

For a better understanding of what the quarterback's numbers mean, take a look at Green Bay Packers quarterback Brett Favre's statistics for the 1997 season. He played in all 16 games.

	Att	Comp	Pct Comp	Yds	Yds/Att	TD	Int	Rating Points
Favre	513	304	59.3	3,867	7.54	35	16	92.6

Examining Favre's statistical numbers, you see that he attempted 513 passes (Att) and completed 304 of those passes (Com) for a completion percentage of 59.3 (Pct Comp). In attempting those 513 passes, his receivers gained 3,867 yards, which equals an average gain per attempt of 7.54 yards (Yds/Att). Favre's teammates scored 35 touchdowns (TD) via his passing while the defense intercepted (Int) 16 of his passing attempts.

The NFL quarterback rating formula is an unusual math problem. So grab your calculator and follow these steps:

1. **Divide completed passes by pass attempts, subtract 0.3, and then divide by 0.2.**

2. **Divide passing yards by pass attempts, subtract 3, and then divide by 4.**

3. **Divide touchdown passes by pass attempts, and then divide by 0.05.**

4. **Divide interceptions by pass attempts, subtract that number from 0.095, and divide that product by 0.04.**

The sum of each step cannot be greater than 2.375 or less than zero. Add the sums of the four steps, multiply that number by 100, and divide by 6. The final number is the quarterback rating.

You should know that Favre's statistics are outstanding. He led the NFL with 35 touchdown passes — he was the only quarterback to throw 30 or more — and was second in yards to the Oakland Raiders' Jeff George. He ranked fourth in *yards per attempt,* the average gain of every pass attempted, and third in the negative category of interceptions. His quarterback rating, which was devised for use in the NFL, ranked third in the NFL behind that of San Francisco 49ers quarterback Steve Young, whose rating was 104.7.

When you see a newspaper article about a football game, the story may state that Favre was 22 of 36, passing for 310 yards. Translation: He completed 22 of 36, pass attempts and gained 310 yards on those 22 completions. Not a bad game.

Chapter 5

The Passing Game

Although the strategy of offenses changes, sometimes favoring running over passing, throwing the football, which first occurred in 1876, is a major part of football's excitement. Some of the most memorable plays in football are those long "bomb" *passes* (or throws) that win games in the final seconds or that pull a team ahead in the score and turn the game around. Who can resist joining in the collective cheer that erupts when the ball is hurtling through the air and looks as though it's about to drop into a receiver's hands? And when the defense catches the ball, known in football parlance as an *interception,* the play can be just as exciting and influential to the outcome of the game.

As Chapter 3 explains, an offense scores points by gaining yards on the field. This chapter focuses on one "half" of the offensive attack: the passing game. The other "half," the running game, is discussed in Chapter 6. During the 1997 NFL season, 54 percent of all plays run by the 30 teams were pass plays, and they accounted for 64 percent of the total offensive yards gained league-wide. In the 1980 NFL season, pass plays exceeded running plays for the first time since 1969, and it's been that way ever since.

The Passing Game

To many fans, the passing game is the most exciting aspect of football. Earl "Curly" Lambeau, the founder and player/coach of the Green Bay Packers, made his offenses throw the football in the mid-1930s. But teams eventually moved away from throwing the ball, and the 1960s and the 1970s saw the running game and zone defenses (where players defended deep and covered every area of the field) choke the life out of this exciting brand of football.

Two significant rule changes in 1978 improved the growth of the passing game in the NFL. First, defenders were permitted to make contact with receivers only within 5 yards of the line of scrimmage. Previously, defenders were allowed to hit, push, or shove ("chuck") a receiver anywhere on the field. Also, offensive linemen were allowed to use open hands and fully extend their arms to block a pass-rusher. The liberalization of this offensive blocking technique led to better protection for the quarterback and ultimately more time for him to throw the football.

Prior to these rules, offenses had begun to rely on running backs as their main pass receivers. Then Bill Walsh became the head coach of the San Francisco 49ers in 1979, and he melded every aspect of these new rules and the running back as a receiver concept into the formations of his West Coast offense. For the first time, teams were running out of passing formations, and the pass was setting up running plays instead of vice versa.

To make a pass successful, quarterbacks and receivers (wide receivers, tight ends, and running backs) must work on their timing daily. To do so, the receivers must run exact *pass patterns* with the quarterback throwing the football to predetermined spots on the field once the receiver *breaks* (deviates to one direction or another) or stops running his pattern. Although passing the football may look like a simple act of the quarterback throwing and a receiver catching the ball, often in full stride, this aspect of the game is very complex. For it to be successful, the offensive linemen must provide the quarterback with adequate protection to throw the football (more than two seconds) while the receivers make every attempt to catch the ball, even if it's poorly thrown. Sometimes, a receiver must deviate from his planned route and run to any open space in the secondary to give the quarterback a target.

Receivers

A quarterback wouldn't be much good without receivers to catch the ball. *Wide receivers* and *tight ends* are the principal players who catch passes, although running backs are used extensively in every passing offense. (See Chapter 6 for more on running backs.) During the 1997 season, on 28 of the 30 NFL teams, wide receivers or tight ends led their respective teams in pass receptions. The other two teams, whose passing offenses ranked in the bottom half of the NFL, had running backs as their leading receivers.

Receivers come in all sizes and shapes. They are tall, short, lean, fast, and quick. To excel as a receiver, a player must have nimble hands (ones that are very good at catching the ball), have the ability to concentrate under defensive duress, be courageous under fire, and be strong enough to withstand physical punishment. Although receiving is a glamorous job, every team expects its receivers to block defensive halfbacks or cornerbacks on running plays as well. (See Chapter 7 to find out.) It wants its receivers to be able to put a defensive cornerback on his back, or at least shield him from making a tackle on a running back.

Tight ends aren't as fast as wide receivers because they play the role of heavy-duty blockers on many plays. Teams don't expect tight ends, who may outweigh a wide receiver by 60 pounds, to have the bulk and strength of offensive linemen, but the good ones — like Green Bay's Mark Chmura and New England's Ben Coates — are above-average blockers as well as excellent receivers.

Basic offenses have five possible receivers: the two running backs, the tight end, and the two wide receivers. The wide receivers are commonly referred to as X and Z receivers. The X receiver normally aligns to the weak side of the formation (split end) and Z aligns to the strength of the formation (normally called the flanker). The tight end is known as the Y receiver. On definite passing downs, many teams substitute another wide receiver if the tight end isn't a very good receiver.

The split end received his name because he was the end (the offenses of the 1930s used two ends) who aligned 10 yards away from the base offensive formation. Hence, he *split* from his teammates. The other end, the tight end, aligned next to an offensive tackle. The *flanker* position was originally a running back, and as offenses developed, he flanked to either side of the formation, but never on the line of scrimmage like the split end and tight end.

In many offenses, on passing downs, the tight end is replaced by another receiver. In Figure 5-1, the Y receiver is the one who replaces the tight end.

Figure 5-1:
The Y receiver replaces the tight end in many offenses on passing downs.

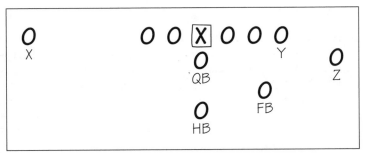

Achieving the proper stance

Before receivers work on catching the ball, they need to learn the proper stance to create acceleration off the line of scrimmage while also using their upper bodies to defend themselves from contact with defensive backs. Receivers must understand, even at the beginning level, that they must get open before they can catch the ball, and the proper stance enables them to explode into the defensive secondary and into position. A quarterback won't throw the ball to a receiver who isn't open, and when it comes to being able to complete a pass to an open receiver, every step counts.

The best way for a youngster to learn the proper stance is to take him to a track meet and show him the sprinters. If you can't go to a track meet, watch one on television or videotape. Watch how a great 100-meter sprinter starts with his or her feet in the starting blocks and then explodes at the sound of the gun. This starting position is the same in football, with the snap of the ball representing the starter's pistol. Teaching receivers their stance by using sprinter's starting blocks is a good idea.

First put the receiver in a *four-point stance,* both hands and feet on the ground, and have him get a feel for the burst out of the blocks, or what football calls the *burst off the line of scrimmage.* His feet should be shoulder width apart. Next, have the receiver try a *three-point stance,* with only one hand on the ground. The receiver should try this stance 100 times before advancing to the stand-up stance that's common on all levels of football, from youth to the pros.

In the *stand-up stance,* the receiver's feet remain shoulder width apart and are positioned like they remain in the starting blocks, his left foot near the line of scrimmage and his right foot back 18 inches. With his shoulders square to the ground, he should lean forward just enough so that he can explode off the line when the ball is snapped. The receiver's lean shouldn't be exaggerated, though, causing him to tip over.

A good receiver uses the same stance on every play because he doesn't want to tip off the defense to whether the play is a run or a pass. Bad receivers line up lackadaisically on running plays. Remember, one wide receiver, usually the split end, lines up on the line of scrimmage. The other receiver, the flanker, must line up 1 yard behind the line of scrimmage. A combination of seven offensive players must always be on the line of scrimmage prior to the ball being snapped. A smart receiver checks with the nearest official to make sure that he's lined up correctly.

The tight end and the split end never line up on the same side. If a receiver is aligned 15 to 18 yards away from the quarterback, he can't hear the quarterback barking signals. Therefore, he must look down the line and move as soon as he sees the ball snapped. Once off the line of scrimmage, a receiver should run toward either shoulder of a defensive back, forcing the defender to turn his shoulders perpendicular to the line of scrimmage to cover him. The receiver hopes to turn the defender in the opposite direction to which he intends to go.

Catching

Practice makes perfect. I know coaches who tell their receivers to catch 500 passes a day. And it doesn't matter how hard, how tough, or how slow the ball is thrown. Playing catch for a couple hours should work, these coaches think.

The one tip to remember, though, is to catch with your hands and with your arms extended away from your body. Never catch a football into your shoulders or chest because it will most likely bounce off. The best technique for using your hands is to take both thumbs and interlock them by placing one thumb behind the other while turning your hands so that the fingers of both hands face each other. Spread your hands as wide as possible while keeping your thumbs together. Then bring your hands face-high, like you're looking through a tunnel (see Figure 5-2). You want the ball to come through your tunnel. You want to see the point of the ball coming down the tunnel and then trap it with your palms, thumbs, and fingers. This technique is called getting your eyes in line with the flight of the ball. If a ball is thrown below your waist, you should turn your thumbs out and your little fingers should overlap. Another good fundamental is to keep your elbows together when catching a football, which adds power to your arms.

Figure 5-2: To catch a ball, put your thumbs together, spread your fingers wide, and bring your hands face-high so that you're looking through a tunnel.

A receiver wants to follow the ball with his eyes from the moment it leaves the quarterback's hands until it comes down his tunnel into his hands. One method of helping a receiver see the ball is to paint the points on both ends of the football with either white or very bright-colored paint. Now train the receiver's hands and eyes to see the paint and track it all the way into his hands or concentrate on the point where the seams meet on the point of the ball.

Another tip is to go into a basketball gymnasium that has a protective pad on the wall at one end of the court. Stand in front of the pad, placing your back against it, and try to catch some passes. With your body against the wall, you must raise your arms and hands. The padded wall prevents your elbows from going past your back, forcing you to catch everything with your hands and not your body.

If you can't find a padded wall, simply lie on the ground. Pull your knees up to protect your groin and stomach area. The person throwing the passes should stand near your feet and throw toward your chest or face. The ground serves as a backstop and prevents your elbows from coming into your body. This drill forces you to catch with your hands. Throwing some passes away from the face, but still within arm reach, is also good.

Beating man-to-man coverage

Basically, *man-to-man coverage* is a style, like in basketball, in which one man guards (or defends) another. The defender stays with this receiver no matter where he runs; his responsibility is to make sure that the receiver doesn't catch a pass. See Chapter 10 for more on man-to-man coverage.

Defensive players use the in-your-face technique of putting their bodies on the line of scrimmage and trying to knock the receivers off stride and out of their routes. A receiver must approach this style as if he's in an alley fight against someone who wants to put him down. The defensive back's objective is to "hurt" the receiver first, and then try to push him out-of-bounds (it's illegal for a receiver to return to the field and catch a pass) while trying to get the receiver's mind off running a perfect route and making a catch. The entire defensive attitude is to take the receiver out of the game, mentally and physically.

When the ball is snapped, the receiver must bring his arms and hands up to his face just like a fighter would. The receiver wants to prevent the defensive player from putting his hands into his chest, by counter-punching his attempts. The working of the receiver's hands is similar to the "wax on, wax off" style taught in the movie *The Karate Kid*. Never, ever let the defensive back get his hand in your chest.

After the receiver has fought off the defensive back's hands, he must dip his shoulder and take off running. This technique is called *dip and rip* — dip your shoulder and rip through the defender's attempt to hold or shove you with a strong punch, like a boxer throwing a great upper cut to his opponent's chin. This move is a favorite of the San Francisco 49ers' Jerry Rice, possibly the greatest receiver of all time.

Another method of defeating man-to-man coverage that many receivers use is the *swim* technique. With the swim, the receiver's arms and hands are still in the same position as the dip and rip. The receiver must again get his hands up in a boxing position. But at the snap of the ball, instead of lowering his shoulder and ripping through, the receiver tries to slap the defensive back's hands one way while heading in the opposite direction. When the defensive back reacts, the receiver uses his free arm and takes a freestyle stroke (raises an arm up and forward and then brings it back to the side) over the defensive back while trying to pull the arm back underneath and behind him. This entire action takes a split second. With the swim technique it's critical that the receiver doesn't allow the defensive back to catch his arm and grab hold under his armpit.

Bigger, stronger receivers use the dip and rip method, whereas smaller, faster receivers usually use the swim.

The Bad and the Ugly Aspects of Passing

This section lists the words and descriptions that are frequently mentioned when discussing the passing game. As a player, my favorite word was *sack:* a defender's dream and a quarterback's nightmare (you can find a definition in the following list). I had 84 sacks in my career, every one a great thrill. I deflected quite a few pass attempts, too. Read on; you'll get my meaning.

- **Deflection:** One of the bad things that can happen when a quarterback throws the ball. A *deflection* is when a defensive player uses his hands or arms to knock down a pass before it reaches the receiver. This act usually occurs near the line of scrimmage when defensive linemen jump, arms raised, into a quarterback's visual passing lane, hoping to deflect the pass, which leads to a possible interception or incompletion.

- **Holding:** Holding is the most common penalty called against the offense when it's attempting to pass. The offense receives a 10-yard penalty (and repeat of down) when any offensive player holds a defensive player by grabbing his jersey or locking his arm onto the defensive player's arm while that player is trying to sack the quarterback. This penalty is also known as illegal use of the hands, arms, or any part of the body.

✔ **Illegal forward pass:** A quarterback cannot cross the line of scrimmage and throw the ball. This penalty often occurs when the quarterback runs forward, attempting to evade defensive players, and forgets where the line of scrimmage is. The offense is penalized 5 yards from the spot of the foul and loses a down.

✔ **Intentional grounding:** This penalty occurs when a quarterback deliberately throws the ball out-of-bounds or into the ground, but it can be interpreted three different ways. The first two drastically penalize the offense.

- *No. 1:* The quarterback is attempting to pass from his own end zone and, prior to being tackled, intentionally grounds the ball, throwing it out-of-bounds or into the ground. The defense is awarded a safety, worth two points, and the offense loses possession of the ball and has to kick the ball from its own 20-yard line.

- *No. 2:* The quarterback is trapped more than 10 yards behind his own line of scrimmage and intentionally grounds the ball for fear of being tackled for a loss. This penalty is a loss of down, and the ball is placed at the spot of the foul, which in this case is where the quarterback was standing when he grounded the ball. Otherwise, the intentional grounding penalty calls for loss of down and 10 yards.

- *No. 3:* The quarterback steps back from the center and immediately throws the ball into the ground, intentionally grounding it. This play is common when an offense wants to stop the clock because it either wants to preserve its time-outs or is out of time-outs. For this type of intentional grounding, the penalty is simply a loss of down.

✔ **Interception:** The act of any defensive player catching a pass. Other than a fumble, an interception is the worst thing that can happen to a quarterback and his team. It is called a *turnover* because the defensive team gains possession of the ball and is allowed to run with the ball in an attempt to score. (Deion Sanders is probably the greatest threat on an interception because of his open-field running ability.)

✔ **Roughing the passer:** This penalty was devised to protect the quarterback from injury. After the ball leaves the quarterback's hand, any defensive player must attempt to avoid contact with him. Because a defensive player's momentum may cause him to inadvertently run into the quarterback, he is allowed to take one step after he realizes that the ball has been released. But if he hits the quarterback on his second step, knowing that the ball is gone, the referee (the official standing near the quarterback) can call *roughing*. It's a 15-yard penalty against the defense and an automatic first down. This penalty is difficult to call unless the defensive player clearly hits the quarterback well after the QB releases the ball; after all, it's pretty tough for a player like Reggie White, who's 6'6" and 315 pounds, to come to an abrupt stop from full sprint.

✔ **Sack:** This is when the quarterback is tackled behind the line of scrimmage by any defensive player. The sack is the most prominent defensive statistic, one that the NFL has officially kept since 1982. (Tackles are considered an unofficial statistic because individual teams are responsible for recording them.) Colleges have been recording sacks for the same length of time.

✔ **Trapping:** Receivers are asked to make a lot of difficult catches, but this one is always disallowed. Trapping is when a receiver uses the ground to help him catch a pass that is thrown on a low trajectory. For an official not to rule a reception a trap, the receiver must make sure that either his hands or his arms are between the ball and the ground when he makes a legal catch. Often, this play occurs so quickly that only television's instant replay shows that the receiver was not in possession of the ball (he trapped it along the ground) when making the reception.

Passing Patterns

When watching at home or in the stands, you can look for basic pass patterns that are used in all levels of football. The following list includes the most common patterns (also known as *pass routes*) that receivers run during games. They may be a single part of a larger play. In fact, on a single play, two or three receivers may be running an equal number of different pass patterns. By knowing passing patterns, you can discover what part of the field or defensive player(s) the offense wants to attack, or how an offense wants to compete with a specific defense. Sometimes, a pass pattern is run to defeat a defensive scheme designed to stop a team's running game by moving defenders away from the actual point of attack.

✔ **Comeback:** Teams use this pass effectively when the receiver is extremely fast and the defensive player gives him a 5-yard cushion, which means that the defensive player stays that far away from him, fearing his speed. On the comeback, the receiver runs hard downfield, between 12 and 20 yards, and then turns to face the football. The comeback route generally is run along the sideline. To work effectively, the quarterback usually throws the ball before the receiver turns. He throws to a spot where he expects the receiver to stop and turn. This kind of pass is called a *timing pass* because the quarterback throws it before the receiver turns and looks toward the quarterback or before he makes his move backward.

✔ **Crossing:** This is an effective pass against man-to-man coverage because it's designed for the receiver to beat his defender by running across the field. The receiver can line up on the right side of the line of scrimmage, run straight for 10 yards, and then cut quickly to his left.

When the receiver cuts, he attempts to lose the man covering him with either a head or shoulder fake (a sudden jerk with his upper body to one side or the other) or a quick stutter-step. This route is designed for two receivers, usually one on either side of the formation. It allows one receiver to interfere with his teammate's defender as the two receivers cross near the middle of the field. The play is designed for the quarterback to pass to the receiver on the run as the receiver crosses in front of his field of vision.

✔ **Curl:** For this 8- to 12-yard pass beyond the line of scrimmage, the receiver stops and then turns immediately, making a slight curl before facing the quarterback's throw. The receiver usually takes a step or two toward the quarterback and the ball before the pass reaches him. The curl tends to be a high-percentage completion because the receiver (this is a favorite route of a big tight end) wants to shield the defender with his back, and the intention is simply to gain a few yards.

✔ **Hook:** This is a common pass play designed mostly for a tight end, who releases downfield and then makes a small turn, coming back to face the quarterback and receive the ball. A hook is similar to a wide receiver running a curl, although it's a shorter pass of between 8 and 12 yards. The quarterback usually releases the ball before the tight end starts his turn. It's a timing route.

✔ **Post:** This is a long pass, maybe 40 to 50 yards, in which the receiver runs down the hash marks toward the goalposts. Most teams use the hash marks as a guiding system for both the quarterback and the receiver. A coach calls this play when one safety is deep and the offense believes that it can isolate a fast receiver against him. The receiver runs straight downfield, possibly hesitating a split second as if he might cut the route inside or outside, and then continues straight ahead toward the post. The hesitation may cause the safety or whomever is positioned in the deep center of the field to break stride or slow down. The receiver needs only an extra step on the defender for this play to be successful. The quarterback puts enough loft on the ball to enable the receiver to catch the pass in stride.

✔ **Slant:** This pass is designed for an inside receiver (a flanker) who is aligned 5 yards out from the offensive line, possibly from a tight end or the offensive tackle. The receiver runs straight 5 to 8 yards and then *slants* his route to the left, angling toward the sideline while running through the middle of the field. Some teams also run an inside slant in which the receiver, should he align on the left side of the field, slants to the right and through the hash marks. A slant is effective against both zone and man-to-man coverage (see Chapter 10) because it's designed to find an open space in either defensive scheme.

✔ **Square-out:** The receiver on this pattern runs 10 yards down the field and then cuts sharply toward the sideline, parallel to the line of scrimmage. The square-out is also a timing play because the quarterback must deliver the pass before the receiver reaches the sideline and steps out-of-bounds. The quarterback must really fire this pass; that's why commentators sometimes refer to it as a *bullet* throw. The route works against both man-to-man and zone coverage. The receiver must roll his shoulder toward the inside before cutting toward the sideline. The quarterback throws the pass, leading the receiver toward the sideline.

✔ **Streak (or Fly):** This is a 20- to 40-yard pass, generally to a receiver on the quarterback's throwing side: right if he's right-handed (and left if he's left-handed). The receiver, who is aligned very wide and near the sidelines, runs as fast as he can down the sideline, hoping to lose the defensive man in the process. This pass must be thrown very accurately because both players tend to be running as fast as they can, and often the cornerback is as fast as the receiver. This play is designed to loosen up the defense, making it believe that the quarterback and the receiver have the ability to throw deep whenever they want to. Moving a defense back or away from the line of scrimmage allows the offense an opportunity to complete shorter passes or run plays. To complete this pass, the quarterback makes sure that a safety isn't playing deep to that side of the field. Otherwise, with the ball in the air for a long time, a free safety can angle over and intercept the pass. When the quarterback sees this, he must throw to another receiver elsewhere on the field.

✔ **Swing:** This is a simple throw to a running back who runs out of the backfield toward the sideline. The pass generally is thrown when the running back turns and heads upfield. This is generally a *touch* pass, meaning that the quarterback doesn't necessarily throw it as hard as he does a deep square-out. He wants to be able to float it over a linebacker and make it easy for the running back to catch. The area in which the back is running is known as *the flat* because it is 15 yards outside the hash marks, and close to where the numbers on the field are placed. The receiver's momentum most likely will take him out-of-bounds after he catches the ball unless he's able to avoid the first few tacklers he faces.

Figure 5-3 shows the many pass patterns and how they funnel off what is called a *passing tree*. The tree is numbered: 4 is a square-out; 5 is a slant; 6 is a curl or a hook; 7 is a post; 8 is a streak or fly; and 9 is a corner route. When calling a pass play, these numbers (which can vary by team) refer to the specific pass route (pattern) called by the quarterback.

The Shotgun Formation

The shotgun passing formation was devised by San Francisco 49ers head coach Red Hickey in 1960. Hickey feared the Baltimore Colts' great pass rush, so he had his quarterback, John Brodie, line up 7 yards behind the line of scrimmage (see Figure 5-4). Hickey figured that Brodie would have more time to see his receivers and could release the ball before the defensive rush reached him. The strategy worked, and the 49ers upset the mighty Colts.

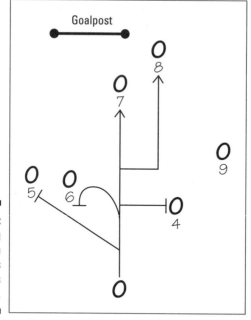

Figure 5-3:
A passing
tree with
the pass
patterns
numbered.

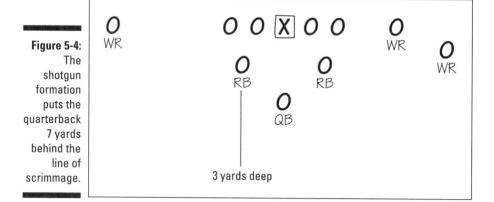

Figure 5-4:
The
shotgun
formation
puts the
quarterback
7 yards
behind the
line of
scrimmage.

The shotgun is used by offenses who may have poor offensive blocking or when an offense is facing superstar-like pass-rushers. Teams use the shotgun when they want to pass on every down. Teams usually opt to pass when they're trailing on the scoreboard. However, many offenses use the shotgun because the quarterback and the coach like to use it. Other teams use the shotgun strictly on third down when they need 4 yards or more for a first down: an obvious passing down.

Today, some NFL teams use the shotgun in obvious pass situations, when they need 10 or more yards for a first down. The shotgun formation does have several downsides, though:

- ✔ The center must be able to make an accurate, chest-high snap to the quarterback.
- ✔ You can't fool the defense; they know that you're throwing the ball, and the pass-rushers won't hesitate to sprint for your quarterback in hopes of a sack.

Teams need a quick-thinking quarterback who can set his feet quickly in order to use this formation effectively.

Reading a Defense

If you flip forward to Chapter 11, you can discover the many defensive schemes and strategies that exist in football. When a quarterback prepares for a game, he wants to be able to look at a specific defensive alignment and instantly know which offense will or won't succeed against it.

Many quarterbacks are taught to read the *free safety,* or the safety positioned deepest in the secondary. (See Chapter 10 for more on the secondary.) If the safety lines up 5 to 7 yards deeper than the other defensive backs, then the safeties are probably playing a zone defense. A quarterback also knows that the defense is playing zone if the cornerbacks are aligned 10 yards off the line of scrimmage. If the cornerbacks are on the line of scrimmage, eyeballing the receivers, they're most likely playing man-to-man. Knowing whether the defense is playing zone or man-to-man is very important to the quarterback because he wants to know whether he's attacking a zone defense with his pass play or a man-to-man alignment in the secondary.

Although a defense may employ 20 to 30 different pass coverages in the secondary, four basic coverages exist. Because most defenses begin with four players in the secondary, the coverages are called *cover one, cover two, cover three,* and *cover four.*

- ✔ **Cover one:** In this coverage (shown in Figure 5-5), one deep safety is about 12 to 14 yards deep in the middle of the field, the two cornerbacks are in *press coverage* (on the line of scrimmage opposite the two receivers), and the strong safety is about 5 yards deep over the tight end. ***Translation:*** one deep safety or secondary player. Cover one is usually a man-to-man coverage. A running play works best against this type of coverage.

✔ **Cover two:** This time, both safeties are deep, 12 to 14 yards off the line of scrimmage. (See Figure 5-6.) The two cornerbacks remain in press coverage, while the two safeties prepare to help the corners on passing plays and come forward on running plays. A deep comeback pass, a crossing route, or a swing pass works well against this type of coverage.

✔ **Cover three:** This coverage, shown in Figure 5-7, has three defensive backs deep. The free safety remains 12 to 14 yards off the line of scrimmage, and the two cornerbacks move 10 to 12 yards off the line of scrimmage. The cover three is obvious zone coverage. The strong safety is 5 yards off the line of scrimmage, over the tight end. This is a stout defense versus the run, but very soft versus a good passing team. A quarterback can throw *underneath passes* (short passes for beating the linebackers positioned underneath the defensive back's coverage). It is difficult for some linebackers to stay with quicker, faster receivers in this area.

✔ **Cover four:** In cover four, what you see is what you get. (See Figure 5-8.) All four defensive backs are off the line of scrimmage, aligned 12 yards deep. Some teams call this coverage "Four Across" because the defensive backs are aligned all across the field. The cover four is a good pass defense because the secondary players are told to never allow a receiver to get behind them. If offensive teams can block the front seven, (a combination of defensive linemen and linebackers that amounts to seven players) running play works against this coverage.

Figure 5-5:
Cover one puts one safety or secondary player deep.

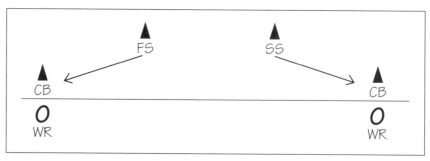

Figure 5-6:
Cover two puts both safeties deep.

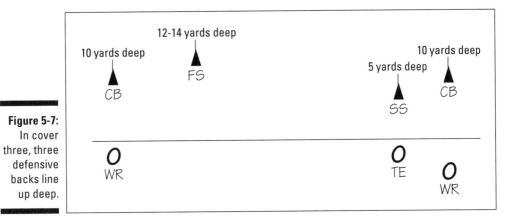

Figure 5-7:
In cover three, three defensive backs line up deep.

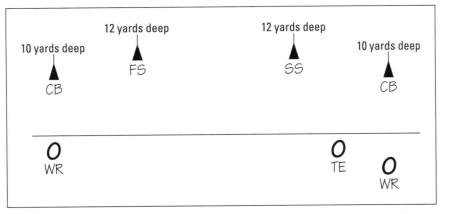

Figure 5-8:
Cover four aligns all four secondary players off the line of scrimmage.

Passing and catching dandies

A football team needs all kinds of warriors to make the passing game work. Here are a few snapshots of the performers who are worth remembering. Many of them mixed style with grace, talent, and toughness.

✓ The San Diego Chargers had a receiver named "Bambi." Lance Alworth hated his nickname, given to him by a teammate who thought that he looked 15 instead of 23. Alworth had short hair and brown eyes and ran like the wind, and right into the Pro Football Hall of Fame. Alworth was the second player to reach 10,000 receiving yards.

✓ Joe "Willie" Namath was the first player to wear white football shoes. He was a flashy bachelor quarterback for the New York Jets in the 1960s and early 1970s who once wore a fur coat on the sidelines. In the 1967 season, he threw for 4,007 yards in just 14 games. And Namath followed through on his guarantee to beat the heavily favored Baltimore Colts in Super Bowl III.

✓ Curley Lambeau was first a quarterback/coach of the Green Bay Packers. Lambeau (the Green Bay stadium is named after him) opted for a wide-open passing game in the 1930s when most NFL teams were still slugging each other with the running game. Lambeau made stars of players like receiver Don Hutson (see Chapter 22).

✓ Johnny Unitas is in the Hall of Fame, but he wasn't always a Baltimore Colts' star. He played minor league football in 1955 for $6 a game. The Pittsburgh Steelers drafted him but didn't believe that he was good enough to make their team and released him from their roster. Unitas, famous for his black high-top football shoes, ended up being the first quarterback to pass for 40,000 yards.

Chapter 6

On the Ground

*R*unning back may be the most physically demanding position in football. A great running back, whose productivity dictates his team's success, is asked to take a tremendous beating on a weekly basis. Every game, he faces 11 angry men who have a license to physically punish him. Rarely does one defensive player bring down a great running back. He gets hit from every angle — high and low. Often, one player grabs hold of the running back while a number of defenders take clean shots at him.

One of the toughest football players I played with was running back Marcus Allen. Despite the continual beating he took, Allen would pick himself off the ground and, without showing any emotion, walk back to the huddle and prepare for the next play. I don't know how many times I saw Marcus look like he'd just gotten his head taken off and then come right back for more on the very next play. He was especially determined at the goal line, scoring an NFL-record 123 rushing touchdowns even though everyone in the stadium knew that he would be running with the ball. But running was just one facet of his game.

Allen was also the best blocking halfback I've ever seen. Although he weighed only 210 pounds, he would be asked to block a man who out-weighed him by 30 to 100 pounds. He was also a gifted pass receiver. Add to this his ability to throw the football because he played quarterback in high school, and you have a rare triple-threat running back. Most great running backs take such a beating that they rarely last more than five seasons in the NFL. Marcus Allen retired in 1998 after playing for 16 seasons.

This chapter goes into detail about what makes a great running back — or a good one, for that matter. Obviously, a running back needs to be able to do more than just run with the football. A running back must know his assignments, know the opposing defenses, and be aware of all the players on the field. I explain the many different running plays and the varied styles and types of people who fit the mold of a running back. Running backs definitely come in all shapes and sizes, and most of them get the job done.

An Overview of the Ground Game

Men have been running with a ball for almost two centuries. Before football, people were fascinated by a sport called *rugby,* which was developed by an Englishman in 1823. Players in this sport are tackled by more than one opponent, and the runner is not protected by a helmet or shoulder pads. Football is based on rugby — but the men who designed this sport were smart enough to add protective gear to the mix.

Running the ball is the basic premise of football, and it's the easiest way to move the ball. A team runs three times and gains 10 yards, and that's good enough for a first down and another set of four downs. What could be easier? In youth football, every team runs. After all, what 11-year-old can pass like Miami Dolphins quarterback Dan Marino? And learning this fundamental is much easier than learning how to run pass routes.

Most championship football teams are excellent at running the football. The Denver Broncos won the Super Bowl in 1998 because they had a better running game than the Green Bay Packers. The Broncos could run, and the Packers couldn't stop them and their talented running back Terrell Davis. In fact, Denver's offensive line was really fired up for that game — they wanted to block and open holes — because they felt that the Packers, the media, and some NFL insiders weren't giving them enough respect.

The New York Giants won their second Super Bowl after the 1989 season, beating a superior Buffalo Bills team, because they could run and keep the clock moving. They also kept the ball away from Buffalo's high-powered offense. This ploy is called *ball control* — a common football term. When a team is ahead, running the ball is the best way to maintain possession and keep the clock moving, because the clock doesn't stop if a player is tackled in-bounds. However, if the quarterback throws an incompletion, the clock stops. Stopping the clock is advantageous to the defense; it gives them a breather and gives them hope that they may get the ball back. So when a team is running the football successfully, usually it is physically whipping the other team. And that's the object!

Fans may think that the NFL is a pass-happy league and that colleges are right behind, imitating that offensive attack. But in 1997, 16 NFL running backs rushed for 1,000 yards or more, tying for the highest total ever in one season. Running backs also ripped off 121 games in which they gained at least 100 yards, the most in any season since 1970. There were also seven different 200-yard rushing games by running backs, an NFL record. Of course, tiny Barry Sanders of the Detroit Lions played a big role in those statistics — he rushed for 2,053 yards, the second highest total ever. Eric Dickerson set the NFL record of 2,105 yards with the Los Angeles Rams in 1984.

The Men Who Play the Ground Game

Understanding what's going on during running plays is much easier when you know who's who. In this section, I explain what each position does, what type of player plays each position, and how each player lines up in the *backfield* (that area of the field behind the quarterback and the line of scrimmage).

The big back (or fullback)

When a team employs two backs in the offensive backfield, the bigger of the two is generally called the *fullback.* He's there to block, to clear the way for the *halfback,* or the main ball carrier. Teams generally don't share the running chores, preferring to have one back receive the majority of the rushing attempts. Any player in the backfield who runs with the ball is called a running back. The halfback is the primary running back in the veer formation, and a tailback is the primary running back in the I formation. Running backs don't like to share, either; most of them want the ball as many times as they can get it.

You may think that the fullback's job is a thankless one, but most fullbacks get a lot of satisfaction from making a great block, generally on a linebacker, and winning the physical battle against players who usually are bigger than them. For example, Howard Griffith signed with the Denver Broncos as a free agent simply to block for Terrell Davis.

In the old days, 30 to 50 years ago, some of the best runners were fullbacks. Marion Motley of the Cleveland Browns in 1949 weighed almost 240 pounds and carried defenders down the field. Cookie Gilchrist was a 252-pound fullback with the Buffalo Bills in the mid-1960s; he was one devastating blocker and could run, too. So could Larry Csonka, a former Miami Dolphin, who was the dominant fullback of the 1970s.

In today's NFL, the best all-around fullback is probably Tampa Bay's Mike Alstott. He's a punishing blocker and also a difficult runner to tackle on short-yardage plays, when the offense needs to gain only a yard or two. When Tampa Bay needs 2 yards for a first down, the ball goes to Alstott, and he does the rest.

But on most teams, the fullback doesn't carry the ball much. On some teams, the fullback blocks for the runner, stays in the backfield to protect the quarterback, and occasionally swings out of the backfield to catch a pass. Some fullbacks actually catch more passes than they rush the ball.

The fullback position has evolved through the years, as offenses have. Many teams employ a simple offensive formation called the *one-back set* (see Figure 6-1). In such an offense, another back still can be in the lineup. If another back is used, he is called the *H-back (HB)*. This player is more of a blocker, though, and he usually lines up close to the line of scrimmage, almost like a tight end. Prior to the snap of the ball, the H-back frequently comes in motion, generally to the side to which he's going to help block. I've heard some people refer to this player as a *GIB*, or *Guard In the Backfield*. He's a big guy who packs the blocking punch of an offensive guard.

Figure 6-1:
This one-back set features a main back (RB) and an H-back (HB), who blocks for the main back.

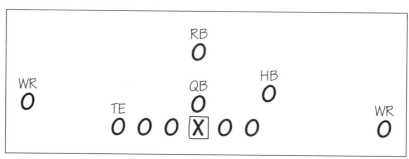

The principal ball carrier (or halfback)

The running back is any team's principal ball carrier. On most teams, he's called the *halfback*, the *tailback*, the main man. When teams — high school, college, or NFL — find a good running back, they give him the ball. And they give it to him as often as he's willing and able to carry it.

Denver's Terrell Davis ran for 157 yards and three touchdowns to beat the Packers in Super Bowl XXXII and was named the game's Most Valuable Player. Runners like Davis are used to being the principal ball carrier. During the 1997 season, Davis carried the ball 369 times. The NFL record for rushing attempts in a single season is 407, set by Tampa Bay's James Wilder in 1984. To show that Davis truly was the main man, quarterback John Elway had the second most carries (50) for the Denver Broncos during the 1997 season, and probably half of those were impromptu runs after he was forced from the pocket. Elway was simply scrambling to escape being sacked.

I unearthed the defining statistics that show how much a team can rely solely on one ball carrier: The top ten rushers in the NFL during the 1997 season rushed for 14,251 yards on 3,061 carries. They averaged 4.66 yards a carry, and their combined rushing total was 69 percent of their teams' entire rushing offense. Seven out of ten carries went to one runner on each team.

Runners like Barry Sanders and Terrell Davis probably would tell you that they wouldn't mind carrying the ball even more often than they actually do. Toting the football is a status symbol, after all. Sanders has led the NFL in rushing four different seasons. The great Jim Brown of the Cleveland Browns led the NFL in rushing eight times (see Chapter 22 for more information about Brown); Sanders and four other runners, who each led the NFL four times, are tied for the second highest mark.

Running Backs Come in All Sizes and Shapes

You may hear football coaches say that a particular player is the prototype performer at a particular position, but no such prototype exists at running back. Running backs come in all sizes and shapes. Little guys like the Detroit Lions' Barry Sanders, ex-Chicago Bear Walter Payton, and the Buffalo Bills' Thurman Thomas, who are quick and slippery players, have excelled at the highest level. Big brutes like Jim Brown of the Cleveland Browns, Earl Campbell of the Houston (now Tennessee) Oilers, John Riggins of the Washington Redskins, and Jim Taylor of the Green Bay Packers also had successful NFL careers.

Current Dallas Cowboys running back Emmitt Smith, who scored a record 25 touchdowns in 1995, is an example of the tough, physical inside runner who weighs only 210 pounds. Pittsburgh Steelers tailback Jerome "The Bus" Bettis is 50 pounds heavier than Barry Sanders, but he's still considered a halfback, not a fullback, because he's the main runner on his team. And I can't forget former Dallas Cowboy Tony Dorsett, the recently retired Marcus Allen, and ex-San Francisco 49ers Roger Craig and Tom Rathman — all good backs, but never listed as little guys *or* big brutes.

Next, let me clear up the myth that you have to be extremely fast to be an excellent running back. Marcus Allen had only average speed; in fact, some scouts thought that he was too slow. But in his outstanding career, he scored 145 touchdowns and gained 12,243 yards rushing, and he'll be in the NFL Hall of Fame in a few years.

Allen was football's finest *north/south runner* — which means that he didn't mess around dancing "east" or "west" behind the line of scrimmage. When trapped by defensive players, the quickest and best way to gain yards is to go straight ahead; that's the primary trait of a north/south runner.

Little guys slip by opponents in the open field. They're difficult to grab hold of and tackle, almost like their shoulder pads are covered with butter. Sanders falls into that group. So did Dorsett and Lionel "Little Train" James, who played for San Diego ten years ago. On the other hand, big brutes like Jim Brown simply run over everyone. Brown never concerned himself with making tacklers miss him. At some point, every coach looks for a big back who can run over everyone in his way.

Regardless of their size or skill level, the common denominator in all these men is that they were physically tough, determined, and talented football players. Any type of runner can be a good running back, as long as he's playing in the right system and gets help from his teammates.

Running Back Fundamentals

On most football teams, the running back is the best athlete on the team. The demands on him, both physically and mentally, are great. Here I list the basic skills that every running back must be able to do well:

✔ **Line up in the right stance:** The most common stance for a running back is the two-point stance. A tailback in the I formation often uses the two-point stance with his hands on his thighs, his feet shoulder width apart, and his weight on the balls of his feet. His head should be up, his legs slightly bent at the knees, and his feet parallel to one another, with his toes pointed toward the line of scrimmage. (For more information about running back stances, see the section "Finding the Perfect Stance for Every Formation," later in this chapter.)

✔ **Receive a handoff:** A runner must receive the football from the quarterback without fumbling. To do this properly, his arms should form a pocket outside his stomach. If the back is right-handed, his left arm should be bent at the elbow in a 90-degree angle with his forearm parallel to the ground. The palm of his left hand should be turned up. His right arm should be up to receive the ball so that when the quarterback places the ball in his stomach area, his right forearm and hand close around it. (Figure 6-2 shows how a receiver takes a handoff and holds the ball while running.) After he has possession of the ball, the back should grip the ball at the tip and tuck the other end into his elbow with one side of the ball resting against his body. His arm should be in somewhat of a V-shape.

Figure 6-2:
One of a running back's main concerns is ball protection. Receiving a handoff properly, as shown here, is essential.

✔ **Run at top speed:** A running back should attempt to be running at near top speed when he grabs a handoff. He should keep his head upright and his shoulders square to the line of scrimmage, and for most backs its best to run with a forward lean to their shoulders. Running with the lean keeps a back's body low and keeps his legs driving forward. When making cuts, the back should plant and accelerate off the foot that is opposite the direction he is running. For example, if he wants to go left, he should plant on his right foot. When running behind a blocker, he should be behind the blocker's outside hip. When the block is made, the back should cut quickly behind the blocker's inside hip when turning upfield. For cut-back running, the back should fake a step away from the defender (trying not to shift too much weight) and then turn quickly to the inside of the defender. The defender must move for the cut-back to be successful.

✔ **See the field:** When you watch Barry Sanders run, you'd swear that he has eyes in the back of his head. How else can you explain his cuts and moves and his escapes from defensive trouble? Like a basketball guard running a fast break, a back needs to have peripheral vision. He needs to be able to see what's coming at him from the corners of the field. Backs with exceptional speed (4.4 seconds in the 40-yard dash) can gain many more yards by seeing where the defensive pursuit is coming from and by running away from it. However, backs without great speed can be successful by sensing danger while trying to maintain a straight line to the end zone (these backs are called *north-south runners*). But backs with great speed can outrun many defenders by heading to the corner of the end zone if a defender is 10 yards away to their left or right.

✔ **Block for another back:** A team's principal running back is rarely a good blocker. The best blockers among the backs are the fullbacks, who are asked to block players 30 to 100 pounds heavier than they are. A running back needs to stay low and explode into the defender's upper body while using his hands (closed-fist) and forearms to make contact. A lot of backs try to block a linebacker or defensive back low (at his legs), but this technique is rarely successful. Many defensive players are capable of jumping up and then shoving the back down to the ground as they move past him. Coaches want their backs to get a piece of the defender and knock him off his line to the quarterback or ball carrier.

Running Backs Have an Assignment for Everything

A running back has a responsibility on every play. I think that running backs have the toughest job on the football field because not only do they have to know every play like a quarterback, but they also make physical contact on virtually every down.

No matter how fast an athlete is, or how big a brute he is, or how slippery or quick he is, he will not be able to play this position if he doesn't have a brain and can't think on his feet. I think the main reason that many outstanding college runners never make it in professional football is that the pro game simply overloads their brains.

Here's a rundown of a running back's job description:

✔ **He's an every-minute player.** While he's on the field, he never has a minute to let up, and he never has a chance to take a play off. He can't afford to line up and merely go through the motions. When he doesn't have the ball, he must follow through with his fakes and pretend that he has the ball.

✔ **On every play, he must know what down it is and how many yards are needed for a first down.** He must know when to lower his shoulder and go for a first down and when to keep a drive alive by making a move and gaining a little extra yardage, helping his team move into scoring range.

✔ **He must know the time on the clock in order to know when to go out-of-bounds and when to turn upfield and gain extra yardage.** Stopping the clock is critical when a team is behind in the score.

✔ **He must know the defense's various alignments and then adjust his thinking to those alignments on pass plays and running plays.** On a pass play, he must know the protection scheme because he may be asked to throw a block to give the quarterback time to pass.

✔ **He must know every play and all its variations.** For example, on one running play, he may have to block a linebacker. But on the same play called against a different defensive front, he may be asked to block a defensive end.

On running plays, a running back must know the opposition's defensive schemes so that he can predict which defender will be the first guy coming to make the tackle. Although this information may not be important to the runner carrying the ball, it is valuable for the other back who is asked to block on the play.

✔ **He must know every pass route called because he may be the first receiving option on a play.** He must know the defense's coverage in order to adjust his route accordingly. For example, if the linebacker goes out, he may have to go in, and vice versa. He must know how deep he has to get on every pass route so that he's timed up with the quarterback's drop. Because the quarterback may throw the ball before the runner turns to catch the ball, he must run the exact distance or the timing of the play will be messed up.

✔ **He must know every hole number in the playbook.** A typical NFL playbook may contain between 50 and 100 running plays. The holes, which are numbered, are the only things that tell the running back where he's supposed to run with the ball. The play will either specify the hole number or already be designed for a specific hole.

VIEWER TIP

Finding a great running back

In college, coaches give a great high school running back a scholarship, and they have him for four years. Now, it doesn't look good for your program if you beg a player to come to your school and then end up cutting him or taking away his scholarship because he doesn't live up to your expectations. This is what I mean when I say that he's yours for four years.

The difference for pro running backs is that the NFL is a big business. Running backs can be signed to big contracts, but teams can always cut them and lose nothing but a few days or weeks of coaching time and a few dollars. Today, such dismissals are viewed simply as bad money deals or bad investments. Therefore, when a head coach finds a runner who can run for over 1,000 yards, score whenever he needs to, and carry the team when the quarterback is having an off day, he knows that he has a winner.

Finding the Perfect Stance for Every Formation

A running back can use two stances: One is the *up stance,* where he has his hands resting on his thighs, a few inches above his knees (see Figure 6-3). This stance is also called the *two-point stance.* The second is the *down stance,* where he puts his right hand on the ground like a lineman (see Figure 6-4). It's also called the *three-point stance* because one hand and both feet are on the ground.

Figure 6-3: A running back's up stance (or two-point stance).

Figure 6-4: A running back's down stance (or three-point stance).

Runners can use the two-point stance when they're in the split-back formation, with one back aligned to the left and one to the right of the quarterback. (For more information about this formation, see "Lining Up: The Formations," later in this chapter.) However, most coaches prefer that their runners use the three-point stance in this alignment, believing that the stance provides the runner with a faster start — like a sprinter bursting from his blocks — than the upright stance. Some runners remain in the two-point stance in split backs, which can tip off the defense that they're going to pass-protect for the quarterback or run out for a pass. The running backs can then resort to a three-point stance with the intention of confusing the defense.

In the I formation, the deep back is always in a two-point stance. The fullback in the I formation is in front of the tailback. He can be in either a two-point or a three-point stance because he's blocking on 95 percent of the plays. The up stance is better on passing downs because it enables the running back to see the defensive alignment better. It enables him to see whether a linebacker may be blitzing, especially if he must block this defender. The three-point stance is better for blocking because the running back can exert his force upward and to the defender's chest and upper body.

Protecting Yourself and the Ball

To be an exceptional runner, a running back must know *pursuit* and *angles*. I'm talking football language here, not physics. What I mean is that the runner must understand where the defensive players are coming from (the pursuit) and from what direction (the angle) they plan on tackling him.

If a runner understands these basic principles, he can protect himself from being injured by bigger defensive players. Knowing which direction the defensive players are coming from is also important so that he can prepare himself for the contact and protect the football.

Before contact, the running back braces the ball against his body while protecting the outside of the ball with his hand and forearm. Some backs prepare for the collision by wrapping their other arm around the football as well. Also, the back dips his shoulders and head and rolls his shoulders inward away from where he expects the first contact to come from. When facing smaller defenders, the running back may use a *stiff arm* (extending his free hand) to jostle the defender in his face mask or shoulder area. A back uses a stiff arm to push a tackler away from him or to reduce the tackler's ability to go after his legs.

Dorsett goes the distance

A player can return a kick or punt for 100 yards or more to score a touchdown, but the longest possible run is 99 yards. Former Dallas Cowboys running back Tony Dorsett, a Heisman Trophy award winner from the University of Pittsburgh, covered exactly that distance in 1983.

The amazing part about the play is that Ron Springs, the Cowboys' other running back, was supposed to get the ball; the play was designed for him. But Springs misunderstood quarterback Danny White's call and left the huddle, returning to the sidelines. With Springs gone, Dallas had only ten players on the field. And because quarterbacks don't do much blocking, only 8 Cowboys were available to block 11 Minnesota Vikings (only 8 because one of the remaining 9 was Dorsett, who was carrying the ball).

Dallas, coached by the highly specialized and inventive Tom Landry, always did a lot of substituting. But White didn't know that Springs had left the huddle. As White turned away from the line of scrimmage, looking for Springs, he instead came face to face with Dorsett. White did what any panicked quarterback would do: He handed the ball to Dorsett. But the play didn't end up being a flop. Dorsett faked left, stopped, and then headed around the right end. He broke through the first line of defenders and was off to the races.

Dorsett's run still stands as the longest run from the line of scrimmage in NFL history. It may be equaled someday, but it will never be surpassed.

The most important aspect of a running back's game is protecting the football. On the first day of practice, the first thing the coach tells his running backs is this: If you don't protect the football, you won't play. By "protecting the football," I'm talking about not fumbling the ball and leaving it on the ground where the opposition can recover it and gain possession. In the 1996–97 NFL season, Pittsburgh's Jerome Bettis lost ten fumbles, or one every 70 carries. Barry Sanders, a much smaller man, lost only four fumbles over those same two seasons, or one every 160 carries. Consequently, how well you protect the football is not a matter of how big you are, but how well you concentrate.

Understanding the Terms of Running

Instead of simply calling every carry a run, the football powers that be have invented a few run terms that you should remember. These are the basic styles of rushing plays, and they're used in all levels of football:

✔ **Blast or dive:** Every team has the blast or dive run in its playbook; it's the simplest of carries. Usually led by a blocking fullback, the running back takes a quick handoff from the quarterback and hits a hole between an offensive guard and a tackle. On some teams, this run ends up between a guard and the center. The offense calls this run when it needs a yard or two for a first down. The runner lowers his head and hopes to move the pile before the middle linebacker tackles him.

✔ **Counter:** A misdirection run by design. The quarterback fakes a lateral toss to one back who's heading right, running parallel to the line of scrimmage. He's the decoy. The quarterback then turns and hands off to the remaining runner in the backfield, generally a fullback, who runs toward the middle of the line, hoping to find an opening between either guard and the center.

✔ **Draw:** A disguised run, which means that it initially looks like a pass play. The offensive linemen draw back like they're going to pass-protect for the quarterback. The quarterback then drops back and, instead of setting up to pass, turns and hands the ball to the runner. After the runner receives the ball, he wants to reach his maximum speed quickly to take advantage of the anticipated huge holes at the line of scrimmage. The goal of every draw play is for the defensive linemen to come charging at the quarterback, only to be pushed aside by the offensive linemen at the last second. To fool the defense with this run, a team must have an above-average passing game. (See Figure 6-5.)

Figure 6-5:
In the draw play, the quarterback (QB) drops back to pass and then hands off to the running back (RB) who's pretending to pass-block.

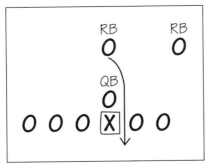

✔ **Off-tackle:** The oldest run around — a by-product of the old single wing offense of 90 years ago (see the sidebar "Single wing," later in this chapter). It's a strong-side run, meaning that the halfback (HB) heads toward the end of the line where the tight end, the extra blocker, lines up. The runner wants to take advantage of the hole supplied by the tackle, tight end, and his running mate, the fullback (FB). He can take the ball either around the tight end (as shown in Figure 6-6) or outside the tackle. He hopes that the fullback will block the outside linebacker.

Figure 6-6: In the off-tackle run, the FB leads the HB around the right side. The FB clears a path for the HB by blocking either the outside linebacker or the defensive end on that side.

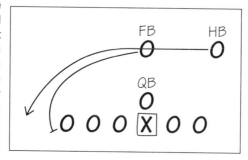

> ✔ **Pitch:** This run is usually from a two-back formation. The quarterback takes the snap and fakes a handoff to the first back (HB), who's heading directly toward the line of scrimmage; then he tosses *(pitches)* the ball laterally to the other runner (FB), who has begun to move to the outside. The runner can either take the pitch outside or cut back toward the inside. Pitch plays can be designed to go in either direction. (See Figure 6-7.)

Figure 6-7: In the pitch run, the QB fakes a handoff to the HB and then tosses the ball to the FB.

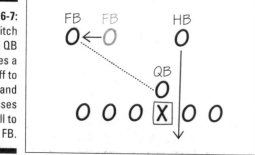

✔ **Reverse:** For this play, the halfback (HB) receives the handoff from the quarterback and then runs laterally behind the line of scrimmage. (The play can be designed for the back to run in either direction.) The ball carrier meets up with a receiver or flanker running toward him and then hands the ball to that receiver or flanker. The offensive line blocks as if the ball were intended for the halfback so that the defensive players follow him. After the receiver comes in motion and has the ball, he runs in the opposite direction, or against the flow of his own blockers. This play really works if the receiver is a fast and tricky runner. It helps if the interior defensive players and linebacker fall for the halfback's initial fake. Also, the weak-side defender, the last line of defense, must leave his position and chase the halfback. Otherwise, this weak-side defender is in perfect position to tackle the receiver. (See Figure 6-8.)

Figure 6-8:
For a reverse, the QB hands off to the HB running to his left. The WR then takes a handoff from the HB and runs the other way.

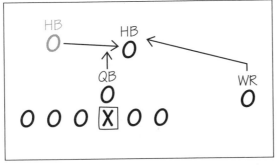

✔ **Slant:** This run is exactly like it sounds. Instead of running straight toward the line of scrimmage, the runner (HB) slants his angle outside after he receives the ball. A slant is used to take advantage of defenses that overpursue, allowing offensive linemen to be more effective by pushing the defenders to one side. (See Figure 6-9.)

✔ **Sweep:** This run is pretty common in every team's playbook. It begins with two or more offensive linemen (in Figure 6-10, LG and RG) leaving their stances and running toward the outside of the line of scrimmage. The ball carrier (HB) takes a handoff from the quarterback and runs parallel to the line of scrimmage, waiting for his blockers to lead the way around the end. The run is designed to attack the defensive end, outside linebacker, and cornerback on a specific side. Most right-handed teams (that is, teams that have a right-handed quarterback) run the

Figure 6-9:
In the slant
play, the HB
takes a
handoff and
slants his
run to the
right side
after
aligning on
the left side.

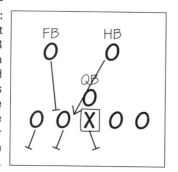

sweep toward the left defensive end. The sweep can begin with the other back faking receipt of a handoff and running in the opposite direction of where the sweep run is headed. Many teams simply have the other back, a fullback, help lead the blocking for the ball carrier.

Figure 6-10:
For a sweep
play, the HB
receives a
handoff from
the QB and
follows the
two pulling
guards and
FB around
the weak-
side end.

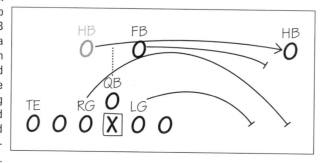

✔ **Trap:** Teams don't use this run very often because it requires quick and agile offensive linemen, and most teams use big blockers these days. The trap is a sucker run that, like the draw, is intended to take advantage of the defensive players' willingness to attack the offense. The trap works well against an aggressive defensive line and linebackers. On the trap, a guard (LG in Figure 6-11) vacates his normal area, allowing the defensive player to cross the line of scrimmage and have a clear lane into the backfield. The guard from the opposite side then moves across the line and blocks the defender. This action by the guard is called *pulling,* hence the term *pulling guard.* The trap play has to be well timed, and after the ball carrier receives the ball, he must quickly dart through the hole behind the trap block.

Figure 6-11:
As the FB takes a handoff for the trap play, the LG pulls to his right. The center blocks the defensive tackle who is left unblocked.

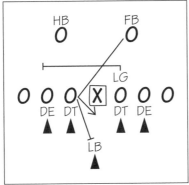

✔ **Veer:** College teams run this play more often than pro teams do because it generally requires a quarterback who is quick-footed and an excellent ball-handler — a quarterback who can run if he has to. The veer is a quick-hitting run in which the ball can be handed to either running back, whose routes are determined by the slant or charge of the defensive linemen. The term _veer_ comes from the back veering away from the defense. In Figure 6-12, the quarterback (QB) hands off to the halfback (HB), who veers to the right behind his blockers.

Figure 6-12:
The QB hands off to the HB, who veers to the right between the guard and tackle.

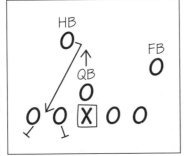

Lining Up: The Formations

An offensive _formation_ is how the offense aligns all 11 of its players prior to using a particular play. A team can run or pass out of many formations, but for this chapter I selected three backfield formations that focus specifically on running backs. One is the _pro-set_, which is also known as the _split-back_ or _split T formation_. Another is the _I formation_ — where both runners are aligned together behind one another and behind the quarterback and center — and its hybrid, the *offset I formation.* Most teams also give these offset formations names like Jack, Queen, Far, Near, and so on.

✔ **Split-back formation:** In the split-back formation, the runners are aligned behind the two guards about 5 yards behind the line of scrimmage (see Figure 6-13). Teams use this formation because it's difficult for the defense to gauge whether the offense is running or passing. With split backs, the backfield is balanced and not aligned toward one side or the other, making it harder for the defense to anticipate what the play will be. This formation may be a better passing formation because the backs can swing out of the backfield to either side as receivers.

Figure 6-13:
In the split-back formation, the two running backs (RB) are aligned behind the two guards.

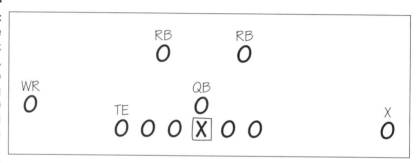

✔ **I formation:** In the I formation, the tailback — the runner who will carry the ball — can place himself as deep as 7 yards from the line of scrimmage (see Figure 6-14). By stepping this far back, the runner believes that he'll be in full stride when he nears the line of scrimmage. Consequently, the I formation is ideally suited to a team with a great running back. Also, the depth allows him to have complete vision of his blockers and the defensive players' first reaction to the run. This formation is called the I because the quarterback, fullback, and tailback form an I, with the fullback between the quarterback and tailback.

✔ **Offset I formation:** In the offset I formation, the running back remains deep, 5 to 7 yards from the quarterback. When the running back is this deep, the majority of the time the team plans to run the ball. The fullback or blocking back can be as close as 3 yards to the line of scrimmage (see Figure 6-15). The other back wants to be close to his target: the defender he must block. A good fullback needs only 2 yards before making blocking contact. Also, he's deep enough should the play require him to go in motion to either side and swing to the outside for a possible reception. The fullback can be set to the strong side or the weak side of the formation.

Figure 6-14:
In the I
formation,
the tailback
(TB) lines
up 7 yards
behind the
line of
scrimmage
with a
fullback
(FB) in front
of him.

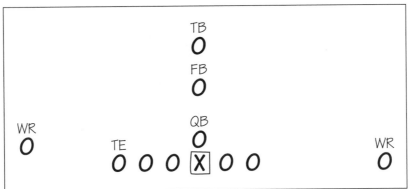

Figure 6-15:
In the offset
I formation,
the running
back (RB)
remains
deep, while
the fullback
(FB) is set 3
yards
behind the
line of
scrimmage.
The fullback
can be set
to the
strong side
(as shown)
or the
weak side.

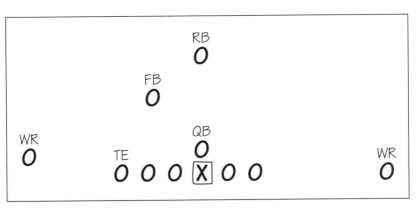

Single wing

The single wing was an offensive formation that was popular in the early years of the NFL. Pop Warner developed the formation around 1908, and it utilized four players in the backfield: the quarterback, tailback, wingback, and fullback. In the single wing, the tailback, not the quarterback, was the primary passer and runner. The quarterback was a blocking back like today's fullback.

In this formation, the quarterback was positioned close to the line of scrimmage and in a gap (the spacing) between two offensive linemen. The wingback was aligned behind and outside the strong-side end. The fullback was a few steps from the tailback and also aligned to the strong side. Back then, the offensive line generally was unbalanced — two linemen were to one side of the center and four were to the other side. The strong side was the side where the four offensive linemen were lined up. The ball was snapped to the tailback, not the quarterback, who was about 4 yards behind the center.

Most of the time, offenses ran the ball from the single wing; it was still a power football formation. However, with the tailback doing a lot of spinning and faking, the single wing added deception. The tailback often would lateral the ball to another backfield teammate. Teams would run reverses, counters, and trap plays from the formation while also passing the ball.

Chapter 7

The Offensive Line

In This Chapter

▶ The purpose of the O line

▶ The center and everyone else's duties

▶ Lineman physiques

▶ The keys to good line play

▶ Blocking, holding, and other things that linemen do

---

*F*ootball is not a relationship-driven business. If any positions could be used to illustrate that point, they would be the offensive and defensive line positions. The offensive and defensive lines are the shark and the dolphin, the mongoose and the cobra, of football: natural enemies. Being a defensive lineman, I never encouraged friendships with offensive linemen, but I always respected them. My job was to beat them, to overpower them, in order to help my team win.

When I was with the Raiders in the 1980s, two opposing offensive linemen stuck out: Anthony Munoz, a tackle with the Cincinnati Bengals, and Dwight Stephenson, the Miami Dolphins' center. Unlike many offensive linemen, both of these men were very athletic in addition to being rugged and physical. That's the ideal physical combination for this position. I've seen Munoz play basketball, and for a 280-pounder, he moved as if he were 100 pounds lighter. Great feet. When the ball was snapped, I wanted to be quicker than the man blocking me. My plan was to beat him off the ball and get by him before he could react.

The job of offensive linemen? To protect the most hunted commodity in the game, the quarterback, and to protect the ball carrier. The line also opens up "holes" in the defense for the running backs (by *blocking,* or impeding the movement of, defenders). Ball carriers try to go through those holes, which also are called *running lanes*. The ability to run effectively in a football game is the end result of the offensive line winning the war at the line of scrimmage. It's man against man, and whoever wants it more usually wins.

The offensive line is also essential to the passing game. Its job is to shield the quarterback, allowing him two or three seconds of freedom in which to throw the ball. The more time the line gives the quarterback to scan the field and find an open receiver, the better chance the QB has of a completion or a touchdown pass. Without the O line, the offense would never get anywhere.

This group, more than any other, needs to work together like the fingers on a hand. The linemen want their offensive teammates to gain yards, the more the merrier. You'll notice that when a team has a great running back, gaining a lot of yards, the offensive line usually is mentioned as doing its job. A great NFL running back usually rewards his offensive linemen with gifts, such as Rolex watches or vacations

In this chapter, I explain the positions that make up the offensive line, give some insight into the personalities of offensive linemen, and talk about some of the techniques that offensive linemen use.

Looking Down the Line

The offensive line is made up of five players, with the man in the middle called the *center.* Every offensive line position is based on the center. To the right of him is the *right guard,* and outside the right guard, is the *right tackle.* To the left of the center is the *left guard,* and outside the left guard is the *left tackle.* Figure 7-1 shows the offensive line and its personnel.

Figure 7-1: The personnel on the offensive line.

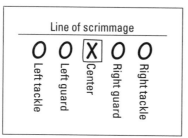

Line of scrimmage

O O X O O

Left tackle | Left guard | Center | Right guard | Right tackle

If the quarterback is right-handed, the left tackle is also referred to as the *blind-side tackle.* Why? Well, a right-handed quarterback generally drops back to pass and turns his head to the right while doing so. He can't see behind him, so his left side is his blind side.

The following sections give some generalities about the players at the three main offensive line positions.

The most special offensive lineman: The blind-side tackle

Most coaches put their best athlete at left tackle if their quarterback is right-handed, which more than 90 percent of quarterbacks are. Different kinds of people play out there (playing this position can feel like being on an island because this tackle receives little or no help), but ideally this player should have quick feet and a good sense of balance.

The blind-side tackle doesn't have to be the biggest, baddest player on the team; he can weigh 300 pounds and be quite adequate. But *reach* (which you get through arm length) is important, and knowing how to use your arms and hands to *jam* (place your hands on the top of your opponent's jersey number) or block is critical. Getting his hands on the defensive player's numbers, so to speak, guarantees that the lineman is keeping a distance between himself and the defensive player. Gaining this advantage is imperative.

By maintaining proper distance, the offensive lineman isn't as susceptible to the defensive lineman's techniques and moves. If he keeps that distance, he has more time to get his feet into position to block the defender again. Also, distance gives the lineman time to adjust laterally and get in front of his man. If the defender is body to body or hip to hip with the offensive lineman, the lineman is beaten because the defensive player can grab him. The closer the defensive player gets to you, the harder it is to recover and get the correct positional leverage on him.

Centers

Like a center in basketball, a football center is in the middle of the action. He's the player who snaps the ball to the quarterback. (By *snaps the ball,* I mean delivers it to the quarterback.) Thus he must know the *signal count* — when the quarterback wants the ball to be snapped, indicated by a series of commands such as "Down. Set. Hut hut hut!"

This center-quarterback exchange initiates every offensive play. Before the play begins, the center stands over the ball and then bends down, usually placing both hands around the front tip of the football. He snaps (or *hikes*) the ball between his legs to the quarterback, who reaches for it with both hands under the buttocks of the center. (Refer to Figure 4-3 for an illustration of the snap.)

The exchange of the football is supposed to be a simple action, but occasionally it gets bungled, resulting in a fumble. A fumble can be caused by the center not snapping the ball directly into the quarterback's hands or by the quarterback withdrawing his hands before the ball arrives. Because hands are essential to good blocking, centers sometimes worry more about getting their hands into position to block than cleanly snapping the ball to the quarterback. Coaches refer to those poor snaps as *short-arming the ball;* the center doesn't bring the ball all the way back to the quarterback's hands.

In addition to delivering the ball cleanly to the quarterback, a center must know the blocking responsibilities of every other offensive lineman. The offense never knows beforehand how the defense will set up. And unlike the offense, the defense may move before the ball is snapped, which allows a defense to set up in a vast array of formations. The center is essentially a coach on the field, redirecting his offensive line teammates as necessary based on how the defense aligns itself. On nearly every play, the center points to the defenders and, using terminology that the defense can't decipher, gives his fellow linemen their blocking assignments.

Centers tend to be quick, smart, and even-keeled. The other linemen look to him for leadership and stability. In addition to being mentally tough, a center needs to be physically tough so that he can absorb hits from defensive players while he's concentrating on snapping to the quarterback and delivering the ball cleanly. Fumbles result from poor exchanges between the center and the quarterback when the center is worried more about being hit.

Center is the most demanding position on the offensive line. So when a coach finds a good center, he hopes that he plays for years and years. For example, the Pittsburgh Steelers have had only three regular centers since 1964, more than 30 seasons, to the present: Ray Mansfield, Hall of Famer Mike Webster, and current Pittsburgh Steelers center Dermontti Dawson, a potential Hall of Famer. Dawson has been one of the finest centers in the NFL. He's quick, smart, and fast enough to leave his area and block for a ball carrier running around the end.

Guards

Guards, who line up on either side of the center, should be some of the best blockers. In a *block,* an offensive lineman makes contact with a defensive player and uses his hands, arms, and shoulders to move him out of the way. A guard is doing his job if he clears the way, creating a hole for a running back to run through. A guard also must be able to fight off his man — stopping the defender's forward momentum — and prevent him from rushing the quarterback on a pass play.

The neutral zone

The *neutral zone* is the area between the offensive and defensive lines. It's the length of the ball in width. Only the center is allowed into the neutral zone until he snaps the ball. If a lineman from either team lines up in this zone prior to the snap of the ball, his team incurs a 5-yard penalty.

Depending on the offense, guards can be big, or they can be small and fast. As I mention in the section "The Lineman Physique: Fat Guys Doing the Job," later in this chapter, the West Coast offense requires finesse blocking and faster guards, and the power blocking style featured by the Dallas Cowboys requires bigger, more physical guards. Larry Allen, who weighs over 320 pounds, was the ideal version of the Cowboys' power-blocking guards. Brian Habib, who started for the world champion Denver Broncos in 1997, suits the West Coast style with his speed and power at the point of attack.

Tackles

Tackles tend to be the biggest linemen, and in the NFL they're generally the most athletic. They should be the stars of the offensive line because their job on the ends of the line is to repel some of the game's best defensive linemen and pass-rushers. They need to have great agility, and they also must possess the strength to seal off the outside when a running play occurs. (*Sealing off the outside* means preventing defensive players from reaching the corner of the line and tackling the ball carrier.)

Sometimes a tackle must shove a defensive player outside when the play is designed toward the middle of the field. He has a lot of responsibility on the *edge* (the outside shoulder of the defensive end or linebacker aligned over him) because there's nothing but open field for the ball carrier if the tackle contains this defensive player(s). Sometimes the tackle must block his man toward the inside, thus allowing the ball carrier to run wide and outside the edge. In some plays, a tackle blocks down on the defensive tackle while the guard pulls to block the defender aligned over the tackle, moving that defender away from the running lane.

 The majority of running plays are designed to go inside the tackles. And *off-tackle* runs are usually run to the strong side of the formation, where the tight end, who serves as another blocker, lines up. On off-tackle runs, the tackle must contain his man and push him inside toward the center of the line as the ball carrier runs wide or outside the tackle. If the tackle can't move his man, he must prevent this defensive end or linebacker from reaching the edge of the line of scrimmage, shielding the ball carrier from the defensive pursuit.

The Lineman Physique: Fat Guys Doing the Job

Fans often look at offensive linemen and say that they're out of shape because they have big, round bodies. But that's the kind of body that most offensive line coaches look for. They don't want sculpted bodies; they want bulky players like Bill Bain, who played for the Los Angeles Rams in the

1980s, and Dallas Cowboys guard Nate Newton. Players like Newton, who weighs over 325 pounds, have great body mass and great natural strength. If you've been carrying that kind of weight around all your life, you tend to develop good leg strength and a powerful torso. If you're a big man, though, you must have quick feet and good athletic ability, too, to play on the O line — that way, you can move the weight and move people out of the way. That's what Newton has.

The perception used to be that you should stick the biggest, least athletic men on the offensive line. A myth? Somewhat. Today's offensive linemen have gone a long way toward shattering that notion. Players like Randall McDaniel, Willie Roaf, and Larry Allen range in size from 290 to 320 pounds, and they're fast, agile, and mean.

Today, an offensive line can be comprised of two different types of players:

✔ **The big, burly (heavyset) lineman:** During the Cowboys' Super Bowl run from 1992 to 1995, when Emmitt Smith was the best runner in pro football, the Dallas line consisted of this type of linemen. These players imposed their will on their opponents and pounded them repeatedly — considered a power offense. Their style was to beat their opponents into submission. They limited their running plays to maybe five or six; they had those plays and stuck with them.

The power offense is a common style when a coach believes that his offensive line is bigger and stronger than the opposition's defensive line. The Cleveland Browns had such an offensive line for Jim Brown. The problem that defensive players face against such a powerfully built line is not the first running play, or the second running play, but the ninth play and beyond. As a defensive player, you start getting tired of 300-pound guys hammering at your head.

✔ **The smaller, quicker lineman:** This type of lineman is light and agile, with the ability to run and block on every play (they call that *pulling*) — he takes more of a surgical approach. The best example of the style of offense that this type of line plays is the classic West Coast offense. This scheme involves a lot of *angle blocking,* which means that an offensive lineman rarely blocks the defensive player directly in front of him; he does everything in angles.

The San Francisco 49ers used this finesse offense exclusively while winning four championships in the 1980s. The Denver Broncos won Super Bowl XXXII in 1998 with what is considered by today's standards to be a small offensive line, with an average size of 290 pounds. The Broncos used a variation of the West Coast offense, which their head coach, Mike Shanahan, incorporated into his offense after serving as the 49ers' offensive coordinator for three seasons.

I see the difference between these two offensive line styles as the difference between heavyweight boxers George Foreman and Muhammad Ali, the West Coast style being Ali and the Dallas Cowboys style being Foreman. Every one of Foreman's body punches is magnified by ten, all brute force, whereas Ali works you over like a surgeon, slicing and picking you apart. So offensive line play can be two different types of games.

What style a team chooses often depends on its quarterback, the size and ability of its offensive linemen, and the coach's offensive preference. If your quarterback has the ability to escape the rush, the West Coast finesse works fine. If you have an immobile quarterback, you may want Foreman-like blockers who are difficult to get past.

Keys to Successful Offensive Line Play

Because the offensive line's job is so important, linemen need to develop certain key characteristics, both individually and as a unit. This section outlines some of those critical traits.

The proper stance

Offensive linemen often use a two-point, or up, stance, especially if the team plans to pass. The best two-point stance for a lineman is to be balanced, meaning that the right foot should not be way back. When the foot is back too far, the lineman has a tendency to turn a little more. A lineman must not turn his body to the outside or to the interior. If he gets caught leaning to the outside, he could give the defensive player the corner, the outside edge. When a lineman gives the defensive player the corner, the defender simply dips his shoulders and then runs forward to that corner. Figure 7-2 shows the proper up stance for an offensive lineman.

On normal downs in which the offense may opt to run or pass the football, many teams put their linemen in a three-point stance, which means right hand on the ground and right foot back (see Figure 7-3). A player must get comfortable in this stance and also maintain his balance so that he doesn't telegraph what he intends to do. The hand on the ground shouldn't be too far forward as to cause a dip in the shoulders; the shoulders should be square. From that stance, you can pull to the right, pull to the left, set up, or drive straight ahead.

But in a definite passing situation, such as third-and-long, being in a two-point stance is perfectly fine. Moving and maintaining positional leverage is easier and quicker from a two-point stance. (See the following section, "Leverage," for more information.) You also can run a draw or trap play from that position.

Figure 7-2:
An offensive lineman's two-point stance ensures that he remains balanced.

Figure 7-3:
On normal downs, offensive linemen assume a three-point stance.

By the same token, if it's first-and-10, an offensive tackle may be able to remain in the up position. Say the play is a run designed away from the tackle. From a two-point, up position, he can pull to the inside and help block for the ball carrier. Linemen want to change stances occasionally to prevent the defensive players from zeroing in on exactly what the offense is doing. This changing is known as *giving the defensive player different looks*.

A solid base

To be an excellent offensive lineman, you must maintain proper balance. The key to proper balance is having a solid base. A lineman's feet should be set a little wider than the width of his shoulders; that way, the torso is set like a perfect upside-down T. If the lineman can maintain this stance, in most cases he will not be knocked off his feet. The same principle applies in boxing and basketball. A boxer always maintains that good base while keeping any leans to a minimum. He doesn't want to overextend his body to one side, thus becoming more susceptible to being knocked off his feet. A basketball player on defense wants to be able to move right and move left while maintaining a good center of gravity. Offensive linemen are the same. If they can maintain a good base, they can utilize their feet and whatever quickness they have.

To maintain that solid base, you have to keep your feet on the ground. If a foot gets caught in the air, a defender can push you aside. Once your foot is in the air, you cannot move laterally. And if an offensive lineman can't move laterally, he is beaten.

Leverage

Maintaining positional leverage is very important for an offensive lineman. He needs to anticipate where the defensive player is going and then get himself between that player and the quarterback, whom he's trying to protect. The point between the blocker and the quarterback, where the offensive lineman wants to meet the defender he plans to block, is called the *intersection point*. The offensive lineman needs to reach that point as quickly as possible. The slower the lineman assumes that position, the easier it is for his opponent to get him turned. That's really what the defensive player is trying to do — turn the offensive lineman. Once the offensive lineman is turned, the defensive player can shorten his distance to the corner. Once he accomplishes that, the defender can make an inside move because he has the offensive lineman pointed in the wrong direction.

Toughness

An important ingredient in offensive line play is toughness. Generally, toughness is an attitude that a player develops over a period of time. He must have a lot of self-pride and tell himself that no one will beat him. Being tough is a big part of every sport, and it's a sign of a true competitor. A player who has a certain degree of toughness can improve if he plays on a team made up of tough, physical, and aggressive players.

So much of that toughness is mental toughness. Tell yourself, "I refuse to give up!" Many times, a game is like a 15-round prizefight. There's a point when one of those boxers slows down. I don't want to say that he quits, but working hard simply becomes less important to him. That phenomenon happens on a football field, too, and that's where mental toughness comes in. Toughness is essential when run-blocking because run-blocking is basically about being tougher than your opponent and wearing him down. Linemen win the fight when they rob their opponents of mental toughness.

Offensive crackups

Offensive linemen tend to hang in a group: They practice together and go out together.

In 1997, the Denver Broncos had a typical group. Denver's offensive line instituted a kangaroo court — no defense attorneys allowed — in which they fined each other for being quoted in newspapers or talking on radio shows. The plan was for them to be anonymous; they were against publicity. In fact, they fined each other if they received a game ball, usually awarded by the captain or coach for a well-played game. And they fined Pro-Bowler Gary Zimmerman for being a prima donna because he missed training camp during a contract negotiation.

Prior to the Super Bowl, when the NFL ordered the Bronco linemen to talk — 2,000 reporters were asking questions every day — they bit their tongues when they heard how the more-talented Green Bay Packers defensive line was too powerful for them. On game day, they opened huge holes for running back Terrell Davis, who scored three touchdowns and rushed for 157 yards in Denver's 31-24 victory.

When their teammates declared that the offensive line deserved the Super Bowl MVP award for blocking for Davis and protecting quarterback John Elway, the linemen thought that was definitely a bad idea. They would have had to fine themselves $1,000 or more for accepting such an honor.

Repetition

Another key to an effective and cohesive offensive line lies in its practice repetition. Take as many snaps as possible in practice, and repeat the same play 10 to 20 times. On any level, many of the best running teams are teams that run three or four basic plays. They keep repeating them, doing them over and over until they're so proficient that no opposition can stop them. In NFL training camps, offensive lines constantly work together, everyone going through the hard times, the long, hot muggy days — everyone working when he's tired. There comes a point when you have to rely on the guy next to you. Working together over and over in the heat of the day can develop real cohesiveness.

A Lineman's Worst Offense: Holding

Holding — when an offensive lineman grabs and holds onto a defensive player — is one of the worst things an offensive lineman can get caught doing. An offensive lineman is whistled for holding when he grabs an arm, a jersey, or even tackles a player who has beaten him. Linemen are allowed to use their hands, but they can't use their hands to clamp onto an opposing player and limit his movement. If a lineman is caught holding a defensive player, the penalty is 10 yards from the spot of the infraction. Now, some people will tell you that offensive linemen hold on every play, but mainly they are defensive guys like myself.

Generally, if the offensive lineman's hands are inside the opponent's shoulder and his chest area (where the jersey number is), he can grab and hold all he wants as long as he keeps the defender in front of him. But if a defender goes down to the ground really fast for no apparent reason, it's obvious that he's being held, even if the offensive lineman's hands are inside.

Other bad things that offensive linemen do

✔ **Clipping:** When an offensive lineman blocks an opponent from behind, hitting him in the back of the legs or in the back. The infraction costs the offense 15 yards. However, clipping is legal within 3 yards of the line of scrimmage.

✔ **Chop blocking:** This is considered a dirty play (a 15-yard penalty) when a lineman dives at an opponent's knees anywhere outside a designated area 3 yards beyond the line of scrimmage. The same block is considered legal when it occurs within 3 yards of the line of scrimmage. Go figure. The worst chop block is when two linemen double-team a defender, one lineman restraining the player around the shoulders while another hits him below the waist.

✔ **Encroachment:** When an offensive player enters the neutral zone before the ball is snapped and makes contact with the opposition. It's a 5-yard penalty, and the offense repeats the down.

✔ **False start:** When an offensive lineman who's in a stance or set position moves prematurely prior to the snap of the ball. Five-yard penalty, replay the down.

✔ **Helping the runner:** After the ball carrier crosses the line of scrimmage, an offensive lineman can't push or pull him forward, helping him gain extra yardage. Ten-yard penalty and replay the down.

✔ **Ineligible receiver downfield:** A quarterback would never throw the ball to his blockers, but the blockers can be penalized for running downfield if they're not trying to block defensive players. Linemen who are no longer blocking or have lost their man can't run past the line of scrimmage when the quarterback is attempting to pass. Five-yard penalty and repeat the down.

✔ **Offside:** When an offensive player lines up over the designated line of scrimmage, trying to gain an edge on blocking or simply forgetting where he should be. Generally, the lineman either places his hand over the line of scrimmage or tilts his upper body over the line of scrimmage. Five-yard penalty and repeat the down.

Some coaches teach holding, but incorporating it as a base teaching principle is a bad idea. If you teach holding and how to get away with it, players will come to rely on it, and it doesn't always work. Linemen who rely on holding can get themselves out of balance. And the essence of pass protection is to stay in balance as long as you can. *But* if holding protects your quarterback from being slammed to the ground, go ahead and do it.

Familiar Blocking Terms

You hear a lot of terms thrown around when it comes to blocking. Knowing one type of block from another really isn't that important unless you're trying to impress the most diehard of fans, but here's the lowdown on some of the common terms:

- **Cut-off block:** Generally used on running plays, which are designed to allow a defensive player to come free, or untouched, across the line of scrimmage. After that happens, an offensive lineman deliberately gets in the way of this on-rushing defender. This block is sometimes called an *angle block* because the offensive lineman hits the defensive player from the side, or from an angle.

- **Chop block:** The legal variety is used within 3 yards of the line of scrimmage to slow down the opposition's pass rush. A lineman blocks down low with his shoulders and arms, attempting to take the defender's legs from underneath him and stop his momentum. If this play occurs 3 yards or more beyond the line of scrimmage, the blocker is penalized 15 yards. Defensive players wish that this type of block would be outlawed permanently on all parts of the playing field.

- **Drive block:** This one-on-one block is used most often when a defensive lineman lines up directly over an offensive lineman. The blocker usually explodes out of a three-point stance and drives his hips forward, delivering the block from a wide base while keeping his head up and his shoulders square. The blow should be delivered with the forearms and not the head, with the head kept to the side of the opponent where the hole for the ball carrier should be.

- **Double-team:** *Double-teaming* is two linemen ganging up on one innocent defensive player. Two against one. It's more common on pass plays when the center and a guard work together to stop the penetration of a talented inside pass-rusher. However, the double-team also works well on running plays, especially at the point of attack or at the place where the play is designed to go. The double-team blockers attack one defender, thus clearing out the one player who might stop the play from working.

✔ **Man-on-man blocking:** The straight-ahead style of blocking a defender who plays directly over you and driving him out of the hole. Most defenses use four linemen, so man-on-man blocking is common on pass plays, with each offensive lineman choosing the opponent opposite him, and the center helping out to either side.

✔ **Reach block:** When an offensive lineman reaches for the next defender, meaning that he doesn't block the opponent directly in front of him but moves for an opponent to either side. The reach block is common on run plays when the play calls for a guard to reach out and block an inside linebacker.

✔ **Slide block:** When the entire offensive line slides down the line of scrimmage — a coordinated effort by the line to go either right or left. This technique is good when the quarterback prefers to roll or sprint right, running outside the tackle while attempting to throw the football. In that case, the line may slide to the right to give the quarterback extra protection to that side. With a talented cutback runner, this scheme may give the illusion of a run to the right, as the line slides that way while the ball carrier takes an initial step to the right and then cuts back to his left, hoping to gain an edge.

✔ **Trap block:** When the offensive line deliberately allows a defensive player to cross the line of scrimmage untouched and then blocks him with a guard or tackle from the opposite side or where he's not expecting it. The intent is to create a running lane in the area that the defender vacated. The trap is a mind game, really. The offense wants the defender to believe that it has forgotten about him or simply missed blocking him. Once the defender surges upfield, across the line of scrimmage by a yard or two, an offensive lineman blocks him from the side.

This block, depending on the play's design, can come from a guard or a tackle. Teams run this play to either side, and it's important that the center protects the back side of this lane, negating any pursuit by the defense. The trap block is also called an *influence block* because you want to draw the defender upfield and then go out and trap him. Good passing teams tend to be good trapping teams because defenders usually charge hard upfield, hoping to reach the quarterback.

✔ **Zone block:** Just like it sounds; each lineman protects a specific area or zone. Even if the defensive player leaves this area, the blocker must stay in his zone because the play or ball may be coming in that direction and the quarterback wants to see that area uncluttered. Blocking in a zone is generally designed to key on a specific defensive player who is disrupting the offensive game plan.

Blocking a 3-4 zone blitz defense is tough

The standard defense is the 4-3 defense, which involves four down linemen and three linebackers. The defense has four guys rushing the passer and everyone else dropping back into zones. That's traditional.

With the 3-4 defense, you have three down linemen, but one of the outside linebackers or defensive backs always rushes, essentially becoming the fourth player on the line of scrimmage. The offensive line seldom knows which player will be this fourth rusher; they can't account for the personnel like they can with a four-man defensive line. In not knowing which defender plans to rush the passer, the offensive line doesn't know which side to protect. This guessing game causes problems for the offensive linemen. The blockers must react after the snap because they need to think of the many combinations, and often they guess wrong. The 3-4 zone blitz defense definitely makes pass protection harder.

The 3-4 zone blitz defense often messes up the quarterback's reads because a safety may become a pass rusher. Most quarterbacks look into the secondary at the safeties and linebackers, hoping to read what areas they plan to cover once the ball is snapped. When these same players switch roles and come charging upfield rather than dropping into pass coverage, the quarterback rapidly must account for which players will now assume the coverage roles of these safeties or linebackers. The defense hopes that the quarterback reads the defense incorrectly and throws a poor pass.

A lot of 3-4 teams drop defensive linemen into pass coverage, which further complicates pass-blocking schemes. To deal with these combinations of zone blitzes, teams use maximum protection, which means using their running backs as blockers. They ask running backs to negate the extra defensive player coming from the outside or inside.

Besides using maximum protection, the best way to beat a zone blitzing team is to call either a draw play or some other running play from the offense's most successful pass formation set. Coaches refer to this as *showing pass*. Draw plays and max protecting hurt those zone blitzing teams.

Chapter 8

Offensive Plays and Strategies

- -

In This Chapter

▶ Why players are the keys to successful offenses

▶ Running specialized pass offenses like the West Coast offense

▶ Beating different defensive fronts

▶ Looking for a score in the final two minutes

▶ Deciding when to gamble on offense

▶ Choosing a goal-line offense

- -

I remember a song by Foreigner called "Head Games." That title would be very appropriate for this chapter.

When I played defense, I knew that the offensive coaches were trying to get into my head and into the minds of my defensive buddies. When calling a specific play, the offensive coaches not only wanted to beat us but also wanted to make us look foolish. This chapter unmasks some of the chicanery that those offensive geniuses come up with when they're burning the midnight oil studying defensive tendencies.

When football teams, especially in the NFL, decide which play or formation to use, they base the decision on the personnel matchups they want. Coaches study the opposition, examining hours of film, hoping to find the weak links in the opposing defense. No defensive team has 11 great players; therefore, the offense's design is to move away from the opposition's strengths and attack the weaknesses.

Here's another thing you should know about offensive strategy: No perfect play exists for every occasion. In strategy sessions prior to a game, a play may look like it will result in a long gain, but in reality it may not succeed for various reasons. It may fail because someone on the offensive team doesn't execute, or because a defensive player simply anticipates correctly and makes a great play. Things happen!

My plan for this chapter is to explain the basic offensive approaches to the game and explain some particular plays and overall schemes. Then I discuss which offensive plays or formations work well against particular defenses and in specific situations. When does a quarterback sneak work? When is play-action passing ideal? What goal-line run plays really work? What does a team do on third-and-long? This chapter has answers for all these questions and a whole lot more.

Understanding That Offense Begins with Players

The first thing you should know about offense is that *players* win games, not schemes or formations or trick plays. If a player doesn't execute, none of the decisions that the coaches made will work. And I'm not talking merely from the point of view of an ex-player; coaches, owners, scouts, everyone knows that this is true.

The opposite scenario applies, too: A play designed to gain the offense only a couple of yards can turn into a score unexpectedly if a defensive player misses a tackle or turns the wrong way, or if an offensive player makes a spectacular move. Having been a defensive player, I know that we sometimes had players placed in the right situations to defend a play perfectly, but the play still succeeded because of an offensive player's outstanding effort.

And look at the size of today's offensive players — who can stop them? So many runners and receivers weigh 200 pounds or more, and they all can run 40 yards in 4.5 seconds or faster. (The 40-yard dash is a common test that teams use to measure players' talents.) Ryan Leaf, quarterback of the San Diego Chargers, weighs over 240 pounds and is 6'5". So is Peyton Manning, quarterback for the Indianapolis Colts.

And it's not just the quarterbacks, runners, and receivers who are growing in size. Some teams have 325-pound offensive linemen who can run 40 yards in 5 seconds flat, and some are as agile as men half their size. They are as big as the defensive linemen, therefore giving the skilled players on offense an opportunity to succeed. Every great ball carrier will tell you that he can't gain his 1,000 yards in a season without a very good offensive line.

Helping Offenses by Enforcing an Important Rule

What has aided offensive production in the last few NFL seasons is the enforcement of the *5-yard bump rule:* when defensive backs are forbidden to push or shove receivers 5 or more yards beyond the line of scrimmage in hopes of pushing the receivers off their pass routes. This rule was originally instituted in 1978, but through the years, officials started to allow defensive backs to again use their hands and arms in this manner. This liberal interpretation of the rule hurt the passing game because it prevented offenses from executing their carefully designed plays.

But because the rule is being enforced properly in the NFL today, offenses seem to be taking charge. They're doing a much better job of spreading out the defenses, knowing that they can throw to their outside receivers. Not only has forcing defenses to defend a larger area of the field improved the passing game, but it also has created more opportunities for running backs. With defenders spread out across the line of scrimmage, a runner now has a chance at a longer run if he breaks through the first line of defense.

College football, particularly teams like Florida, Florida State, and UCLA, tend to pass more and have copied many of the NFL formations (and vice versa). What often makes for bigger plays in college football is the fact that not every college team has the defensive backfield talent of an NFL team.

Specialized Pass Offenses

It's important to remember that few passes travel more than 10 or 12 yards. I'm sure you've heard about *the bomb* — a reference to a long pass — but those 35- to 40-yard or longer pass plays are pretty rare. To put this in perspective: Green Bay Packers quarterback Brett Favre led the NFL during the 1997 season with 37 pass plays that covered 25 yards or more. Favre attempted 513 passes, so 7 percent of them were big plays.

With the 5-yard bump rule being enforced, offenses like Favre's are using the pass more and more. As a fan, you should be aware of three types of pass offenses, which I describe in this section.

West Coast offense

Brett Favre and about ten other NFL quarterbacks operate a short, ball-control passing game that's called the *West Coast offense* because it was developed by coach Bill Walsh, who directed the San Francisco 49ers to three Super Bowls. Packers coach Mike Holmgren learned the offense as an assistant under Walsh, and its popularity has spread throughout the NFL as other Walsh disciples have begun to use it. Many college teams use variations of this offense, depending on the talent of their receivers.

The West Coast offense uses all the offense's personnel in the passing game, as opposed to an I-formation team that is structured to run the ball and rarely throws to the running backs. Rather than running long routes downfield, the wide receivers run quick slants or square-out patterns toward the sidelines, hoping to receive the ball quickly and gain extra yards after the catch. The receivers run a lot of *crossing routes,* meaning that they run from left to right in front of the quarterback, maybe 10 yards away. Crossing routes are effective because they disrupt many defensive secondary coverages.

If a running back is good at catching the ball, he becomes a prime receiver in the West Coast offense, which also utilizes a tight end on deeper routes than most other offenses. Because there are so many potential pass catchers (two receivers and two running backs, or three receivers and one running back) on a typical pass play, the tight end often can find open areas after he crosses the line of scrimmage — the defensive players in the secondary tend to focus their attention on the wide receivers. The West Coast offense incorporates the tight end into most pass plays, and that player is required to be an above-average receiver.

The premise of this offense is to maintain possession of the ball. Although it does have quick-strike scoring possibilities, the West Coast offense is designed to keep offensive drives alive via passing rather than running the ball. One of the basic theories of the offense is: If the defense is suspecting a run, pass the ball to the running back instead.

Shotgun offense

For obvious passing downs, some teams use the *shotgun offense.* In the shotgun, the quarterback lines up 5 to 7 yards behind the center and receives a long snap, as shown in Figure 8-1. The pass plays used in this offense are identical to the ones that are used when the quarterback is under center; offenses use the shotgun simply to allow their quarterbacks more time to visualize the defense, particularly the secondary's alignment. On an obvious passing down, nothing can be gained by keeping the quarterback under center. Why have him spend time dropping back to pass when he can receive a long snap and be ready to throw?

To run this offense, you want a quarterback who's quick with his decisions and also able to run with the football if the defense's actions make it possible for him to gain yardage by carrying the ball himself.

Figure 8-1:
In the shotgun offense, the quarterback lines up 5 to 7 yards behind the center, which enables him to see the defense better.

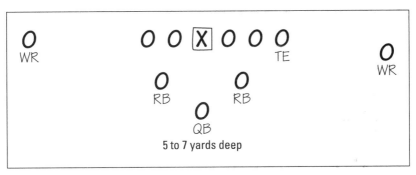

The best shotgun quarterback I ever saw was John Elway of the Denver Broncos. Jim Kelly of the Buffalo Bills truly excelled in the shotgun, too. Elway and Kelly seemed more comfortable and confident in this formation than other quarterbacks. Elway, like the Pittsburgh Steelers' Kordell Stewart, is always a threat to run if a pass play fails to develop. From my perspective, Elway never seemed excited. He stood back in the pocket with poise, looked around, and scanned the whole defense. You couldn't get him to panic. He would just catch the snap, read the defense, and throw.

But from a defensive lineman's viewpoint, the shotgun is okay because you don't have to concentrate on defending the run; you know that the offense is going to pass. In other formations, a defender has to be prepared for both possibilities: run or pass. He has to think before reacting. When facing the shotgun, a defensive lineman has only one mission: to get to the quarterback as fast as he can.

Red gun (or run-and-shoot) offense

The *red gun offense*, or *run-and-shoot offense*, utilizes four receivers, one running back, and no tight end. The Houston Oilers and the Atlanta Falcons used this offense in the early 1990s, but both teams have since abandoned it for a more conventional approach because it places too much emphasis on passing. (Heck, Houston has since moved out of Texas, and now they're called the Tennessee Oilers with a home in Nashville.) Some good high school teams in California and Florida that love to throw the football use variations of the red gun, as does the University of Florida and its talented coach, Steve Spurrier.

The red gun is a great offense for fans to watch because it utilizes so many pass plays. Also, only five offensive linemen are blocking on every play, which creates more opportunities for the defense to place more pass-rushers to one side (called *overloading*); the offensive lineman can't possibly block every one of these pass-rushers. These types of gambles may lead to a sack or a big play — feast or famine. When a red gun offense gives the ball to a running back, he has a chance to make a big play because the defense is concentrating on pressuring the four wide receivers. Depending on how deep the receivers run their patterns, the running back may have a lot of open area on the field to run.

I never thought that a team could win a championship with this offense because the players spend too much time on the passing game in practice. No NFL team has won with the red gun, but the University of Florida recently won a national championship with it. Defenses need to practice and prepare for running offenses, too, and with a limited amount of practice time on a typical weekday, the red gun offense never gives the defense that opportunity. Instead, the defensive players become accustomed to defending the pass. Defenses have to be very good at stopping the run, too, in order to win. Also, the red gun doesn't employ a tight end — another thing the defense needs to know how to defend.

I always had problems with this scheme as a player because it was an unconventional system. In the red gun, it was difficult to key on the lone running back and anticipate what the play was going to be. This running back usually was in the same alignment, so, to me, some passes looked like run plays, and run plays ended up being pass plays. Offenses often ran draw plays (running plays) from an unusual perspective. For example, the team would run a draw as the quarterback was faking like he was going to run around the end (called a *bootleg*), but actually he had already given the ball to the running back; the quarterback was simply pretending to have the ball while running wide. I know that this offense disrupted our defensive coaches. They never seemed sure of which defense worked best against it, especially for us defensive linemen.

Beating a Defense

One of the primary factors that helps a coach decide what offense to run and what plays to call is how the defense sets up. Various defenses call for different strategies to beat them. This section talks about some defenses and the offensive plays or formations that may work against those defensive schemes. For more information about any of these defenses, see Chapter 11.

Teams with good offensive lines

If your team has a strong offensive line, you use more four-wide-receiver formations and spread out the defense — split the receivers out and force the defensive backs to play as wide as you can get them. You use such a formation because you know that you have an offensive line that can protect the quarterback. You don't have to worry about your offensive linemen losing the physical battle up front.

If your offensive line is better at run-blocking than pass-protecting, you run the ball and probably use a formation that utilizes two tight ends at once. The running offense can be either from the I formation or the split-back formation. Basically, an offense can use a combination of two tight ends, two receivers, and one back (the I formation). Or the offense can mix things up and use two tight ends, two backs, and one receiver (a variation of the split-back formation).

Battling a 3-4 front

When facing a 3-4 front (three down linemen and four linebackers), the offense's best strategy is to run *weak side,* or away from the tight end (which is always the strong side of any offensive formation). One possible running play is called the *weak-side lead.* With this play, the defensive end (DE) usually attempts to control and push the offensive tackle (LT) inside toward the center of the line, leaving the linebacker behind him (OLB) to defend a lot of open area. The offense is in the I formation, and the fullback (FB) runs to the weak side and blocks the linebacker, shoving him inside. The left offensive tackle allows the defensive end to push him a little, letting the defender believe that he's controlling the play. However, the offensive lineman then grabs the defender, containing him, and moves him out of the way to the right. The ball carrier should have a clear running lane after he hits the line of scrimmage. (Figure 8-2 diagrams this play.)

Running against a 4-3 front

An offense can attack a 4-3 defense formation (four down linemen, three linebackers) in many different ways, but one common strategy is to attack what coaches call the "bubble" side. Remember, the 4-3 defense employs both over and under slants that the four-man defensive line uses. Overs and unders are basically the alignments of defensive linemen to one particular side of the offensive center. (See Chapter 11 for further details.) When the defensive front lines up in an under look, the offense should attack the defensive side where the two linebackers are positioned, which is known as the bubble.

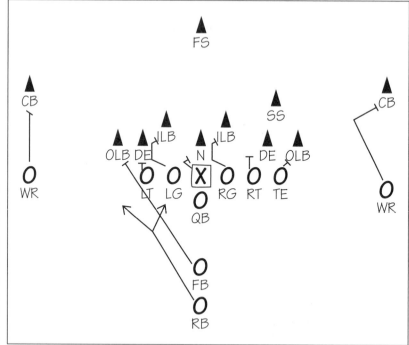

The offensive play shown in Figure 8-3 is called a *delay draw* to the strong side (the tight end side) of the offensive formation. When the defense is positioned like this, three defensive linemen line up over the center, left guard, and left tackle. These offensive linemen are also called the weak-side guard and tackle. This defensive alignment leaves only one lineman and two smaller linebackers (DE, ILB, and DLB) to defend the strong side of the offense's I formation.

On the delay draw, the right guard (RG) blocks down on the defensive nose tackle (N), and the fullback (FB) runs into the hole and blocks the front-side linebacker (ILB). The right tackle (RT) blocks the defensive end (DE), keeping him out of the middle, and the tight end (TE) blocks and contains the outside linebacker (OLB). This approach is known as *running at the defense's weakest point*. When the ball carrier reaches the line of scrimmage, he should find open space between the offense's right guard and right tackle.

Beating the four-across defense

In the four-across defense, the defense plays all four secondary players deep, about 12 yards off the line of scrimmage. To beat this defense, the offense wants to have two wide receivers (WR) run comeback routes, have the tight end (TE) run a 16-yard in route, and have the two backs (RB)

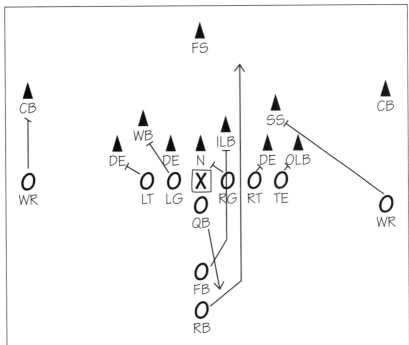

Figure 8-3:
The delay draw takes advantage of there being only one lineman and two linebackers on the strong side.

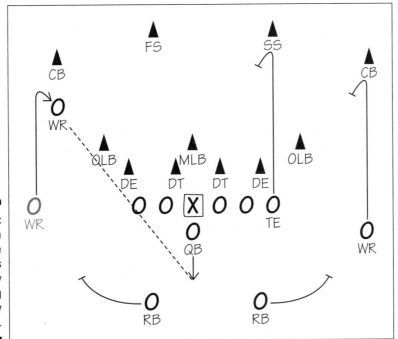

Figure 8-4:
You can beat the four-across defense by running a play like this.

swing out to the right and left. The running back to the quarterback's left side should run more of a looping pass pattern. The quarterback (QB) throws the ball to the wide receiver on the left. (See Figure 8-4.)

The quarterback throws to his left because the ball is placed on the left hash mark, which is the short side of the field. Throwing a 15-yard comeback pass to his left is much easier than throwing a 15-yard comeback to the right, or the wide side of the field. The pass to the wide side would have to travel much farther, almost 42 yards, as opposed to just 15 yards. From the left hash mark to the numbers on the right side of the field, the distance is more than 19 yards. And the comeback to the right is always thrown beyond those numbers (10, 20, 30, 40), going down the length of the field.

If the defense senses that the quarterback is going to throw to the wide receiver on the left side and then decides to drop a linebacker into underneath coverage, hoping to intercept, the quarterback can't throw that pass. By *underneath,* I mean that the linebacker is dropping back to defend the pass, but safeties are still positioned beyond him. Hence, the linebacker is underneath the safeties. Instead, the quarterback throws to the running back on the same side. The quarterback simply keys (watches) the linebacker. If the linebacker drops into coverage, the QB throws to the running back because he won't be covered. If the linebacker takes the running back, then the QB throws to the receiver.

Beating press coverage

In discussing press coverage, I'm not talking about dealing with newspaper reporters or the media. *Press coverage* is when the defensive team has its two cornerbacks on the line of scrimmage, covering the outside receivers man-to-man.

One tactic against this defense is to throw to the tight end (TE), who runs to the middle of the field. (See Figure 8-5.) Another option is to throw to the running back (RB) who is swinging out to the left. The wide receivers (WR), who are being pressed, should run in the opposite direction, away from the area in which either the tight end or the running back is headed. (See Figure 8-6.)

Passing against a zone coverage

When I say "passing against a zone coverage," I'm talking about a defensive secondary that's playing zone — meaning that the cornerbacks are playing off the line of scrimmage. They are not in press coverage. The best pass against a zone coverage is the curl, and the best time to use it is on first-and-10. A receiver (WR) runs 10 to 12 yards and simply curls or hooks back toward the quarterback (QB), as shown in Figure 8-7. He usually curls to his left and attempts to run his route deep enough to gain a first down. The coverage should be soft enough (the defensive back, CB, is playing 5 to 7 yards off the receiver) on these routes that the receiver's size shouldn't matter. However, against a man-to-man scheme, a smaller receiver may be ineffective running patterns against a taller, stronger defensive back.

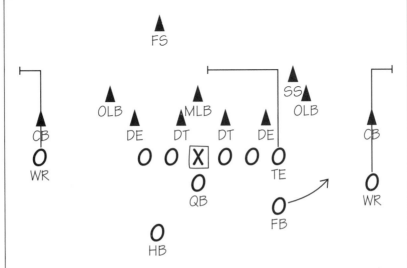

Figure 8-5: One option for beating press coverage is to throw to the tight end in midfield.

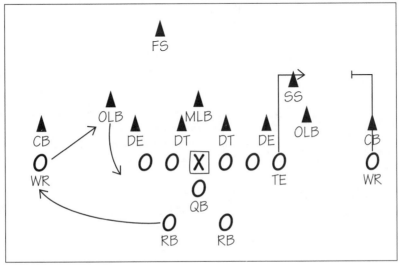

Figure 8-6: Another option for beating press coverage is to throw to the running back, who swings out to the left.

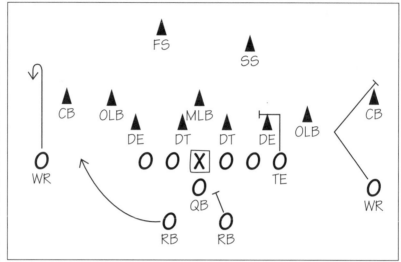

Figure 8-7:
Against a zone coverage, the receiver(s) should run 10 to 12 yards out and then curl back toward the quarterback.

Selecting an offense versus a zone blitz

The two best zone blitz teams in the NFL are the Pittsburgh Steelers and the Carolina Panthers. (See Chapter 11 for more on zone blitz). Against either of these defenses, sustaining a running offense is very difficult. Some offenses have had success running against zone blitz defenses, but I don't think that you can beat them consistently by running the ball.

When facing a defense that blitzes a lot off the corner (linebackers or safeties coming from either wide side of the line of scrimmage against your offensive tackles), your offense should align with two tight ends in order to help pass-protect. To beat a zone blitz with a passing attack, you must find your opponent's weakest defender in the passing game. Find the player — cornerback, safety, or linebacker — that your offensive players can block and handle.

Your quarterback must throw to the side opposite where the defense overloads. For example, if the defense positions four players to your quarterback's left, as shown in Figure 8-8, he should throw to his right. But the offense must still block the side from which the defense is attacking.

Throwing the post versus blitzing teams

Most defenses protect against quarterbacks attempting to throw the *post route,* when a receiver fakes to the outside and then runs straight down the field toward the goalpost. The quarterback lines up the throw by focusing on the hash marks. When he releases the ball, the quarterback tries to lead

Figure 8-8:
With the defense overloaded (having more players) to the quarterback's left side, the QB attempts to avoid the zone blitz from that side by throwing a short pass to the wide receiver on his right.

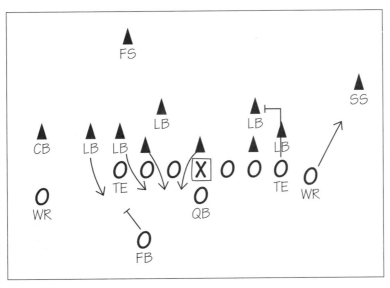

the receiver, or throw the ball slightly in front of him, so that the pass drops to him over his shoulder. That way, if a defensive player is chasing the receiver, the defender shouldn't be able to intercept the pass.

The deep post doesn't really work well against zone blitz scheming defenses like the ones that the Carolina Panthers and the Pittsburgh Steelers play. Why? Because these teams rarely leave the post open. They defend it pretty well.

However, other teams that blitz from a basic 4-3 defense may use a safety to blitz the quarterback. When a team uses a safety to blitz, usually the defense is vulnerable in the center of the field, where both safeties should be. Still, very few teams leave the deep post wide open because it can give the offense a quick six points. The Dallas Cowboys, who have a great cornerback in Deion Sanders, occasionally leave the post open because they believe in their defense's ability to recover.

Although it may look like a throw-and-catch play on television, the post is a tough throw because the quarterback must lead the receiver and align his throw with the goalpost. When you watch games on television this season, you'll see some receivers running wide open down the middle of the field, but the pass won't be on target and will fall incomplete. In this case, usually the quarterback put too much depth on his pass (threw it too far) or was off-line. Sometimes, the receiver doesn't run his route in a continuous straight line, making the pass look off-line.

Gaining Better Field Position

Of course, a score is always an offense's ultimate goal, but to score, you have to move down the field toward your opponent's end zone. In this section, I talk about various strategies for gaining yards and thus better field position.

A field position pass

When offenses face third down and more than 6 yards, known as *third-and-long,* the safest play is for the quarterback to throw to a running back who is underneath the coverage of the defensive secondary. Why? Because in such situations, the defensive secondary, which is aligned well off the line of scrimmage, is always instructed to allow the receiver to catch the ball and then come out and tackle him, preventing a first down.

Early in the game, when your offense is down by ten points or less, you want to run a safe play on third-and-long, knowing that you'll probably end up punting the ball. Your offense is raising its white flag and giving up. That's why this pass to the running back is called a *field position pass.* Maybe the back will get lucky, break a bunch of tackles, and gain a first down, but basically you're playing for field position. The odds are pretty slim that you'll beat a good defensive team under third-and-long conditions.

Possession passes

Most of the time, a *possession pass* is a short throw, between 8 and 10 yards, to either a running back or a tight end. The intent isn't necessarily to gain a first down but to maintain possession of the ball while gaining yardage. Often, teams call possession passes several times in a short period to help the quarterback complete some easy passes and restore his confidence.

If you want to throw a possession pass to a wide receiver and the defensive secondary is playing off the line of scrimmage, the best pass to throw is a 5-yard *hitch.* The receiver runs up the field 5 yards, stops, and then turns his back so that he is facing the quarterback. When he turns, the ball should almost be in his hands. You call these throws when the quarterback has thrown some incompletions, giving him a chance to calm down and complete a few easy passes.

The money receivers

"Money time" is when the game is on the line and you need a catch to keep a scoring drive alive or win the game. The ball has to be caught, or your team loses. The two best money receivers, I think, are still playing today: Jerry Rice of the San Francisco 49ers and Michael Irvin of the Dallas Cowboys. Both of these players are very physical, meaning that it may take two defensive backs to stop them. These receivers usually overpower everyone in single coverage.

My other three top receivers have retired. In no particular order, they are Fred Biletnikoff of the Oakland Raiders, who was always a clutch receiver; Steve Largent, whom I played against a lot when he was with the Seattle Seahawks; and Paul Warfield, who played for both the Cleveland Browns and the Miami Dolphins more than 25 seasons ago.

Play-action passes

In a *play-action pass,* the quarterback fakes a handoff to a running back and then drops back 4 more yards and throws the football. The fake to the running back usually causes the linebackers and defensive backs to hesitate and stop coming forward after they realize that it's not a running play. They stop because they know that they must retreat and go and defend their pass responsibility areas.

If neither team has scored and the offense is on its own 20-yard line, it's a perfect time to throw the football. As an offensive coach, I would prefer that the ball is out of my own territory. But you run this play when you believe the defense is generally thinking that the offense will run, which is considered the safer option. Some conservative offensive teams run play-action only in short-yardage situations (for example, second down and 3 yards to go). But play-action works whenever the defense places its strong safety near the line of scrimmage, wanting to stuff the run. Because the defensive pass coverage is likely to be soft, the offense has a good opportunity to throw the ball. And the defense shouldn't be blitzing, which in turn gives the quarterback plenty of time to throw.

Offenses for Sticky Situations

One of the biggest challenges of being a coach — or a quarterback, for that matter — is to lead your team out of the sticky situations that arise. This section explains some of the strategies that offenses use to gain the necessary yardage for a first down, move downfield with little time left on the clock, and more.

Deciding whether to gamble on fourth-and-1

The game is tied. On fourth-and-1, should your team kick a field goal or go for it — try to make a first down and maintain possession, hoping to end your offensive possession with a touchdown?

For most coaches, the decision depends on the time of the game and the team they're playing. If a team is on the road against a solid opponent, one that has beaten the team consistently in the past, most coaches elect to kick a field goal. In the NFL, some teams are especially difficult to beat at home. For example, the Green Bay Packers have won 27 consecutive home games (including playoff games) through the 1997 season. The thought process is that any lead, even a small one, is better than risking none at all against such a team on the road. So, at Lambeau Field, you kick the field goal and take your three points.

However, a coach's strategy may change drastically when his team is playing the same opponent in its own stadium. If I'm playing in my stadium and I'm leading 17-7 in the fourth quarter, I may go for it — especially if we're inside the other team's 20-yard line. I may let my team take a shot, especially if the offense hasn't been very effective. If my team doesn't make the first down, the other team has to go more than 80 yards to score, and it has to score twice to beat me. You'd rather be in the other team's territory when you gamble. Never gamble in your own territory — it could cost your team three points or a touchdown.

The toughest area to make a decision is between your opponent's 35- and 40-yard lines, a distance that may be too far for your field goal kicker but too close to punt. If your punter kicks the ball in the end zone, for example, your opponent begins possession on the 20-yard line, giving you a mere 15-yard advantage. When you're making that decision whether to kick or punt in this 35- to 40-yard line area, you may as well toss a coin.

Making a first down on a fourth-down gamble

It's fourth down and 1 yard to go for a first down, and your offense just crossed midfield. You want to gamble, believing that your offense can gain enough yards for a first down. The best play to call in this situation is a run off the tackle and the tight end on the left side of the formation, as shown in Figure 8-9.

Your offense has three tight ends in the game: the standard short-yardage personnel. These players always practice running a few specific plays during the week. Your offense knows that the defense plans to plug up the middle;

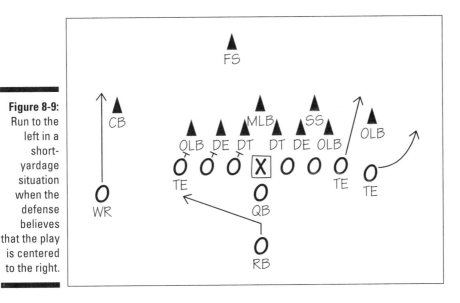

Figure 8-9:
Run to the left in a short-yardage situation when the defense believes that the play is centered to the right.

they don't want an interior running play to beat them. They will defend that area. To fool the defense and maximize the offense's chance to succeed, the offensive alignment puts two tight ends to the right, hoping that the defense will react to the formation and slant its personnel to that side because it believes that the play is centered there. With the defense slanted to prevent a run to the right, the offense runs to the left.

Running a quarterback sneak

The *quarterback sneak* is one of the oldest plays in the book. But it isn't that simple to execute, and it doesn't always succeed. The play is designed for the quarterback to run behind one of his guards, using the guard as his principal blocker. Teams run the sneak when the yardage needed for a first down is less than a full yard, sometimes only a few inches.

To be successful with the sneak, the quarterback delays for a moment and sees from what angle the defensive linemen are coming. Then he dives headfirst, pushing his shoulders into the crack behind whichever guard (the right or left side) is called in the huddle.

Teams call this play *quarterback sneak left* or *right* — the defense determines which side. The quarterback wants to run at the weakest defensive tackle. For example, you don't want to run at the Dallas Cowboys' Leon Lett; you want to run at the other tackle. If the Minnesota Vikings' John Randle is aligned over your right guard, you want to sneak over your left guard. You make the sneak work by having your center and guard double-team the defensive tackle, or whoever is playing in this gap opposite the two offensive linemen. These two blockers must move the defensive tackle or the defender in that gap.

Granted, the defense knows this plan as well, but they tend to stick to their scheme. During the 1997 season, I don't remember any team successfully running a quarterback sneak against the San Francisco 49ers because the 49ers had two great defensive tackles in the middle, Bryant Young and Dana Stubblefield. There was no weak link. Therefore, no offensive team risked a quarterback sneak because they couldn't effectively block those linemen.

Doing the two-minute drill

Your team has two minutes left in the game to drive 70 yards for a score. You must score a touchdown (and successfully kick the extra point) to tie the game. As an offensive coach, you're hoping that the defense decides to play a *prevent defense,* which means that they use seven players in pass coverage while rushing only four linemen or linebackers at the quarterback. When a defense plays a prevent defense, you may want to run the ball because the running back has plenty of room to run after he crosses the line of scrimmage.

The best pass play to use in this situation is the *triple stretch* or *vertical stretch:* One receiver runs a deep pattern through the secondary, another receiver runs a route in the middle, and another simply runs underneath. (See Figure 8-10.) The underneath route may be only 5 yards across the line of scrimmage and *underneath* the linebackers' position in pass coverage.

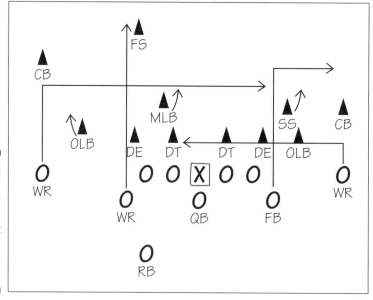

Figure 8-10: The triple (or vertical) stretch pass play is great for a two-minute offense.

HOWIE SAYS

The best two-minute quarterbacks

Some quarterbacks operate the two-minute drill as close to perfectly as possible. Number one, in my opinion, is Denver Broncos quarterback John Elway. The second best I ever saw was Joe Montana when he played with the San Francisco 49ers. Montana directed a 92-yard scoring drive in the final minutes to beat the Cincinnati Bengals in Super Bowl XXIII. Also at Notre Dame, in the 1979 Cotton Bowl, Montana rallied his team from a 34-12 deficit to a 35-34 victory in the final 6 minutes.

The next guy would be Dan Fouts, a Hall of Fame quarterback with the San Diego Chargers; when I played, he seemed to score every two minutes. The Chargers won and lost a lot of games by scores like 38-35 — they didn't have a great defense when Fouts was playing. Then I'd pick Roger Staubach of the Dallas Cowboys, Kenny Stabler of the Raiders, and Dan Marino of the Miami Dolphins to round out my top two-minute quarterbacks list.

The intermediate receiver runs a route behind the linebackers and in front of the secondary coverage players. Teams don't necessarily want to throw deep, knowing that the defense is focused on preventing a huge gain, but that receiver must *stretch the defense,* or force the defense to retreat farther from the line of scrimmage. You use the deep receiver as a decoy.

The quarterback's intention is to find the intermediate receiver (WR who comes in from the left). If the intermediate receiver can run behind the linebackers and catch the ball, he'll probably have a 15-yard gain, but he'll have to make sure that he runs out-of-bounds to stop the clock and conserve time. If your short receiver catches the ball, the linebackers are probably playing very, very deep to prevent the intermediate receiver from catching the ball. In this situation, you dump it to the running back. He catches it and has a chance to run, but he'd better make sure that he gets out-of-bounds, too. If the defense blitzes, you may be able to complete the deep route for a long touchdown pass. The quarterback normally reads progression from deep to intermediate and underneath, knowing that the defense is set up for the middle route.

Scoring Offenses

After you get the ball downfield and get out of all those sticky situations, your offense is ready to score. In this section, you can find plays for various scoring situations.

The best run play on the goal line

Actually I can't tell you the *best* run play on the goal line because there is no best play. But I can tell you that teams that have the most success running on the goal line have a great back like Jim Brown or Marcus Allen (both retired) in their backfield. Teams are always searching for a great running back, someone who can fight through three defenders, for example, and still reach the end zone. Mike Alstott, the young Tampa Bay fullback, is that kind of runner.

The best running back in the NFL today may be Barry Sanders of the Detroit Lions. But Sanders is not a great goal line runner because he's a dodger and a dancer. Barry is not a "pour it in there guy," meaning that he can't physically power his way into the end zone like Jerome Bettis of the Pittsburgh Steelers, who probably weighs 50 pounds more than Sanders. Down on the 1-yard line, you need a powerful runner — a tough, very physical player — who can run over people. Because he's going to be hit, he needs to be able to bounce off one or two tacklers.

Well, okay. The best play at the goal line is always something straight ahead.

Inside the opponent's 10-yard line

One pass in today's NFL offenses is perfectly suited to this part of the field: the *quick out* (see Figure 8-11). The outside receiver (WR on the left) runs straight for 5 to 7 yards and then breaks quickly to the outside. Offenses use this pass play a lot because many defenses play the old college zone defense of putting their four defensive backs deep and back, which is called the *four-across alignment*.

If you have a big, physical receiver, the quick out is the ideal pass. The receiver and the quarterback have to be in unison and *time it right*. If the quarterback completes the pass, the receiver has a chance to break a tackle and run in for a touchdown. The opportunity to score is there because in the four-across alignment, the defensive back doesn't have help on that side; he must make the tackle all by himself. If he doesn't, the receiver can score an easy six points. Of course, the quick out is also a dangerous pass to throw. If the cornerback reads the play quickly and the quarterback fails to throw hard and accurately, the ball is likely to be intercepted by the defensive player and returned for a touchdown.

Two-point conversions

After scoring a touchdown, a team has two options: kick the ball or try for a two-point conversion. The team earns two points if it successfully reaches the end zone on either a pass or a run after a touchdown.

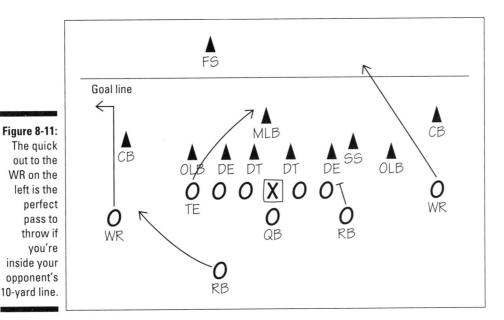

Figure 8-11: The quick out to the WR on the left is the perfect pass to throw if you're inside your opponent's 10-yard line.

For a two-point conversion in the NFL, the ball is placed on the 2-yard line, the same spot as for a kick. (College and high school teams must score from the 3-yard line.) You would think that the two points would be automatic, but in 1997, NFL teams converted only 47 of 109 attempts, well under 50 percent, whereas kickers converted 993 of 1,007 extra-point attempts, or 98.6 percent.

There's a universal chart on when to kick and when to attempt a two-point conversion. Coaches like this because they dislike being second-guessed by players and the media for making the wrong choice, a decision that may result in a defeat.

- **Behind by 2, 5, 9, 11, 12, or 16 points:** Attempt a two-point conversion.
- **Ahead by 1, 4, 5, 12, 15, or 19 points:** Attempt a two-point conversion.
- **Behind by 1 or 4 points:** The dreaded judgment call — it can go either way.

Teams elect to go for two points when they need to close the point differential with their opponent. For example, if a team is behind by five, kicking the extra point would close the gap to four. That means that a field goal (worth three points) would still have them losing the game. But a two-point conversion would reduce the deficit to three, and a field goal would tie the game. When behind by nine points, a two-point conversion reduces the deficit to seven, meaning that a touchdown and an extra point could tie the game.

The two-point conversion, with the right multiples of field goals and touchdowns, can close a deficit or widen it, depending on the situation. It's a gamble. But when a team is trailing, it may be the quickest way to rally and possibly force overtime. Most coaches prefer to tie in regulation and take their chances with an overtime period. However, some coaches, especially if their teams have grabbed the momentum or seem unstoppable on offense, may elect to try two points at the end of the game and go for the win instead of the tie. That play is more common in high school and college football than in the NFL, where coaches tend to be conservative because of the playoff implications — and a loss might mean unemployment.

Most teams use zone pass plays in two-point conversion situations because defenses aren't playing man-to-man coverages as much anymore. So the following play was designed to succeed against a zone defense. Remember, the offense simply has to gain 2 yards (or 3 in high school and college) to reach the end zone, which doesn't sound complicated.

To attempt a two-point conversion, you line up three receivers to one side. One receiver runs the flat; another receiver runs up about 6 or 7 yards and runs a curl; and the third receiver runs to the back of the end zone, turns, and waits. Say you put three receivers to one side — the right side. They can be a tight end and two wide receivers, as shown in Figure 8-12 — it doesn't matter. Just make sure that you bunch them together in a close group. Have one receiver head straight ahead and about 2 yards deep into the end zone. Another receiver is the inside guy. Just run him straight up the field. He heads first to the back of the end zone and turns to run a deep square-out. The other receiver just releases into the flat area, outside the numbers on the field. The receiver whom you're looking to come open is the receiver running the little 6-yard curl. Now, that's if your quarterback looks into the secondary and believes that he is facing a zone defense.

If the defense is playing a man-to-man coverage, the quarterback wants the receiver in the flat to come open immediately. If the defense reads the play perfectly, then the quarterback is in trouble because he must find a secondary target while under a heavy pass-rush. Still, this pass is almost impossible to defend because the offense is prepared for every defensive concept.

If the coverage is man-to-man, the offense opens with a double pick, which is illegal if the officials see it clearly. By a *pick,* I mean that an offensive receiver intentionally blocks the path of a defensive player who is trying to stay with the receiver he's responsible for covering. Both the tight end and one receiver on the right side attempt to pick the defensive player covering the receiver (refer to Figure 8-12) running toward the flat area. If the receiver benefiting from the illegal pick doesn't come open, the first receiver attempting a pick runs 2 yards into the end zone and curls, facing the quarterback. After trying to pick a defender, the tight end should settle and stop to the right of the formation. He should wave his arm if he believes that he's wide open so that the quarterback can see him.

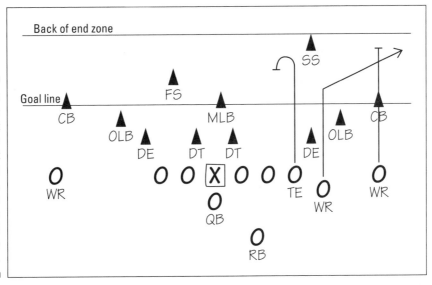

Figure 8-12: A common two-point conversion play against a zone coverage, with three receivers (TE and WR) to one side.

Disguising a Successful Play

During the course of a game, a team often finds that one pass play works particularly well against a certain defense and matchup. To keep using the play in that game and continue to confuse the defense, the offense often runs the pass play out of different formations while maintaining similar pass routes.

Here's what an offense does: It lines up with three receivers (WR), a tight end (TE), and a running back (RB), as shown in Figure 8-13. One receiver is to the left, and the running back is also behind the line to the left, behind the left tackle. The tight end is aligned to the right, and two other receivers are outside of him. The receiver on the left runs down the field 18 yards and runs a square-in. (For more on this passing route, see Chapter 5.) The tight end runs a crossing route, about 7 or 8 yards from the line of scrimmage. The running back swings out of the backfield to the left.

The receiver located in the slot to the right simply runs right down the middle of the field. He's the deep decoy receiver. He's going to pull all the defensive players out of the middle. The quarterback wants to hit the receiver who lined up on the left side. If he isn't open, he tries the middle with the tight end, and lastly he dumps the ball to the running back.

Now, to modify this successful play, the same receiver on the left runs the same 18-yard square-in, as shown in Figure 8-14. The running back on the left releases to that side, but this time he runs across the line of scrimmage 7 or 8 yards and curls back toward the quarterback. The back is now assuming the role of the tight end in the previous formation. This time, the tight end runs down the middle of the field. The receiver in the slot now runs right between the two hashes and hooks. So it's pretty much the same play. The offense's target remains the receiver to the left. And all those other receivers are simply decoys.

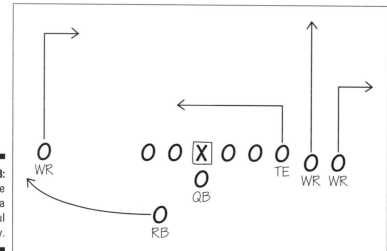

Figure 8-13:
An example of a successful play.

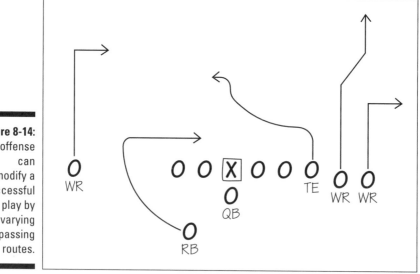

Figure 8-14:
An offense can modify a successful play by varying passing routes.

Part III
The Big D

The 5th Wave   By Rich Tennant

"Yeah, I've seen large defensive linemen before, but these are the only guys I've ever seen who can carry 6-digit numbers on their jerseys."

In this part . . .

This part is my favorite — but of course, I'm biased. Without the defense, football wouldn't be a very interesting sport, because teams would score a touchdown on every play. What makes touchdowns exciting is that the offense must overcome the opposition to earn them! This part walks you through the three components of the defense: the line, the linebackers, and the secondary. I also talk about some common defensive strategies and alignments so that, when you're ready to look a little deeper into the game, you'll be able to recognize what the defensive coach is trying to do.

Chapter 9

These Guys Are Huge: The Defensive Line

*T*he game of football has changed a lot since I entered the NFL in 1981. Today's defensive linemen are bigger, and maybe faster, than those who played 17 years ago. Of course, they've had to keep pace with their main opposition, the offensive linemen. When I played in the NFL, you could count the number of 300-pound offensive linemen on one hand. Now, you need more than two hands to count a single team's 300-pounders!

Defensive linemen have to battle these huge offensive linemen. Then they have to deal with running backs and quarterbacks, whose main function in life is to make the defensive line look silly. Few linemen can run and move, stop and go, like running back Barry Sanders of the Detroit Lions and Green Bay Packers quarterback Brett Favre, two of the best offensive players in the NFL and also superb all-around athletes. Linemen, who generally weigh 100 pounds more than Sanders, have a difficult time catching and tackling him. The few who can are the great linemen. However, many linemen have the ability to put themselves in position to stop a great offensive player. The key is: Can they make the tackle?

For the defense to do its job effectively, the linemen and linebackers (the players who back up the defensive linemen) must work together. This collaboration is called *scheming* — devising plans and strategies to unmask and foil the offense and its plays. To succeed as a group, a defensive team needs linemen who are selfless, men who are willing to go into the trenches and play the run while taking on two offensive linemen. These players must do so without worrying about not getting enough pass-rushes and sack opportunities.

In this chapter, I address the responsibilities of every defensive lineman and talk about all the linebacker positions, explaining how those two segments of the defense interact. I cover many names and combinations, but if you watch football on television, the terms may already be familiar.

Lining Up on Defense

To better understand the inner workings of defensive football, you need to know how a defense lines up. Most defenses line up according to where the tight end on offense lines up. A defensive player, generally a linebacker, yells "left" or "right," and the remaining players react and align themselves. Alignments are critical to a defense's success. If the defense isn't in the proper alignment, the players put themselves at a great disadvantage prior to the snap of the ball.

Here are some helpful explanations of terms used to describe defensive players and their alignments:

- ✔ **On or over a player:** The defensive player is directly across from the offensive player and no more than a yard apart — virtually helmet to helmet.

- ✔ **Inside a player:** The defensive player lines up with his right shoulder across from the offensive player's right shoulder. The defensive player's right shoulder can be directly across from the offensive player's helmet.

- ✔ **Wide of a player:** The defensive player is facing forward, and his entire upper body is outside the nearest shoulder of an offensive player. When the ball is snapped, the defensive player wants a clear path forward so that he can use his quickness to beat the offensive blocker off the line of scrimmage.

- ✔ **Over defense:** In this defensive alignment, four members of the defensive team shift position in order to put themselves directly over each player aligned on the strong side (tight end side) of the offensive formation.

- ✔ **Under defense:** This is exactly the opposite of the over shift. This time, three defensive players line up directly over the center, guard, and tackle on the weak side (non–tight end side) of the offensive formation, leaving only a defensive end over the offensive tackle on the strong side of the formation.

The *open end side,* or *weak side,* is opposite the tight end, where the split end lines up on offense. Most defenses design their schemes either to the tight end or to the open end side of the field. When linebackers and defensive linemen line up, they do so as a group. For example, they align *over* to the tight end or maybe *under* to the open end.

Those Big Guys Called Linemen

Defensive linemen are big players who position themselves on the line of scrimmage, across from the offensive linemen, prior to the snap of the ball. They're usually in a *three-point stance* (one hand and two feet on the ground); in rare situations, they align themselves in a *four-point stance* (both hands and both feet on the ground) to stop short-yardage runs. The latter stance is better because the lineman wants to gain leverage and get both of his shoulders under the offensive lineman and drive him up and backward. He needs to do anything he can to stop the offensive lineman's forward charge.

Defensive linemen are typically a rare combination of size, speed, and athleticism, and, in terms of weight, they're the largest players on the defense. A defensive lineman's primary job is to stop the run at the line of scrimmage and to *rush* (chase down) the quarterback when a pass play develops.

Defensive linemen seldom receive enough credit for a job well done. In fact, at times, a defensive lineman can play a great game but go unnoticed by the fans and the media, who focus more on offensive players, like quarterbacks and wide receivers, and defensive play-makers, such as defensive backs and linebackers. Defensive linemen *are* noticed in some situations, though:

- ✔ When they record a *sack* (tackle a quarterback for a loss while he's attempting to pass)
- ✔ When they make a tackle for a loss or for no gain

Often, defensive linemen *contain* an opponent (neutralize him, forcing a stalemate) or deal with a *double-team* (two offensive linemen against one defensive lineman) block in order to free up one of their teammates to make a tackle or sack. The defensive lineman position can be a thankless one because very few players succeed against double-team blocks. The only place where one guy beats two on a regular basis is in the movies.

Great defensive linemen, like Bruce Smith of the Buffalo Bills and Reggie White of the Green Bay Packers, are very rare players. Their combination of size, speed, strength, and durability is not found in many players. A good defensive lineman has the majority of these qualities:

- ✔ **Size:** A defensive lineman needs to be big. As I mentioned earlier, most offensive linemen are over 300 pounds (at least at the pro level), and most NFL running backs weigh over 200 pounds.
- ✔ **Durability:** Defensive linemen must be able to withstand the punishment of being hit or blocked on every play. Because they play 16 or more games a season, with an average of 70 plays per game, defensive linemen are hit or blocked at least 1,120 times a season.

✔ **Quickness:** Speed is relative, but quickness is vital. A lineman's first two steps after the ball is snapped should be like those of a sprinter breaking from the starting blocks. Quickness enables a defensive lineman to react and get in the proper position before being blocked. I call this "quickness in a phone booth." A defensive lineman may not be fast over 40 yards, but in that phone booth (5 yards in any direction), he's a cat!

✔ **Arm and hand strength:** Linemen win most of their battles when they ward off and shed blockers. Brute strength helps, but the true skill comes from a player's hands and arms. Keeping separation between yourself and those big offensive linemen is the key not only to survival but also to success. You have to use your hands and arms to maintain separation, which cuts down on neck injuries and enables you to throw an offensive lineman out of your way to make a tackle.

✔ **Vision:** Defensive linemen need to be able to see above and around the offensive linemen. They also need to use their heads as tools to ward off offensive linemen attempting to block them. A defensive lineman initially uses his head to absorb the impact and stop the momentum of his opponent. Then, using his hands, he forces separation. But before the ball is snapped and before impact, the opponents' backfield formation usually tells him what direction the upcoming play is going in. Anticipating the direction of the play may lessen the impact that his head takes after the ball is snapped.

✔ **Instincts:** Defensive linemen need to know the situation, down, and distance to a first down or a score. And they must be able to read and know the stances of all the offensive linemen they may be playing against. For example, if an offensive lineman is leaning forward in his stance, the play is probably going to be a run. The offensive lineman's weight is forward so that he can quickly shove his weight advantage into his opponent and clear the way for the ball carrier. If the offensive lineman is leaning backward in his stance (weight on his heels, buttocks lower to the ground, head up a bit more), the play is usually going to be a pass, or the O lineman may be preparing to *pull* (run to either side rather than straight forward).

In an effort to move those big bodies where they need to go a little more quickly, offensive linemen "cheat" in their stances more than any position in all of football. By doing so, they *telegraph* their intentions. Defensive linemen must assess these signs prior to the snap in order to give themselves an edge.

The types of defensive linemen

The term *defensive lineman* doesn't refer to a specific position, as you might think. A player who plays any of the following positions is considered a defensive lineman:

- ✓ **Nose tackle:** The defensive lineman who lines up directly across from the center, "nose to nose," as shown in Figure 9-1. Like in baseball, you build the strength of your team up the middle, and without a good nose tackle, your defense can't function. This player needs to be prepared for a long day because his job is all grunt work, with little or no chance of making sacks or tackles for minus yardage.

  The nose tackle knows that he'll be double-blocked much of the game. He's responsible for both gaps on each side of the center (known as the *A gaps*). Prior to the snap, the nose tackle looks at the ball. When the center snaps the ball, the nose tackle attacks the center with his hands. Because the nose tackle is watching the ball, the center can sucker him into moving early by suddenly flinching his arms and simulating a snap.

Figure 9-1:
The nose tackle (N) lines up opposite the center and covers the A gaps.

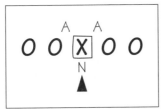

- ✓ **Defensive tackles:** The two players who line up inside the defensive ends (see the following bullet) and usually over (football lingo for "across from" or "opposite") the offensive guards. The defensive tackles' responsibilities vary according to the defensive call or scheme; they can be responsible for the A gaps or the B gaps. (See Figure 9-2.)

  Defensive tackles do a great deal of *stunting,* or executing specific maneuvers that disrupt offensive blocking schemes. They also adjust their alignments to the inside or outside shoulders of the offensive guards based on where they anticipate that the play is headed. Often, they shift to a particular position over the offensive linemen when the game unfolds and they discover a particular weakness to an offensive lineman's left side or right side.

Figure 9-2:
The defensive tackles (DT) line up inside the defensive ends (DE) and watch the A or B gaps.

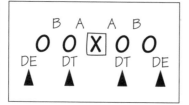

✔ **Defensive ends:** The two defensive linemen who line up over the offensive tackles or on those players' outside shoulders. Where the defensive ends line up varies according to the defensive call or scheme. For example, in a 4-3 defense, the defensive ends align wide because they have two defensive tackles to the inside of them (refer to Figure 9-2). In a 3-4 defense, the defensive ends align tighter, or closer to the center of the line, because they have only a nose tackle between them, as shown in Figure 9-3. If you have no idea what a 3-4 or a 4-3 defense is, turn to Chapter 11, where I talk about defensive setups and strategies.

Figure 9-3:
The defensive ends (DE) line up closer together in a 3-4 defense because only a nose tackle is between them.

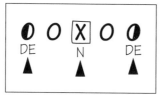

The ends are responsible for chasing the quarterback out of the pocket and trying to sack him. These players are usually smaller than nose tackles and defensive tackles in weight (that is, if you consider 290 pounds small), and they're generally the fastest of the defensive linemen. The left defensive end is usually a little stronger against the run, a better tackler, and maybe not as quick to rush the quarterback.

He is generally tougher for an offensive lineman to move off the line of scrimmage. The right defensive end (who's usually on the blind side of the quarterback) is the better pass-rusher. On a few teams, these ends flop sides when facing a left-handed quarterback, making the left defensive end the better pass-rusher.

D line lingo: Did he call me "Liz"?

Every football team has its own vocabulary for referring to different positions. For example, some teams give male names to all the defenders who line up to the offense's *tight end side* — they call these defenders Sam, Bart, Otto, and so on. The defenders who align on the *open end side* (away from the tight end) are occasionally — but not always — given female names like Liz, Terri, and Wanda.

Here are some of the most common terms that teams use to refer to defensive linemen and their alignments:

✔ **Under tackle:** A defensive tackle who lines up outside the offensive guard to the split end side, as shown in Figure 9-4. The entire defensive line aligns under (or inside) the tight end to the split end side. Some of the NFL's best players, like Minnesota's John Randle and Tampa Bay's Warren Sapp, are positioned as the under tackle. They possess strength and exceptional quickness off the ball, but they are not powerful players.

Figure 9-4:
The under tackle (UT) lines up outside the offensive guard to the split end side.

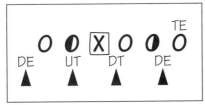

✔ **Open end:** A defensive end who lines up to the split end or open end side of the formation — away from the tight end side. (See Figure 9-5.) If the offensive formation has two tight ends, there is no open side, thus no open end. Coaches generally put their best pass-rusher at the open end position for two reasons: He has the athletic ability to match up with the offensive tackle, and if he's positioned wide enough, a running back may be forced to attempt to block him, which would be a mismatch. Detroit Lions end Robert Porcher, who had 12 sacks in 1997, typifies the all-around open end.

Figure 9-5:
The open
end (OE)
lines up to
the split end
side and
goes head-
to-head
with the
offensive
tackle or a
running
back.

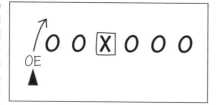

✔ **Elephant end:** The elephant end lines up on the tight end side of the offense, as shown in Figure 9-6, and attempts to disrupt the tight end's *release* (his desire to escape the line of scrimmage and run down the field) on each play. This position was made famous by the San Francisco 49ers and was suited to the specific skills of Charles Haley, the only player to have earned five Super Bowl rings. Haley was ideal for the position because he was a great pass-rusher as well as strong, like an elephant, which enabled him to hold his position against the run. This position gives the defense an advantage because the tight end generally has trouble blocking this talented defensive end.

Figure 9-6:
The
elephant
end (EE) is
the tight
end's
greatest foe.

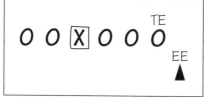

✔ **Pass-rushing end:** A player on the defense who has superior skills at combating offensive linemen and pressuring the quarterback. A pass-rushing end is usually a substituted player who makes sure that he doesn't jump offside by looking at the football and remaining still until the ball is snapped. His primary job is to get the best possible pass-rush, although he reacts to the run if a pass play doesn't develop. If the quarterback is in a shotgun formation, the pass-rushing end must focus on where he expects the quarterback to be when he attempts to throw his pass. This player can line up on either side (or both sides) of the defensive line.

Keys to a defensive lineman

A *key* is what a defensive player looks at prior to the snap of the ball. For example, if it's first-and-5, odds are that the offense will attempt to run the ball. The defensive lineman must key (watch) the offensive lineman and be prepared to react to his movements.

In a pass situation, such as second-and-7 or more, most defensive linemen key the ball and begin their pass-rush moves after the ball is snapped. When keying the ball, a defensive lineman wants to penetrate the line of scrimmage as quickly and deeply as he can. He should never use an offensive lineman as his primary key on a pass play, because that would slow him down. *Being quick off the ball* — or moving as quickly as possible after the snap — is impossible when you're reacting to another player's movements.

Here's a quick rundown of a defensive lineman's thought process prior to any play:

1. **Alignment:** Am I aligned correctly?

2. **Stance:** Is the stance that I'm using to my advantage?

3. **Assignment:** Do I know exactly what to do?

4. **Key:** What/whom should I be looking at?

5. **Get off:** Be quick off the football.

6. **Attack:** Attack and control the offensive lineman with my hands; then escape by using my arms and shoulder to push by him.

7. **Execute:** Execute my stunt to a specific area or gap and then react to where the ball is.

8. **Pursue:** Follow the football.

9. **Tackle:** Make the tackle.

And you thought tackling was the only chore of a defensive lineman! Now you know that they have many responsibilities, some of them thankless tasks, and they really have to be thinking to put themselves in a position to make a tackle. The play of the defensive linemen (as a group) can decide the outcome of many games. If they can stop the run without much help from the linebackers and defensive backs, they allow those seven defensive players to concentrate on pass defense (and their coverage responsibilities). Ditto if they can sustain a constant pass-rush on the quarterback without help from a defensive back or linebacker blitzing the quarterback.

Linebackers: The Leaders of the Defense

Linebacker has become one of the most complicated terms in football. Because of their wide variety of responsibilities and enormous talent, linebackers have become football hybrids.

Football is in the age of specialization, and linebackers are used a great deal because they're superior athletes who can learn a variety of skills and techniques. Some of them are suited to combat specific pass or run plays that the coaches believe the opposing offense plans to use. For that reason, coaches make defensive adjustments mainly by putting their linebackers in unusual alignments, making it difficult for the opposing quarterback and offensive players to keep track of the linebackers. Sometimes in a game, three linebackers will leave the field and be replaced by two defensive backs and one linebacker who excels in pass defense. The roles are constantly changing as defenses attempt to cope with the varied abilities of a team's offense.

Because linebackers play so many different roles, they come in all sizes, from 215 pounds to 270 pounds. Some are extremely fast and capable of sticking with a running back. Others are very stout and strong and are known for clogging the middle of a team's offensive plans. Still others are tall and quick and extremely good pass-rushers. All linebackers must be smart on their feet, have good instincts, and be able to react immediately when the offense snaps the ball.

Linebackers must dominate each individual opponent they face. Football is a tough, demanding game, and linebackers are taught to defeat the offensive line and get to the ball. Their intention, still the basic premise, is to tackle the offensive player with the ball.

By the design of the defense, linebackers are the leaders of that 11-man squad. They are the defensive quarterbacks and coaches on the field, beginning every play by giving the defensive call. They set the standard for every defense by being able to get to the ball before anyone else. They usually are emotional leaders who excel in leading by example. If they play hard, their winning attitude carries over to the rest of the defense. Linebackers should stand out on a defensive team. They should have an aura about them.

What linebackers do

The job description of all linebackers is pretty lengthy: They must defend the run and also pressure the quarterback. (Vacating their assigned areas to go after the quarterback is called *blitzing.*) They must execute stunts and defend against the pass in a zone or what are paradoxically known as *short-deep areas* on their side of the line of scrimmage. Also, the middle linebacker generally makes the defensive calls (informs his teammates of what coverages and alignments they should be in) when the offense breaks its huddle.

Linebackers are often responsible on pass defense to watch and stay with the tight end and backs. In other pass defense coverages, a linebacker may be responsible for staying with a speedy wide receiver in what is known as *man-to-man coverage* (see Chapter 10).

To fully understand linebacker play, you need to be aware that every linebacker wants to coordinate his responsibilities with those of the defensive line. A linebacker is responsible for at least one of the *gaps* — the lettered open spaces or areas between the offensive linemen — in addition to being asked to ultimately make the tackle.

Every team wants its linebackers to be the leading tacklers on the team. It doesn't want its players in the *secondary,* the last line of the defense (see Chapter 10), to end up as the top tacklers.

To keep your sanity when watching a game, just try to remember which players are the linebackers, and remember that the bulk of their job is to do what old-fashioned linebackers like Chicago Bears Hall of Famer Dick Butkus did: make tackles from sideline to sideline and constantly pursue the ball carrier.

Dealing with the senses

Linebackers must take full advantage of what they can see, feel, and do. Every drill that they do in practice, which carries over to the game, is based on these things:

- ✔ **Eyes:** Linebackers must train their eyes to see as much as possible. They must always focus on their target prior to the snap of the ball and then mentally visualize what may occur after the snap. Using your vision properly often gives you an edge in making a tackle or helping to stop a play.

- ✔ **Feet:** Everything linebackers do involves their ability to move their feet. Making initial reads of what the offense is going to do, attempting to block offensive linemen and defeating them, and tackling the ball carrier are all directly related to proper foot movement.

- ✔ **Hands:** A linebacker's hands are his most valuable weapons. They also protect him by enabling him to ward off blockers and control the offensive linemen. A linebacker uses his hands to make tackles, recover fumbles, and knock down and intercept passes.

Naming all the linebackers

The following definitions can help you dissect the complex world of the linebacker:

- ✔ **True linebacker:** Linebackers who line up in the conventional linebacker position — behind the defensive linemen. They align themselves according to the defensive call. Their *depth* (or distance) from the line of scrimmage varies, but usually it's 4 yards.

- ✔ **Sam linebacker:** A linebacker who lines up directly over the tight end and keys the tight end's movements (see Figure 9-7). His responsibility is to disrupt the tight end's release off the line of scrimmage when he's attempting to run out for a pass. The linebacker must then react accordingly. Depending on the defensive call, he either rushes the passer or moves away from the line of scrimmage and settles (called a *pass drop*) into a specified area to defend potential passes thrown his way. The ideal Sam linebacker is tall, preferably 6'4" or taller, which enables him to see over the tight end. (Tight ends also tend to be tall.)

Figure 9-7:
The Sam linebacker disrupts the tight end during the play.

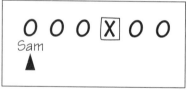

When he played with the New York Giants in the 1980s, Carl Banks was a perfect fit for the Sam linebacker position. He had long arms and viselike hands, giving him the ability to control the tight end or *shed* him (push him away) if he needed to run to a specific side. The Sam linebacker needs to immobilize the tight end as well as have the athletic ability to pursue any ball carrier.

- ✔ **Willy linebacker:** The macho term for a weak-side linebacker (see Figure 9-8). The Willy linebacker has the most varied assignments of any linebacker; he rushes the passer or drops into coverage, depending on the defensive call. He tends to be smaller, quicker, and faster than most other linebackers.

Two perfect examples of Willy linebackers playing in the NFL today are Dexter Coakley of the Dallas Cowboys and Jessie Armstead of the New York Giants. Although these players are smaller than the average linebacker, they have been successful NFL players because they use their speed, and their teams' defensive alignments usually protect them from being blocked.

Figure 9-8:
The Willy
linebacker
(W) covers
the weak
side.

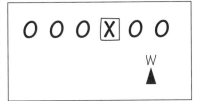

▶ **Mike linebacker:** The glory position of the linebacker corps. Every
defensive player — from boys playing pickup games on the sandlot to
men playing in the NFL — wants to play this position. The Mike linebacker is also known as the *middle linebacker* in 4-3 defenses (Chapter 11
explains what a 4-3 defense is). He lines up in the middle, generally directly
over the offense's center and off him 3 to 4 yards (see Figure 9-9). His job is
to make tackles and control the defense with his calls and directions. Mike
should key the running backs and the quarterback. Because he's in the
middle of the defense, he wants to go where the ball goes.

Figure 9-9:
The Mike
linebacker
(M) lines up
across and
back from
the center
and follows
the ball.

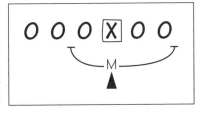

The linebackers line up in a variety of ways, depending on the defensive
scheme that's being used and their specific abilities. See Chapter 11 for
information about how these players are aligned in various defenses.

Sacks, Tackles, and Other Defensive Gems

Defensive players work all game hoping to collect a tangible reward: a sack.
Former Los Angeles Rams defensive end Deacon Jones coined the term *sack*
in the 1960s when referring to tackling the quarterback for a loss behind the
line of scrimmage. (The name comes from hunting: When hunters go into the
field planning to shoot a quail or pheasant, they place their trophies in a
gunny sack.) Unfortunately for Jones, who had as many as 30 sacks in some of
his 14 seasons, the NFL didn't begin to officially record this defensive statistic
until the 1982 season. Consequently, Jones doesn't appear on the all-time sack
leader list, which is currently headed by the Green Bay Packers' Reggie White.

When two defensive players tackle the quarterback behind the line of scrimmage, they must share the sack. Each player is credited with half a sack; that's how valuable the statistic has become. In fact, many NFL players have performance clauses in their contracts regarding the number of sacks they collect, and they receive bonuses for achieving a certain number of sacks.

Alan Page, Hall of Famer and defensive end of the Minnesota Vikings, was so quick that opposing quarterbacks often rushed their throws in anticipation of being tackled. Some quarterbacks would rather risk throwing an incompletion — or an interception — than be sacked. Page's coach, Bud Grant, called this action a *hurry*. The term remains popular today in football, and pressuring the quarterback remains the number-one motive of defensive linemen on pass plays.

The term *tackling* has been around for almost 100 years. A player is credited with a tackle when he single-handedly brings down an offensive player who has possession of the ball. Tackles, like sacks, can be shared. A shared tackle is called an *assist.* Many teams award an assist whenever a defensive player effectively joins in on a tackle. For example, some offensive players have the strength to drag the first player who tries to tackle them. When that occurs, the second defensive player who joins the play, helping to bring down the ball carrier, is credited with an assist.

You may have heard the term *stringing out a play*. Defenders are coached to force the ball carrier toward the sideline after they cut off the ball carrier's upfield momentum. The sideline may be the best "tackler" in the game.

A lineman who preferred keyboards to QBs

Mike Reid was raised in Altoona, Pennsylvania — about the craziest high school football town in the country. Reid became an All-State defensive lineman and a punishing fullback. Before football, his mother made him take piano lessons. So when Penn State offered him a football scholarship, he accepted and majored in classical music.

Reid was a demon on the football field. In 1969, he won the Outland Trophy, emblematic of the best lineman in college football. The next April, he was the first-round draft choice of the Cincinnati Bengals. He enjoyed football, but music remained his passion. He taped his fingers before every game, hoping to prevent them from being broken so that he could play the piano on Monday afternoons. After playing five pro seasons and twice being named to All-Pro teams, Reid quit the Bengals in 1975 to join a little-known rock band. Five years later, he moved to Nashville, Tennessee, and began writing country-and-western songs.

Reid has since written such hits as "There You Are" for Willie Nelson and "I Can't Make You Love Me" for Bonnie Raitt. He has won two Grammys and even wrote an opera about football, titled *Different Fields.*

Chapter 10

The Secondary

In This Chapter

▶ Cornerbacks are the most athletic members of the secondary

▶ Safeties are the defense's quarterbacks

▶ Two nickels equal a dime back

▶ The difference between zone and man-to-man

▶ The bump and run and stemming around

▶ Eight men in a box and the Nickel 40

Secondary is the word given to the group of players who make up the *defensive backfield*. The basic defensive backfield consists of four position players: a right and left cornerback, a strong safety, and a free safety. The secondary is the final line of defense, right after the defensive line and the linebackers. (See Chapter 9 for more on these defenders.) The players who make up the secondary are known collectively as *defensive backs,* or *DBs;* later in this chapter, I explain the specific types of defensive backs. Basically, their job is to tackle runners who get past the defensive line and the linebackers and to defend — and hopefully break up — pass plays.

Depending on the defensive scheme that the coaching staff employs, the secondary can consist of three, four, five, six, or seven defensive backs on the field at the same time. In rare instances, I've even seen eight defensive backs on the field at once. However, most conventional defensive alignments utilize four defensive backs, two cornerbacks and two safeties.

When an extra (that is, a fifth) defensive back is substituted into the scheme, he's referred to as a *nickel back.* Substitute in a sixth defensive back, and he's called a *dime back.* The *nickel* term is easy to explain — five players equal five cents. The dime back position received its name because, in essence, two nickel backs are on the field at once. And everyone knows that two nickels equal a dime.

Whether you find the phraseology cute or confusing, the play of the secondary is rather complex and difficult to understand. Try to remember the points in this chapter, because they can help you understand how and why a secondary acted in a particular way. If you're female, I guarantee that you'll sound more knowledgeable than your husband or boyfriend if you refer to these points periodically.

Also, be aware that a majority of big offensive plays (gains of 25 yards or more) and touchdowns come from the offense's ability to execute the passing game. Therefore, on the defensive side of the ball, a great deal of attention on television is devoted to the secondary. Often, a defensive back is in proper position or has good coverage technique, but the offensive receiver still catches the pass. Other times, the secondary player is out of position, failing to execute his assignment, or is physically beaten by a better athlete. If you know the difference and what to look for, you'll be regarded as an expert.

The Performers

All the players who make up the secondary are called defensive backs, but that category is further divided into the following positions. Basically, all these players are responsible for preventing the opponent's receivers from catching the ball. If they fail, they must make the tackle, preventing a possible touchdown. But they do so in slightly different ways.

Cornerbacks

The *cornerback* is typically the fastest of the defensive backs. Deion Sanders, who has played on Super Bowl championship teams in the 1990s with the San Francisco 49ers and the Dallas Cowboys, has Olympic-caliber speed and the explosive burst necessary for this position. The *burst* is when a secondary player breaks (or reacts) to the ball and the receiver, hoping to disrupt the play.

The ideal NFL cornerback should be able to run the 40-yard dash in 4.4 seconds, weigh between 180 and 190 pounds, and be at least 6 feet tall. However, the average size of an NFL cornerback was 5'10" during the 1997 season. Although speed and agility remain the necessary commodities, height is becoming a factor in order to defend the ever-increasing height of today's wide receivers. How many times have you seen a great little cornerback like Mark McMillian, who is 5'8", put himself in perfect position simply to be out-jumped for the ball by a much taller receiver with longer arms?

The ultimate thrill for a cornerback is the direct challenge he faces on virtually every play, but especially on passing downs. A defensive lineman can win 70 percent of his battle against an offensive lineman and leave the field feeling relieved; however, the same odds don't necessarily apply to a cornerback. He can't afford to lose many challenges because he's exposed one-on-one with a receiver. If his man catches the ball, everyone in the stadium or watching on television can see. And if he's beaten three out of ten times for gains over 25 yards, he may be on the unemployment line or find himself demoted come Monday. Cornerback is a job that accepts no excuses for poor performance.

Cornerbacks in man-to-man coverage

Most defensive schemes employ two cornerbacks in man-to-man coverage (explained further in "Man-to-man coverage," later in this chapter) against the offense's wide receivers, as shown in Figure 10-1. The cornerbacks align on the far left and right sides of the line of scrimmage, generally at least 10 to 12 yards from their nearest teammate (usually a linebacker or defensive end) and opposite the offense's wide receivers. The distance varies depending on where the offensive receivers align themselves. Cornerbacks must align in front of them.

Figure 10-1:
In most defenses, the two cornerbacks (CB) line up on the far left and right sides of the line of scrimmage.

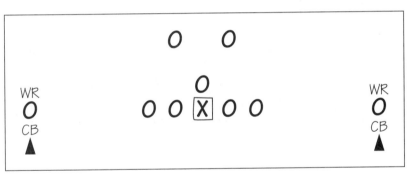

Most teams attempt to place their best cornerbacks against the opposition's best receivers. Coaches generally know who these players are and design their defenses accordingly. Often, they simply need to flop cornerbacks from one side to the other. Some offensive formations place a team's two best receivers on the same side of the field, requiring the defense to place both of its cornerbacks accordingly, as in Figure 10-2. This offensive alignment usually forces the cornerbacks into man-to-man coverage.

Cornerbacks in zone coverage

Cornerbacks are also used in zone coverage (see the section "Zone coverage," later in the chapter). If a team's cornerbacks are smaller and slower than its opponent's receivers, that team usually plays more zone coverages, fearing that fast receivers will expose its secondary's athletic weaknesses. If you

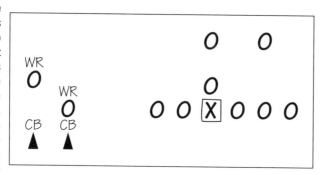

Figure 10-2:
Some offenses place two great receivers (WR) on the same side of the field, forcing the defense to place both cornerbacks on that side.

have two talented cornerbacks, like the Washington Redskins had during the 1997 season with Darrell Green and Cris Dishman, your team can play more man-to-man coverage.

Two excellent cornerbacks can alter a defensive coordinator's intentions when he's planning a defensive scheme. Although teams don't want to play with athletically inferior players in the secondary, great cornerbacks can allow a team to employ safeties who are better tacklers than pass defenders. Often, a particular team's talent pool consists of those types of safeties. On most levels of football, from high school to the NFL, it's impossible to find four super athletes capable of playing each and every position in the secondary.

Safeties

Most defenses employ two safeties — a *strong safety* and a *free safety*. Safeties often are called the defense's quarterbacks, or the quarterbacks of the secondary. They must see and recognize the offense's formations and instruct their teammates to make whatever coverage adjustments are necessary. These instructions are different from what the middle linebacker (see Chapter 9) tells his teammates.

The middle linebacker focuses more on his fellow linebackers and the alignment of the defensive linemen. Also, he is generally too far away from the defensive backs to yell to them. The safeties must coordinate their pass coverages after finding out what assistance the linebackers may offer in specific situations. They often have to use hand signals to convey their instructions in a noisy stadium.

HOWIE SAYS

An outstanding cornerback pair

To win in the NFL today, a team needs to have a good pair of cornerbacks. When I played for the Raiders, we had an excellent pair: Mike Haynes, who was inducted into the Pro Football Hall of Fame in 1997, and Lester Hayes. When you have two great players like Haynes and Hayes — guys who can cover the best receivers one-on-one without surrendering any long gains — your front seven defensive players (some combination of linemen and linebackers) are all the more effective.

Cornerbacks are a special breed of athlete. They must be both physically gifted and mentally strong. Haynes was an effortless player, with a fluid stride and graceful movements. And *graceful* is not a term that's generally associated with football players. Sometimes an opposing coach — the type who likes to take a hit on 17 when playing blackjack — would decide to test him and throw the ball his way, but rarely with any success. More often than

not, when you throw toward a great cornerback, your play doesn't succeed. And in the worst-case scenario, the corner intercepts the ball and returns it for a touchdown. Haynes never talked much on or off the field, but he was deadly as a player.

Hayes was just the opposite. He enjoyed talking to newspaper and TV reporters and seemed to have an opinion on most subjects. He loved talking on the field, too. He also believed in putting tacky goo on his hands and uniform. We called it "stickum." Stickum was so sticky that it was like having a Velcro glove or playing with a Velcro ball. Hayes covered himself with the stuff. When a pass would come Lester's way, it generally would stick to his body, and then he would grab hold of it. One season, he had 13 interceptions, the second-best total in NFL history. Soon after, the NFL outlawed stickum, claiming that it gave players an unfair advantage.

Strong safety

Of the two safeties, the strong safety is generally bigger, stronger, and slower. LeRoy Butler of the Green Bay Packers and Darren Woodson of the Dallas Cowboys are currently the NFL's two best strong safeties. And neither one of these players is slow. However, unlike many defensive backs, these two players are extremely good tacklers and seem to thrive on making hard hits.

Coaches often refer to (and judge) their safeties as small linebackers. They should be above-average tacklers and have the ability to backpedal and quickly retreat in order to cover a specified area to defend the pass (which is called *dropping into pass coverage*). The strong safety normally aligns to the tight end side of the offensive formation (also known as the *strong side,* hence the name *strong safety*), and 99 percent of the time, his pass coverage responsibility is either the tight end or a running back who leaves the backfield.

VIEWER TIP

Good strong safeties like Butler and Woodson are superior against the run offense. Many strong safeties are merely adequate in pass coverage, and below average when playing man-to-man pass defense. When you hear a television analyst inform viewers that the strong safety "did a great job of run support," he means that the strong safety read his key (the tight end) and quickly determined that the play was a run rather than a pass. (See Chapter 8 for more on keys.)

The sole reason that strong safeties are more involved with the run defense is because they line up closer to the line of scrimmage. Coaches believe that strong safeties can defend the run while also having the necessary speed and size to defend the tight end when he runs out on a pass pattern.

Free safety

The free safety is generally more athletic and less physical than the strong safety. He usually positions himself 12 to 15 yards deep and off the line of scrimmage, as shown in Figure 10-3. He serves the defense like a center fielder does a baseball team: He should have the speed to prevent the inside-the-park home run — in football, the long touchdown pass. He also must have the speed and quickness to get a jump on any long pass that's thrown in the gaps on the field. Merton Hanks of the San Francisco 49ers is a quality free safety.

When I mention the 49ers, I would be remiss if I didn't talk about Ronnie Lott. What made Lott, a future Hall of Famer, so special is that he could play either safety position. And he was so fast that he began his career as a cornerback. Never has a more intuitive player played in the secondary than Lott, who always seemed to know where the pass was headed. (Chapter 23 talks more about Ronnie Lott.)

Figure 10-3:
The free safety (FS) lines up deep and off the line of scrimmage, hoping to prevent the long pass.

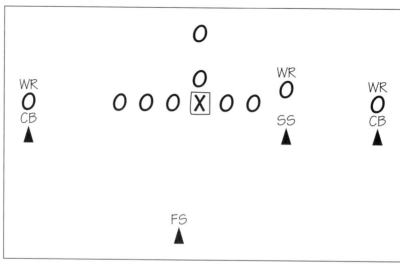

Being the final line of the defense against the long pass, the free safety must be capable of making instant and astute judgments. Some people say that a free safety can interpret the quarterback's eyes, meaning that he knows where the quarterback is looking to throw the football. The free safety is the only defensive back who is coached to watch the quarterback as his key. The quarterback directs him to where the ball is going.

A free safety also must be able to cover a wide receiver in man-to-man coverage because many offenses today employ three wide receivers more than half the time. (The first two are covered by the cornerbacks.)

Nickel and dime backs

Some experts try to equate learning the nickel and dime defensive schemes with learning to speak Japanese. Not so! All it's about is making change. When defensive coaches believe that the offense plans to throw the football, they replace bigger and slower linebackers with defensive backs. As mentioned earlier in this chapter, the fifth defensive back to enter the game is called the *nickel back,* and the sixth defensive back to enter is termed the *dime back*. No universal football terminology for nickel and dime backs exists, though; each team has its own vernacular. For example, the Oakland Raiders refer to their nickel back as the "pirate." These players generally are the second-string cornerbacks; there is no designated "nickel back" or "dime back" job.

By substituting defensive backs for linebackers, defensive coaches ensure that faster players — who are more capable of running with receivers and making an interception — are on the field. The one downside of using a defensive scheme that includes nickel and dime backs is that you weaken your defense against the running game. Today, many offenses opt to run the ball in what appear to be obvious passing situations because they believe that their powerful running backs have a size and strength advantage over the smaller defensive backs once the ball carrier breaks the line of scrimmage. Although defensive backs should be good tacklers, the prerequisite for the position is being able to defend pass receivers and tackle players who are more your size.

Substituting nickel and dime backs is part of a constant chess game played by opposing coaching staffs. Defensive coaches believe that they have prepared for the occasional run and that these extra defensive backs give the defense more blitzing and coverage flexibility.

Figure 10-4 shows a common nickel/dime alignment that has a good success rate against the pass, especially when offenses are stuck in third-and-20 situations. This alignment enables teams to utilize many different defensive looks, which help to confuse the quarterback. But this scheme is poor versus the run, so the defense has to remain alert to the possibility that the offense will fake a pass and run the ball instead.

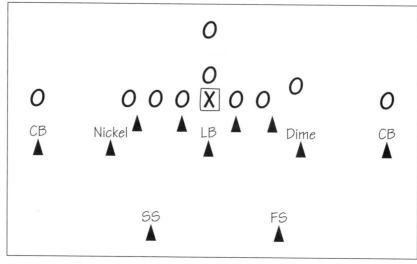

Figure 10-4:
A common nickel/dime alignment that works well against the pass.

Secondary Tricks and Techniques

Being a defensive back is pretty scary. Often, the entire weight of the game is on your shoulders. One misstep in pass coverage or one missed tackle can lead to a touchdown, or six points against your team. A defensive back may be the only player between the ball carrier and the end zone. Consequently, the defensive back has to be a good, smart tackler rather than an aggressive one.

When defensive backs line up, they rarely know whether the play will be a pass or a run. In a split second, after the ball is snapped, they must determine the offense's intentions and, if it's a pass play, turn and run with one of the fastest players (the wide receiver) on the field. In the following sections, I discuss some of the tricks of their trade.

The bump and run

The meaning of the term *bump and run* has been altered through the years. Twenty-five years ago, a cornerback could bump a receiver and then bump him again. Many cornerbacks held on for dear life, fearful that the receiver would escape and catch a touchdown pass. Mel Blount, a Hall of Fame cornerback with the champion Pittsburgh Steelers of the 1970s, may have had the strongest hands of any defensive back. When he grabbed a receiver, even with one hand, the man could go nowhere; Blount would ride him out of the play. By riding him, I mean Blount (or any strong defensive back) could push the receiver away from his intended pass route. Most defensive backs tend to ride their receivers, if they can, toward the sidelines.

Blount perfected his hands-on technique so well that in 1978, the NFL's Competition Committee (coaches, owners, and general managers who are appointed to study and make rule changes) rewrote the chuck rule, or what is known as the *bump* in bump and run. Consequently, defensive backs are still allowed to hit receivers within 5 yards of the line of scrimmage, but beyond that, hitting a receiver is a penalty. This illegal use of the hands penalty gives the offense an automatic first down and 5 free yards.

Today, you may catch defensive backs with their hands on receivers beyond 5 yards. Sometimes the officials catch them, and sometimes they don't. The intent remains the same; defensive backs want to get in the faces of the receivers and chuck them or jam them (using both hands) as they come off the line of scrimmage. The idea is to disrupt the timing of the pass play — to force the receiver to take a bad step — by hitting the receiver in the chest with both hands. Often, the defensive back pushes the receiver in order to redirect him. A defensive back generally knows which way a receiver wants to go. By bumping him to one side, the defensive back may force the receiver to alter his pass route.

Staying with a receiver

After bumping or attempting to jam a receiver, a defensive back must be able to turn and run with the receiver. Sometimes, the defensive back (especially a cornerback) ends up chasing the receiver. When he needs to turn, the defensive back should make half-turns, rotating his upper body to the same side as the receiver. When the receiver turns to face the ball in the air, the defensive player should turn his body to the side of the receiver to which his arms are extended.

A defensive back must practice his footwork so that he can take long strides when backpedaling away from the line of scrimmage while covering a receiver. When he turns, he should be able to take a long crossover step with his feet while keeping his upper body erect. This technique is difficult because the defensive back often has to move backward as quickly as a receiver runs forward. When he turns to meet the receiver and the pass, the defensive back should be running as fast as he can to maintain close contact with the receiver.

Stemming around

The term *stemming around* sounds foolish, and defensive backs may appear foolish while they're stemming around. Well, at least they're not standing around. Anyway, *stemming* describes the action of the defensive backs when they move around after appearing to be settled in their alignments prior to the offense's snap of the ball. By stemming, they attempt to fool the quarterback and force him into making a bad decision about where to throw the football. This tactic is becoming very popular in defensive football (all players can do it, although it is most noticeable in defensive backs and linebackers) because it creates an uncertainty in the quarterback's mind, thus disrupting his decision-making.

The most successful stemming ploy by the secondary is to give the quarterback the impression that they're playing in man-to-man coverage when they're really playing a zone coverage. This ploy usually results in a *poor read* (an inaccurate interpretation of the defense) by the quarterback. A poor read can lead to a deflected pass, an incomplete pass, or an interception — the secondary's ultimate goal.

It's Been a Good Day

Quarterbacks and receivers tend to pick on defensive backs. Miami Dolphins quarterback Dan Marino has passed them silly, and receivers like the Detroit Lion Herman Moore and the Minnesota Viking Cris Carter simply push them aside with their size and strength. The only way a defensive back can retaliate is to make a play.

Here are some of the positive plays with which a defensive back can make his mark. The first three of these plays are reflected on the statistical sheet after the game; the rest just go into the receiver's or quarterback's memory bank. Of course, all tackles are recorded, but the ones that I list here have a unique style of their own.

- ✔ **Interception:** The ultimate prize: picking off a pass intended for a receiver. An even bigger thrill is returning the catch for a defensive touchdown.

- ✔ **Pass defensed:** A statistic that a defensive back achieves every time he deflects a pass or knocks the ball out of a receiver's hands. You can also say that the defensive back *broke up a pass.* A pass defensed means an incompletion for the quarterback.

- ✔ **Forced fumble:** Forcing the ball away from a receiver after he gains possession of the ball. Defensive backs have been known to use both hands to reach and pull the ball away from the receiver's grasp. This play is also known as *stripping the ball.* Any defensive player can force a fumble, and forced fumbles can happen on running plays, too.

- ✔ **Knockout tackle:** The ultimate tackle that puts a wide receiver down for the count. Every safety in the league wants a knockout tackle; it's a sign of intimidation. Defensive backs believe in protecting their (coverage) space, and protecting it well. Cornerbacks wants these hits, too, but many of them are satisfied with bringing an offensive player down any way they can.

- ✔ **Groundhog hit:** A perfectly timed tackle on a receiver who's leaping for the ball. Instead of aiming for the body, the defensive back goes for the feet, flipping the receiver headfirst into the ground.

Pass interference

When a pass is in the air, a defensive player cannot push, shove, hold, or otherwise physically prevent an offensive receiver from moving his body or his arms in an attempt to catch the pass. If he does, he is called for pass interference. Except for being ejected from a game, pass interference is the worst penalty in football for any member of the defensive team. Why? Because the number of yards that the defense is penalized is determined by where the penalty (or foul) is committed. So when the officials call pass interference against a defensive player on a pass attempt that travels 50 yards beyond the line of scrimmage, the penalty is 50 yards. The offensive team is given the ball and a first down at that spot on the field. If a defensive player is flagged (penalized) in the end zone, the offensive team is given the ball on the 1-yard line with a first down. The offense is not awarded a touchdown.

This penalty is a judgment call, and you often see players from both sides arguing for or against a pass interference penalty.

Officials do not usually call pass interference when a defensive player, who also has a right to any ball, drives his body toward a pass, gets his hand or fingers on the ball, and then instantaneously makes physical contact with the receiver. The critical point is that the defensive player touched the ball a split second before colliding with the receiver. On these plays, the defensive back appears to be coming over the receiver's shoulder to knock down the pass. Often, you can't tell whether the official made the right call on these types of plays until you see them in a slow-motion replay on television. These plays (called *bang-bang plays*) occur very quickly on the field.

Coverages to Remember

Football teams employ two types of pass coverage: man-to-man coverage and zone coverage. Both coverages have many variations and combinations, but the core of every coverage begins with either the man-to-man concept or a zone concept.

Man-to-man coverage

Simply stated, *man-to-man coverage* is when any defensive back, or even some linebackers, is assigned to cover a specific offensive player, such as a running back, tight end, or wide receiver. The defender must stay with *(cover)* this player all over the field until the play ends; his responsibility is to make sure that the receiver does not catch a pass. The most important rule of man-to-man coverage (known for short as *man coverage*) is that the defensive back must keep his eyes on the player he's guarding or is responsible for watching. He's allowed to take occasional peeks toward the quarterback, but he should never take his eyes off his man.

Here are the three main types of man-to-man coverage:

✓ **Man free:** All defensive backs play man coverage except the free safety, who lines up or drops into an area and becomes a "safety valve" to prevent a long touchdown completion. This style of coverage is used when the defense *blitzes,* or rushes four or five players at the quarterback. So, man free is man coverage with one roaming free safety. Linebackers also cover running backs or even tight ends man-to-man.

✓ **Straight man:** The free safety does not serve as a safety valve in this alignment — or, as coaches say, no safety help is available. Each defender must know that he (alone) is responsible for the receiver he's covering. The phrase "the player was stuck on an island" refers to a cornerback being isolated with an offensive receiver and having no chance of being rescued by another defensive back. This style of man coverage generally is used when the defense is blitzing or rushing a linebacker toward the backfield, hoping to sack the quarterback. Defenses use it depending on the strength and ability of their own personnel and the receiving talent of the offense they're facing. So, straight man is pure man-to-man coverage with no roaming free safety.

✓ **Combo man:** Any number of combinations in man-to-man coverage. For example, when a team wants to double-team a great wide receiver (with two defensive backs), it runs a combo man defense. A great receiver is someone like the San Francisco 49ers' Jerry Rice, who owns virtually every pass-receiving record in the history of pro football. The object of such a defense is to force the quarterback to throw the football to a less-talented receiver than Jerry Rice. Throw it to anybody but him!

In Figure 10-5, the cornerback (CB) is responsible for Rice's outside move, while the safety (S) is prepared should Rice decide to run his route inside, or toward the middle of the field. A team's pass defense may be vulnerable on the opposite side of the field from where it is double-teaming a receiver. Also, the pass defense may be vulnerable to a short pass on the same side of the field and underneath the double-team.

Figure 10-5:
Combo man coverage aims to prevent a talented receiver from making a big play.

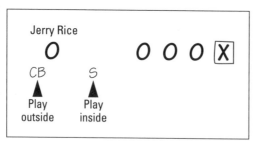

What's fun about man-to-man coverages, especially for players, are the endless personnel matchup possibilities that they provide. Also, against an excellent throwing quarterback like the Miami Dolphins' Dan Marino or the Green Bay Packers' Brett Favre, these combinations create something of a chess match between the quarterback and the defensive secondary.

Zone coverage

In *zone coverage,* the defensive backs and linebackers drop into areas on the field and protect those *zones* against any receivers who enter them. The biggest difference between zone coverage and man-to-man coverage is that in man coverage, a defender is concerned about only the player he's covering. In virtually all zone coverages, two defensive backs play deep (12 to 15 yards off the line of scrimmage) and align near the hash marks.

In a zone coverage, each defensive back is aware of the receivers in his area, but his major concentration is on the quarterback and reacting to the quarterback's arm motion and the ball in flight. Teams employ zone coverage against teams that love to run the football because it allows them to better position themselves to defend the run. Other teams use zone when the talent level of their secondary personnel is very average and inferior to that of the offensive personnel they're facing.

For defensive backs, zone coverage is about sensing what the offense is attempting to accomplish against the defense. Also, in zone coverage, each defensive player reacts when the ball is in the air, whereas in man coverage, he simply plays the receiver. In man coverage, he turns to the ball when he sees the receiver turn, expecting the ball.

The simplest way to recognize a zone defense is to observe how many defenders line up deep in the secondary. If two or more defensive players are aligned deep (12 to 15 yards off the line of scrimmage), the defense is in a zone.

Eight men in the box

I'm sure that you've heard television commentators mention the term *eight men in the box.* They're not talking about a sandbox, and they're not discussing a new pass coverage. Actually, eight men in the box is a setup that enables a team to defend the run more effectively when it has a strong secondary.

The *box* is the imaginary area near the line of scrimmage where the defensive linemen and linebackers line up prior to the offense putting the ball into play. Usually, a team puts seven defenders, known as the *front seven,* in that box. But a team can put an eighth man — the strong safety — in the box, as shown in Figure 10-6, if it has two outstanding cornerbacks like James Hasty and Dale Carter of the Kansas City Chiefs.

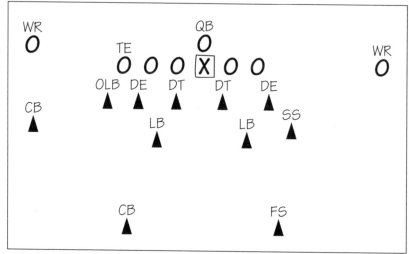

Figure 10-6:
The
defense
puts an
eighth man
(SS) in the
box to
improve its
odds
against
six run
blockers.

So how does a talented pair of cornerbacks drastically improve a team's defense against the run? By allowing the defense to play an extra (eighth) man in the box, where the runner has to be dealt with. By placing eight defenders against six blockers — five offensive linemen and a tight end — the odds are pretty good that the running back will have trouble finding open territory. And when a team has talented cornerbacks who can defend the pass effectively, the defensive linemen and linebackers perform with the utmost confidence. They know that they can attack without worrying about their pass coverage responsibilities.

Speaking of Hasty and Carter, the Chiefs led the American Football Conference (AFC) with 21 interceptions in 1997. Hasty and Carter combined for only four of those interceptions, which you may think is a low number. You're right. Mark McMillian, the nickel back, led the Chiefs with eight interceptions. He was able to make those interceptions because quarterbacks preferred to throw away from Carter and Hasty, hoping to find a weaker spot in the secondary. McMillian became that target, and he cashed in, stealing eight quarterback passes.

The Nickel 40 defense

By definition, the Nickel 40 defense is strictly a pass defense that can employ either a linebacker or another defensive back as the sixth player in pass coverage. It's a substituted defense (one that generally is not used on every down) by skill and ability level. A defensive team wants to put its four best pass-rushers on the line of scrimmage, with one linebacker and six defensive backs.

The pressure of being a cornerback

A matchup between a great cornerback and a great receiver is as eagerly awaited as an Old West gunslinger's final duel. Back in 1990, the Los Angeles Rams and New York Giants were in overtime of a playoff game. With the ball on their own 30-yard line, the Giants had their defensive backs on the line of scrimmage (called pressing), hoping to prevent the Rams from moving into ideal field goal range.

Rams receiver Willie "Flipper" Anderson was lined up on the right side, and Giants cornerback Mark Collins had him one-on-one. If Anderson were to run past Collins, no safety would be available to help. Rams quarterback Jim Everett recognized the coverage and elected to try for the home-run play (a "bomb" pass) rather than a Greg Bell run.

When the ball was snapped, Collins missed his bump or jam on Anderson. The game was now on the line. Everett floated a rainbow (a high-arching pass) down the right sideline toward Anderson, who had a 1-yard advantage on Collins. Near the goal line, Collins jumped, praying that he could deflect the pass. His fingertips missed the spiraling ball by 6 inches. Anderson caught the ball, the officials raised the touchdown signal, and the Rams won a playoff game. Anderson actually ran through the end zone, through the Giants Stadium tunnel, and into the locker room, the ball firmly in his grasp.

Afterward, Collins stood in his locker room aware of his failure, but his confidence wasn't shattered. "That's the life of a cornerback," Collins said. "You make ten good plays and one bad one, and all anyone wants to talk about is the bad. If you're going to play cornerback in this league, you've got to accept that this is your life."

The sixth, or dime, position (DB in Figure 10-7) can end up being a defensive back as well as a linebacker at times. In this alignment, the linebacker aligns in the middle about 5 yards away from the line of scrimmage. He should be one of the team's fastest linebackers as well as a very good tackler. Most teams use four defensive backs near the line of scrimmage with two safeties playing well off the ball, toward the middle of the field near the hash marks.

The object of the Nickel 40 is to pressure the quarterback, hoping to either sack or harass him. Teams use their four best pass-rushers on the field in this alignment, and these four players will most likely be opposed by only five offensive linemen. Defenses use a Nickel 40 defense only when the offense uses three or more receivers in its alignment.

From this defensive look, the pass-rushers may stem or *stunt* (move about on the line of scrimmage), trying to apply pressure by using their best linemen against the offense's weakest blockers. Defenses have been known, too, to blitz the quarterback with one of the defensive backs or a linebacker in order to overwhelm the offensive blocking scheme. The defensive pass coverage in the secondary can be a mixture of man-to-man and zone alignments.

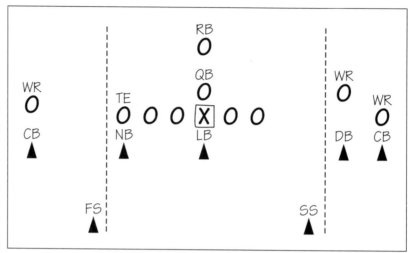

Figure 10-7:
In the
Nickel 40,
the defense
puts a sixth
player (DB)
in pass
coverage.

The Nickel 40 is also a good defense against an offense that is fond of *play-action passes* (when the quarterback fakes a handoff to a running back, keeps the ball, and then attempts a pass) or against an offense that likes to substitute a lot of receivers into the game. I'm talking about offenses that use formations that employ four wide receivers rather than the customary two wide receivers. The Nickel 40 defense, with faster personnel, can compensate and deal with an offense that prefers to always have a player in motion prior to the snap of the ball. It's also adept against other unusual formations.

Chapter 11

Defensive Tactics and Strategies

● ●

In This Chapter

▶ What the different types of defenses are

▶ Why the four-man line (the 4-3 defense) is the in thing

▶ Why the Flex worked only in Dallas

▶ How the 46 made the Bears monsters

▶ What the appeal of the over/under is for the patient coach

▶ Why the 3-4 defense was great with Taylor

▶ How Kansas City survives with speed

● ●

This chapter may not be the most entertaining read, and it's not filled with clever one-liners, but it covers really important stuff. Coaches will tell you that defenses win championships, and I'm not prejudiced when I say that I agree with that statement. When I was in the right defense, in the proper alignment, that was when I had the best chance to succeed. When you're in the right defense, it comes down to you beating the man in front of you. As an athlete, that's all you can ask for.

I may get a little sophisticated and sound like a businessman in this chapter, but pro football is a big business. When I played for the Raiders in the 1980s, I brought computer printouts to the locker room to glance over on game days. Those computer sheets showed every formation that the opposition planned to use against us (or so we thought).

When I went on the road, I carried my own VCR and brought tapes that Johnny Otten, the Raiders' film guy, had put together for me. I had him put every run play the team used on one tape, called a *run cut-up,* and every pass play on another, called a *pass cut-up.* The cut-ups showed every play that the opposition ran from a two-back formation. Every play they ran from the I-formation. And every play they ran from the one-back formation.

We watched hours of film during the week, but on Saturday nights I watched a couple more hours on my own and broke down every formation. By studying and reviewing all the formations, I was prepared. For example, when the opposition's offense came to the line of scrimmage in a split-back formation, my mind immediately computed to "full left, 18 Bob Tray O," a run play.

I know that jargon means nothing to you, but it tipped off my mind. I knew which play was coming, which is more than half the battle as a player. The other half is stopping the play.

The defense's battle plans are exactly what this chapter is about. Every team enters a game with a basic strategy. This chapter explains the common strategies — the defense's alignment and look — and how the defense really can be "offensive" by dictating the style of play in a game. Here, I cover all the basic defenses and help you figure out which defensive package works best against which offense.

Choosing a Base Defense

NFL coaches love to copy one another, primarily when a coach is successful with a particular offense or defense. For example, a lot of winning teams in the 1970s began to use the 3-4 defense (which utilizes three down linemen and four linebackers) as their *base,* or primary, defense. The 3-4 was the defense of choice in the 1980s; only Dallas, Chicago, and Washington preferred a 4-3 scheme (four down linemen and three linebackers). As the 1990s come to a close, the 4-3 defense is back in vogue, thanks mostly to the success that Jimmy Johnson had with the Dallas Cowboys earlier in this decade. In the 1998 season, 25 of the 30 NFL teams utilize some form of the 4-3 as their base defense.

Basically, what you need to understand is that the goals of any type of defense are to

- Stop the opposition and get the ball back for the offense.
- Seize possession of the ball via a turnover. A *turnover* occurs when the defense recovers a fumble or secures an interception.

To compete with sophisticated offenses, defenses have had to keep pace. In fact, some rules have changed simply to negate suffocating defenses. These rule changes have caused defensive coaches to return to the chalk-boards and film rooms — they even use computers to uncover offensive tendencies — to devise more dastardly plans.

The rest of this chapter attacks the most common defensive schemes and *fronts* individually. Most defenses are named by their fronts, or the number of defensive linemen and linebackers who align in front of the defensive backs. The most common front is the *front seven:* four defensive linemen and three linebackers, or three defensive linemen and four linebackers. It's assumed in football parlance that a front seven also includes four defensive backs: 7 + 4 = 11 players on the field.

I want you to fully understand the history, the reason, and success/failure rate for each scheme. Knowing *why* a team uses a specific strategy is important. Choosing a defense is like a game of checkers. A coach wants his team to stay a few offensive moves ahead of its opponent, anticipating the opponent's next move or play. The defense wants to prevent the offense from jumping over its defenders and reaching the end zone (or like they say in checkers, "King me!"). And, like checkers, you may sacrifice a piece in one area of the board (or field) to prevent the opponent from reaching your end of the board. The ultimate goal with any defense is to prevent a touchdown, so sometimes surrendering a field goal is a moral victory.

4-3 Front

The majority of NFL teams use the 4-3 defense, which consists of two defensive tackles (DT), two defensive ends (DE), two outside linebackers (LB), a middle linebacker (MLB), two cornerbacks (CB), and two safeties (S) as shown in Figure 11-1. The 4-3 was devised in 1950 by New York Giants coach Steve Owen, who needed a fourth defensive back to stop the Cleveland Browns from completing long passes. Owen, whose defensive captain was future Dallas Cowboys head coach Tom Landry, called the 4-3 his *umbrella defense* because the secondary opened in a dome shape as the linebackers retreated into pass coverage. In the first game in which the Giants used it, the defense clicked, and the Giants beat Cleveland 6-0, shutting out this Paul Brown–coached team for the first time.

Figure 11-1:
The 4-3 defense consists of four linemen (DE and DT), three linebackers (LB and MLB), and four defensive backs (CB and S).

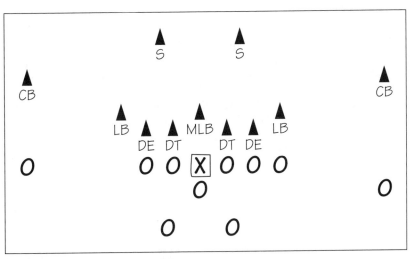

Although it was initially devised to stop the pass, this defense should be able to stop both the pass and the run. The 4-3 was first widely used in the late 1950s, when Sam Huff became the Giants' middle linebacker and the Detroit Lions, who also liked the scheme, made Joe Schmidt their middle linebacker. Both of these Hall of Fame players were instinctive and played run defense well because they were strong and exceptional at lateral pursuit of the ball carriers. But they also played the pass well. They could move away from the line of scrimmage *(drop into coverage)* and effectively defend a team's short-passing game.

On paper, this defense is very balanced. As with all defenses, having talented personnel is important. The defense needs ends who are strong pass-rushers as well as physically tough against the run. The ideal middle linebacker is someone like ex-Bear Dick Butkus (see Chapter 21), who could single-handedly make defensive stops and possessed the all-around savvy to put his team-mates in favorable positions. The defensive tackles should be strong against the run and agile enough to sustain pass-rush pressure on the quarterback.

The stronger and more physical of the two outside linebackers lines up over the tight end, leaving the other, quicker outside linebacker to be more of a pass-rusher. With the exception of all-star teams, it's almost impossible for a team to have superior players at every position. However, teams tend to use a 4-3 when they have four pretty good defensive linemen and a good middle linebacker. If three of those five players have all-star potential, this scheme should be successful.

As you go along in this chapter, you'll discover that there are variations of the 4-3, including the Dallas 4-3, the over/under, and the Chicago Bears' 46 defense of the mid-1980s. Some teams also use four-man lines but use more defensive backs rather than linebackers behind their four-man fronts.

3-4 Front

Bud Wilkinson created the 3-4 defense at the University of Oklahoma in the late 1940s, but the 1972 Miami Dolphins were the first NFL team to begin using it. And the Dolphins did so out of necessity; they had only two healthy defensive linemen. Chuck Fairbanks, another Oklahoma coach, used the 3-4 as an every-down defense with the New England Patriots in 1974, as did Houston Oilers coach O. A. "Bum" Phillips.

Unlike the 4-3, this defense uses only three defensive linemen, with the one in the middle (N) called the *nose tackle* (see Figure 11-2). The prototype nose tackle was the Oilers' 260-pound Curley Culp, who combined strength with exceptional quickness; he was an NCAA wrestling champion. The 3-4 also employs four linebackers (LB), with the other two defensive linemen (DE) usually consisting of one superior pass-rusher and a rugged run-defender. In some 3-4s, all three down linemen are *two-gappers,* meaning that they plug the gap between two offensive linemen and aim to neutralize those two blockers, allowing the linebackers to go unblocked and make the majority of the tackles.

Figure 11-2:
The 3-4
defense
lines up
with three
linemen (DE
and N) and
four
linebackers
(LB).

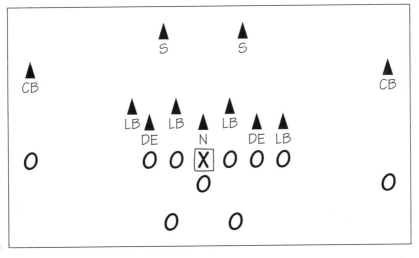

NFL teams in the 1970s adopted the 3-4 because they lacked quality defensive linemen, plus they had more players who were suited to play outside linebacker. This is also true today in high school and college, where teams may lack quality defensive linemen but have no shortage of athletes who are capable of playing linebacker. The outside linebacker position fits an NFL player who is at least 6'3", 240 pounds (the bigger and taller, the better). This player should have the ability to play the run and rush the passer like a defensive end.

The 3-4 can be a very flexible defense. In some instances, the defense may decide to drop seven or eight players into pass coverage. Conversely, the interchangeable personnel of a 3-4 could end up sending three to five players to rush the quarterback. Miami actually called its 3-4 defense "the 53" after linebacker Bob Matheson's jersey number. Matheson moved around, but he was primarily a pass-rushing linebacker.

The 3-4 defense is ideally suited to defending multiple offensive formations, meaning that a defensive coordinator can match his personnel with that of the offense. Also, the physically dominant nose tackle can prove to be a nightmare for the offensive center. The nose tackle can neutralize the center's pass-blocking attempts by constantly shoving his strong head and shoulders to the ground or moving the center sideways, thus negating his effectiveness as a blocker. In other instances, the center is asked to move to either side *(pull)* to assist on a wide run toward either end.

The 3-4 defense also spawned the term *two-gap style*. With this technique, the defensive linemen and inside linebackers actually block the offensive linemen to either side, opening a lane for the untouched outside linebacker to make the play. The 3-4 defense focuses on the outside linebackers; they are the stars of this defense.

The greatest defensive player I ever saw, Lawrence Taylor of the New York Giants, was essentially an outside linebacker in a 3-4 scheme. Although Taylor was great at sacking the quarterback in this scheme, the 3-4 defense generally is better at stopping the run than rushing the passer. And Taylor was exceptional at both aspects of the game; he could rush but also stand his ground and contain the run. Plus, he had the speed to pursue a running back moving away from him and still make the tackle.

NFL teams have moved away from the 3-4 defense because, to be successful, they need a tall, 250-pound outside linebacker who is capable of containing the tight end to play opposite a player like Taylor. Taylor had Carl Banks. Chip Banks and Duane Bickett were also players of that sort, but finding the likes of them has become harder and harder.

3-4 Eagle

Green Bay Packers defensive coordinator Fritz Shurmur started using the 3-4 Eagle defense with the Los Angeles Rams in the early 1980s. Shurmur's defense used another linebacker in the role of the nose tackle (see Figure 11-3). Instead of having a 300-pound player over the center, Shurmur inserted a 240-pound linebacker, a player who was susceptible to the run because most offensive centers outweighed him by 60 pounds. To succeed against the run, this linebacker needed to use his quickness and guile to shoot offensive line gaps. However, this linebacker was a solid tackler and also good at dropping into pass coverage. The remainder of the personnel were identical to a typical 3-4 scheme.

Shurmur devised this defense to confront and hopefully confuse San Francisco 49ers quarterback Joe Montana, who had an exceptional ability to read a defense correctly and complete a pass to the open man. Having a nose tackle (really the lighter and faster linebacker) drop into passing lanes was a totally foreign concept to any quarterback, who was used to that player remaining along the line of scrimmage rather than roaming in the defensive backfield like a defensive back.

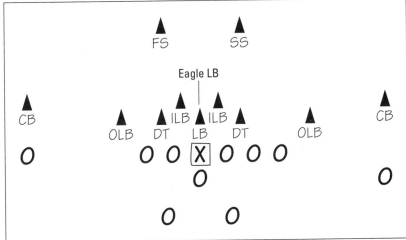

Figure 11-3: The 3-4 Eagle defense uses a linebacker in place of the nose tackle.

The 3-4 Eagle evolved from Buddy Ryan's 46 defense (described in detail later in this chapter), which is all about applying pass-rush pressure at the end of the offensive line. The Eagle places a premium on above-average linebackers who can sack the quarterback by rushing around the last blocker at the end of the offensive line. Most pass-rushers in this scheme prefer to line up away from the outside shoulder of the man responsible for blocking them. Outside linebacker Kevin Greene, who collected 46 quarterback sacks in three seasons, was the star (and benefactor) on Shurmur's Rams teams. Greene used his speed and exceptional strength for a 248-pounder to later lead the NFL in sacks twice (in 1994 and 1996). His 133 sacks are the most ever by a linebacker.

The Eagle is more successful with above-average cornerbacks who can play man-to-man defense. Man coverage complements the deep zone drops of two of the five linebackers. To me, it makes more sense to drop a 240-pound linebacker into pass coverage than to use a 310-pound nose tackle, which is what some zone blitz defenses do. That's one of the big differences (pun intended) between these two defenses. This defense can be very effective against a team running the West Coast offense (see Chapter 8), especially one that has a versatile running back who can damage a defense with his receiving as well as his running ability. Linebackers are better suited to catching and tackling this kind of ball carrier, while also being capable of defending the tight end, who is always an important performer in the West Coast offense.

Despite the lack of a fat body over the center, the Eagle 3-4 defense isn't susceptible to the run because it employs two very physical inside linebackers and can bring a strong safety close to the line of scrimmage to serve as another tackler (or linebacker). This maneuver allows the Eagle to put eight defensive players in the *box,* the area near the line of scrimmage where the defense is most effective at stopping the run. However, San Francisco, particularly with running back Roger Craig, had tremendous success running the football against this defense in some games because the offense was able to neutralize the light linebacker playing nose tackle and also run the ball from formations from which it had always thrown the football. Such tactics confused the defensive personnel, who were unable to predict what the offense intended to do.

Dallas 4-3

I want to make a distinction here: When Jimmy Johnson coached the Dallas Cowboys to two consecutive Super Bowls, Dallas's defense had an abundance of talented players among the front seven but didn't have cornerback Deion Sanders and safety Darren Woodson. Now, the Dallas 4-3 defense utilizes four down linemen and three linebackers but gambles more than Johnson would have allowed, and occasionally uses more of a nickel scheme, inserting another defensive back in place of a linebacker. (See Figure 11-4.) This defense is predicated more on a team's personnel than on a particular alignment.

Figure 11-4:
The Dallas 4-3 defense uses four linemen (DE and DT) but may use an extra defensive back in place of one of the three linebackers (OLB, MLB, and LB).

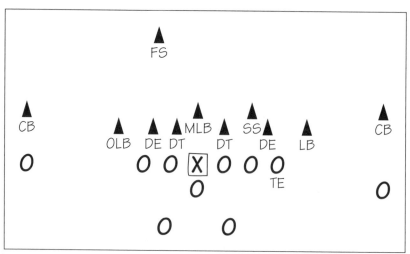

But what Dallas was able to accomplish, and what has been copied, was the scheme *cover four* or *four across* in the secondary. Because Dallas's front seven was so talented and could apply extreme pressure on the quarterback, the secondary was able to play deeper and prevent the deep pass. Of course, this scheme puts extreme pressure on the two cornerbacks, who are expected to be able to take the opposition's two best receivers man-to-man and shut them down without any help.

In the Dallas 4-3 defense, the safeties also can creep up toward the line of scrimmage to provide support against running plays. Basically, this defense allows the safeties to cheat, to overplay one aspect of the offense when they anticipate the play correctly. With the rest of the defense attempting to funnel almost every running play toward these physical safeties, the back goes down if the safeties make good reads. In modern football, in which teams may have physically gifted tight ends, the Dallas 4-3 defense puts the safety in a better position to defend the *seam pass,* the throw right down the hash marks to the tight end or to a receiver running straight upfield.

Flex

Coach Tom Landry invented the Flex defense for the Dallas Cowboys teams of the 1970s and 1980s. It is a 4-3 alignment, too, but it *flexes* (moves back) two defensive linemen off the line of scrimmage by 2 or 3 yards (see Figure 11-5). These two offset linemen read the blocking combinations of the offense and attempt to make the tackle (or the sack), while their teammates try to break down the offense's blocking patterns.

However, this defense works only if you have talented defensive tackles like Bob Lilly and Randy White, who was nicknamed "The Manster." Interpretation: White was half man, half monster. These flexed defensive linemen must have exceptional speed and the ability to react. By being a couple of yards off the line of scrimmage, they should be able to see how an offensive play is developing. But to be able to stop a play from their positions, they also must have the speed to recover these 2 yards while moving forward. Being off the line makes it harder for offensive linemen to block them. The blockers have to run a couple of yards to strike them, but meanwhile the defensive linemen also are moving, quite possibly in a different direction.

Lilly (see Chapter 21) was one of the greatest defensive tackles of all time, and White was very close to him in ability. The keys to both players were their exceptional quickness and strength. White was a converted linebacker playing defensive tackle; you don't find many players capable of making that change. Shifting White's defensive position was a bold move by Landry 20 years ago, but this defensive scheme wouldn't work very well today. The

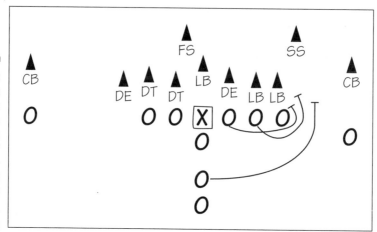

basic premise of the Flex — to have defensive linemen reading — hinders the pass-rush. A player can't be sitting and reading and waiting for something to come his way; he has to react and attack if he wants to tackle the quarterback. The Flex seemed like a great defense against the run until Eric Dickerson of the Los Angeles Rams ran for 248 yards against it in a playoff game at the end of the 1985 season.

Zone Blitz

Zone blitz sounds like a contradiction in terms: Teams that like to play zone pass coverage generally don't blitz. Zones are safe; blitzes are all-out gambles.

The Pittsburgh Steelers and the Carolina Panthers were the proponents of the exotic zone blitz in the mid-1990s. From a base 3-4 alignment, they would overload one side of the offense by placing as many as three of the four linebackers to that side, as shown in Figure 11-6. They might stick a cornerback there, too, or put a safety there in place of a linebacker. The object was to confuse the quarterback and the offensive linemen, forcing them to wonder: How many people (four, five, or six) are really coming at the quarterback?

The down linemen in this scheme usually engage the center and guards. Their intent is to occupy these players and to give them the impression that they may be rushing the quarterback. Often, the defensive linemen merely hold their ground, waiting for the run, or stop and then peel back off the line of scrimmage (5 yards or so) and attempt to cover that area *(short zone coverage)* against a possible pass play. The object of a zone blitz is to create one or two free lanes to the quarterback for the linebackers or defensive backs who do the blitzing.

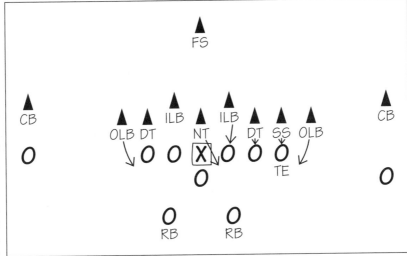

Figure 11-6:
In a zone blitz, the defense lines up like this.

The zone blitz is an ideal defense against an inexperienced or gun-shy quarterback. The defense wants to get the quarterback thinking. Before any quarterback drops back to pass, he scans the secondary to try to figure out what kind of defense it's playing. This is called *reading the secondary*. When a quarterback looks at a zone secondary, he doesn't usually equate it with blitzing. But in this defense, the quarterback checks out the defensive front, too. He wants to have an idea where the blitz or the most pass-rush pressure will come from. A good quarterback believes that he can move away from the pressure from the suspected overloaded side and gain enough time to complete his pass.

The combinations and varieties of zone blitzes are endless. However, offenses have discovered that a short pass play to the *flat* (outside the hash marks) may be effective against this defense. Most zone blitzing teams give offenses considerable open areas to one side or the other underneath their final line of pass defense. Often, blitzing teams send a player who normally would be in pass coverage toward the quarterback. When a defense blitzes like that, it always keeps two people deep. It doesn't want to surrender a home run — that is, a long touchdown.

Smart offenses have learned that you can run at defensive linemen who are stopping, waiting, and then dropping into coverages. Teams that are patient against the zone blitz can find running room to the opposite side of the overload. And a missed assignment by a defender in a zone blitz package can spell doom quickly.

46

The team that's most often associated with the 46 defense is the Chicago Bears of the 1980s. The 46 didn't receive its name from its alignment, but rather because Bears free safety Doug Plank wore jersey number 46 and often lined up as a linebacker. Buddy Ryan, the Bears' defensive coordinator, altered Chicago's original personnel in the 46 defense — five defensive linemen, one linebacker, and five defensive backs — to four defensive linemen, four linebackers, and three defensive backs (see Figure 11-7). The fourth "linebacker," the "46," is generally considered a cross between a linebacker and a strong safety.

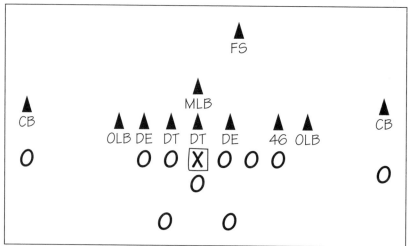

Figure 11-7:
The Bears'
46 defense
utilized four
down
linemen,
four
linebackers,
and three
defensive
backs.

In the 46, three defensive linemen line up across from the offense's center and two guards, making it impossible for those offensive players to double-team the defender opposite the center. In Chicago, this defensive player was Dan Hampton. When Ryan became head coach of the Philadelphia Eagles, the player over the center was Reggie White. Hampton and White were the strongest linemen on their teams and also were excellent pass-rushers. Their exceptional ability made it possible for them to collapse the offense's pocket, thus ruining the quarterback's protection. They were good enough to beat two blockers in their prime, paving the way for teammates to have a clean shot at the quarterback as White and Hampton preoccupied the others.

The Bears had sensational success with the 46 defense. In 1984, they recorded 72 quarterback sacks, an NFL record. And the following year, they allowed only ten points in three playoff games en route to their Super Bowl XX championship. In one five-game stretch, the defense scored 25 points and allowed only 20 points. When the Bears won the Super Bowl, the defensive players carried Ryan off on their shoulders, while the offensive players took care of head coach Mike Ditka. The Tennessee Oilers also use the 46 defense because Oilers head coach Jeff Fisher played for Buddy Ryan.

In the 46, no defender lines up over the two offensive tackles. Instead, defenders are placed off both of the offensive tackles' outside shoulders. From there, their intentions are straightforward: rush and sack the quarterback.

The biggest downsides to the 46 defense are the limitations from a pass coverage standpoint. Your cornerbacks are stuck in man-to-man coverage 90 percent of the time, with only one safety back to help. You can drop an inside linebacker or two into zone coverage; however, when you line up with basically only three defensive backs on the field, often a linebacker gets stuck one-on-one with the tight end. If the tight end can run, this matchup may be a mismatch for the defense. Also, the 46 defense can struggle against a three-wide-receiver offense because of the man coverage situations. However, the philosophy of this defense is to attack the quarterback before he can pick apart the secondary.

The 46 is a good defense against offenses with two-back sets. Why? Because such an offense doesn't spread the 46; it condenses it. And that's perfect, because the 46 is an aggressive defense that's designed to attack. The two-back offense affords the 46 defense the opportunity to send its pass rushers off the corner. When they come off the corner, the edge of the offensive line, there's no one to impede their path into the backfield, where they can cause the most damage.

The 46 defense can have a soft spot if the offense believes that it can run wide against it, particularly in the direction of one of the offensive tackles. If the offense can block the two outside defenders, pushing them outside, the runner can cut inside the offensive tackle and run through that lane. And when the cornerbacks drop deep, the back may be able to gain a lot of yards. In college football, offenses beat the 46 defense by having the quarterback run an option play, something the pros don't allow their quarterbacks to do. In the *option,* the quarterback starts running around the end. He can either turn upfield or lateral the ball back to a running back.

Kansas City Falcon

Kansas City head coach Marty Schottenheimer developed this multiple defense, in which he can utilize highly versatile players in a variety of interchangeable roles, for the 1997 season. Both the players and the scheme have multiple variations. It begins in a 3-4 alignment with three defensive linemen and four linebackers (see Figure 11-8). The Kansas City Falcon is very multiple, meaning that the defense is capable of 20 different looks in a typical 70-play game.

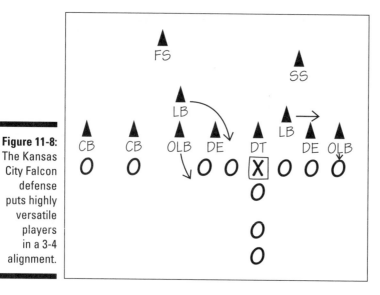

Figure 11-8:
The Kansas
City Falcon
defense
puts highly
versatile
players
in a 3-4
alignment.

The Kansas City Falcon is a personnel defense. Schottenheimer went to this defense because he believes that the NFL draft offers an abundance of smaller, faster linebacker-safety types. He puts these players in positions to create confusion, allowing them to simply run around and make plays. The downside to this defense is that it is not capable of beating the offense with size; a battering run-oriented team can wear down these defensive players.

Kansas City does some abstract formations with this defense — inserting another linebacker for a defensive lineman or simply using five defensive backs a lot. I've seen them put two linebackers on the line of scrimmage. The linebacker who blitzes is generally Derrick Thomas, a tremendous speed rusher, and the other linebacker drops into coverage. This defense plays a tremendous amount of man coverage in the secondary; it can do that because its cornerbacks, James Hasty and Dale Carter, are superior players. It's an in-your-face defense. The attitude of this defense is "We might give you 15 yards, but so what? We're going to sack you on the next play and get those 15 yards back."

Over/Under 4-3

The over/under 4-3 is basically a four down linemen and three linebacker scheme — what I call a Sam linebacker on the tight end and then two inside linebackers. The object of this defense is to shift more defensive linemen to the offense's suspected point of attack, which is called the *over,* or to shift the linemen *under,* to the weak side of the offensive formation. The down linemen are the stars of this show.

In the under 4-3, shown in Figure 11-9, one defensive lineman is on an offensive tackle, another is on the guard and center, and another is on the *open side* offensive tackle (where there's no tight end). In the *over shift,* three of the four defensive linemen shift toward the strong side of the offensive formation (the tight end side), as shown in Figure 11-10. There is always a defender directly opposite the tight end in both of these over/under defenses.

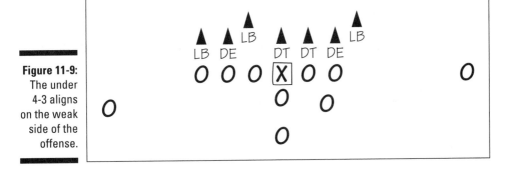

Figure 11-9: The under 4-3 aligns on the weak side of the offense.

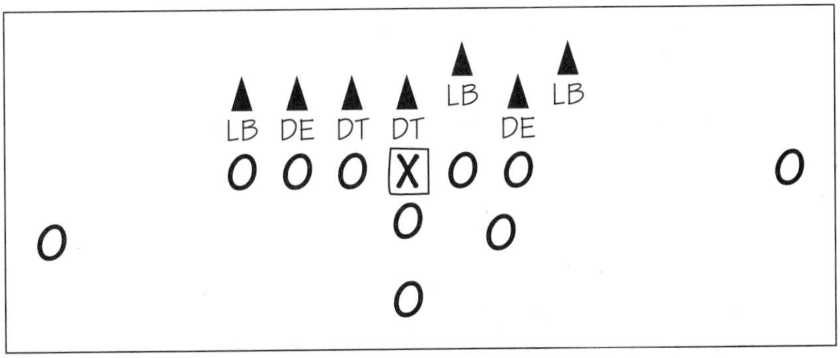

Figure 11-10: In the over 4-3, the down linemen shift toward the strong side of the offensive formation.

The over-and-under scheme gives the defense flexibility in how it uses its players in the secondary. Coach Tony Dungy does this with his Tampa Bay Buccaneers: He brings his strong safety close to the line of scrimmage, and suddenly he has an eight-man front. For a change-up look, defenses can drop safeties to their traditional spots 12 yards off the line of scrimmage and roll the two cornerbacks up to or within 3 yards of the line of scrimmage, making the defense look like a nine-man front.

For this defense to succeed, you need to have very talented people up front, players who are capable of dominating the line of scrimmage. This scheme works only if your down linemen are special players like defensive tackles Warren Sapp of the Tampa Bay Buccaneers and John Randle of the Minnesota Vikings, a team that Dungy also coached. This defense can survive with average linebackers, decent safeties, and good cornerbacks, but it must have hard-charging linemen who are physically capable of beating offensive linemen.

The over/under 4-3 is a perfect defense for Dungy. Unlike Dungy, some teams and their coaches are very impatient; they want to attack and be aggressive, maybe pushing the panic button and blitzing the opposition before the time is right. But a coach like Dungy can sit back. He's not going to be emotional. He's going to fold his arms and let the offense keep the ball for seven or eight plays, believing that sooner or later the offense will panic and make a mistake. This defense can force an offense into making mistakes, too. Believe me, some NFL offenses have trouble running eight plays without screwing something up.

Tackling Tricky Situations

Defenses are under constant pressure in every game: one mistake (a missed tackle in the open field or a blown assignment, for example) and the opponent has points on the board. These sections tackle a couple of the tricky situations that defenses face and gives advice for handling them.

Stopping a superstar

I think the best way to play against a standout offensive player, such as Detroit Lions running back Barry Sanders, is to do what the Green Bay Packers have done in the last few seasons. When playing against a superstar, whether he's a running back or a quarterback, the defense must decide what facet of the offense it wants to focus on. In other words, the defense says, "I'm stopping Barry Sanders and forcing the quarterback to throw the ball to beat me." Defenses can't do both — stop the run and the pass — against great offensive teams.

Because they have such a great safety in LeRoy Butler, the Packers move Butler closer to the line of scrimmage. He becomes another linebacker, the eighth man in the box. In other words, you have four defensive linemen and three linebackers, and you bring an extra run defender out of the secondary. If your safety reacts poorly, the defense can be susceptible to being beaten consistently by the pass. The consolation, though, is that Sanders isn't going to run for 200 yards.

The other thing against a great back like Sanders is that your defenders must at least attempt to tackle him. They should never stand and wait for a good shot; they should fly at him. If they miss, they miss, but they're definitely not going to bring him down if they don't at least give it a shot.

Stopping the two-point conversion

First, I want to say that bringing the two-point play into the NFL (which was done in 1994) has helped teams play better defense inside their own 20-yard line, an area known as the *red zone*. The two-point play can make or break a game, and ultimately make or break a season. Offensively, what teams are attempting to do on this play is to spread the defense and then run some kind of *pick pass pattern*. Here's how that pattern starts: The offense aligns two receivers on one side of the formation. The outside receiver runs toward the middle of the field, while the inside receiver runs, stops, and then heads in the direction of the outside receiver. When the two receivers cross, that's called a *pick play* because the inside receiver tries to rub the man guarding him against the defender who's covering his teammate. The desired result is an open receiver in the *flat*, the area beyond the defensive linemen but in front of the secondary.

In an effort to prevent the pick play, defenses trying to prevent two-point conversions are playing more and more zone coverage in the secondary. The reason is that they just can't stop all the combination pass routes (when a receiver can improvise and vary his route in three different ways on the same play) — especially impossible to cover when offenses use a three-wide-receiver set. And the pick play is particularly successful against man-to-man coverage. So in trying to prevent a two-point play, the defense anticipates that most teams won't run. Most offenses line up in a one-back formation with three receivers to one side.

The key for the defense is not to blitz, and instead use a four-man line and play a zone defense behind it. You can play as many as six or seven defensive backs across because the defense doesn't have to worry about the depth of the field. Remember, the end zone is only 10 yards deep.

Stuffing short yardage

The first thing you have to realize in *short-yardage situations* (third down and 1 yard or fourth down and 1 yard or less) is that you can't stop everything. So you have to prepare your defensive front people, the defensive line and the linebackers, to stop one or two particular plays. Usually, you have eight defenders on the line, a combination of linemen and linebackers, and defensive players over both tight ends. The key play that you have to be able to stop is the offense's isolation play.

What I mean by *isolation* is what happens on a blast play, when a fullback runs inside to block a defensive player standing by himself before the quarterback hands off the ball to the running back behind him. (Chapter 6 explains this play in more detail.) The running play is called the *blast play,* but it works because the fullback *isolates* a specific defensive player. On this type of play, the defensive linemen must establish positive gap control. What does that mean? In addition to lining up across from an offensive lineman and defeating his block, each defensive lineman must get his body into a gap, either by *stunting* (see the following sidebar) or by lining up on the shoulder of an offensive lineman and securing the gap. That's the first thing.

The second thing is that someone on defense must get some penetration across the line of scrimmage in order to have any chance of disrupting the play. Remember, offensive linemen have trouble blocking quicker players who are charging straight ahead into a gap.

Stunting: It's like baseball

You may have heard the term *stunting.* Stunting involves defensive linemen being up to some tricks. What I mean is that we defensive linemen don't necessarily move straight ahead. We don't always go where the offensive linemen anticipate us to go.

When I played, I was pretty good at reading formations. I had good instincts for anticipating what direction the offense was going with the ball. On passing downs, when we thought that the quarterback was going to throw the ball, we may have had 14 different stunts or games among us four defensive linemen. For example, I (DE) would go inside, and the player next to me (DT) would drop and circle around me, as shown in the figure. We made these movements to confuse the offensive line.

We used word signals among ourselves for what we wanted to do. We also received signals from the sideline from our line coach, Earl

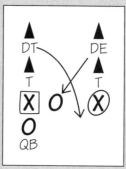

Leggett. He would signal us like a third base coach does in baseball — you know, touching his shoulder, slapping his head, waving his arms — basically telling us which stunt to use. And sometimes we would shake him off, just like in baseball. We wouldn't do what he asked us to do, and he'd call us all kinds of ugly names after we returned to the sidelines.

Part IV
Meet the Rest of the Team

The 5th Wave

By Rich Tennant

@RICHTENNANT

TOMP 55

27

GUN 7

"Not the most accurate kicker we've ever had, but definitely the strongest."

In this part . . .

A football team wouldn't be complete without coaches, the main masterminds and motivators behind the players. All sorts of other people play roles as well: managers, trainers, and, in the NFL, owners. This part talks about all those folks and what they do. Also in this part, you can find out about that part of football that lies somewhere between offense and defense: the kicking game, also known as special teams.

Chapter 12

The Kicking Game

As Chapter 3 explains, every football game begins with a kickoff. More than 97 percent of the time, a team kicks an extra point after scoring a touchdown. And after every touchdown that a team scores, the team must kick off again. These are just some examples of what is known as the *kicking game*. The proper name for the group of players who take care of these tasks is *special teams*.

Overall, this group of players is remarkable. A lot of effort, skill, and courage is involved in manning these positions. But you can play ten years in the NFL, be a tremendous special teams performer, and play in virtual anonymity. Kickers and some return men garner attention, but for the other players — the guys who cover kicks and punts and block for kickers — the job is pretty thankless even within the team. And on most occasions, the job certainly is a thankless one with the media and the public. Special teams players generally are noticed only for doing a poor job — when a punt or field goal attempt is blocked or when the opposition returns a kickoff for a touchdown.

After you read this chapter, however, you should have a much greater appreciation for these fine athletes and the important tasks that they do.

My own special teams experiences

I was a special teams player during my first two years in the NFL. Being a small-college player from Villanova, playing on special teams gave me the opportunity to work my way up through the ranks on the Raiders. The NFL is kind of like the Army: You have to prove that you belong.

I was on most of the special teams units. I covered punts and kickoffs, plus I was part of the unit that tried to block field goal and extra point attempts. Matt Millen and I were the two bulldozers on the kick-blocking team. We used to get down in a four-point stance (both hands and feet on the ground) and line up on either side of the center, who snaps the ball. Ted Hendricks, who was over 6'7" and had the longest arms I'd ever seen, would stand right behind us. Millen and I would basically function as a snowplow and clear a path for Hendricks. Ted was in charge; he'd tell us where to line up and what to do, and I remember him blocking a number of kicks.

When I became an All-Pro player in my third year in the NFL, my defensive line coach wouldn't allow me to play on special teams anymore; he didn't want me getting hurt. That's pretty much the philosophy in the NFL today. Quarterbacks used to be the holders for field goals and extra points, but it's pretty rare to see any of them holding these days. They don't want to hurt those pretty fingers!

Getting to Know the Men Who Make Up the Special Teams

The players who put their foot to the ball are the *placekickers, punters,* and *field goal kickers,* also known as *specialists.* On some teams, the punter handles kickoff duties and the placekicker is responsible for field goal and extra point attempts. Other teams have players for all three positions. But there's a lot more to the kicking game than these two or three players.

When a punter attempts a punt, for example, 21 other players are on the field. The ten remaining men on the punting team have two responsibilities: to protect the punter's kick from being blocked and then to run down the field and cover the punt. However, these tasks are difficult ones. They face ten players who are trying to slow them down and, lastly, the player catching the punt (the *punt returner*). The returner generally is one of the fastest, quickest runners on a team; he's a specialist in his own right. The punting team wants to prevent the return man from gaining a single yard, whereas the punt returner obviously wants to go the distance: score a touchdown. At the very least, he wants to place his team's offense in good field position, shortening the distance that the offense must travel to score.

This group has its own coach, a special teams coach, who serves in a capacity similar to that of an offensive and defensive coordinator. (Chapter 13 explains the coaching lineup in more detail.) Like them, he coaches a large group of players, not merely a specific position. Some teams, like the Dallas Cowboys, also have a kicking coach who coaches basically two players, his punter and kicker.

Special teams is *so* specialized that a single group of players can't cover every situation. Four special teams units exist:

- Basically, the same group of players handles punts, kickoffs, and punt returns.
- Another unit handles field goal and extra point attempts.
- Another group takes care of kickoff returns.
- A final group attempts to block field goal and extra point attempts.

Generally, great special teams players are unusual. Green Bay's Travis Jervey, who has been selected for the Pro Bowl, had a pet lion. They're often the wild and crazy guys on a team, too. When coverage men stop a returner in his tracks, for example, they're usually as excited as offensive players scoring touchdowns.

Understanding What's So Special about Special Teams

A key thing to know about special teams is that these 11-man units typically are on the field for about 20 percent of the plays in a football game. But coaches often say that special teams play amounts to one-third of a football game — by that, they mean its total impact on the game.

Take scoring, for example — how games are won and lost:

- In 1997, NFL **offenses** scored 1,001 touchdowns, or 60.32 percent of the 9,957 points scored in 240 regular-season games (a full season). Remember, teams earn six points for every touchdown.
- **Special teams** accounted for 3,318 points, or 33.32 percent of all scoring. Punt and kick returners scored only 29 touchdowns, but kickers made 993 extra points (worth one point each) and 708 field goals (worth three points each). Also, five punts/kicks were blocked and returned for touchdowns.

OFFICIALLY SPEAKING

Field position terminology

The main line of demarcation on a football field is the 50-yard line. The area on both sides of the 50 is known as *midfield territory*. Remember, a lot of football terms are defense-oriented. Consequently, when a commentator says, "The Chicago Bears are starting from their own 18," he or she means that the ball is on the 18-yard line and that the opposition, should it recover the ball, is only 18 yards away from scoring a touchdown. The Bears may be on offense, but they should be mindful of the precarious offensive position they're in. They want to move the ball away from their goal line, and probably in a conservative fashion (such as by running the ball rather than throwing risky passes that could be intercepted).

Another important function of the special teams unit is to maintain good field position and to keep the opposition in bad field position. The main object of the kickoff, for example, is to pin the opponent as far away from its end zone, and thus a score, as possible. In 1997, the typical NFL team started on offense 72 yards away from its end zone, or on its own 28-yard line. Kickoff coverage teams strive, though, to put the opponent 80 yards or more away from scoring.

Placekicking

Placekicking, one "half" of the special team's duties, involves kickoffs, field goal attempts, and extra point attempts (also known as a *PAT*, or *point after a touchdown*). Unlike punting, which I describe later in this chapter, a kicker boots the ball from a particular spot on the field. In this section, you can read about these three types of kicks and the rules and objectives behind them.

Kicking off

Have you ever heard the phrase *kicked off* used in regard to something that started off something else, as in "The Bon Jovi show kicked off the summer concert season"? Well, that phrase could well have originated from the football kickoff, which starts off every game.

VIEWER TIP

For fans, the opening kickoff is an exhilarating start to any game. There's the two-sided thrill of one team attempting to block the other, helping its returner run through, over, and past 11 fast-charging players of the kicking team. (Well, make that ten players. The kicker usually stands around the 50-yard line, hoping that he doesn't have to make a tackle.) And the kicking team wants to make a statement by stopping the returner inside his own 20-yard line. This is the object on every level of football, from peewee to college to the NFL.

Deciding whether to kick or to receive

At the coin toss, when captains from both teams meet the referee in the center of the field, the captain who correctly calls the flip of the referee's coin decides whether his team is to receive or to defend a particular goal. For example, if the captain says that he wants to defend a certain end zone, then the opponent automatically receives the ball. If the winning captain wants the ball, the opponent chooses which end of the field his team will kick from (and the goal it will defend). Except in bizarre weather conditions — when it's snowing, raining, or extremely windy — most teams elect to receive the kickoff. They want the ball for their offense.

On rare occasions, a team may allow the other team to receive after winning the coin toss. They *defer* their right to kick off because the head coach probably believes that his defensive unit is stronger than the opposition's offense and wants to pin them deep in their own territory, force a turnover, or make them punt after three downs. Adverse weather conditions are also a factor because they may jeopardize the players' ability to field the kick cleanly, and some kickers have difficulty achieving adequate distances against a strong wind. In these conditions, a team may opt to receive the ball at the end of the field where the weather has less impact.

Setting up for the kickoff

For kickoffs, an NFL kicker is allowed to use a 1-inch tee to support the ball; college and high school kickers may use a 3-inch tee. The kicker can angle the ball anyway he prefers while using the tee; most kickers prefer to have the ball sit in the tee at a 75-degree angle rather than have it perpendicular

PLAYER TIP

Improving your kicking skills

To be a good kicker, you must practice every other day. While practicing kicking, make sure that your plant foot remains behind the ball. Also, keep your head down and your shoulders square to your target. At the point of striking the ball, your kicking leg should lock out. It should be straight, and your right arm should never swing beyond the ball until after impact; your left arm should pull your body through the kick. Your left arm should go up when your plant foot goes down. For kickoffs, most kickers take five or more steps before striking the ball.

On the days you're not kicking, head to the weight room and do power squats, leg presses, and leg extensions, in which you lift and then hold the weight for two counts. Weight work should stress quads, plus you should do reverse curls for your hamstrings. But never do any exercise that puts too much stress on your knees.

to the ground. During some games, strong winds prevent the ball from remaining in the tee. In those instances, a teammate holds the ball steady for the kicker by placing his index finger on top of the ball and applying the necessary downward pressure to keep it steady.

The kickoff team generally lines up five players on either side of the kicker. These ten players line up in a straight line about 8 yards from where the ball is placed on the kicking tee. If the kicker is a soccer-style kicker (see the section "Soccer-style kicking," later in this chapter for more information), he lines up 7 yards back and off to one side (to the left if he's a right-footed kicker, or vice versa). As the kicker strides forward to kick the ball, the ten players move forward in unison, hoping to be in full stride when the kicker makes contact with the ball.

In the NFL, the kickoff recently was moved back to the 30-yard line, whereas the 35-yard line is still used in college football, and high school teams kick off from the 40. The pros moved to the 30-yard line for a twofold reason: Kickers were placing too many kicks deep in the opposite end zone. This forced the players who return kicks to make a wise judgment call: They either took a knee once in possession of the ball in the end zone (known as *downing the ball*) or allowed the ball to bounce past the end line. Both actions result in a *touchback,* meaning that the officials declare the ball dead. Touchbacks automatically give the offense the ball on its own 20-yard line. NFL owners wanted to restore kickoff returns — the exciting attempt of one man trying to score from 90 to 100 yards away — to the game. The extra 5 yards also mean that the men attempting to tackle the returner are farther away from their target.

Still, after the kickoff was moved back 5 yards, not only did NFL kickers continue to reach the end zone, but 14.13 percent of all kickoffs resulted in touchbacks during the 1997 season. And, as mentioned earlier, the average starting point for NFL offenses was their own 28-yard line. Kickers, and the players sent to tackle the kick returner, are doing their jobs extremely well.

Kicking the ball

When the referee blows his whistle, the kicker approaches the ball. His objective is to hit the ball squarely in the lower quarter in order to get the proper loft and distance. As soon as his foot makes contact with the ball, his ten teammates are allowed to cross the line of scrimmage and run downfield to *cover* the kick — basically, to tackle the player who catches the ball and attempts to return it back toward the kicking team. The ideal kickoff travels about 70 yards and hangs in the air for over 4.5 seconds. Maximizing the loft time, known in football parlance as *hang time,* is important because it enables players on the kicking team to run down the field and cover the kick, thus tackling the return man closer to his own end zone.

Kicking their way to the top

Kicking is a fine science. For example, John Carney of the San Diego Chargers led the NFL in 1997 by averaging 64.5 yards on his kickoffs. But the Chargers weren't able to cover his kicks very well, allowing the opposition to start their offensive drives beyond the 30-yard line. The Dallas Cowboys led the NFL in this special teams category — their opponents, on average, started at the 22½-yard line.

Again, the kicking team's objective in a kickoff is to place the ball as close to its opponent's end zone as possible. After all, it's better for your opponent to have to travel 99 yards to score a touchdown than it is for them to have to move the ball only, say, 60 yards. Plus, if you can keep the ball close to your opponent's end zone, your defense has a better chance of scoring a touchdown if it recovers a fumble or intercepts an errant pass. And by pinning the opposition deep in its own territory and possibly forcing a punt, a team can expect to put its offense in better field position once it receives a punt.

OFFICIALLY SPEAKING

To keep the kick returner from making many return yards, kickers may attempt to kick the ball to a specific side of the field (known as *directional kicking*) to force the return man to field the kick. The basis of this strategy is the belief that your kick coverage team is stronger than your opponent's kick return unit and that the return man isn't very effective. In this situation, the returner is often restricted, and the defense can pin him against the sidelines and force him out-of-bounds.

The kickoff formation shown in Figure 12-1 typifies directional kicking. Instead of simply kicking the ball straight down the middle of the field, the kicker angles the ball to the left side. This style is ideal against a team that lines up with only one kick returner. The directional kick forces the returner to move laterally and take his eyes off the ball in flight. The kicking team's purpose is to focus its coverage to one side of the field, where it hopes to have more tacklers than there are blockers.

Following the rules of the kickoff

Like virtually everything else in football, kickoffs are governed by a strict set of rules:

- The receiving team must line up a minimum of 10 yards from where the ball is kicked.

- Members of the kicking team can recover the ball after the kick travels 10 yards or the ball touches an opponent. However, if the kicked ball goes out-of-bounds after it travels 10 yards or more from the line of scrimmage, the receiving team takes possession at that spot. If the kicked ball goes out-of-bounds before traveling 10 yards, the kicking team is penalized 5 yards and must rekick. If a member of the kicking team touches the ball before it travels 10 yards, the kicking team must rekick and is penalized 5 yards.

✔ A member of the kicking team can recover the ball in the end zone and be awarded a touchdown.

✔ Members of the kicking team must give the receiving team's returner the opportunity to *fair catch* the ball. If he signals for a fair catch, they cannot touch him and cannot come within 3 feet of him until he touches the ball.

✔ The receiving team gets the ball on its own 35-yard line if the kickoff goes out-of-bounds before reaching the end zone. If it bounces out before the 35-yard line, the receiving team receives the ball where it went out-of-bounds.

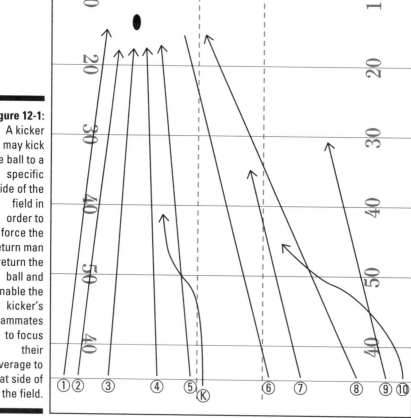

Figure 12-1:
A kicker may kick the ball to a specific side of the field in order to force the return man to return the ball and enable the kicker's teammates to focus their coverage to that side of the field.

The wackiest kickoff ever

Alumni and fans of the Stanford/University of California at Berkeley rivalry know it simply as "The Play." It is also the only known touchdown scored while running through the opposition's band. As in *marching band.*

These schools have faced each other in more than 100 games in the rivalry, and The Play occurred in the 85th meeting, on November 20, 1982. Stanford went ahead 20-19 with four seconds remaining, and most of the 75,662 fans were heading for the exits in Cal's Memorial Stadium when Stanford's Mark Harmon kicked off from his own 25-yard line because his team had been assessed a 15-yard penalty for excessive celebration following its go-ahead field goal. Given the field position and in attempt to prevent a runback, Harmon made a *percentage kick* — a low-bouncing squibber. Such kicks are usually difficult to field and, because the ball is not kicked a great distance, allow the coverage team a shorter distance in which to tackle the opposition. At the time of the kick, the Stanford band, a legendary group known for its zany attire and performances, poured onto the south end of the field (Cal's end zone), believing that the game was over.

What happened next goes into football history under the "pretty unbelievable" category. Cal's

Kevin Moen caught the bouncing ball on his own 43-yard line and ran forward 10 yards, where he was surrounded by Stanford tacklers. But before he was downed, Moen lateralled back (a legal play in which the ball is passed or tossed backwards; it is illegal to pass forward on any type of running play) to Richard Rogers. Rogers kept the ball briefly before tossing it back to running back Dwight Garner, who carried the ball to the Stanford 48-yard line. Garner was being tackled when he flipped the ball back to Rogers, who started running forward again and, before he was tackled, lateralled back to Mariet Ford, who sidestepped two tacklers and rushed to the Stanford 25-yard line.

As Ford was being tackled and falling to the ground, he tossed the ball up in the air, and backward, to Moen, the player who had originally fielded Harmon's kickoff. By this time, Moen and the players who remained were running through the Stanford band. Moen sidestepped some tacklers and then smashed through the Stanford trombone player to score the winning touchdown.

Final score: Cal 25, Stanford 20.

Returning the kickoff

The ultimate purpose of a kickoff return is to score or advance the ball as close to midfield (or beyond) as possible. A team's ability to start out on offense in better-than-average field position greatly increases its chances for success.

For example, during the 1996 season, Desmond Howard was a major reason the Green Bay Packers were Super Bowl champions. Howard returned only one kickoff for a touchdown that season, but his long returns always supplied tremendous positive momentum swings for his team. When he didn't go all the way, Howard was adept at giving his team excellent field position. Anytime he advanced the ball to his own 30-yard line or beyond, he put his offensive teammates in better field position and, obviously, closer to the opponent's end zone and a score.

During the 1997 NFL season, the average kickoff was returned 22 yards. However, the Atlanta Falcons Byron Hanspard returned two kickoffs for touchdowns, and Carolina Panther Michael Bates, a former Olympic runner, led the NFL with a 27.3-yard return average.

Gale Sayers, who played for the Chicago Bears in the 1960s, is the only NFL player to average over 30 yards on kickoff returns. In the 1990s, Eric Metcalf, who is playing for his fourth team, the Arizona Cardinals, in 1998, has been one of the finest kick and punt returners in NFL history. Metcalf returned two punts for touchdowns in 1997 while with the San Diego Chargers, giving him an NFL record of 11 career touchdown returns (nine on punts, two on kickoffs).

Both Sayers and Metcalf possess the innate ability to sense where the tackling pursuit is coming from (I'm sure you've heard the phrase, "He has eyes in the back of his head") and move quickly away from it. A great returner follows his initial blocks and, after that, relies on his open-field running ability or simply runs as fast as he can through the first opening. Both Sayers and Metcalf were excellent at changing directions, stopping and going, and giving tacklers a small target by twisting their bodies sideways.

Teams want their kick returners to be able to run a 4.3-second 40-yard dash, but also to have enough body control to be able to utilize that speed properly. Being the fastest man doesn't always work because there's rarely a free lane in which to run. Usually, somebody is in position to tackle the kickoff returner. Great returners make a few of these potential tacklers miss them in the open field.

It's best to keep two players deep to receive the kick. This way, the player not catching the ball can serve as the initial blocker. Some teams place just one man back, but only teams with truly gifted returners like the aforementioned Eric Metcalf should consider that strategy. Teams should place experienced returners in return positions — never a rookie.

Understanding the kickoff return rules

The following rules govern the kickoff return:

- ✔ No member of the receiving team can cross the 40-yard line (or the 45-yard line in college football) until the ball is kicked.
- ✔ Blockers cannot block opponents below the waist or in the back.

✔ If the momentum of the kick takes the receiver into the end zone, he doesn't have to run the ball out. Instead, he can down the ball in the end zone for a touchback, in which case his team takes it at the 20-yard line.

✔ If the receiving team catches the ball in the end zone and downs the ball, the kickoff results in a touchback, and the receiving team's offense takes possession on its own 20-yard line.

✔ If the receiver catches the ball in the field of play and retreats into the end zone, he must bring the ball out of the end zone. If he's tackled in the end zone, the kicking team records a safety and collects two points.

Setting up a blocking wedge

Good return teams set up a *blocking wedge* with two or three huge players aligned together. These huge players are usually offensive linemen, but I've seen defensive linemen be part of the wedge, too. These players stand together, separated by two arm lengths, between the 15- and 25-yard lines, approximately 10 yards in front of the kick returner. They must adjust their position on the field based on the depth of the kickoff. Most coaches like their wedge blockers to do a 90-degree turn and then accelerate forward prior to making blocking contact.

The wedge's objective is to assist the return man in breaking free from the initial pursuit by creating a hole or lane in which the returner can run freely. Coaches want these blockers to remain on their feet and work together to free their man.

Figure 12-2 shows a common kickoff return strategy involving a blocking wedge, the Trap 3 Right. This strategy involves five blockers, listed as tackle (T), guard (G), and center (C), slightly inside the 45-yard line. Four other blockers (A, B, C, and D) are deeper, aligned between their own 25- and 30-yard lines. Once the ball is kicked, C and D retreat to a position 10 yards in front of R2, who has the ball near the right hash. (X marks the receiving spot.) R1 on the left hash runs faster, positioning himself with C and D to form a blocking wedge. B runs horizontally and blocks kick cover man 3, and blocker A retreats in order to prevent any cover man from breaking through and tackling R2. Then R2 has the option of running ahead or cutting back to his left. R2 must find his own running lane if one doesn't materialize between C and D.

Covering the kickoff return

Coverage men (the guys whose job is to tackle the kick returner) must be aggressive, fast, and reckless in their pursuit. They must avoid the blocks of the return team. Special teams coaches believe that a solid tackle on the opening kickoff can set the tone for a game, especially if the return man is stopped inside his own 20-yard line.

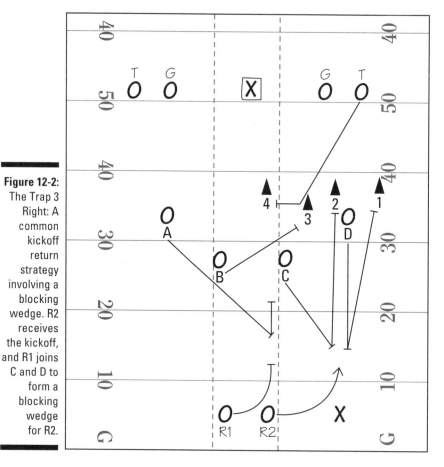

Figure 12-2: The Trap 3 Right: A common kickoff return strategy involving a blocking wedge. R2 receives the kickoff, and R1 joins C and D to form a blocking wedge for R2.

Hidden yardage

Jimmy Johnson, who has coached the Dallas Cowboys and the Miami Dolphins, calls positive return yards *hidden yardage*. For example, Johnson equates a 50-yard advantage in punt/kick return yards to five first downs. In some games, it may be extremely difficult for an offense to produce a lot of first downs, so return yardage is key.

Johnson says that his teams have won games while making only 12 first downs because they

played great both defensively and on special teams. The team with the best field position throughout the game, attained by excellent punt and kick coverage, generally wins, Johnson says. Also, he believes that if you have a great punt and kick returner, opponents may elect to kick the ball out-of-bounds, thus giving your offense fine field position.

Kicking field goals and PATs

Most special teams scoring involves the placekicker or field goal kicker. During the 1997 NFL season, the 30 teams attempted 906 field goals and converted 708 of them, a .781 percentage. For the last 20 years, field goal kicking has played a pivotal, often decisive, role in the outcomes of NFL games. Kickers can become instant heroes by converting a last-second field goal to win a game.

Once an NFL offense has driven to within 30 yards of scoring a touchdown, the coaches know that the team is definitely within easy field goal range. In the 1997 NFL season, field goal kickers converted 263 of 277 attempts inside 30 yards, an impressive .949 percentage. Between 30 and 39 yards, NFL kickers made 83.9 percent of their attempts. However, teams saw a significant drop-off beyond 39 yards. Kickers made only 169 of 271 (.624) attempts between 40 and 49 yards. Despite the decline in accuracy, you can see that coaches were still willing to at least attempt to score three points, knowing that a missed field goal gives the defensive team the ball at the spot of the kick.

Reliable kickers can claim a job for a decade or more because their ability to convert in the clutch is so essential. For example, Gary Anderson completed his 16th NFL season in 1997 with his third team and set a league record when he made his 385th career field goal. In another NFL record set in 1997, kicker Norm Johnson extended his streak of consecutive PATs to 255, bettering the old mark by 21 kicks.

Who does what

On field goal and extra point (PAT) attempts, the kicker has a holder and a snapper. He has a wall of nine blockers in front of him, including the snapper, who is generally the offensive center. On many teams, the player who snaps the ball for punts also snaps for these kicks. The snap should take approximately 1.3 seconds to reach the holder, who kneels on his right knee about 7 yards behind the line of scrimmage. He catches the ball with his right hand and places the ball directly on the playing surface. Tees are allowed in high school and college football, but not in the NFL. The holder uses his left index finger to hold the ball in place.

The kicker's leg action, the striking motion, takes about 1.5 milliseconds, and the ball should be airborne for 2 seconds after being snapped.

It's good!

For an extra point or a field goal try to be ruled good, the kicked ball must clear the crossbar (by going over it) and pass between (or directly above) the uprights of the goalpost, which is placed 10 yards from the goal line and positioned directly in the center of the field. Two officials, one on each side of the goalpost, stand by to visually judge whether points have been scored on the kick.

Most college and NFL teams expect to convert every extra point, considering that the ball is snapped from the 2- or 3-yard line. A field goal is a different matter because of the distance involved.

The rules

A few rules pertain strictly to the kicking game. Most of them decide what happens when a kick is blocked or touched by the defensive team. Because three points are so valuable, special teams place a great emphasis on making a strong effort to block these kicks. The team kicking the ball works just as diligently to protect its kicker, making sure that he has a chance to score.

The byproduct of these attempts often leads to the defensive team *running into* or *roughing* the kicker. This infraction occurs when a player hits the kicker's body or leg while he's in the act of kicking. A penalty also is enforced when a player knocks down the kicker immediately after he makes the kick. The rules are fairly strict because the kicker cannot defend himself while he's concentrating on striking the ball.

Here are some other rules regarding field goals and extra points:

- A blocked field goal recovered behind the line of scrimmage may be advanced by either team.

- A blocked field goal that crosses the line of scrimmage may be advanced only by the defense. If the ball is muffed or fumbled, however, it's a free ball.

- On a blocked PAT in an NFL game, the ball is immediately dead. Neither team is allowed to advance it. In college football, the defense can pick up the ball and return it to the kicking team's end zone for a two-point score (if they're lucky).

- The guards may lock legs with the snapper only. The right guard places his left foot inside the snapper's right foot after both players assume a stance so that their legs cross, or lock. The left guard places his right foot on the opposite side of the center. By locking legs, the guards help stabilize the snapper from an all-out rush on his head and shoulders while he leans down over the ball. All other players on the line of scrimmage must have their feet outside the feet of the players next to them.

- The holder or kicker may not be roughed or run into during or after a kick. The penalty for doing so is 5 yards and an automatic first down for the kicking team.

- Roughing the holder or kicker is legal if the kick is blocked, the ball touches the ground during the snap, or the holder fumbles the ball before it's kicked.

- On a missed field goal, the ball returns to the line of scrimmage if it rolls dead in the field of play, is touched by the receiving team, goes into the end zone, or hits the goalpost. The defensive team assumes possession at that time.

A lost art

Before the ball was made thinner and distinctly more oblong to assist passers, the plumped version was easily drop-kicked. Yes, players would simply drop the ball and kick it after it touched the ground. The action was perfectly timed.

The last NFL drop-kick attempt occurred in the 1941 championship game, when the Chicago Bears' Ray "Scooter" McLean successfully drop-kicked an extra point conversion. The current rules still allow drop-kicking, but the ball's tapered design probably negates anyone trying a drop-kick. Jim McMahon, Chicago's starting quarterback in Super Bowl XX, converted many drop-kicks in practices before he retired, but none of his coaches would allow him to attempt a drop-kick in a game.

Blocking field goals and PATs

Blocking either a PAT or a field goal attempt can change the momentum of a game and eventually decide its outcome. To block kicks, players must be dedicated, athletic, and willing to physically sacrifice themselves for the good of the team. To have a successful block, everyone must do his job.

Blocked kicks may appear easy, but a play such as the middle field goal block (see Figure 12-3) requires talented defensive linemen who can win the battle up front. These defensive linemen position themselves near the center snapping the ball because the quickest way to any field goal or extra point attempt is up the middle. With the ball 7 yards off the line of scrimmage, teams place their best pass-rushers — like Bruce Smith of the Buffalo Bills — in the middle, believing that one of them can penetrate the blocking line a couple of yards and then raise his arms, hoping to tip the booted ball with his hands. If the kicker doesn't get the proper trajectory, the kick can be blocked.

In Figure 12-3, the three interior defensive linemen (RT, N, and LT) are over the two guards and the snapper. RT must align on the inside shoulder of the guard opposite him. N lines up directly across from the center. LT aligns on the inside shoulder of the guard opposite him. These linemen want to be able to gain an edge, an angle, on those blockers. Their attempts to block the kick won't work if the two tackles align squarely on top of the guards. They must pick a particular shoulder of the guard and attack to that side.

Both L and R drive through the tackles' outside shoulders. Their objective is to apply enough individual pressure, thus not allowing the tackle to slide down the line and help his buddies inside. Both players should attempt to

Figure 12-3:
In the
middle field
goal block,
the
defensive
linemen
position
themselves
near the
center in
hopes of
penetrating
up the
middle and
blocking
the kick.

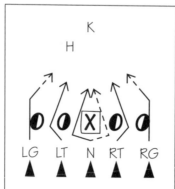

Figure 12-3: In the middle field goal block, the defensive linemen position themselves near the center in hopes of penetrating up the middle and blocking the kick.

block the kick if they break free. If not, they contain late in case of a fake field goal attempt. In containing, they simply jostle with the player blocking them and hold their ground, keeping their eyes on the kicker and holder.

The only chance that the middle block has of succeeding is if the pass-rush moves that the three interior linemen (RT, NT, and LT) make on the offensive linemen work. It's critical that all three players are isolated on one blocker. The defenders can decide to double-team a blocker, hoping that one of them breaks free and penetrates the line.

On other kick blocks, teams attempt to break through from the outside, using two men on one blocker and hoping that the single blocker makes the wrong choice and allows the inside rusher to get free.

Soccer-style kicking

One of the biggest developments in kicking came in the late 1950s, when soccer-style kickers began surfacing at U.S. colleges. Before the soccer style came into vogue, the straight-on method was the only way to kick a football. This American style of kicking was totally different. American kickers approached the ball from straight on, using their toe, the front of their foot, to strike the ball and lift it off the ground. A soccer-style kicker, on the other hand, approaches the ball from an angle. In soccer, the instep of the kicker's foot makes contact with the ball.

Like most everything else, football coaches have Americanized soccer's kicking style to suit the shape of the football. Your foot should be turned down and out upon impact with the ball. The top part of your foot, where you find solid bone cartilage, should strike the ball. On your shoe, the striking point is the middle of the laces. Your foot is also wider at this spot, allowing for more square inches of striking power on impact. Hitting the ball with your big toe doesn't allow for full compression, and the ball doesn't travel as far.

Today, you rarely, if ever, see the straight-on style used in the NFL, as Americans have embraced soccer and the benefits of this style. In 1997, not one NFL kicker used the straight-on method. For starters, the soccer style creates quicker lift off the ground. But basically, it has simply stuck and become the pervasive kicking style.

What makes the soccer style of kicking useful is how accurate soccer kickers are. In NFL history, eight of the top ten field goal kickers of all time are ex-soccer players. The most accurate ones convert 75 percent of their field goal attempts and rarely miss within 40 yards of the goalpost. No straight-on kicker ranks among the NFL's all-time top 40 most accurate field goal kickers. George Blanda, who ranks sixth all-time with 335 field goals, was a straight-on kicker. But he was a 50/50 kicker, with a field goal percentage of 52.5. Conversely, current Cincinnati Bengals kicker Doug Pelfry enters the 1998 season with the NFL's all-time best accuracy mark of 80.6 percent (116 of 144 field goal attempts).

Punting

Punting occurs when a team's offense is struggling, which means that the offense is failing to generate positive yardage and is stuck on fourth down. Teams punt on fourth down when they're in their own territory or are barely across midfield. By punting, the team relinquishes possession of the ball.

One of the most difficult aspects of football to understand initially is why teams punt the ball. A team has four downs to gain 10 yards, and after accomplishing that, it receives a new set of downs. Why not gamble on fourth down to gain the necessary yardage to maintain possession of the football?

Field position is the answer.

Unless it's beyond the opponent's 40-yard line, a team would rather punt the ball on fourth down, hoping to keep the opponent as far from its end zone, and consequently scoring points, as possible. Teams punt routinely at the beginning of the game, especially when there's no score or the score is close. Teams tend to rely on their defenses in such situations, believing that the benefits of field position outweigh any offensive risk-taking. Punting in these situations is not a conservative tactic, but a smart one.

Are you kicking dead center?

Here's a nifty trick to learn whether you're kicking the ball squarely, or "dead center," as they say:

Divide the ball's length in half with white tape. Then do the same with tape around the middle. Then divide the lower quarter of the ball with tape. Now dab some washable white paint on the toe area of your kicking shoe. After every kick, examine the ball for paint; it's the best way to find out exactly where you're hitting the ball. The key is to put as much white paint as possible on the center spot of the ball on the lower quarter. For example, if the paint is right of center, the ball is probably going left, and vice versa.

Punting is a critical part of football because some coaches believe that it can change the course of a game. And no facet of the game alters field position more than punting. In the NFL, each punt is worth an average of 36 yards per exchange. However, some punters are capable of punting farther than that, thus pinning opponents deep in their own end of the field and far, far away from a score.

Setting up and kicking the ball

The punter stands about 15 yards behind the line of scrimmage and catches the ball after the snapper hikes it. The center's snap of the ball must reach the punter, who generally stands 15 yards behind the line of scrimmage, in 0.8 seconds. Every tenth of a second longer further risks a blocked punt.

The punter takes two steps, drops the ball toward his kicking foot, and makes contact. This act requires a lot of practice and coordination because the velocity of the punter's leg prior to striking the ball, as well as the impact of his foot on the ball, is critical. The punter needs to strike the ball in the center to achieve maximum distance. When the punter strikes the ball off the side of his foot, the ball flies sideways. Such a mistake is called a *shank*.

A punt, from the snap of the ball to the action of the punter, requires no more than 2 seconds. Most teams want the punter to catch, drop, and punt the ball in under 1.3 seconds.

VIEWER TIP

Today's punters must be adept at kicking in all weather conditions and must strive for *hang time* (4.5 seconds in the air) and for booming the ball at least 45 yards from the line of scrimmage. Most punters also serve in a dual role as holder for the field goal kicker.

Key performers on the punt team

The punter isn't the only important player during a punt play — although it may seem like it sometimes, especially on a bad punt. Following are some of the other key performers:

- **Center or snapper:** Must be accurate with his snap and deliver the ball to where the punter wants it. On most teams, he makes the blocking calls for the interior linemen, making sure that no one breaks through to block the punt.

- **Wings:** The players on both ends of the line of scrimmage, generally 1-yard deep behind the outside leg of the end or tackle. They must block the outside rushers but worry more about anyone breaking free inside of them.

- **Ends:** There's one end on each side of the line of scrimmage, and they're isolated outside the wings at least 10 to 12 yards. On some teams, these players are called *gunners*. Their job is run downfield and tackle the punt returner. Often, two players block each end at the line of scrimmage in hopes of giving the punt returner more time to advance the ball.

- **Personal protector:** The last line of protection for the punter. The personal protector usually lines up 5 yards behind the line of scrimmage. If five or more defensive players line up to one side of the snapper, the personal protector shifts his attention to that side and makes sure that no one breaks through to block the punt. Most coaches prefer that a fullback or safety play this position. Regardless, the personal protector must be a player who can react quickly to impending trouble. The personal protector makes adjustment calls for the ends and wings.

Figure 12-4 shows a basic punt formation involving these players against what coaches call *man coverage*. X is the snapper; he stands over the ball. PP is the punter's personal protector, and P is the punter. The wings are labeled with Ws, and the Es (ends) are on the line of scrimmage about 10 to 12 yards away from the wings.

Punt rules

As with everything else in football, there are rules for the punt:

- In the pros, only the players lined up on the ends are permitted to cross the line of scrimmage after the ball is snapped to the punter and before the ball is punted. In college and high school, all players on the punting team may cross the LOS after the snap.

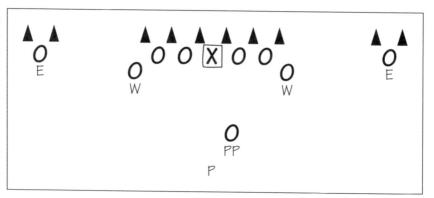

Figure 12-4:
A basic punt formation involving a personal protector (PP), ends (E), and wings (W).

✔ Once the ball is punted, everyone on the punting team is allowed to cross the line of scrimmage with the intent of tackling the player fielding the punt (the *punt returner*).

✔ Players are not allowed to block below the waist on punt returns. Such an illegal block is a 15-yard penalty and is marked off from where the punt team gained possession of the ball.

✔ If a punt does not cross the line of scrimmage, either team may pick up the ball and run toward its end zone.

✔ A *touchback* occurs when a punt touches the end zone before the ball touches a player on either team, or when the punt returner catches the ball in the end zone and drops to one knee. The ball is then spotted on the receiving team's 20-yard line.

✔ Either team can *down* a punt after it hits the ground or after one of its players touches the ball past the line of scrimmage. To down the ball, a player must be in possession of the ball, stop his forward movement, and drop to one knee. Such action leads to an official blowing his whistle, signaling the end of action.

✔ A partially blocked punt that crosses the line of scrimmage is treated like a typical punt.

Several times during a game, you see the punt returner stand and simply catch the ball. He doesn't run. In this case, he's probably calling for a *fair catch*. To signal for a fair catch, the player who's preparing to receive the punt must clearly extend his arm over his head and then wave it from side to side to let the officials and the defensive players know that he doesn't plan to run with the ball after catching it. After signaling for a fair catch, the punt returner cannot advance the ball. If the defenders tackle him after he signals a fair catch, the kicking team incurs a 15-yard penalty.

However, the player signaling for a fair catch is not obligated to catch the ball. His only worry is not touching it. Once he touches it or loses control and the ball hits the ground, either team is allowed to recover the ball.

If the returner "muffs a kick," meaning that he fails to gain possession, the punting team may not advance the ball if they recover it. If the returner gains possession and then fumbles, however, the punting team may advance the ball.

Punting out of trouble

When I played with the Raiders in Super Bowl XVIII, our punter, Ray Guy, won the game for us. Now, what role can a punter have when you beat the Washington Redskins 38-9? Well, after a bad snap early in the game, Guy jumped as high as he could and grabbed the ball one-handed. When he landed, he boomed his punt way downfield. We were deep in our own territory, and if the ball had gone over Guy's head, the Redskins might have recovered it in our end zone for a touchdown. Who knows?

Guy was a fabulous athlete. He was a first-round draft choice (who ever heard of a punter being taken in the first round?) and a tremendous secondary performer at Southern Mississippi. All I remember about him was that he was like "Cool Hand Luke," the role Paul Newman played in the movie. No matter the situation, even if he was punting from our own end zone, Guy never got frazzled. In all my years in the NFL, he was head and shoulders above every punter I saw. He was such an exceptional athlete that he served as the quarterback on the scout team in practices, but all he ever did for us in games was punt. Guy led the NFL in punting during three seasons and retired after 14 years with a 42.4-yard average.

Like Ray Guy, a punter must remain calm and cool when punting out of trouble — that is, anywhere deep in his own territory. Any poor punt — a shank or a flat-out miss — can result in the opponent scoring an easy touchdown, especially if they get the ball 40 yards away from their end zone. Although the result isn't as bad, poor punts inevitably mean an automatic three points via a field goal. A dropped snap can mean a defensive score; ditto for a blocked punt — and little sympathy when that punter returns to the sideline. In 1997, NFL teams averaged slightly more than five punts per game, so coaches and players fully expect punts to happen without a hitch.

Punt returning: A dangerous art

Punt returning isn't always as exciting as returning a kickoff because the distance between the team punting and the punt returner isn't as great. A punt returner needs either a line-drive punt or a long punt (45 yards or more from the line of scrimmage) with under four seconds of hang time — or spectacular blocking by his teammates — to achieve significant positive return yards.

To produce positive return yards, the receiving team must concentrate on effectively blocking the outside pursuit men and the center — the players who have the most direct access to the punt returner. The rest of the unit must peel back and attempt to set up a wall or some interference for the returner. A good return happens almost immediately, because every second counts. Whenever the return unit can hold up four or five players from the punting team, the returner has a chance.

A returner needs to be a fearless competitor, willing to catch a punt at or near full speed and continue his run forward. If the defense isn't blocked, the collisions between a returner and a tackler can be extremely violent, leading to injuries and concussions.

A returner's other necessary qualities are superior hands and tremendous concentration. Because of the closeness of the coverage and the bodies flying around, the returner usually catches the ball in traffic. Several players are generally within a yard of him, so the sounds of players blocking and running tend to surround him. He must close out these sounds in order to catch the ball and maintain his composure. To catch the ball and then run with it, under such conditions, takes guts. A returner's final fear is losing the ball via a fumble, thus putting his opponent in favorable field position.

Punt returns during the 1997 NFL season averaged 9.9 yards. The two best punt returners were Jermaine Lewis of the Baltimore Ravens and Darrien Gordon of the Denver Broncos. Lewis led the NFL with a 15.6 average while Gordon returned three punts for touchdowns. Amazingly, both players returned two punts for touchdowns in the same quarter of the same game. Only nine players in NFL history have had two punt returns for touchdowns in the same game.

Truly special

In 1986, the NFL and its players began awarding Pro Bowl invitations to each conference's best special teams player. Mainly, the award winner is the player who's best at covering punts and kickoffs — a fearless open-field tackler. Steve Tasker of the Buffalo Bills was even named the MVP of the 1993 Pro Bowl for forcing a fumble and blocking a field goal attempt, preserving a three-point victory for his AFC teammates. Peter King, the senior pro football writer for *Sports Illustrated,* believes that Tasker is worthy of being voted into the Hall of Fame because he was a dominant special teams player. Prior to the 1999 vote, no player has ever been inducted into the Hall of Fame based exclusively on his special teams contributions. King's support, however, might swing some votes in Tasker's direction someday.

Chapter 13

Coaches, General Managers, and Other Important Folks

In This Chapter

▶ What coaches do

▶ Different coaching styles

▶ The functions of general managers and the front-office staff

▶ Scouting opponents and college prospects

▶ How trainers take care of players

I'd be the first to tell you that players win championships. But I say that with a little hesitation. Depending on the football franchise, a coach, a general manager, or even an owner has the ability to put the team in the best possible position to win. Each person's primary function is to help the team win, assisting the players in any way possible.

I'm proud to say that I became an All-Pro player because of Earl Leggett, who coached the defensive linemen for the Raiders. I had quickness and strength, the skills that I needed to play in the National Football League, but Earl Leggett was the one who taught me how to harness my ability. He showed me how to anticipate an offense's intentions and use my talents on every single play. He was my mentor.

Probably hundreds of coaches, maybe not as gifted as Leggett, have the same impact on players throughout high school, college, and pro football. If a player is willing to commit himself to a coach's system, a good coach can develop him into a very good player.

In this chapter, I discuss how coaches, from the head coach to the strength coach, work together toward one goal: winning. And for NFL coaches to win, they need a personnel department — headed by a general manager and supported by ownership — that has the ability to scout and find players and then sign them. A college coach needs the support of the school's administration to be able to recruit good players. I guess I'm saying that there's more to playing football and winning than simply the players — coaches, general managers, scouts, and all the rest play important roles on winning teams.

Coaches

Every army has a general and a group of lieutenants, which is similar to a football team's head coach and coaching staff. The coaches are the leaders of the team, the men who put the players in the position to win games. They decide what offenses and defenses the team will use, and good coaches devise these schemes to get the most out of the talent of their players. In the NFL, the coach is highly visible because the television cameras show him on the sidelines every Sunday or Monday night.

Some coaches are stars, like Miami Dolphins coach Jimmy Johnson, New York Jets coach Bill Parcells, and Pittsburgh Steelers coach Bill Cowher. All three men have perfect personalities for coaching football because they are charismatic and emotional. Not only do they know the game, but they also understand how to motivate players, make them tough, and extract every ounce of desire and ability from them. A great coach can make a difference.

I'm using NFL coaches as examples because covering them is part of my job, and I know these men personally. I can relate to their powerful impact on a football team. However, hundreds of high school and college coaches have the same impact on their teams. Coaches are special. They devote countless hours to preparing practice schedules and game strategies, working with players in practice and in film sessions, and dealing with them one-on-one when necessary. In high school and college, a coach can be stern and fair like a father. And many coaches, like Penn State's Joe Paterno, have earned players' respect because of their success and longevity and are revered for being great for the game of football.

A good coach is a special man, one who is supremely confident in his ability to build, prepare, and focus a team on winning a championship. Because the season is long and the games are few in comparison to other sports, a football coach must cope with the mood swings of his players during the week and know when and how to be assertive and when to be relaxed. He sets the tone for his team. The assistant coaches must believe in the overall focus of the program because they deal individually with the players in practice groups.

What coaches do

Though high school and college football teams are restricted to a certain number of off-season practice days, NFL coaching staffs work virtually year-round making free-agency decisions, scouting potential draft choices, monitoring selective mini-camps (three or four days of on-field practice), and attending countless organizational meetings. Most NFL coaches take their vacations in late June and early July, right before the opening of training camp. And from that point on, they work virtually every day, although some days aren't as full as others, throughout the season.

With the head coach leading the way, the coaches meet during the players' off-day, preparing the game plan for the next week and reviewing hours of film of their own players and the opposition, looking for tendencies, strengths, and weaknesses. Before players take the practice field, they may attend meetings for a couple of hours (quarterbacks a whole lot more) to review last week's game and then discuss how they will deal with this week's opponent. During training camp, the coaching staff dissect what they want to accomplish during the season in all phases of the game: offense, defense, and special teams. At the same time, they test to see how the players are adapting to specific plays and strategies. From there, they refine their plan, tinkering with minute details in order to guarantee success.

In the NFL, every play is analyzed and dissected until the coaching staff knows exactly how they want to instruct the players on the practice field. A coach can break down a single play on videotape to show a player taking the wrong first step, or backing up too much, or angling his shoulders improperly, or failing to recognize a specific read.

Coaching personnel

Almost every football team has more than one coach — 22 positions plus special teams is a lot to monitor. The Dallas Cowboys, for example, have two coaches monitoring special teams: One coach handles the punter and placekicker, and another coach handles coverages and kick protection. The typical NFL team averages 12 assistant coaches. (A college team generally has 6 to 8 full-time assistants and 2 or 3 graduate assistants.) Here is a common NFL coaching staff:

- ✔ **Head coach:** The main man who gets most of the credit for winning — or losing. Most head coaches are over 40 years old and have 20 or more seasons of playing and coaching experience. Their styles of coaching vary. Some head coaches demand control over what alignments and plays the team uses on defense and offense. Others delegate one aspect of the game plan, preferring to focus on their particular expertise, whether it's defense or offense. Most head coaches are experts on one side of the ball or the other. Depending on the franchise's power structure and ownership, the head coach may have a lot of flexibility and control over personnel, or he may have a rather limited role.

- ✔ **Offensive coordinator:** The coach in charge of the offensive players. He usually calls the plays and works directly with the quarterbacks. He's responsible for developing the offensive game plan (what plays he believes will be successful against the upcoming opponent) and works with the head coach on how practice is organized, especially if some of the plays are unusual or somewhat unfamiliar to the offensive personnel. Some coordinators do all the work and are becoming almost as valuable as the head coach. On some NFL teams, the owner is as involved in the hiring of the offensive coordinator as in the hiring of the head coach.

- **Defensive coordinator:** The coach in charge of the defensive players. He usually decides what defensive schemes to run. Like the offensive coordinator, the defensive coordinator meets with half the team on a typical practice day and prepares them for the upcoming opponent. I've always thought that a good coordinator is one who can adapt his system to his players' talents rather than the other way around. But sometimes teams want to find players that fit their particular system. The best coordinators are the ones who are really flexible and simply strive to put their players in the best possible situation to succeed.

- **Special teams coach:** The coach who supervises the kickers, punters, kick return team, field goal protection team, punt block team, and so on. Generally, he is coaching the younger players on a team, and he must find a way to motivate them to do their jobs, considering that many of the special teams' stars are backups and reserves, players not talented enough to be offensive or defensive starters. On some units, the special teams coach may have starters mixed in with rookies, and he must find a way to get these players to complement one another. He must study the strengths and weaknesses of how teams return kicks and cover kicks. Also, he studies film to discover whether a team is particularly weak in kick protection so that he can prepare his team to attempt a block in a specific game.

- **Quarterback coach:** An assistant coach who monitors the physical and mental aspects of a quarterback's game. He works on the quarterback's footwork, pass-drop technique, and throwing motion. He makes sure that a quarterback doesn't fall into bad mental or physical habits. In training camp, if the starting quarterback is an experienced veteran, the quarterback coach may devote extra hours to the backup and third-string quarterback, hoping to develop them for the future and prepare them to play in an emergency. On some teams, the quarterback coach serves as a sounding board between the quarterback and the head coach. On NFL teams, the head coach and the quarterback are usually under the greatest scrutiny.

- **Offensive line coach:** A coach who works with the offensive linemen and generally has a solid understanding of the team's running game. The line coach and the offensive coordinator spend time discussing what running plays may work, depending on what the line coach views are his unit's strengths and weaknesses against the upcoming opponent. A good offensive line coach can mold five blockers, all with different or varied levels of skill, into a solid, efficient unit. On some teams, the line coach is more valuable than the offensive coordinator.

- **Defensive line coach:** A coach who works exclusively with the defensive linemen. He works on individual technique (run stopping, gap control, pass rushing, and so on) and whatever stunts the coordinator wants from these players.

✔ **Linebacker coach:** A coach who works with linebackers and, depending on the style of defense, ranks a step below the coordinator. Defenses that exclusively utilize four linebackers need a coach who can teach all the variations necessary for this scheme to work. This coach must work on tackling, pass-rushing off the corner, and particular pass coverage drops.

✔ **Secondary coach:** A coach who works with the defensive backs and must have a total understanding of pass offenses. He works on all aspects of pass coverage, from footwork and deep zone drops to how to prepare players for the particular receivers that they will face.

✔ **Strength coach:** A coach who specializes in weight training and conditioning. He makes sure that the players are strong and in shape throughout the season and often coordinates off-season training programs. A strength coach also works with team doctors to prepare and monitor rehabilitation exercises following player surgeries.

A team may also have specific position coaches, such as a receiver or running backs coach, depending on how many coaches the team can afford to keep on staff. On smaller staffs, the head coach also may serve as the offensive coordinator, or the special teams coach may also be the strength coach. On some large NFL staffs, the head coach calls the offensive plays instead of the offensive coordinator.

Coaching styles and philosophies

Without question, a coach can have a dramatic impact on a football team. Some coaches want to control the emotional pulse of their teams; others attempt to use their influence via selected team leaders with whom they establish good rapport. A coach needs to stand apart as an authority figure, especially if he coaches younger players. He makes the rules, and the players must follow his orders. Still, a coach can't be as demanding as an army sergeant because he wants his players to feel comfortable talking to him about any serious off-the-field problems that they may be facing. A pro coach may allow himself to become friendly with his players and treat them like the adults they are.

No one set standard for being a head coach exists, nor is there a particular philosophy that a coach should adhere to. Good head coaches learn from the men for whom they have worked in the past, absorbing the good qualities and tossing out the bad ones that don't work with their personality. A coach needs to be himself and be true to how he would want to be treated. Players can spot a phony as soon as he walks into the team meeting room.

The yell-your-head-off coach

Players don't like coaches who yell and scream all the time. But I've known some coaches who can communicate only by screaming. They're not screaming because their angry; screaming is the only way that they can get their point across to a player. The screamers are generally defensive coaches; offensive coaches tend to be calmer and more cerebral.

Many of these screamers are good coaches. When Jimmy Johnson screams at any of his Miami Dolphins, everyone at practice knows that he means business. Johnson isn't a screamer by nature, but he, like many other coaches, yells when a player or unit constantly repeats the same mistake. A coach can be patient for only so long. These vocal coaches believe that yelling is the only way their instructions are going to sink into a player's head. Granted, players can barely think on the practice field when their bodies are tired and aching from a long day, so that's why some frustrated coaches start to yell. It's a sign of exasperation.

Here are some examples of the yell-your-head-off coaching style:

- ✔ Whenever these coaches believe that their teams have been penalized unfairly, you can bet that they're yelling at the referee or some official along the sidelines.

- ✔ Whenever a player misses an assignment and causes a critical play to fail, you may see these coaches actually grab the player and tell him, inches away from his face, how and why he screwed up.

- ✔ These coaches often grab a player's face mask and rattle his cage before telling him how poorly he's playing or practicing.

- ✔ These coaches throw things. Coaches who scream a lot love to toss their hats, clipboards, or whatever they're holding to get everyone's attention.

The kinder, gentler coach

You find kinder, gentler coaches on the youth level and in high school football, and a few in college football. They rarely yell and seem more interested in raising good football players than worrying about their own win-loss record. These coaches work at schools where football's reality is not in how many games are won, but how the game is played. Hundreds of high schools and colleges fit into this category, where football is not a big-time operation. The administrators believe in the values of the game and want to have it on campus.

I've seen NFL assistant coaches who use this kinder, gentler coaching style. They mostly coach receivers, quarterbacks, and kickers. They are more cerebral and deal with players who have a lot to learn or have fragile egos. They realize that yelling defeats the learning process and detracts from a player's concentration. Most great coaches have shown glimpses of this kinder, gentler side to their players, but not for long. Football is a tough, physical game, and nice guys do finish last in football.

The smash-mouth football coach

Smash-mouth coaches love nothing better than to see a tremendous block by an offensive lineman and then watch their running back gain 10 yards while running over the opposition. Most of these coaches began as defensive coaches, and they believe in dominating the line of scrimmage and want their defense to decide the outcome of a game. On offense, they'd rather win by running the football. Bill Cowher of the Pittsburgh Steelers and Bill Parcells of the New York Jets are examples of the smash-mouth coach. They prepare their teams to be the stronger, dominant teams, and that's why they're successful.

Here are some examples of the smash-mouth coaching style:

✔ When the game is close and the offense needs to convert a play on fourth-and-1, these coaches are likely to gamble, believing that their offensive line and running back can pick up the first down.

✔ These coaches are more apt to continue to run a successful play until the opposition stops it.

✔ These coaches' football teams usually focus on both the offensive and the defensive linemen. Their teams may not always win the game, but they plan on winning the war along the line of scrimmage.

✔ These coaches rarely waiver from their beliefs in how to approach a game or a particular opponent. They're very strong-minded coaches.

The offensive genius coach

You see a lot of offensive genius coaches in the NFL. Mike Shanahan, who directed the Denver Broncos to their 1998 Super Bowl win, typifies this caliber of coach. His coaching counterpart in Super Bowl XXXII, Green Bay's Mike Holmgren, uses the same approach. An offensive genius is a coach who seems to have an unlimited ability to develop new plays; defensive coaches know that these coaches will try more than one new play or variation of an old play every week. Offensive coaches aren't always viewed as tough guys because they are so cerebral. But both Holmgren and Shanahan are also tough guys; though their minds may be working overtime on the sidelines, they don't tolerate a lack of discipline or shoddy play on the football field.

This kind of coach is constantly looking for an edge on the field. One example of Shanahan's genius took place in the 1997 season when the Broncos had to beat the Kansas City Chiefs to reach the Super Bowl. The Chiefs have a great pass-rusher in Derrick Thomas, and they prefer to line up Thomas on the weak side, away from the tight end. The Chiefs have a strong linebacker, Wayne Simmons, who demolishes most tight ends.

Prior to the snap, Shanahan would move his tight end off the line of scrimmage and motion him over until he was in front of Derrick Thomas. Then he'd call a running play directly at Thomas. That simple formation adjustment prior to the snap gave Shanahan's offense the matchups that he wanted on a running a play. In such a short period of time, Thomas and Simmons couldn't switch sides before the ball was snapped. Denver had success running at Thomas while negating the Chiefs' greatest asset, his pass-rushing ability.

Here are some typical actions of the offensive genius coach:

- ✔ These coaches generally wear headsets on the sidelines to communicate with their assistants upstairs in the press box, and they always have a *playsheet* (the game plan of offensive plays) in their hands. They are more involved with the offensive team than the defensive team during a game.

- ✔ These coaches tend to be more thoughtful and under control during sideline sessions with their players. They don't rattle easily.

- ✔ When they talk during practice, these coaches explain the whole play and show how a small aspect can lead to a gigantic reward. For example, each player's alignment dictates a defensive alignment response. Anticipating the defense's alignment to a certain formation or pass route can lead to an opening to spring a big play.

- ✔ At the training facility, these coaches work alone most of the time. They have a daily staff meeting, but they like to think and tinker with the offense for hours on their own.

What coaches do when they're not yelling on the sidelines

Coaches have a lot of work to do. An NFL head coach spends his days in the off-season preparing practice schedules for training camp and the regular season. Coaches at all levels prepare playbooks — many include more than 200 plays for the offense alone — that every player receives. They meet with the general manager and other college and pro scouts regarding personnel — whom to trade for, whom to acquire, and whom to release. I know a lot of talented coaches whose days are so long that they actually sleep on their office couch rather than go home at night.

The college coach devotes much of his off-season to recruiting high school players and hosting clinics for high school coaches. Recruiting means visiting a potential player in his hometown (which necessitates a lot of traveling) and meeting with his parents, guardians, and high school coaches. During the season, a college coach may even show up at a Friday night game to check out a player.

College and high school coaches meet regularly with their school's athletic director and administrators regarding financial budgets and player eligibility status. They oversee travel schedules and are involved in picking hotels and

Being unemployed

Coaches work long hours because they're usually under enormous pressure to win. If they don't win, even on the high school level, they will be fired. There's constant changeover. From the end of the 1995 season to the start of the 1998 season, 19 NFL head coaches lost their jobs. Some teams, like the Oakland Raiders, are on their third head coach in that short span of time.

When a head coach is fired, usually his coaching staff of 10 to 13 assistants is also out of work. Sometimes, a head coach saves his job but is forced by management to fire some or all of his assistants. This situation doesn't happen a lot, but it does occur enough to make assistant coaches realize that coaching is more about business than it is about loyalty. Besides being fired, coaching staffs are constantly turning over as assistants move on to different teams and receive promotions to coordinator jobs. Changing teams creates a lot of upheaval for a coach's family, especially if he's married with children. Coaches who begin their careers dreaming of the NFL usually bounce around to several colleges, sometimes as many as eight different jobs, before landing a pro position. And I know good NFL assistants who have worked for five different teams throughout their careers.

meals for road trips. College and high school coaches usually work all day on Sunday, examining film of the weekend's game and preparing for the next week. They have staff meetings in preparation for meeting the players on Monday. And, of course, they devote a lot of time to motivating their players on a daily basis (see Chapter 19 for more info).

Coaches also deal with the media. In the NFL, coaches may have regular press briefings with newspaper, radio, and television reporters every day except Tuesday and Saturday. However, on Saturday, they must meet with network television producers and commentators and discuss their opinions of what may occur in Sunday's or Monday's game. College and high school coaches also deal with local reporters, although on a smaller scale.

General Managers

On many NFL teams, general managers are the eyes and ears of the owner, and they oversee the day-to-day operation of the team. They must be cold and calculating people because they have to make a lot of difficult personnel decisions. They make the player trades and free agent acquisitions, decide what salaries will be paid, and ultimately decide which players to select in the NFL draft. General managers must be excellent judges of every player's ability because they are responsible for doing what's best for the organization. They must have a feel for what the team needs and must be able to work in conjunction with the head coach and his needs.

The best possible scenario is to have a solid general manager and a great head coach, who can put their egos aside and work together. But this situation is very rare these days because head coaches usually want total control over personnel, like Mike Shanahan has in Denver and Bill Parcells has with the New York Jets.

General managers oversee a large front-office staff. Some teams have business, marketing, and public relations personnel. The people who report to the general manager are the following:

- **Capologist:** The person who monitors a team's salary scale and knows how every player's contract fits under the salary cap. When a trade is made or a player is released, the capologist reports how much more (or less) room is available under the cap. This person is also responsible for keeping track of the cap situations of the other teams.

- **Business manager:** This person is responsible for the marketing and overall business needs of a franchise.

- **Contract negotiator** (also known as club vice president): This person is responsible for negotiating with players and their representatives when contracts expire or when the team is pursuing an unsigned free agent player. Often the negotiator and general manager work in tandem on a superstar player or during a contentious salary squabble.

- **Personnel people:** Most teams have a personnel staff that oversees college and professional players. The college personnel chief collects and organizes the files of the many scouts who are traveling the nation, going to practices and games. The pro personnel chief monitors the NFL games, looking for players who may fit well on the team should they be released or offered in trade. A winning franchise may have as many as eight employees in the personnel department, excluding secretaries and office workers.

- **Public relations director:** On most matters, this person is the public voice of the team. He or she relays important information regarding the owner, coaches, and players to the media. He or she oversees the printing of an annual media guide, which includes statistics and personal information for every player and coach on the team. On many teams, this position is very high-profile.

Owners

People buy teams for many different reasons, but most owners want to be public figures. The NFL is structured financially so that every club receives an equal share of television revenue and splits the ticket revenue 60/40 — it's more or less a socialist system. The concept is that the weakest franchise can gross as much revenue as the strongest franchise. A team's revenue from local radio broadcasts, luxury boxes, parking, concessions, and private seat licenses (fans pay a fee for the right to own a season ticket) is not totally shared with the other teams. But the revenue from NFL Properties (income generated from selling NFL logo clothing, hats, and so on) and the Super Bowl is shared. Therefore, you don't have to own a Super Bowl team to do pretty well financially.

After the head coach and the stars on the team, the owner may be the next most visible person. Most football fans know, for example, that Jerry Jones owns the Dallas Cowboys. Jones has his own television show in Dallas and also writes a newspaper column. He's very visible in marketing his football team and is very active in network television negotiations.

However, many franchise owners are rarely interviewed and remain behind the scenes, preferring that their coach and general manager speak for the franchise. The NFL requires one person to own at least 30 percent of a particular franchise and prefers that this person has no financial interest in any other professional sports leagues. Some franchises, like the Baltimore Ravens, Pittsburgh Steelers, and Chicago Bears, have been owned for decades by members of one family. The New York Giants have two owners, each with a 50 percent stake in the franchise.

I don't think that any owner in pro football knows more about the game than Al Davis of the Raiders. In pure Xs and Os, the strategy of a game, Davis is like a coach. He actually started in football as a coach and was a very good one. And in terms of making the financial commitment, Davis is always bringing in great players. He makes every possible effort to improve his team. You can't say that about every NFL owner.

With the value of most franchises at between $150 million and $300 million, you must be extremely wealthy to own an NFL franchise. Although the financial return is generous, many businesspeople would tell you that better ways exist to invest that amount of money. Many NFL owners are actually sports fans, people who love the game as much as their pursuit of financial success. Many of them contribute their time, energy, and financial resources to their respective communities, believing that football is part of their region's social fabric.

Scouts

Every NFL team has all kinds of scouts. Some scouts are responsible for tracking college talent, and some cover the other pro teams. The pro scout's job is to attend NFL games and study a team's opponents.

A team can have a great week practicing, but if the players don't know what to expect from their opponents, they may find themselves behind by 14 points or more in a hurry. Pro scouts exist so that teams can anticipate what each opponent will do. Scouts attend games of upcoming opponents and take copious notes, tracking every offensive and defensive tactic, keeping an eye on key players, noting who gets injured, and so on. Then they bring this information back to the coaches, who may devise parts of their game plans around the scouts' input.

A college scout examines a pro prospect's every move. He times the player in the 40-yard dash, studies his ability and decisions on every play, and monitors him off the field. NFL teams want to know whether a prospect has ever been arrested, and for what crime. They're concerned about illegal drug use and also about how the player performs in the classroom. They want to know about his attitude, his personality, and his approach to football and to life in general. A good scout watches the prospect in practice and games and also watches film of all his games. The scout then interviews the prospect and members of the college coaching staff. He may even interview opposing coaches to find out their views of the player, and athletic trainers to check on a player's past injuries or training room habits. When scouting the top 100 college players, teams often have two or more scouts examine a prospect.

Trainers and Team Doctors

A team isn't very good if its players don't stay healthy or recover quickly if they do get injured. Trainers and team doctors step in to help alleviate these concerns. Most teams have their own orthopedic surgeon and general practitioner. Unless these doctors have total autonomy, they are often put in really difficult positions because their job is to take care of the player, but their employer, who is the owner, wants the player on the field all the time.

A trainer's job is to monitor every injury and then work with the doctor on the rehabilitation process. In some instances, players seek outside medical opinions, especially if the injury is considered serious or the team doctor prescribes surgery. The league monitors injuries and has several medical groups that assist on serious injuries, particularly injuries involving the head and neck.

A trainer also works with the strength trainer to make sure that injured players aren't overextending themselves in the weight room or exercising too much. Most pro and college teams have at least two full-time trainers, and some have part-time assistants for training camps. Trainers are responsible for dispensing and monitoring all medicine prescribed by the doctors and all dietary supplements that players are taking. A trainer also inspects team meals, making sure that they contain the proper proteins and carbohydrates.

The best trainer is trusted by both the players and the coaching staff. The worst thing a trainer can do is to inform the head coach that a certain player isn't hurting as badly as he claims to be. If the trainer feels that way, he must confront the player as well. Players need to believe that the trainer is concerned about their welfare, regardless of how that concern (possibly in the form of keeping a player off the field) may impact the team's win-loss record.

Part V
Football for Everyone

The 5th Wave • By Rich Tennant

"I'm really happy to hear your team won, but I still can't let you on the bus with that thing."

In this part . . .

You can make football a part of your life in many ways. Football exists at many levels, from peewee teams all the way up through the NFL and other professional leagues in Canada, Europe, and all over the world. This part talks about the game and how it works at each level.

Chapter 14

Armchair Quarterbacks and Other Fabulous Fans

In This Chapter

▶ Watching a game at home or in the stands

▶ Keeping up with the game in various ways

▶ Indulging your football fandom

*F*ootball is a great sport because you don't have to be *playing* it to enjoy it. In fact, after you watch a few of the hits that football players take, you may decide that you'd *rather* watch.

This chapter gives you tips for making the most out of the viewing experience, whatever your vantage point. I also tell you about all the ways that you can keep up with your favorite teams when no games are being played — through newspapers, magazines, and even the Internet. Finally, if you want to check out a game in person, I include telephone numbers for major football organizations throughout the U.S.

Following a Game on Television

In a way, television is the best way to watch a football game; you can see up close what's happening on the field and watch replays of the big plays if you missed them the first time around. My innovative bosses at FOX Sports devised the scoreboard clock, which appears in the upper corner of your television screen and gives you a stadium feel. It gives you the score, the down and distance, and how much time is remaining in a particular quarter.

Excellent football analysts, such as FOX's John Madden, add humor along with their insight into the game. They're also good with a device known as a *telestrator,* which allows them to circle players on the screen or to demonstrate how a certain play was successful by diagramming it on the screen.

Knowing what to watch for

I like to watch a game from the inside out; first I look at the quarterback and then I check out the action away from the ball. Because the networks use so many cameras, you can follow the entire game and not miss a play. What's great about television are the replays — you can watch a replay of a critical play from two or three different angles. These different views are often necessary to determine whether a player was in possession of the ball, especially on really close plays involving receptions and fumbles. Also, the different angles help fans interpret whether the officials called the correct penalty, especially on penalties like pass interference (see Chapters 3 and 5).

Here are some tips to help you become a more savvy and informed viewer when you're watching a game on television:

✔ Start at the line of scrimmage. Look wide to see how many receivers you spot and where they're located. Scan to see how many players are lined up on the defensive line and in the defensive backfield. Where and how the players line up gives you an indication of what the play may be.

✔ In the upper corner of the television screen, check out what the down is, how far the offense needs to go for the first down, how much time is left on the clock, and what the score is. The score and the time left on the clock often dictate whether a team will run or pass.

✔ Check the quarterback. If he's positioned 5 yards behind the center, he's in the shotgun formation, meaning that there's a 98 percent chance that he'll pass the ball. The other 2 percent of the time, the quarterback will drop back and then lateral or hand off the ball to a running back.

✔ Look for movement among the linebackers and defensive backs. If defenders appear to be creeping toward the line of scrimmage, they're probably going to either blitz the quarterback or fill all the running lanes to neutralize a run play.

✔ Look at the defensive fronts, paying particular attention to the defensive tackles. If only three linemen are lined up close to the line of scrimmage, the defense expects the offense to pass the ball. If the defense has four down linemen on the field and the linebackers are within a couple yards of the line of scrimmage, the defense expects the offense to try to run.

✔ Count the number of defensive backs. If more than four defensive backs are in the game, the defense is geared toward preventing a pass completion. If the offense has four receivers on the field, the majority of the time the quarterback will be throwing the football.

Deciphering the announcers' slang

One of the hardest and most intimidating parts about watching a football game on television is that the announcers sometimes seem to be speaking a foreign language known only to true football junkies. But if you remember a few key terms, you'll be way ahead of the game. Here are some terms that you'll hear and what they mean:

✔ **Corner blitz:** The blitzing linebacker or defensive player rushes the quarterback from the outside edge of the offensive alignment or the *corner* of the offensive line.

✔ **Dime back:** When the defense has six players in the secondary, the sixth player is called a dime back because he's the second nickel back (two nickels equal a dime).

✔ **Forklift:** A defensive lineman lifts an offensive lineman off the ground, moving him aside as he rushes the quarterback.

✔ **Franchise player:** Although this term is also used as a collective-bargaining description, the meaning here is different. Commentators routinely refer to the most important player on a team as the franchise. In Detroit, running back Barry Sanders is the franchise; the team can't win without him. In Green Bay, quarterback Brett Favre is the franchise; he drives the Packers' offense.

✔ **He's a player:** Yes, they're all players. But some commentators use this phrase to single out players that they really like or are impressed with.

✔ **Looking off a defensive back:** Commentators say this when a quarterback eyeballs a defensive back, giving the defensive player the impression that he's throwing the ball toward his area. In actuality, the quarterback intends to throw in a different direction. He fools the defensive back by *looking him off.*

✔ **Muscling his way through:** When a commentator says this, he means that a player managed to gain a physical advantage over an opponent. Dallas receiver Michael Irvin is a very physical receiver, and he often muscles his way through or past a defensive back.

✔ **Nickel package:** The defensive team is using five defensive backs in the secondary to defend the pass.

✔ **Running to daylight:** The running back has found the soft spot in the defense and is running freely down the field toward the end zone.

✔ **Shooting a gap:** A defensive player somehow runs untouched through a space that should have been blocked by an offensive player. The gap often is between two offensive players or to the outside shoulder of one player.

✔ **Zeroing in on a receiver:** The quarterback is focused on throwing to one specific receiver. The quarterback watches the receiver while he's running his route and then releases the ball when he's open.

Watching a Live Game

I love to watch a game from the sidelines. It's too bad that more fans don't have that same opportunity at least once in their lives. Standing on the sidelines, you see firsthand the speed of the players and the velocity of their hits. The contact occurs — and the overall game is played — at such a high speed. The players move like bullet trains plowing through a cornfield.

Obviously, the really good seats in every stadium are near the 50-yard line, 25 rows up, where you can scan the entire field. But those great seats usually belong to longtime season ticket holders. If you aren't a longtime season ticket holder or lucky enough to have an official NFL sideline credential, the end zone can be a good place to watch a game. The best seat in the house, from my perspective, is in the end zone about 20 rows up. Of course, you need good binoculars. I like to see plays developing and watch the line play on both sides of the ball, and the end zone offers the best vantage point to see this action.

Sitting in the end zone, you can focus on a matchup of two linemen, like a defensive end battling an offensive tackle, and watch how they attack each other. Whoever wins this battle is going to win the war (the game). These individual wars can teach you a lot about football, even when the play or ball is going in the opposite direction. For a team to win, its players need to win these individual battles.

Make sure that you buy a program or check your local newspaper for team depth charts and numbered rosters — these rosters are the only way to identify the many players on the field. A depth chart lists the starting lineups for both teams by their positions on offense and defense. The chart also lists the punter, placekicker, snapper for punts and kicks, and kickoff and punt return specialists. The reserves are listed alongside the starters on the depth chart, so when a player is injured, you can figure out who will replace him.

The beauty of watching a game in person is that you can see the entire play develop. As soon as the ball is snapped, all 22 players are moving. Television can't possibly capture that singular moment and every player, too. And at the stadium, you can watch what happens to a quarterback after the ball is released. On television, the camera follows the ball. In person, you can see whether the quarterback is hit after he releases the ball. Occasionally, the quarterback and a pass-rusher exchange words (or even swings).

The special teams play, especially kickoffs and long punts, is exciting to watch in person because you can follow the flight of the ball and the coverage players running full speed toward the kick returner. Because kickoff and punt plays cover so much of the field, often 50 to 70 yards, television can't capture all the action.

Talk radio

I enjoy being a guest on most sports talk shows. There are some really good talk radio sports shows, such as WFAN in New York City and XTRA in San Diego and Los Angeles. I enjoy exchanging opinions with XTRA's Jim Rome and WFAN's Mike and the Mad Dog (otherwise known as Mike Francesa and Chris Russo), both of whom are plugged into the New York Jets and Giants. To me, talk radio is another way to get information about pro football. These shows discuss the inside scoop and address all the serious issues.

Sports talk radio has altered the landscape of sports journalism. Players and coaches listen to these shows. One season, Philadelphia's WIP radio station was so critical of the Philadelphia Eagles that the team declined to issue game credentials to some of the station's commentators. I know that coaches on the team quit listening to the morning shows because they would get too upset to go to work. This shows you the power of talk radio and how it can irritate people.

However, I recommend listening to the pro football reports in most NFL cities. If the talk radio show includes a lot of conversations about your team and regular player interviews, then the program probably is worth listening to. Some talk radio hosts can be more insightful than some newspaper reporters; they do their homework on the team.

During commercial time-outs during a game, scan the sidelines with your binoculars. You can spot coaches talking strategy with players, and sometimes you can capture an animated conversation or debate. The more games you attend, the better you'll be able to follow the action and observe the sidelines. The pace is fast during plays, but there's enough down time between plays in which to check out what's happening on the sidelines and to figure out, by how teams are substituting, which play may be called next.

Following a Game on the Radio

The first time I saw a fan listening to a radio in a ballpark was during a Los Angeles Dodgers game. Although the fans were watching the action in person, they wanted to hear Vin Scully, the radio announcer, describe it. Many football fans also enjoy listening to the radio when attending a game. Every NFL team and most major college teams have a local radio station that owns the rights to their broadcasts. And because of the growing popularity of sports talk radio, many fans want to tune in to their favorite broadcasters.

Perhaps the best thing about listening to the radio is that you get the home-team announcers' insights into what strategy your team plans to use. These announcers know the players and can immediately tell you what player has the ball and who made the tackle. They also have access to the injury reports, so you receive player updates throughout the broadcast. You hear important statistics — such as how many total yards and first downs each team has collected — faster than most scoreboards can provide them.

Keeping Up with Your Favorite Teams

The fun of football doesn't end when the last seconds of the fourth quarter tick away. Diehard fans love to analyze the statistics of today's games and also find out all about the upcoming ones. You can get this type of information from a wide variety of sources. In this section, I list some of my favorites.

Newspapers

Newspapers are a great way to find out about upcoming matchups or to analyze how your team did in its most recent game. They're also a good source for discussing player trades, free-agent signings, and coaches whose jobs are in trouble. Most newspapers give you a shortened, statistical version of key football games after the games have been played, in addition to discussing the matchups before they occur. This statistical breakdown is actually an abbreviated story, telling you who scored and how and providing details about the performances of individual players. Scores of college games are placed in the region (East, South, Midwest) in which they are played.

Newspapers often provide a much more in-depth review of a particular player or a team's internal troubles than any television or radio program. Here are some good national papers to try:

- *The Atlanta Journal-Constitution*
- *The Sun (Baltimore)*
- *The Boston Globe*
- *The Dallas Morning News*
- *Rocky Mountain News*
- *San Jose Mercury News*
- *USA Today*

Magazines and books

Numerous football books, periodicals, and magazines are published, ranging from histories of football and biographies to fan guides and statistics-oriented tomes. Most major sports and football magazines — including the NFL magazine, called *Team NFL* — publish preview issues in July devoted to the upcoming college and NFL season. These magazines feature predictions, rosters, schedules, and articles for all the major college and NFL teams. For a complete view of the season, I suggest purchasing one magazine devoted to the college game and one to the NFL game.

If you're looking for current information about football or in-depth feature articles on many of the game's players, coaches, and teams, here's a list of my favorite football magazines. You can purchase them on any newsstand or convenience store magazine rack, at most bookstores, and via mail subscriptions.

- ✔ *College and Pro Football Newsweekly*
- ✔ *ESPN Magazine*
- ✔ *Football Digest*
- ✔ *Inside Sports*
- ✔ *Pro Football Weekly*
- ✔ *Sport Magazine*
- ✔ *The Sporting News*
- ✔ *Sports Illustrated*
- ✔ *Street & Smith's Yearbook*
- ✔ *The War Room*

In-depth football information

In the preceding section, I mentioned some weekly and monthly publications, but here I note some historical record books worth checking out. They're full of statistical updates of either current players or players throughout the history of the NFL.

Unlike Major League Baseball, which seems to have records for every moment, football hasn't been quite as exacting. For example, defensive statistics tend to be unofficial, and the league has recorded sacks (when defensive players tackle a quarterback behind the line of scrimmage) for less than 20 seasons. Some players' records, such as New York Giants linebacker Lawrence Taylor's, are not complete because they played before sacks were officially tracked.

Football's popularity

In 1997, *The Sporting News* conducted one of the most extensive research studies about the popularity of different sports among fans nationwide and discovered that the NFL is the most popular sport/league. According to the survey, sports fans (on a scale of 1 to 10) are most interested in the NFL (which received a 9.12 rating) followed by college football (7.87), Major League Baseball (7.79), the NBA (7.45), men's college basketball (7.42), and the National Hockey League (5.73).

The Sporting News began as the baseball bible, but times have changed; the St. Louis-based publication now views professional football as its top sport. The magazine produces an annual Player Register with updated individual statistics and a Pro Football Guide that includes statistics of every game from the preceding season. Another excellent player register is the *STATS Pro Football Handbook,* which is published annually. The new edition is available each year in late February. Both of these player registers, which include statistics of that season's draft choices and their college statistics, are available in bookstores. To order by telephone, call *The Sporting News* at 314-997-7111 or 800-825-8508 or STATS at 800-637-8287.

Total Football, the official encyclopedia of the National Football League, was printed for the first time prior to the 1997 season and will be updated annually prior to the start of each season. The book lists more than 17,000 players (and that number is growing) and includes the statistics from every season since 1920. The book is more than 1,650 pages long and weighs $7^{1}/_{2}$ pounds.

Following Your Team on the Net

You can find more football-related information on the Internet than you could read in a whole season — everything from who's being traded to who's been injured to who is predicted to go to the playoffs and more. The following Web sites are great sources of up-to-the-minute football info:

- ✔ **ABC Monday Night Online** (`www.abcmnf.com/`): Includes a schedule of the current season's Monday night NFL games and offers previews of the matchups.

- ✔ **CBS SportsLine** (`cbs.sportsline.com`): The online home of CBS Sports. Covers the NFL, the CFL, and college football. Offers both free and subscriber-only areas. Even if you don't have a subscription, this site is an excellent source for information such as team updates, schedules, injury reports, and statistics.

- ✓ **CNN/SI** (`www.cnnsi.com`): An online collaboration of CNN and *Sports Illustrated*. Includes comprehensive coverage of the NFL, college football, Arena football, and NFL Europe.

- ✓ **College Football Weekly On-Line** (`www.ncaacollegefootball.com/`): The online version of *College Football Weekly*. Provides both free and subscriber-only areas. The free area gives a rundown of different conferences, polls, bowl schedules, and more.

- ✓ **ESPN SportsZone** (`espnet.sportszone.com/`): Offers in-depth information about the NFL and college football. Some ESPN on-air personalities — such as Andrea Kremer, Tom Jackson, and Chris Mortensen — contribute feature articles. Even without subscribing to this site, you can access lots of information, including scores, statistics, standings, and news.

- ✓ **The Football Server** (`www4.nando.net/sportserver/football`): Focuses mainly on the NFL and NCAA but also includes standings and scores for NFL Europe, the CFL, and Arena football. This site is an excellent source of NFL and NCAA statistics.

- ✓ **FOX Sports** (`www.foxsports.com`): Covers the NFL, CFL, NFL Europe, and Arena football. If you're interested in knowing what's going on with your favorite NFL team during the off-season, check out the Team Notebooks area. You get full coverage of the signings, trades, and contract negotiations for each team.

- ✓ **MSNBC** (`www.msnbc.com/news/SPT_Front.asp`): The online home of NBC Sports. This easy-to-navigate site covers both the NFL and college football. Hold your cursor over Sports in the left-hand column to see the full array of features that this site offers.

- ✓ **NFL.COM** (`www.nfl.com`): The official site of the NFL. In addition to scores, statistics, and news, this site gives in-depth team coverage, including audio and video clips. The individual team pages offer links to your favorite teams' official Web sites. The Player Tracker enables fans to follow, in real time, the performance of players with instantaneously updated statistics on game days.

- ✓ **The Sporting News** (`www.sportingnews.com`): The online version of the magazine. This site provides an abundance of information about NFL and college football. You can customize this site so that it displays your favorite sports and teams.

In addition to these sites, you may also want to check out the Web sites of your favorite college teams and conferences. The College Sports Internet Channel at `www.sportscom.com/colsport/` provides links to many college teams' sites.

Checking Out the Football Halls of Fame

Visiting one of the football halls of fame — there's one for college and one for professional football — is a terrific way to find out more about how football became what it is today. Both are filled with memorabilia from players and teams from the turn of the century to the present. The many exhibits include uniforms and pictures of Hall of Famers in action. There are also screening rooms in which fans can enjoy films of legendary players and teams. The Pro Football Hall of Fame has been expanded four times since it was first constructed; a fan could spend an entire day walking through its many exhibits and halls. Following is the contact information for each hall of fame:

College Football Hall of Fame
South Bend, IN
219-235-9999 or 800-440-FAME
hof@CollegeFootball.org

Pro Football Hall of Fame
Canton, OH
330-456-8207
www.canton-ohio.com/hof/

Get Your Tickets Here

Another great way to increase your enjoyment of football is to splurge for tickets to a pro game, either in your home city or in a city that you're visiting.

I like going to a stadium that has a lot of history. A few years ago, I was in Green Bay's Lambeau Field for a championship game, and the outside temperature must have been 20 degrees. When the hometown Packers won the game, their loyal fans didn't rush the field; they simply stood in the stands cheering. Thirty minutes after the game had ended, many of them remained in their seats, applauding the accomplishments of the players and coaches as my colleagues and I at FOX Sports conducted on-the-field interviews. I was amazed by the fans' enthusiasm because of how cold it was. Lambeau is a great place to watch a game. Packer fans consider it a shrine.

My preference is open-air stadiums. I like stadiums that create a football atmosphere, where you can count on being surrounded by super fans. Off the top of my head, here are some stadiums that I highly recommend, that offer a lively and entertaining experience and where you'll find great fans: Denver's Mile High Stadium; Chicago's Soldier Field; Dallas's Texas Stadium; Kansas City's Arrowhead Stadium; the Giants Stadium in East Rutherford, New Jersey; Philadelphia's Veterans Stadium; Pittsburgh's Three Rivers Stadium; and San Francisco's 3Com Park.

Here are the names and addresses of all the NFL stadiums, plus the phone numbers of the ticket offices so that you can order your tickets right now:

Arizona Cardinals
Sun Devil Stadium
Tempe, AZ
602-379-0102

Atlanta Falcons
Georgia Dome
Atlanta, GA
404-223-8444

Baltimore Ravens
Ravens Stadium at Camden Yards
Baltimore, MD
410-261-7283 or 888-919-9797 or
410-243-9994 (hearing impaired)

Buffalo Bills
Rich Stadium
Orchard Park, NY
716-649-0015

Carolina Panthers
Ericsson Stadium
Charlotte, NC
704-358-7800

Chicago Bears
Soldier Field
Chicago, IL
847-615-2327

Cincinnati Bengals
Cinergy Stadium
Cincinnati, OH
513-621-3550

Dallas Cowboys
Texas Stadium
Irving, TX
214-579-5000

Denver Broncos
Denver Mile High Stadium
Denver, CO
303-433-7466

Detroit Lions
Pontiac Silverdome
Pontiac, MI
810-335-4151

Green Bay Packers
Lambeau Field
Green Bay, WI
920-496-5719

Indianapolis Colts
RCA Dome
Indianapolis, IN
317-297-7000

Jacksonville Jaguars
ALLTEL Stadium
Jacksonville, FL
904-633-2000 or 800-618-8005

Kansas City Chiefs
Arrowhead Stadium
Kansas City, MO
816-924-9300

Miami Dolphins
Pro Player Stadium
Miami, FL
305-620-2578 or 800-255-3094

Minnesota Vikings
Hubert H. Humphrey Metrodome
Minneapolis, MN
612-333-8828 (season) or
612-989-5151 (single game)

New England Patriots
Foxboro Stadium
Foxboro, MA
508-543-8200

New Orleans Saints
Louisiana Superdome
New Orleans, LA
504-731-1700

New York Giants
Giants Stadium
East Rutherford, NJ
201-935-8222

New York Jets
Giants Stadium
East Rutherford, NJ
516-560-8200

Oakland Raiders
Oakland-Alameda County Coliseum
Alameda, CA
510-615-1875

Philadelphia Eagles
Veterans Stadium
Philadelphia, PA
215-463-5500

Pittsburgh Steelers
Three Rivers Stadium
Pittsburgh, PA
412-323-1200

St. Louis Rams
Trans World Dome
at America's Center
St. Louis County, MO
314-982-7267

San Diego Chargers
Qualcomm Stadium
San Diego, CA
619-280-2121

San Francisco 49ers
3Com Park
San Francisco, CA
415-656-4900

Seattle Seahawks
Kingdome
Seattle, WA
888-NFL-HAWK or 425-827-9766

Tampa Bay Buccaneers
Raymond James Stadium
Tampa, FL
813-879-BUCS or 800-282-0683

Tennessee Oilers
Vanderbilt Stadium
Nashville, TN
888-313-8326 or 615-341-7600

Washington Redskins
Jack Kent Cooke Stadium
Raljon, MD
301-276-6060

Here's how to contact some major college teams:

Florida State University
Doak Campbell Stadium
Tallahassee, FL
Ticket office: 888-FSU-NOLE

Penn State University
Beaver Stadium
University Park, PA
800-833-5533 or 814-863-5500

University of Michigan
Michigan Stadium
Ann Arbor, MI
Ticket office: 313-764-0247

University of Nebraska
Memorial Stadium
Lincoln, NE
402-472-3111 or 800-8BIGRED

University of Notre Dame
Notre Dame Stadium
South Bend, IN
219-631-7356

University of Texas
Darrell K. Royal Texas
Memorial Stadium
Austin, TX
800-986-2386 or 512-477-6060

Chapter 15

Youth Leagues and High School Football

In This Chapter

▶ Deciding when to let your child play football

▶ Teaching the fundamentals to kids

▶ Understanding and succeeding in the high school game

*O*n the youth level, football is not like baseball or basketball. My experience with those sports is that it's okay if you don't play well — you're not putting yourself in danger. With football, on the other hand, you can really get hurt if you're not physically and mentally equipped to handle the game — especially if you're a young kid.

But football can teach you a lot about life; it's a character-building sport. Young players can learn about the rewards of hard work, dedication, team-work, and discipline. Football, like a lot of sports, is a great way to bring families together and can create a special bond between a father and a son.

In this chapter, I discuss a wide range of the benefits of youth football, from Pop Warner and flag football to high school football. I offer my own thoughts on coaching, the father-son relationship, and what young players need to focus on to be successful with the game and with life.

When to Start Kids in Football

I didn't start playing football until I was 15 years old. But if your young son has the desire to play the game, then let him play; just don't push him to play. Either football will be the right sport for him or it won't, and everyone will know quickly whether he made a good choice.

My oldest son played football for the first time when he was 12. Because of his size (he's bigger than most boys his age), he couldn't play with his friends and other 12-year-olds; he had to play on the junior varsity football team with boys 15 and 16 years old. Because of his age difference, he got physically whipped. But I tried to help and support him.

If you want your son to play at a young age, you must be committed to supporting and consoling him during the tough times. Young players — particularly the ones who have talent but who haven't had a lot of success — need encouragement. However, fathers who care *too much* and try to live vicariously through their children often ruin the experience for them. Find a good balance.

Pop Warner Football and other local junior tackle programs have teams for 7-year-olds. I think that starting football at age 7 is a little too young — they are too small and may get hurt. But if your child is mature for his age, he may have fun. With kids at that young an age, though, every parent should monitor practices and make sure that the coach both knows what he's doing and encourages the players to have fun.

Signing Your Kids Up for Youth Football

When you're signing your child up for youth football, you need a copy of his birth certificate and a current report card. (Most leagues won't enroll students who are failing their school work.) Also, examine your health insurance and make sure that your child is covered for all forms of injury.

If you can't find sign-up information in your local newspaper, check with your town or city's recreation department. Most recreation departments know how to locate league officials and know where teams are practicing.

Pop Warner and other similar programs

The nation's largest youth football organization is Pop Warner Little Scholars, Inc., which is the legal name for Pop Warner Football. In 1996, Pop Warner had leagues in 38 states and in Japan and Mexico. More than 270,000 boys and girls (who take part in cheer and dance teams) participated in those programs.

Pop Warner has stringent safety rules, including an age-weight schematic. This system ensures maximum safety, because players are evenly matched in size and physical maturity. Pop Warner also has a no-cut rule, which means that players don't have to try out. "First-come, first-on" is how Pop Warner operates.

Pop Warner has different age-group divisions from age 7 to age 14. Players move up through the different divisions until they reach the Bantams division in which the 14-year-olds play. In many areas of the country, school districts no longer have junior high/middle school football programs, so youth leagues fill that void.

To find a Pop Warner program in your area, check your local phone book or e-mail the organization at PWLSREG@aol.com. For more information, you can write to Pop Warner Football, 920 Town Center Drive, Langhorne, PA 19047, or call 215-752-2691.

A national touch football league is a good option if you want your boy to play football but not tackle football. Contact the United States Flag and Touch Football League at 7709 Ohio Street, Mentor, OH 44060, or call 216-974-8735.

Both Pop Warner and national youth touch football leagues play on fields that are shorter than the 100-yard regulation one used in high school and higher levels. Some Pop Warner fields are 80 yards long, and some flag and touch fields are only 40 yards long. The smaller field is good for youngsters under 12 and enables coaches to be closer to the action for instructional purposes and in case of injury.

Punt, Pass & Kick

More than 600,000 youngsters, including 150,000 girls, participated in the 1997 NFL Gatorade Punt, Pass & Kick competition. Since this competition began in the early 1960s, numerous participants — including quarterbacks Dan Marino, Drew Bledsoe, and Randall Cunningham — have gone on to play in the NFL.

Kids compete by age group (6 to 14) in this competition, which is offered on the local level in every NFL city. The competition is then regionalized, and those winners compete at the end of the NFL season in a prearranged NFL city. Every young athlete is judged on how far he throws a pass, punts a football, and kicks a football off a tee. Points are awarded by distance, and most winners have won one if not two of the three categories.

Youth camps

In the summer of 1998, the NFL conducted its second NFL/Starter Youth Training Camps in a dozen NFL cities. Boys and girls ages 8 to 14 can participate in drills based on the NFL's televised skills programs, such as "The Quarterback Challenge" and "Run to Daylight." Local NFL players and coaches offer instruction and tips. Registration generally takes place in May at local sporting goods stores that feature Starter sports apparel.

Boys who have completed the sixth through eleventh grade used to have many national summer camps to choose from. However, insurance problems have closed down many of those camps because of injuries to youngsters playing contact football in full uniform. However, check your local newspaper or football magazines for youth camps that develop skills without contact. Many high school teams spend a week at summer camps prior to beginning practice at school. These camps are organized by the school districts in conjunction with the high school coach.

Coaching a Youth Football Team

To coach any youth team, you must be able to give your time freely and want to do it for the kids. You must be committed to making the game fun; to helping develop a player's physical, mental, and social skills; and to winning the game. There's nothing wrong with trying to win, as long as you encourage the team to play the game fairly and teach your players good sportsmanship. Nothing can be gained from whipping an opponent 40-0 in a league of 10-year-olds. Think of how those kids on the losing team would feel!

A successful coach must have a genuine concern for the welfare of his players. You must make sure that *every* child has an enjoyable and successful experience. You need a lot of patience because you have to play every child, and sometimes you have to play a child in a position that he isn't very good at. Your job is to make sure that the player can cope with his limitations, or to place him a position where he can succeed. Try to get to know your players individually — every kid is different.

To be a coach, you must know the rules of the game and understand the tactics of the game. If you don't, you may want to buy some coaching books and attend coaching clinics, which are held in every state. Check with local high school coaches about available clinics.

Your practices need to be well organized, and you need to start the season with a set of rules that applies to each and every member of the team. One rule should be that if a player misses a certain number of practices, he has to sit out a certain number of minutes during the game, even if he's your star player. Rules about players being on time for practices and remembering their equipment teach them how to be responsible. And in the end, football is about building character. Remember, too, that children view most adults' actions from a right-or-wrong perspective. They can tell when a coach is playing favorites; that's why your rules need to be uniform.

Teaching the fundamentals of offense

The main objectives of offensive football are to move the ball down the field — either by running or by passing it — and to put your team in a position to score. To make this happen as a coach, you need to have an offensive philosophy. Develop strategies that make sense to you and your players. For example, if you have one super-fast, tough kid and six big players who can block, running the football should be your strategy.

One positive slogan to keep in mind and stress to your players when you're working on offense comes from the word *score:*

✔ **S = Simple**; make everything as simple as you can make it.

✔ **C = Complete** diagrams and instructions of every play for every player.

✔ **O = One** player who executes poorly messes things up for the team.

✔ **R = Repeat** every play until the players run it flawlessly.

✔ **E = Every** player must have the same commitment to making a play succeed.

To execute plays consistently, football teams must run the same plays from the beginning of preseason practice to the end of the season. Select a simple offense because even a few well-executed plays can give your opponents problems. You may even want to run a few plays as many as 20 times in practice. To win a football game, your offense must believe that it can move the football against anyone. When preparing your offense, you may want to put your defense in the formation that you expect your opponent to use. This way, your players can visualize what may happen in a game situation.

The passing game is easy to teach if you have a player who can accurately throw the ball a good distance. If no player can throw adequately, focus on the running game. But if you can practice the passing game with a quarterback and a few receivers while the rest of the team practices other techniques. The quarterback needs to work on his pass drop and learn how to pass the ball with the correct timing while building accuracy. He can practice these techniques while the receivers run their patterns, the same ones that they'll use in a game.

You need to know what your game plan is every week and install it prior to the first practice session. If you know your opponent's defensive strengths, you must devise a few plays that exploit its weaknesses. Often, by adding a variation of a basic play to your game plan, you can surprise the opposition when you need a big gain during the game. Also, only two or three well-executed plays are necessary for your goal-line offense. Remember, maintaining possession of the football, moving the ball down the field, and scoring are the principal objectives of offensive football.

Teaching the fundamentals of defense

When you're putting together your defense, you need to find your most aggressive players — the ones who love to run and aren't afraid of contact. These players will form your defensive unit. Playing defense is about loving to hit and being aggressive.

After assembling your defense, you need to teach the players how to tackle ball carriers. Start them in a wide stance; have them keep their feet moving with short, choppy steps and keep their heads up. Good tacklers extend their arms and drive their faces through the numbers on the ball carrier's jersey, using their arms and shoulders to put him on his back. Always teach the tackler to slide his head to the outside just before making contact to protect himself from jarring helmet-to-helmet contact.

After your defensive players learn how to tackle, teach them that the basic premise of defensive football is to stop the opposition from collecting first downs. Their goal is to prevent the opposition from gaining 10 yards and to force them to punt, getting the ball back for the offense. (On some levels, the field is smaller, and therefore offenses don't resort to punting. They try another play on fourth down, relinquishing the ball if they fail to gain a first down.) If your defense can't stop a team from moving the football, have the players concentrate on keeping the opposition out of the end zone. Surrendering three points on a field goal is better than allowing the opposition to score a touchdown, and the offense will get frustrated if they don't reach the end zone.

In youth football, you want to develop an attacking defense, one that's designed to focus on the particular strength of the opposition and negate it. Also, an attacking defense can easily exploit an offense's weak links, such as poor or slow-footed blockers. If you can beat the offensive linemen, then how fast the running backs are shouldn't matter. Your defenders should get to them before they can accelerate into fourth gear.

Try to stick with only a few defensive alignments. Like an offense, a defense performs better when the players don't have to think about a lot of formations.

A good defensive player is one who reacts instinctively. Make sure that your defensive linemen and linebackers know, for example, that when the offensive guards start moving sideways, the offense is running a sweep. They must look for tendencies from the running backs as well. When the running backs line up a certain way, the defense should have an idea of what play is going to be called. Defenses must have a basic understanding of how to read and understand an offense and then react to it.

What Sets High School Football Apart

Some high school principals still believe that football is the most important extracurricular activity on campus. Football generally starts off the school year in September, and a winning football team can create a positive attitude on the campus. The spirit and enthusiasm that a football program generates can form the building block for a positive school environment.

At most high schools, the number of students who participate in the sport (including student managers and cheerleaders) can amount to 10 percent or more of the student body. For these youngsters, the football experience can create a special bond that lasts forever. Because of its physical and mental demands, football is a sport that can make men out of boys. Of course, it's essential that the young men have the proper role models and authority figures in the head coach and his assistants.

All across America, high school football teams are part of small towns' identities. The team can serve as a rallying point for the community, mainly because of family ties to the players. In small towns, most people know everyone else; consequently, a lot of people take pride in a successful high school football team. Local businesses usually purchase advertising in the football program or donate services that help the program succeed financially.

Every state has its own high school federation or association that governs football and other sports. These federations oversee all-state awards, name district all-stars, and compile records of achievement.

Rule differences

The rules governing high school football differ from the NFL rules in the following areas:

- In high school football, any ball carrier whose hand or knee touches the ground is ruled down; the ball is dead at that spot. In the NFL, a ball carrier is considered down when he's touched by an opponent while on the ground. If an NFL runner slips and inadvertently touches the ground, he can get up and keep moving forward.

- In the NFL, the offense and defense can return fumbles, but in high school football, the defense can't advance a fumble. The ball is ruled dead where the defensive player recovers it.

- A high school player is considered in-bounds on a pass reception if he catches the ball with one foot down inside the sideline. In the NFL, a player must catch the ball with both feet down inside the sideline to be considered in-bounds.

- The high school goalposts are 23 feet, 4 inches wide; the NFL width is 18 feet, 6 inches. The NFL posts are 30 feet high, whereas high school uprights need be only 10 feet tall.

- The hash marks in high school are marked 53 feet, 4 inches from each sideline — they're closer to each sideline than in the NFL. Therefore, high school offenses can attempt more running plays to the wide side of the field.

- High school games are 48 minutes long, 12 minutes shorter than college and NFL games.

Style of play

With a few exceptions, high school offenses generally run the ball more often than they throw it. Developing a good running game is easier than finding a quarterback who is capable of accurately throwing 25-yard passes and finding receivers who are fast enough to get off the line of scrimmage and catch the ball. Limited practice time (most states allow only 14 days of practice prior to the first game) is another reason high school teams opt for a run-oriented offense; they can develop this type of offense more quickly.

Offense seems to be the priority in high school football. Coaches gamble more often on fourth down, believing that they can easily gain a yard or two to get the first down and keep the ball. Unlike in the pros, most high school quarterbacks are good runners. You see more old-style offenses in high school, too: You see a full-house backfield (three running backs lined up straight across behind the quarterback) and double-wing formations as coaches attempt to use more blockers in the backfield to better the chances of the play succeeding. For the most part, high school teams concentrate more on offensive preparation than on defensive preparation unless they're facing an opponent that operates a formation that's totally unfamiliar to them.

High school teams don't kick as often as pro teams because finding an accurate high school field goal kicker can be difficult. Some high school teams can't find a player who can even convert an extra point, which is basically a 20-yard kick. Plus, they don't have the time to concentrate a lot on special teams play because of the time constraints on high school athletes. To make the kicking game work, you must spend hours on blocking or send your kicker to a summer kicking camp. Another possibility is to talk to the soccer coach about possible kicker candidates.

Player lineups

The players on a high school roster may not compare in size to those on an NFL team, but high school players are definitely getting bigger and bigger. Today, a high school offensive line averaging 260 pounds is not uncommon, whereas 20 years ago that average may have been 220 pounds. In the last few years, more illegal use of steroids has been reported among boys 18 and under than among college and professional football players. Unlike college and the NFL, no mandatory testing system for steroids is in effect at the high school level, although some schools do test for marijuana and other drugs.

You find more two-way players at the high school level because most high school teams don't have enough quality players. These players play both an offensive position and a defensive position. Here are some examples of the different combinations of positions:

> ✔ A receiver may also play defensive back.
>
> ✔ Many quarterbacks lead the offense and spark the defense at safety.
>
> ✔ Many blocking backs are also linebackers.

When a school is forced to use a lot of two-way players, you may see sloppy play in the fourth quarter when the young players tire and begin to lose their concentration, which may lead to injury. Although two-way players don't always run out of steam at the end of a game, an opponent that doesn't need to use two-way players may have an advantage.

Making the Most of the High School Game

The first thing that parents and young men should realize about high school football is that players experience many ups and downs. You win a game against your rival and nothing feels better. Then the next week, you may lose and feel down and depressed. But you have to bounce back. Football teaches you to be humble about success because when games go badly, you have to work hard to battle back.

Losing a football game is not unlike some experiences that you go through in other aspects of life. You have to learn to deal not only with success but also with failure. I think that football is a great teacher of those lessons, more so than any other sport. Unlike high school baseball and basketball teams that play multiple games every week, in football you play only one game, which heightens each game's importance. You focus all week on one game, and if you lose, the pain may linger for days before you get an opportunity to redeem yourself in the next game.

This section gives some tips to help players, coaches, and parents keep the game in the proper perspective and enjoy football to the fullest.

Players

If you're interested in playing high school football, go to the school's main office and ask where and how you sign up. They can send you in the direction of the athletic director's or head football coach's office.

As a player, you need to adhere to the team rules and most likely get involved in a weight-lifting program. Most schools have programs that are monitored by a coach or teacher. In most parts of the country, football players have a few weeks in the spring in which they work out without equipment. To make it, you must take advantage of these training opportunities. Coaches like to see athletes working year-round and attending every practice. If your coach recommends that you attend a football camp, ask your parents for permission and find a way to earn the money to pay your way.

If a modern high school team played against a great high school team of 25 years ago, today's team would win. Twenty-five years ago, most of a school's good athletes were three-sport stars. Today, coaches demand that athletes play one sport almost year-round. This may sound overly demanding, but if you love the game, try dedicating yourself for at least one year.

Remember, you play football (or any sport, for that matter) to have fun. It should be a worthwhile experience, not drudgery. But if you possess special athletic ability and your goal is an athletic scholarship, remain focused and work as hard as you can. Good things come from hard work.

Coaches

Coaching is a demanding career. High schools are having more and more trouble finding quality coaches because coaching is a time-consuming, low-paying profession. High school head coaches also are teachers, and teachers aren't paid well. More and more young college graduates are deciding that the long hours and relatively small financial rewards of teaching and coaching don't make up for the lost time with family and friends.

A high school coach has to make a lot of personal sacrifices, especially if he's married and has a family of his own. As his children grow up, he misses out on their activities because of his commitment to his job, especially if he wants to have a winning team. And if he wants to make a career out of coaching, having a winning record is imperative in order to advance from high school to college or wherever the better positions are.

But regardless of the financial rewards (or lack thereof), a high school football coach's chief reward is the personal satisfaction of working with young people and watching them grow. And that satisfaction is so meaningful to many high school coaches that they would gladly work for minimum wage rather than give up coaching.

If you coach high school football, make a point of recruiting other teachers. Get them on your side so that they understand what your values are and how hard your athletes are working. Every week, invite one or two teachers to the pregame meal and ask them to ride on the bus to away games, making them feel like a part of your program. You must educate them about the game and what's happening with your team. If they know how much time the kids and coaches spend practicing and working at football and are aware of the discipline that you're teaching, they may view your program more favorably. Remember, you're a teacher, too, not just some jock.

The other benefit of building a good relationship with other teachers is that you need to know when players are failing classes. You need to do grade checks every four to six weeks — some schools don't allow students to play sports if they're flunking one or more classes. Developing a good relationship with the other faculty members helps everybody.

Parents

I think that most fathers make their sons go out for football because they played the sport in high school. Often, football is a family tradition. The grandfather played, the father played, and the uncles and cousins played, so a boy grows up wanting to emulate his relatives, particularly his father. Kids quickly learn how tough playing football is. Going to football practice is like going to boot camp. It's much different than practicing baseball, where you play catch and run around and have fun, or basketball, where you're mostly playing the sport all the time. With football, you spend a great deal of practice time working on conditioning, as well as hitting, and two to three hours of practice a day is hardly fun.

This is where parents can have some influence. When your child starts asking you why should he bust his butt for three hours a day and have people hit him and yell at him when he can stay home and play video games, you must step in. But what do you say? I believe that you should preach the benefits of teamwork and of not quitting something you start. Remind your child how much pride he'll feel in being successful at such a difficult sport.

Here are some other tips for parents:

- ✔ A football player has to make a lot of sacrifices, so try to give your son some slack with chores; he has made a huge commitment to the team.

- ✔ Encourage your son to have a good work ethic and to study hard and maintain good grades.

- ✔ If your son has the talent to earn an athletic scholarship, consider sending him to summer football camps during his high school career. Many colleges and universities offer these types of camps.

Making the Jump from High School to College or Pro Football

Even with the scholarship cutbacks that the NCAA is making, high school players still have many opportunities to play college football and receive financial assistance. In fact, if you include the smaller division schools, I think that more colleges and universities are giving scholarships today to play football than 30 years ago. Just as many schools are recruiting high school players, and the entire recruitment process has really advanced.

Twenty years ago, the University of Southern California (USC) could give as many football scholarships as it wanted. Now, all Division I schools are restricted to 85. Although not as many players have the opportunity to earn football scholarships at big-time schools like USC and Notre Dame as in the past, other colleges are picking up the slack. Colleges like Idaho State and Montana go to small suburbs in California to find good players. Good athletes don't get overlooked anymore. Colleges find them.

If you believe that your son has the ability to play college football, meet with the school's guidance counselor when he's a freshman and find out what course work is required by colleges that your son may be interested in. Doing so is a must to ensure that he is eligible to play at the college level when he graduates from high school.

And for players, remember that you go to school to receive an education. Of the thousands of young men who play college football, only 240 are drafted by the NFL each year. Because college players have only a 1 percent chance of having a professional football career, education should be the number-one priority.

Parents and coaches need to prepare young athletes for the realities of college by stressing the importance of academics and keeping track of athletes' academic records. To find out about the eligibility requirements for your son, check with your high school guidance counselor or the NCAA Initial-Eligibility Clearinghouse (you can write to them at P. O. Box 4044, Iowa City, IA 52243-4044, or phone 319-337-1492). And start your research in his junior year if you believe that he has the ability to play college football.

Very rarely does a high school football player jump directly to the NFL. However, a few players have had successful NFL careers without playing college football. For example, Arizona Cardinals defensive tackle Eric Swann didn't play college football, but he did play a couple years of semi-pro football.

Chapter 16

College Football

In This Chapter

▶ Taking a look at the NCAA and what it does

▶ Understanding why there are so many conferences

▶ Exploring the Bowl Alliance and other attempts to determine a national champion

▶ Recruiting and underclassmen

▶ Leveling the playing field with fewer scholarships

▶ Coaches, they are a-changin'

Although my own major football accomplishments occurred in the National Football League, the NFL's rules, traditions, and growth were nurtured by college football. In fact, the sport itself began on the collegiate level. The first college football game was played in 1869 between Princeton and Rutgers, and it took professional football almost a century to match America's love affair with college football.

Although the NFL and college football attract many of the same fans today, some of the rules are different, and the levels of competition are different (four separate divisions exist in college — I explain them in the section "Big, Medium, and Small," later in this chapter). In this chapter, I discuss the differences between the college and professional game, the powerful impact of college coaches, and the recruiting process.

Why People Love College Football

Fans are passionate about college football because of its local and regional flavor, and also because it's built on more than a century of tradition. A fan doesn't have to be an alumnus of a particular college to become a serious fan, either. For example, if you're raised in Ohio and your father is passionate about football, you'll probably hear about Woody Hayes (a legendary coach) and root for Ohio State. In every pocket of America, fans are loyal to their state universities, both big and small, and when two state schools collide, a rivalry emerges. Ohio State's major rival is the University of

Michigan; in Alabama, nothing is bigger than the matchup between the University of Alabama and Auburn, the state's other college football team; and in Florida, life stops for three-plus hours when Florida State and the University of Florida play.

Another primary appeal of college football is its young, amateur players. Even in major college football, you see smaller-sized athletes performing at a high level, who aren't big enough, strong enough, or fast enough to play in the NFL. And the style of the college game generally isn't as structured as the NFL game. College teams are more open about their approach to the game; coaches will try anything new if they think it will work. They use offenses and defenses that NFL teams would never consider, such as the wishbone, which features three running backs and emphasizes the run by using a ball-handling running quarterback. Because not every college team is stacked with great players at every position, superior coaching decides a lot of outcomes because offensive and defensive game plans can exploit specific weaknesses.

Plus, the college game offers pageantry — the tailgate parties, the marching bands, and the Friday night pep rallies. In many cases, a college campus mushrooms to twice its normal size on a Saturday afternoon as thousands of adult fans join students at the game. Major college sights and sounds include

- ✔ **The Notre Dame Victory March ("Cheer, cheer for old Notre Dame . . ."):** This is said to be the fourth most famous song in the United States, finishing right behind the national anthem, "God Bless America," and "White Christmas."

- ✔ **The Stanford and Yale bands:** These bands are known for their zaniness, wacky attire, and willingness to attempt any outlandish halftime show imaginable.

- ✔ **The Trojan Horse:** The symbol of Southern California (USC) football, a white horse with a man dressed like a Trojan warrior riding him. The horse's name is Traveller.

- ✔ **Dotting the *i* in Ohio State:** The Buckeye band ends every home pregame performance by spelling out *Ohio* on the field, with the drum major completing the spelling by running to dot the *i*.

- ✔ **Best mascots:** The Falcons at the Air Force Academy, which fly at halftime; the real-life Buffalo at Colorado; the ugly-faced bulldog at Georgia; and the little Irish leprechaun at Notre Dame.

- ✔ **Best atmosphere games:** Any night game at LSU; the Florida-Georgia game, usually played in Jacksonville; Ohio State versus Michigan before 103,000 in Ann Arbor; Florida-Florida State and Notre Dame-USC anywhere; and any home game at Tennessee.

- ✔ **Battle of the bands:** The Grambling-Southern University game offers the finest strutting, dancing, and rhythm halftime show in college football.

Rule differences between college and NFL football

If you watch a lot of NFL games, you should know that pro and college rules differ in three important areas:

✔ In college football, the hash marks are 10'9" closer to the sidelines than in the pros.

✔ In college football, a receiver is ruled in-bounds when he has possession of the ball and has one foot in-bounds. In the NFL, the receiver must have both feet in-bounds.

✔ In the NFL, any offensive player in possession of the ball — whether a running back, a quarterback, or a kick returner — can fall down, get back on his feet, and continue running if he isn't touched by a defensive player. A college player is considered down whenever one knee touches the ground, whether or not another player has touched him. Consequently, you'd better not slip in college football.

Big, Medium, and Small

NCAA is the abbreviation for the *National Collegiate Athletic Association,* which is the governing body of college athletics. Although it oversees every sport and both men's and women's teams, the NCAA got its start in college football. In 1906, representatives of 26 colleges who were not members of the Inter-collegiate Football Association met to establish their own rules. Eventually, the two organizations merged, forming what eventually became the NCAA.

The NCAA reports that 600 member colleges fielded football teams during the 1997–98 season. These colleges are divided into divisions that are based on enrollment, financial commitment, and the competitive level of the conference to which they belong. The NCAA doesn't want big-time Division I-A powers like Nebraska and Penn State playing small schools like Union College and Wabash. It wants a level playing field, which correlates to a more competitive game.

Consequently, the 600 colleges are divided into Division I-A, Division I-AA, Division II, and Division III programs, as shown in Table 16-1. The NCAA holds national playoffs for the smaller schools, from Division I-AA to Division III. But no such format has been adopted in Division I-A (see the section "The Bowl System and the Search for a National Champ," later in this chapter). The NCAA claims that playing more than 11 or 12 games is too much for Division I-A schools, but its Division I-AA champions of 1996, Marshall University, played 15 games and won them all.

Table 16-1	Schools and Players in Each Division, 1997 Football Season	
Division	*Number of Schools*	*Number of Players*
I-A	112	12,802
I-AA	119	11,186
II	152	12,631
III	217	17,143
Totals	600	53,762

The number of Division I-A teams increased to 112 for 1998, with several schools jumping up from the Division I-AA ranks. The most successful team to make the move was Marshall. The perennial national title contender in I-AA, the Thundering Herd won nine games and the Mid-American Conference title in its first season as a Division I-A football school. It also hosted the Motor City Bowl, which it won, in 1997.

Hundreds of junior colleges (two-year programs) also have football teams, as do National Association of Intercollegiate Athletic (NAIA) schools, a group of smaller four-year colleges not associated with the NCAA. Unable to qualify academically to receive a four-year scholarship to a four-year college, many athletes attend junior colleges, particularly in California, hoping to land a scholarship to a four-year school. O.J. Simpson, one of the finest running backs of all time, played junior college football before attending the University of Southern California. Many of the NAIA teams are based in Kansas, North and South Dakota, Pennsylvania, Ohio, Nebraska, and Oregon.

Big-time schools

Although 112 colleges and universities played Division I-A football in 1997, less than half of them had a realistic chance of finishing in the top ten or being voted the national champion by either the Associated Press (a group of national sportswriters and broadcasters) or the *USA Today*–ESPN Coaches Poll. These two polls are the most respected college football polls.

Nebraska, Florida, Michigan, Notre Dame, Florida State, Ohio State, Penn State, North Carolina, LSU, Tennessee, Washington, and UCLA probably have the best college programs in the country. I could name another dozen, but if you want to pick the national champion in any of the next five years, the winner probably will come from among those first dozen schools. As you can see in Table 16-2, many NFL players come from these 12 schools (in bold in the table).

Table 16-2	Where NFL Players Came From, 1997
College	*Number of Players*
Notre Dame	44
Miami (Florida)	37
Penn State	36
Ohio State	35
Tennessee	35
Colorado	32
Florida State	32
USC	31
Texas A&M	39
North Carolina	28

Notre Dame, a Roman Catholic university of about 8,000 students in South Bend, Indiana, historically has been the most recognized college football power. It began its rise in the 1920s and has maintained a lofty hold on the college scene ever since. Notre Dame's support is nationwide — it recruits high school players from virtually every state — and nearly all of its games are televised nationally. The term *subway alumni* is used to describe the many fans who support Notre Dame football, acting very much like they attended or even graduated from the school.

The reputations of big-time schools help with recruiting because many of the best high school players want to play for a school where they have a chance to compete for a national championship, possibly prepare for the NFL, and also receive a good education. Every one of the 12 schools mentioned earlier in this section adheres to those criteria. And because of television, California boys now may consider playing for faraway schools like Notre Dame, Michigan, or Nebraska.

Small college powers

Although small schools may not achieve national prominence, they certainly play tough football. Some of the winningest teams and coaches are not giants like Florida and Nebraska but smaller colleges:

✔ Just 18 miles east of the Pro Football Hall of Fame is the small Ohio town of Alliance, home of the winningest college football team of the 1990s. Division III powerhouse **Mount Union College** has won 94 of 101 games through the 1997 season. The Purple Raiders play before capacity crowds in a stadium that holds 5,800 people, three times the school's enrollment. Head coach Larry Kehres doesn't believe in cutting any player who wants to participate — a choice he can make because the team doesn't give out athletic scholarships — forcing the team to dress as many as 170 players for home games.

✔ In 1998, former Washington Redskins Super Bowl MVP quarterback Doug Williams replaced retiring **Grambling University** coach Eddie Robinson, who won more games (408) than any other college coach. Among predominantly black colleges, Grambling has been the best producer of NFL players, sending more than 100 to the pros. Robinson, who coached 55 seasons at Grambling, was inducted into the College Football Hall of Fame in 1998.

Remember, too, that two of the greatest players of all time, Walter Payton and Jerry Rice, were small-college players. Payton starred at Jackson State in Mississippi, and Rice, another first-round draft choice, played at Mississippi Valley State in Itta Bena, Mississippi. Bigger doesn't always mean better!

College Conferences

Although some intersectional games are played, usually early in the season, college football teams play most of their games against schools in their own conferences and geographic regions. An *intersectional game* generally is a matchup of teams from two major programs from two different conferences and geographic regions. However, the shapes of conferences are changing all the time (and ignoring geographic areas) as colleges search for schools that are compatible athletically.

Some conferences, such as the Ivy League, formed because the colleges in the conference have a shared focus on academic excellence and do not award athletic scholarships. Harvard, Yale, Dartmouth, Brown, Columbia, Cornell, Penn, and Princeton are in the Ivy League. These schools — particularly Harvard, Princeton, and Yale — helped spawn football in America. They all have fielded teams for more than 100 years, and their students and coaches created many of the rules and styles of play. The Ivy League competes in Division I-AA rather than Division I-A, and its teams still attract many good football players. Their student-athletes simply have goals other than reaching the NFL.

The best-known Division I-A conferences are the Big Ten, Pac-10, SEC (Southeastern Conference), ACC (Atlantic Coast Conference), Big XII (a recent merger of the Big Eight and the Southwest Conference), and the Big East. In 1997, these five conferences supplied over 55 percent of the players on NFL rosters.

Here is the lowdown on these well-known football conferences:

✔ The **Big Ten** is located mostly in the Midwest and actually has 11 members: Illinois, Indiana, Iowa, Michigan, Michigan State, Minnesota, Northwestern, Ohio State, Penn State, Purdue, and Wisconsin.

✔ The **Pac-10** is located in the western states and has ten members: Arizona, Arizona State, Oregon, Oregon State, Stanford, UCLA, USC, University of California–Berkeley, Washington, and Washington State.

✔ The members of the **SEC** are situated mostly in the southeastern states. The conference is divided into East and West divisions: Florida, Georgia, Kentucky, South Carolina, Tennessee, and Vanderbilt are in the East; and Alabama, Arkansas, Auburn, LSU, Mississippi, and Mississippi State are in the West.

✔ The **ACC** schools are mostly in the Carolinas and along the East Coast. They include Clemson, Duke, Florida State, Georgia Tech, Maryland, North Carolina, North Carolina State, Virginia, and Wake Forest.

✔ The **Big XII,** the merger of the old Big Eight schools and the Southwest Conference (which produced some of the great teams in the 1940s and 1950s), is divided into North and South divisions. The North includes Colorado, Iowa State, Kansas, Kansas State, Missouri, and Nebraska; and the South includes Baylor, Oklahoma, Oklahoma State, Texas, Texas A&M, and Texas Tech.

✔ The **Big East,** like the ACC, has long been known as a basketball conference. But it includes the University of Miami (Florida), which has had a strong football program, and Syracuse, a program that's reemerging as a football power. Also in the Big East are Boston College, Pittsburgh, Rutgers, Temple, Virginia Tech, and West Virginia.

Other conferences that you may have heard of are the Mid-American Conference, which includes schools like Ball State, Marshall, and Toledo; the Western Athletic Conference (WAC), which features BYU (Brigham Young University), Colorado State, Fresno State, New Mexico, San Diego State, and Utah; and Conference USA, led by Louisville and East Carolina. Army, Navy, and Notre Dame head the surviving group of football independents. These three schools don't have any trouble scheduling games because of their excellent football heritage. Plus, Notre Dame is the only football power with its own network television contract.

Some of these conferences, like the WAC, have realigned in the last ten years in order to create a more balanced football league, as well as to assist the growth of women's sports. Colleges are focusing more on geographic areas and similar student-athlete goals as they shift conferences around. The WAC appears to be undergoing another realignment, but it won't affect the football programs until the 1999 season.

New leagues, new teams

The 1990s produced the most geographical changes in conferences since before World War II. One legendary independent, Penn State, joined the Big Ten, which retained its name despite growing to 11 members. One legendary conference, the Southwest, ceased to exist. Four Southwest Conference (SWC) schools — Baylor, Texas, Texas A&M, and Texas Tech — united with the Big Eight to form the Big XII, splitting that new conference into two divisions.

Three SWC schools — Rice, SMU, and TCU — joined the Western Athletic Conference, along with ex–Big West members San Jose State and UNLV and independent Tulsa, to create a cumbersome 16-team conference with Mountain and Pacific divisions. The SEC (Southeastern Conference) added Arkansas and South Carolina to become a 12-team conference with two divisions. The Big East created itself out of thin air in 1991 with eight eastern seaboard schools, including Florida's University of Miami. The ACC, meanwhile, added Florida State in 1992, and the Seminoles have lost just one conference game since. Conference USA was born in 1996 out of seven disenfranchised teams, most of them former independents.

The only conference not to have changed in the '90s is the Pac-10, which last expanded in 1978.

Although it isn't a national championship, winning a conference championship is a major accomplishment and assists in postseason honors and invitations to bowl games (in Division I-A) or playoff games (in the other divisions).

The Bowl System and the Search for a National Champ

College basketball has a national tournament — "March Madness" — in which 64 schools receive automatic berths via league championships or at-large invitations. The tournament games are spread out in different parts of the country, and the winners from the four geographic regions meet over a weekend to earn the right to play for the national championship. The tournament has become so popular that the Final Four has been played in domed football stadiums. More than 50,000 fans attended the 1998 Final Four in San Antonio's Alamodome.

Instead of a national title tournament, college football has a bowl system: a series of matchups between teams selected by bowl committees and the individual bowl's association with particular conferences. For example, the Big XII conference champion plays in the Orange Bowl.

At one time, only four major bowl games were played. The Rose Bowl, taking place in Pasadena, California, was first played in 1902. It has been played annually, though, only since 1916. The Orange Bowl, held in Miami, Florida, and the Sugar Bowl, played in New Orleans, both began in 1935. The Cotton Bowl, held in Dallas, had its inaugural game in 1937.

These games are played after the regular season, many of them around the Christmas holidays and on New Year's Day. Some bowls feature a particular matchup every year. For example, the Rose Bowl, played every New Year's Day, pits the Pac-10 conference champion against the Big Ten champion. Other matchups vary from year to year as the bowls (there were 23 in 1997) look for viable candidates around the country. When a bowl doesn't have a marquee matchup, it looks for colleges with a strong following — fans who would be willing to pay airfare and hotel expenses in order to travel.

Because the bowl system proved to be so flawed in elevating a clear-cut national champion, college football has spent most of this decade searching for a solution to the annual national title debate without going to a bowl-busting playoff system. But most of the proposed solutions have only further annoyed fans, players, coaches, and newspaper columnists.

- ✔ The first plan offered was the 1992 bowl coalition. Seven of the holiday bowl games — which have dominated college football for 60 years — agreed to select teams from a pool of champions and second-place teams from the Big Eight, Atlantic Coast, Big East, Southwest, Southeastern (SEC champ only), and Pac-10 (runner-up only), and to include independent Notre Dame.

   This plan solved nothing. Colleges didn't like being nudged into any of the bowls designated "Tier Two," or second-level bowl games: less money and no real chance at claiming the mythical national championship. And without the powerhouse conferences the Pac-10 and Big Ten, this bowl plan didn't resolve the national title debate.

- ✔ In 1995, a more elitist bowl coalition was created in the wake of Penn State — who had a perfect 12-0 season after winning the Rose Bowl — finishing the season number two behind another unbeaten team, Nebraska. The controversy over who deserved a first-place ranking (Penn State or Nebraska) stemmed from the obvious problem that the teams hadn't played one another, thus leaving the coaches and media to decide who deserved to ranked number one. With this new coalition, called the Bowl Alliance, the champs of the ACC, Big Eight, Big East, SEC, and two at-large teams would fill the Fiesta and Orange bowls, traditionally the two bowl games that feature the year's best teams. Because of the Bowl Alliance, the Fiesta Bowl in Tempe, Arizona, has featured games to determine the unofficial national championship.

Once again, it didn't work. In 1996, Florida State beat Florida early in the season in a nonconference game. But a series of upsets in the SEC wound up mandating a rematch between the two teams in the Sugar Bowl. Florida, which eventually won the SEC championship, then knocked Florida State, champions of the ACC, from the ranks of the unbeaten with its victory in the Sugar Bowl.

These coalitions and alliances have been unable to resolve the debate about who should be number one. And in the process, they have devalued the once-popular bowl games that are not a part of the alleged number-one versus number-two matchup.

Most of the major bowls have suffered poor attendance and low television ratings for games mandated by the alliance structure. The January 1, 1997, Fiesta Bowl between Penn State and Texas drew 65,106 fans, almost 15,000 less than the 1996 crowd. The 1993 Orange Bowl between Florida State and Nebraska drew 57,324, or 25,000 fans under capacity. And the New Year's Eve 1995 Sugar Bowl matching Virginia Tech and Texas posted a 4.3 Nielsen rating (a low rating) and saw about 15,000 people eat their tickets; they paid, but they were no-shows in the New Orleans Superdome.

A new alliance, this one called the Bowl Championship Series, is on tap for 1998, with the Rose Bowl, for the first time ever, agreeing to participate. The champions of the six major conferences — Pac-10, Big Ten, ACC, Big East, SEC, and Big XII (the result of the Big Eight and Southwest Conference merger) — will automatically qualify for six of the eight berths in the four major bowls: Rose, Sugar, Orange, and Fiesta. Another provision is that any school that does not have an automatic bowl bid conference association, which would include independent Notre Dame and the recently splintered Western Athletic Conference, can earn a bowl series championship bid with a top-six ranking.

However, for the first time, a statistical rating system will be used to select two teams to play in what the Bowl Championship Series wants to call college football's national championship game. The Fiesta Bowl will be the host of the first title game (under this system) on January 4, 1999. The Bowl Championship Series will use a four-point plan to determine which teams play for the national title and for the first time, the polls will have less of an impact, being only one-fourth of the total solution:

- **Polls:** The ranking of each team in the Associated Press media poll and the *USA Today*-ESPN coaches' poll will be added and divided by two. For example, a team ranked number one in one poll and number four in another poll would receive 2.5 points.

- **Computer rankings:** An average of three computer rankings supplied by *The New York Times, The Seattle Times,* and statistician Jeff Sagarin will be used, but with a 50 percent adjusted deviation factor as a safety net. For example, if a team is ranked number 4 and number 6 on two computers and 14 on the other, the number 14 ranking will be adjusted to a number 7, and that team will get 5.67 points.

✔ **Strength of schedule:** This takes into account the win-loss record of a team's opponents *and* the records of the opposition's opponents. The opponent's record is two-thirds of the mark, and the opposition's opponents comprise the other third. The national strength of schedule placing, once determined, is then divided by 25.

✔ **Team record:** Each loss counts as one point.

At the end of the 1998 conference championship games, the four components will be added, and the schools with the two lowest point totals will be paired in the national title game. Initial rankings won't be released until early November, to allow the strength of schedule component to develop more meaning. Representatives of the Bowl Championship Series believe that having a tie for the top two spots will be impossible.

Is this new Bowl Championship Series a viable solution? Maybe, maybe not. The Rose Bowl, which attracts 100,000 fans every January, will be very nervous the first time its game does not feature the Big Ten or Pac-10 champ. And what happens the first time three teams finish the regular season unbeaten? Or the first time no one goes unbeaten? With each passing year, a playoff looks more and more reasonable. Many fans of the old bowl system, in fact, are starting to support the idea of a playoff simply to get the decision-making out of the hands of the bowls, the coaches, the national media, and now computers.

Recent Trends in College Football

As the popularity of football has grown, some disturbing trends have emerged in college football. Hundreds of players view college football as simply a stepping-stone to the NFL. They are interested in playing — not studying. This trend puts even more pressure to win on the top 20 to 30 college football programs.

Coaches are having a more difficult time exerting their authoritarian measures, which never would have been questioned 20 years ago. Many of these men are giving up coaching, either retiring or finding easier work elsewhere. Players are looking for positions, other than quarterback and running back, that may generate a huge NFL paycheck. I discuss some of these trends in the following sections.

Underclassmen leaving school early

Aside from the attempts to create bowl alliances and avoid a playoff system, the biggest change in college football has been in the number of underclassmen leaving school early. The NFL opened its doors to juniors in 1989, when Barry Sanders — currently the superstar running back for the Detroit Lions — threatened to test the legality of prohibiting underclassmen from turning pro. Because of the National Basketball Association's decision to accept undergraduates, the NFL believed that its legal position against admitting juniors was untenable. Rather than prepare for a legal fight, the NFL let Sanders enter the league. And Sanders, a Heisman Trophy winner at Oklahoma State, proved that he belonged in the NFL by rushing for 1,470 yards and 14 touchdowns in his rookie season. (See the section "The Heisman and Other Trophies" for more information about this coveted award.) Since then, more than 300 players have opted to forgo their college careers and depart early.

The schools hurt most by players leaving early have been Ohio State, Florida State, and Southern California (USC). However, the people who have been hurt the most have been the underclassman who never should have considered the move. Although some underclassmen have had success in the NFL, many did not make it big. Underclassmen quarterbacks Andre Ware (Houston), Tommy Maddox (UCLA), and Todd Marinovich (USC) serve as three prime examples of first-round draft choices who failed in the NFL. All three players should have stayed in school.

The NFL has installed a college relations committee that deals directly with colleges and tells prospective players what round they can expect to be drafted in, before they officially declare for the draft. The NFL also maintains that it would go to court rather than allow college sophomores to enter its college draft. An uneasiness still exists between NFL scouts and college coaches regarding access to college practices and players. But probably a greater fear among college coaches is reserved for football agents, who often work college campuses illegally in search of talent. There are said to be more agents than there are players — 1,600 — in the NFL.

To combat the loss of underclassmen, colleges have opted to play freshmen, which can place academic strain on first-year students. Colleges, though, still have the luxury of issuing a *redshirt* season, in which a player doesn't play but maintains his scholarship funds. The redshirt policy gives some athletes five years to graduate. During a redshirt year, a player has time to rehabilitate from an injury, improve his academic standing, or gain a year of maturity.

Cornering a new star

Quarterback and running back have always been the glamour positions in football, but in the 1990s, a serious trend toward star-quality cornerbacks has emerged. Former Florida State star Deion Sanders, now with the Dallas Cowboys, is considered the player who sparked this trend. Whether or not "Prime Time" is responsible, cornerback has become an impact position and the position of choice for many players.

In 1997, Michigan's Charles Woodson became the first full-time defensive player to win the Heisman Trophy (see the section "The Heisman and Other Trophies" for more information), out-pointing quarterbacks Peyton Manning and Ryan Leaf in the national voting. Woodson's Heisman win was seen as confirmation that a cornerback is worth as much as a good running back, let alone a number-one-drafted quarterback. Michigan used Woodson on offense and special teams at times, which helped his candidacy. But when the 1998 NFL draft came along, Manning and Leaf were selected first and second, while Woodson was the fourth overall selection, drafted by the Oakland Raiders.

Three of the top cornerbacks playing in 1998 are North Carolina's Dre' Bly, USC's Daylon McCutcheon, and Arizona's Chris McAlister. Both Bly and McCutcheon were offensive stars in high school who chose to play corner in college, undoubtedly thinking that they might become another Deion.

Twenty-six cornerbacks were taken in the first round of the NFL draft between 1991 and 1997, including Ohio State's Shawn Springs, who was the third player taken in the 1997 NFL draft. Sanders, who may be the best coverage cornerback ever, was only the fifth player taken in 1989.

Changes at the top

Another notable trend in college football has been the entry of new names in the Top 25 polls. Parity, enhanced by the rollback of scholarships to a maximum of 85 per season, has spread the talent around the nation and has been an integral part of several teams' fortunes. In the early 1980s, the NCAA permitted member schools to award as many as 105 full-tuition scholarships. That total first dipped to 95, and the present figure is 85. And no school can award more than 25 athletic scholarships in a given year.

Although 20 may not seem like a huge number of scholarships to lose, it has prevented big-time schools from stockpiling talent like they did in the past, and it places a higher premium on not making a mistake with any student-athlete. If a prospective player doesn't perform to the playing standards the college coaches predicted, his college has no recourse but to keep him on scholarship and hope that he develops eventually.

College football firsts

- White lines are placed on the field at 5-yard intervals in 1882. As a result of the pattern, the playing field is called a *gridiron*.

- Yale stages a night college football game in 1891.

- A game is played on the West Coast between the University of California Berkeley and Stanford in 1892.

- *Collier's* magazine publishes the first All-American team in 1898. Collier's remains the official selection holder of teams through 1924.

- The length of the football field is reduced to today's standard of 100 yards in 1912.

- The University of Wisconsin erects an electronic scoreboard in 1926, and it is used in a game against Iowa.

- Although a Fordham practice was shown in the preceding year, the game between Maryland and the University of Pennsylvania on October 5, 1940, is television's first game. Saturday afternoon telecasts emerge nationwide in the 1951 season.

Because of these scholarship reductions, schools that were perennial losers have emerged as nouveau powers in the 1990s. Kansas State, once a doormat in the Big Eight, went to the Fiesta Bowl at the end of the 1997 season. Northwestern won the 1996 Big Ten title and went on to the Rose Bowl. North Carolina, traditionally a basketball power, finished 10-1 in the 1997 season, and Colorado State has replaced Brigham Young as the best program in the WAC. Meanwhile, teams like Oklahoma, Texas, USC, and Miami (Florida) have fallen from the highest tier and are having difficulty returning to their familiar spots among the top ten programs. In the 1960s, it was common for college football powers like Oklahoma, Texas, and USC to have more than 110 players on scholarship.

Recruiting becoming more competitive

The wars between colleges to sign the best high school talent have intensified as a result of the reduced number of scholarships that schools can give out, which has made stockpiling all the top players impossible. An uneven science at best, a team's future can now swing on the strength of two or three top recruits.

Recruiting has spawned its own industry as a result. Many major newspapers have reporters who cover football (and basketball) recruiting on a full-time basis. Three services and publications keep tabs on the pulse of recruiting and are respected for their insight and coverage: Chicago-based *Tom Lemmings*, California-based *Super Prep* (published by Allan Wallace), and the *National Recruiting Advisor*.

The college game turning into more of a business

The NCAA spends a lot of time investigating colleges and universities, attempting to verify that student-athletes who are receiving scholarships for room, board, and tuition are not being paid or receiving gifts from influential alumni or booster clubs. The NCAA spends millions of dollars monitoring member schools. And the NCAA can place member schools on probation, forbidding them to appear on television or to compete for a conference championship because of recruiting violations and illegal payments and eligibility standards.

Penalties can cause tremendous financial harm to college and university athletic departments because revenue from big-time college football generally funds other athletic programs within the school. Severe penalties can result in the forfeiture of scholarship awards, lost television revenue, and the ultimate deterrent, the so-called "death penalty." When slapped with this penalty, a school cannot compete in football and is forbidden to award scholarships. Southern Methodist University in Dallas, Texas, was given the death penalty in the 1980s for illegal recruiting practices, including giving financial gifts (from cash to cars) to potential recruits. Although football has returned to SMU, the caliber of the team hasn't equaled its illustrious past.

Some administrators, coaches, and players view the NCAA as an entity of do-gooders, crusading against athletic programs that it views are outside the mainstream of American life. College athletes are supposed to be amateurs, but that's difficult to comprehend sometimes when they play before as many as 100,000 paying customers or before a national television audience. Also, some college coaches are being paid salaries that are comparable to those of NFL head coaches. Florida's Steve Spurrier earns about $2 million a year, a figure that only three NFL coaches currently are paid. With shoe contracts and local radio and television shows, 30 college head coaches earned more than $350,000 during the 1997 season.

Typical of the big money in college sports is the University of Colorado receiving $2.74 million from sports apparel company Nike to wear its equipment. Nike will also pay the school an additional $3 million until the year 2001. And the football team will receive a $100,000 bonus from Nike if it wins the national championship between 1997 and 2001.

Those Father Figures: College Coaches

Unlike the current NFL, college football has had a history of long-term associations with head coaches. A team's coach and his beliefs are more well-known than its star quarterback. A school's identity is forged through its coach; he's the star of the show.

Although some coaching crossover does occur between the professional leagues and the college system, many talented and respected coaches prefer the college game where they often can have two consecutive .500 seasons without being squeezed out by the alumni or college president. This atmosphere exists at 75 percent of the colleges. Now, at Michigan, Notre Dame, USC, Texas, and Alabama — colleges that are used to competing for a national championship and have been football powers for decades — the atmosphere is more like the NFL, with constant national attention and media scrutiny.

After the 1997 season, two of the sport's most successful coaches retired. Eddie Robinson, who won 408 games in 55 seasons at Grambling University in Louisiana, and Nebraska's Tom Osborne, who won 255 games in 25 seasons, both decided to retire. The retirement of Osborne — announced before Nebraska's Orange Bowl victory over Tennessee that gave the school an unbeaten season and a share of the national championship — accents the number of veteran (and successful) head coaches leaving the game.

Osborne and Robinson follow Notre Dame's Lou Holtz, Alabama's Gene Stallings, Colorado's Bill McCartney, Washington's Don James, and UCLA's Terry Donahue off the sidelines. Holtz left Notre Dame because of strained relations with the new athletic director as well as his wife's illness. Stallings also grew apart from the Alabama's administration and decided that he would be better off spending more time with his son. McCartney gave up a secure spot in Colorado for personal reasons and to become a leader of the Promise Keepers, a national Christian group for men. James resigned after Washington was hit with NCAA probation penalties that he thought were excessive, and Donahue left to take a job in broadcasting.

The departure of these coaches leaves Penn State's Joe Paterno, Florida State's Bobby Bowden, BYU's Lavell Edwards, and Iowa's Hayden Fry as the current 60-something legends of the game. Paterno, known as "Joe Pa," is 298-77-3 in 32 seasons at Penn State after the 1997 season. When he wins 300, he'll be one of six coaches to reach that mark in college football, four of which coached in Division I-A. The others are Bear Bryant (323), Pop Warner (319), and Amos Alonzo Stagg (314).

The new wave of coaching stars includes Sonny Lubick at Colorado State; Northwestern's Gary Barnett; Kansas State's Bill Snyder, who gave new life to the ill program; and Steve Spurrier at the University of Florida, who has given the game an offensive goose with his high-scoring offense. Several NFL teams have attempted to lure Spurrier away, with offers ranging from as high as $2 million a season, but he's opted to remain at Florida, where he earns almost the same amount. Other coaches with good futures ahead of them:

- Colorado's Rick Neuheisel, a former quarterback at UCLA

- Auburn's Terry Bowden and Tulane's Jeff Bowden, sons of Bobby Bowden

✔ Texas's Mack Brown, who left North Carolina in 1998 after a 10-1 season

✔ Stanford's Tyrone Willingham, one of Bill Walsh's disciples

✔ Oklahoma State's Bob Simmons, a product of McCartney's Colorado program

✔ Purdue's Joe Tiller, an offensive specialist

✔ Georgia's Jim Donnan, Kentucky's Hal Mumme, Michigan State's Nick Saban, and Boston College's Tom O'Brien

The Heisman and Other Trophies

The Heisman Trophy is awarded annually to America's most outstanding college football player. The trophy is named in honor of John W. Heisman, a legendary football coach, who was a member of the Downtown Athletic Club in New York City. The first Heisman was given to halfback Jay Berwanger of the University of Chicago in 1935. Over the years, the award has traditionally gone to running backs and quarterbacks and some wide receivers. The three exceptions were Larry Kelley of Yale in 1936 and Leon Hart of Notre Dame in 1949 who were both two-way (offense and defense) players at end, and Charles Woodson — a cornerback from Michigan — who in 1997 became the first full-time defensive player to ever win. Woodson also returned kicks and played wide receiver on offense.

More than 900 people vote every year for the Heisman, which is announced in mid-December. The former winners and 865 college football broadcasters and sportswriters cast votes. To vie for the award, a player's college sports information department wages what is tantamount to a political campaign, producing tons of brochures, handbooks, and campaign literature on its star player. The campaign for the next year's Heisman winner actually begins during spring practice prior to the start of the football season.

Besides the Heisman, college football has other prestigious awards. The Outland Trophy has been awarded since 1946 to the nation's top interior lineman. Two years younger than the Heisman, the Maxwell Award, which began in 1937, also goes to the top college player. Often, the Maxwell and the Heisman don't agree. The Lombardi Award is given to the nation's top lineman, and the Davey O'Brien Award is given to the best quarterback.

Remembering my college days

I went to Villanova on a football scholarship, and we never played on television. Our home stadium's capacity was around 7,000. We took buses to a lot of our games and stayed three to a room at motor lodges with two beds a lot of the time. We didn't have all the fancy training facilities that a Nebraska or Penn State or Florida has. No film rooms or big weightlifting rooms. I was just happy to have hot water for my shower.

But we played some big games at Villanova. We played Boston College twice, and Clemson was in the top ten when we faced them. The Boston College game was a big game for me because I was from Boston and was supposed to play for them. I always had some animosity for that game because the day after I had originally signed with Boston College, the head coach told me I was going to play offensive guard. I didn't want to play that position. That's how I ended up at Villanova, playing defense.

When we played Clemson, they had something like seven first-round draft choices on their roster, and they beat us 30-0 with their third team. Clemson had the Bostic brothers (Jeff and Joe) playing center and guard, and they simply wore me out. They didn't beat me with athletic ability; they just knew a whole lot more about playing than I did. But I got my revenge in the Super Bowl, playing against Jeff, who was with the Washington Redskins. And our previous matchup definitely was on my mind.

College football has gotten bigger since I played — more television, more money, and more exposure. Villanova, though, hasn't changed much. It's still a small college program, but in 1997 the team went 12-1 and made the playoffs.

All-American and Other All-Star Teams

The Associated Press All-American team is the most prestigious All-American team, followed by the Walter Camp All-American team. The American Football Coaches' All-American Team, which is selected by the coaches for all NCAA divisions and the NAIA, is also considered a very accurate gauge of the best college talent.

These teams are all-star teams. They don't play anybody; they merely honor the best players at their respective positions on a national scale. The Associated Press lists first-, second-, and third-team All-Americas. The selections are very subjective. Often, coaches and football writers vote for players they know personally. Voters have their favorites and also their prejudices. Consequently, some deserving players may be ignored or fail to receive the recognition they deserve. In many ways, it is a popularity contest.

Because many of these all-star teams include players who are flunking classes and ones who have no intention of ever graduating, Academic All-American teams have emerged to recognize student-athletes who have had great careers and been successful in the classroom.

The Blue-Gray game is one of four major all-star games in which college seniors perform and are studied and watched by NFL scouts, coaches, and general managers. The college kids spend a week practicing before the weekend game. The other college all-star games are the Senior Bowl in Mobile, Alabama; the East-West Shrine Game in Palo Alto, California; and the Hula Bowl in Hawaii.

I was fortunate to receive an invitation to the Blue-Gray All-Star game in Birmingham, Alabama. I think that another player canceled out, and I got in, sort of as a novelty. I don't think that I projected very high in the NFL draft, maybe a tenth-round pick, until I played in this all-star game.

The week of practice and the game itself helped me a lot. It gave me the opportunity to compete with the top college prospects in America; something I couldn't do every weekend at a smaller school like Villanova, a Division I-AA school. Every NFL team had scouts at this game; very few came to my Villanova games. I ended up playing well against a guy from Texas A&M who was considered to be a high draft choice, a first- or second-round pick. Jimmy Johnson, whom I ended up working with at FOX, coached me in the game. During the game, I blocked a punt and scored a touchdown, and my team won.

I had the opportunity to run for a lot of pro scouts at that game. I was running 4.7s and 4.8s and doing all their little eraser drills where you run 10 yards, pick up an eraser, drop it in a basket, and do it again. Run 20 yards, and pick it up. . . . I was really good at those drills. My vertical jump was good. I had all the intangibles, but I wasn't a good football player. So someone had to take a chance, and the Raiders did, drafting me in the second round. All-star games give a lot of unknown players like me a chance to prove that they belong at the next level.

Chapter 17

The NFL and Other Professional Football

The National Football League is the pinnacle of football — the ultimate high, the purest acceptance of anyone's ability as a football player or coach.

When I was a young player in the NFL, I thought that I would always enjoy team success. I thought that my team, the Los Angeles (now Oakland) Raiders, would go to the Super Bowl every year because we had so much talent. But so many intangibles are involved in reaching that game, things that you can't control: injuries, complacency, and the loss of talent to free agency. Looking back on my playing career now, I understand and appreciate how lucky I was to play in and win one Super Bowl.

No professional sports league is more impressive or more powerful than the National Football League. It is a multibillion-dollar empire. The NFL virtually transformed pro sports into a big business, marketing its on-field product through the magic of television. Walking down the street anywhere in the U.S., you're likely to see a fan wearing a ball cap or jersey featuring his or her favorite player or team.

The NFL and television have grown and expanded together in the last 40 years. Unlike baseball, which is always referred to as the national pastime, football captures the imagination of Americans who respect toughness, true grit, and determination. The constant action on every snap of the ball is appealing. And television allows cities and states to close ranks; it brings Miami to tiny Green Bay, Wisconsin, and Los Angeles to New York. The immediacy of television is picture-perfect for a national league full of nationalized teams. For example, no matter where in the U.S. you live, you can follow the exploits of your favorite team on television on Sundays or whatever day they play in a particular week. When the Cleveland Browns played in the early 1990s, for example, one of their biggest fan clubs was in southern California.

Television is a powerful medium that's perfectly suited to NFL football and its many lengthy time-outs and delays. The time-outs and commercials enable fans to discuss strategy with friends who are watching or simply to sit there and think about what the teams will attempt to do on the next play. The fans watching at home actually have a better view of what's going on in a game than the fans sitting in the stands. Television allows fans to see clear replays and up-close shots of the action. Every play is so critical in football. And because each team plays only 16 games per season, not including playoff games, every game becomes an event. In many cities, thousands of fans arrive at the stadium hours prior to kickoff for tailgate parties in the parking lots.

Although regular-season games begin in September and end in December, followed by a month of playoffs culminating in television's number-one attraction, the Super Bowl, the NFL is active year-round. During the *off-season,* players usually continue to work out to remain in condition. The league also experiences coaching changes, players switching teams via free agency, the drafting of college players (another television event in late April), and various organized training sessions called *mini-camps,* which last three to four days. Teams report to training camps in mid-July, where players practice twice a day in preparation for the long season ahead. Preseason games, generally four per team, are played in August, prior to the start of the regular season.

In this chapter, I explain how the NFL works, how teams reach the playoffs, and how the money filters down to the players. I also demystify the salary cap, player movements, practice schedules, and life in general in the greatest league on earth.

The Birth of Pro Football

The first national professional football league was created in 1920 by seven owners/players of what was known as the Ohio League. Prior to that time, pro football was disorganized because of the lack of a league-wide constitution and guidelines. Player movement was rampant, with teams routinely bidding on players. The contracts for star players ranged from $50 to $250 a game, a considerable amount of money for that time. Many college players assumed aliases so that they could earn some of that money by playing on Sunday afternoons with pro teams.

Before 1920, the Ohio League had the strongest professional teams, featuring such legends as the Canton Bulldogs and Olympian Jim Thorpe. The original league, which was called the American Professional Football Association for the first two seasons, consisted of 14 teams. After the 1921 season, the league officially changed its name to the National Football League. In the first few years of the league, the championship wasn't decided on the field; it was awarded based on a vote at league meetings.

The league didn't have a playoff system to decide its champion until 1932, and it wasn't until 1936 that every team in the league played the same number of games. The NFL divided into a two-division alignment in 1933 with the winners of each division meeting for the league championship.

In the first 13 years of the NFL, the league lacked franchise stability; numerous teams folded because of a lack of money or fan interest. Nineteen teams lasted only one year, and another 11 managed just two seasons. Only two teams, the Chicago Bears (originally the Decatur Staleys) and the Chicago Cardinals, whose franchise today resides in Phoenix, Arizona, started with the league in 1920. The Green Bay Packers are the third oldest team, joining the league in 1921.

The AFL Joins the NFL

The American Football League (AFL) started in 1960 with eight teams. The pursuit of the same players by both leagues led to escalating salaries, which was great for the players, but not for the financial welfare of pro football team owners. The NFL wasn't used to this kind of competition over talent. When the AFL, strengthened by its own network television contract, considered signing away many of the NFL's top quarterbacks, it forced the more established NFL to consider peace; a merger of the two leagues was the solution. The AFL and NFL agreed to merge in 1966 under the umbrella of the NFL. The American Football Conference (AFC) was formed to maintain a connection to the old league and its rivalries. The two leagues held a common draft in 1967 and began interleague play in the 1970 season. The first four Super Bowls were actually between the champions of the NFL and the AFL.

To balance out the conferences, the Pittsburgh Steelers and the then Cleveland Browns and Baltimore Colts moved to the American Football Conference, each franchise receiving $3 million for its troubles. (The following section gives a rundown on which teams are in which conferences.)

The NFL Conferences

Today, the National Football League is divided into two conferences, the American Football Conference and the National Football Conference. Each conference consists of 15 teams and is divided into three divisions — East, Central, and West — of five teams each. These division titles don't necessarily correspond to geographic parts of the country, though.

For example, the Atlanta Falcons, New Orleans Saints, St. Louis Rams, Carolina Panthers, and San Francisco 49ers comprise the NFC West. And four of those cities are either *east* of the Mississippi River or right on it.

- The **American Football Conference** includes nine franchises (in bold) that once were part of the old American Football League.

  - *East Division:* **Buffalo Bills,** Indianapolis Colts, **Miami Dolphins, New England Patriots, New York Jets**

  - *Central Division:* Baltimore Ravens, Cincinnati Bengals, Jacksonville Jaguars, Pittsburgh Steelers, **Tennessee Oilers**

  - *West Division:* **Denver Broncos, Kansas City Chiefs, Oakland Raiders, San Diego Chargers,** Seattle Seahawks

- The **National Football Conference** includes eight franchises that formed the old NFL, including the Chicago Bears, Green Bay Packers, New York Giants, Washington Redskins, and Detroit Lions.

  - *East Division:* Arizona Cardinals, Dallas Cowboys, New York Giants, Philadelphia Eagles, Washington Redskins

  - *Central Division:* Chicago Bears, Detroit Lions, Green Bay Packers, Minnesota Vikings, Tampa Bay Buccaneers

  - *West Division:* Atlanta Falcons, Carolina Panthers, New Orleans Saints, St. Louis Rams, San Francisco 49ers

The Schedule

The first half (or first eight games) of the NFL schedule is easy to remember: Every team plays the four other teams in its division twice, once at home and once away. The next four games are filled from a single division from the other conference; these divisions rotate every three seasons. The final four games are played against teams within a franchise's own conference, based on the team's finish the preceding season.

A first-place team plays the first-place team from each of the other two divisions, plus a second- and a third-place team in the conference. A second-place team plays the other two second-place teams, plus a first- and a fourth-place team in the conference. And so on. The fifth-place team ends up with the weakest schedule for the following season, playing the other two fifth-place finishers and a third- and a fourth-place finisher from the conference. The NFL follows a formula for devising the schedule, which is published in the annual *NFL Record and Fact Book*.

For example, although the Denver Broncos were the Super Bowl champions in 1997, they finished second in the AFC West. Therefore, they play a second-place schedule in 1998. Teams in the AFC West play teams in the NFC East this season, in addition to eight games against teams within their own division. Here's what Denver's 1998 schedule looks like:

Sept. 7	New England	1st place team
Sept. 13	Dallas	NFC East
Sept. 20	At Oakland	Division team
Sept. 27	At Washington	NFC East
Oct. 4	Philadelphia	NFC East
Oct. 11	At Seattle	Division team
Oct. 18	Open (no game)	
Oct. 25	Jacksonville	2nd place team
Nov. 1	At Cincinnati	4th place team
Nov. 8	San Diego	Division team
Nov. 16	At Kansas City	Division team
Nov. 22	Oakland	Division team
Nov. 29	At San Diego	Division team
Dec. 6	Kansas City	Division team
Dec. 13	At New York Giants	NFC East
Dec. 21	Miami	2nd place team
Dec. 27	Seattle	Division team

Playoff format

The NFL schedules all those games — 240 in a typical season — to separate the good teams from the bad. On every level of sports, people want to declare a champion. In the NFL, a total of 12 teams qualify for what amounts to the Road to the Super Bowl.

Six teams from each conference qualify for the playoffs. The three division winners qualify automatically. They are joined by three teams called *wildcard* teams, who qualify based on the win-loss records of the remaining teams in each conference that didn't finish first in their respective divisions. The two division winners with the highest winning percentages host second-round games, skipping the first round of competition. The third division winner hosts the number-three wildcard team in the first round, and the other two wildcard teams meet in the other game.

The winners of the two wildcard games advance to the second round of contests, called Divisional Playoff games. The lowest-rated wildcard winner plays the division winner with the best record, and the other wildcard winner plays the division winner with the second-best record. Both division winners enjoy *home field advantage,* meaning that they host the games. For the conference championship games (the third round), any surviving division champion automatically hosts the game. If two division winners survive, the team with the better winning percentage hosts the championship game. If the two surviving teams have identical records, home field is based on how the two teams performed in head-to-head competition during the season, and then on who had the best winning percentage in conference games.

In many instances, potential wildcard teams have identical records. When that situation occurs, the NFL has tie-breaking procedures to determine which teams advance to the playoffs. These procedures are extremely complicated; even the league has difficulty sorting out the survivors until the final two weekends of the season. I'll stick with a fairly simple example for this book. If three teams from different divisions finish with 9-7 records and only two wildcard spots remain, the NFL follows these steps:

1. **Head-to-head, if applicable.**

2. **Best won-lost-tied percentage in games played within the conference.**

3. **Best won-lost-tied percentage in common games with a minimum of four necessary.**

4. **Best net points in the conference games.**

   Net points is when you subtract a team's points scored during the regular season by the total points it allowed.

5. **Best net points in all games.**

By this point, any tie between teams is usually broken.

The Super Bowl

The Super Bowl is really the NFL championship game, pitting the winner of the American Football Conference against the champion of the National Football Conference. The game was born out of the merger of the former American Football League with the National Football League in 1966. In the first two years of the championship, the game was billed as the AFL-NFL World Championship Game. But not until the third championship meeting between the two leagues in 1969 did the name "Super Bowl" stick for good. Kansas City Chiefs owner Lamar Hunt coined the name after a toy, the super ball. The game itself figured to be "super," and "bowl" came from the college game, where bowl games remain common post-season rituals (see Chapter 16).

HALL OF FAME

NFL quarterbacks

Entering the 1998 season, the best quarterback under 30 years old was Brett Favre of the Green Bay Packers. Favre, a three-time winner of the league's Most Valuable Player award, will turn 29 during the season.

Following is a list of what some would call the Over-the-Hill bunch. However, the eight quarterbacks listed here rank as some of the NFL's all-time greats, and every one of them ranked in one, two, or three different top ten quarterback passing categories during the 1997 season. Although the average length of an NFL career is about four seasons, such is not the case with quarterbacks in general, and these players in particular. These eight players have an average age of 35 years and have played an average of 11.5 years and counting. Moon and Young also played two or more seasons in other professional leagues before joining the NFL.

✔ **Dan Marino (37):** Has played 15 seasons, thrown for 55,416 yards and 385 touchdowns, and completed 59.8 percent of his pass attempts

✔ **Warren Moon (41):** 14 seasons; 47,465 passing yards and 279 touchdowns; 58.6 completion percentage

✔ **Steve Young (36):** 13 seasons; 28,508 passing yards and 193 touchdowns; 64.8 completion percentage

✔ **John Elway (38):** 15 seasons; 48,669 passing yards and 278 touchdowns; 56.8 completion percentage

✔ **Troy Aikman (31):** 9 seasons; 26,016 passing yards and 129 touchdowns; 62.0 completion percentage

✔ **Jeff George (30):** 8 seasons; 22,042 passing yards and 120 touchdowns; 58.1 completion percentage

✔ **Chris Chandler (32):** 10 seasons; 15,372 passing yards and 94 touchdowns; 57.7 completion percentage

✔ **Erik Kramer (33):** 8 seasons; 12,726 passing yards and 81 touchdowns; 57.0 completion percentage

---

The Super Bowl is such a huge television and fan attraction that cities routinely bid for the game, offering to defray many of the league's expenses for hotels and travel expenses. The city of San Diego believes that the 1998 game had an economic impact to its city of over $230 million. The Super Bowl is such a large event that cities have been selected through the year 2002, which gives them the necessary time to prepare.

In the two weeks between the two conference championship games and the Super Bowl, plenty of hype and hoopla about the game arises. The two teams usually arrive in the host city on the Sunday prior to the game, along with more than 2,500 members of the media. The event has a national flavor to it. Week-long events, such as the NFL Experience (an interactive theme park that features more than 50 attractions, including games like Quarterback Challenge, the Extra-Point Kick, and the Super Bowl Card Show) are planned for youngsters and older fans alike. Parties are held at hotels and venues throughout the host city.

With ticket prices at $300 and most fans paying five times that amount via ticket scalping, the Super Bowl has become more of a corporate event than a bastion for hard-core football fans. You almost have to be somebody important or know somebody important to attend. The Commissioner's Party — which owners, coaches, and NFL executives attend on the Friday night prior to the game — often is an even tougher ticket to acquire than one to the game.

Building a Team

Building an NFL team is no easy task. Most teams focus first on acquiring a solid quarterback and then making sure that they have highly skilled players at the running back and wide receiver positions. The offensive line is generally built to suit the specific offensive strategy of the team — for example, if the team likes to pass, it pays a premium for linemen who are better pass-protectors than run-blockers. Having linemen equally suited to both styles is best, but sometimes that's a luxury when you're selecting your roster for today's game. Injuries are a factor when most teams have only eight linemen on their 45-player rosters.

Free agency requires teams to change their strategy

Now that player movement via free agency is part of the league, many teams attempt to fill a personnel need by bidding for a particular player's services during the off-season. Free agency began prior to the 1993 season, and more than 600 players have switched teams under the system in the first six years. Similar to its impact on Major League Baseball, free agency has improved player contracts not only for players who switch teams but also for those stars who can negotiate salaries that equate to what the most highly paid players in their same positions earn.

About 1,650 players compete in the NFL each season, which almost equals the number of agents certified with the NFL Players Association. Using players' statistics and overall performance records, these agents debate players' values with an individual team's financial negotiators.

The free-agent period begins in February. Most of the top players agree to new contract terms in the first six weeks of the negotiating session, which ends in mid-July, usually prior to the start of training camp. A top free agent usually decides on a few teams he'd like to play for and then visits each club's facility to meet the coaches and general manager. His agent then begins negotiations with the clubs that are interested. A free agent usually makes his decision based on money, but occasionally his choice is affected by the offensive or defensive system that the team uses, how he fits in with the other players, his city preference for his family, or whether he likes the coach. Some players accept less money to play with a team they think has the potential to make the playoffs.

The quarterback position is the most difficult one to develop. Many coaches and general managers — the two most important decision-makers — prefer quarterbacks with experience. (See Chapter 13 to find out how general managers, coaches, and scouts interact on personnel decisions.) So if the starting quarterback is young and inexperienced, usually his backup, the player who would replace him in the event of injury or a bad performance, has either more game-time experience or years in the league than he does.

In terms of the defense, teams need at least five star performers interspersed among players on the defensive line, linebacking corps, and secondary. These players should rank among the top ten players at their respective positions. Most NFL teams have a core of seven to ten superstar-potential players, an average of six rookies, and a group of veterans, players with at least one year of pro experience, to round out the roster. Many teams have at least 20 players with five or more years of NFL experience.

All teams acquire players through the draft (explained in detail in the following section), and their plan is to develop the players that they draft in a couple seasons. They also acquire players by making trades for players with other teams. In most seasons, fewer than 40 trades are made, most of which involve second-line players whom their former teams want to unload.

Many trades involve the simple exchange of draft choices as teams want to move either up or down from their assigned selecting spots. For example, the San Diego Chargers, a team in desperate need of a quarterback in 1998, traded two veteran players (running back Eric Metcalf and linebacker Patrick Sapp) and three draft choices (their first-round picks in 1998 and 1999 and a 1998 second-round draft choice) simply to move into the Arizona Cardinals' position in the 1998 draft. This was a blockbuster trade, considering that the Chargers surrendered a lot for the rights to draft Washington State quarterback Ryan Leaf.

If a team doesn't want to wait for the draft or can't make a trade, it usually opts to find what it considers a star player by signing a free agent, a player who sells himself to the highest bidding team. Because of salary-cap restrictions, a team must be careful how it pursues free agents because it may not be able to afford a particular player — that player's salary may jeopardize the team's salary scale with its current players, who often are upset when a new player earns more than they do, especially if they're considered team leaders or star players.

If a particular draft choice doesn't become a starter by his third season, he's generally considered a *bust*. The team then attempts to replace him with a veteran or another rookie and starts the process anew. The typical NFL team has an average of eight players with ten or more years of experience.

Player Designations

While listening to commentary or reading about the NFL, you hear many of the following terms that relate directly to a player's status. Knowledgeable fans frequently toss around these terms. Many of the terms were agreed upon by the NFL owners and the NFL Players Association, a union that legally represents the interests of the players.

In 1998, both management and the Players Association agreed to extend the current collective bargaining agreement an additional five years (from 1998 to 2002). The owners voted to extend the agreement at their annual meeting in March. The extension of this agreement ensures labor peace in the NFL through the 2002 season. The agreement includes improved pension benefits for retired players and health coverage for post-career players.

The following list explains some of the key principles in the agreement and frequently heard words that describe players:

- ✔ **Accrued season:** When a player spends six or more regular-season games on a club's active or inactive list, meaning that he was on the injured reserve list or was physically unable to perform.

- ✔ **Agent:** A person who represents players during contract negotiations. Many agents are attorneys; some are friends and relatives of the players they represent. Agents are banned from most college campuses.

- ✔ **First-year player:** A player who spent the preceding season on an NFL practice squad, was injured and never played before, or played in another league — the CFL or Arena (both of which are described later in this chapter) — and isn't considered a rookie by professional standards.

- ✔ **Franchise player:** A team can designate only one of its players as a franchise player. This player must be paid a minimum of the average of the top five salaries at his position or 120 percent of his previous salary, whichever is greater. If the player declines this salary increase and wants even more money, the club can designate him as an exclusive rights player, and the player can negotiate with other teams for a better contract. However, his team can match the new club's offer or receive two first-round draft choices as compensation.

- ✔ **Injured reserve:** A special category in which a team can place an injured player who is deemed a physical risk. Usually, these players require surgeries for their injuries. This player cannot return to the active roster (and play again) during that season.

- ✔ **Practice squad:** Each team can place five players on this squad, and they are eligible only to practice. These players are paid $3,300 a week and are free agents. Teams routinely sign players from other teams' practice squads in order to complete their 45-man active rosters when they lose players due to injury or release them due to poor performance.

✔ **Pro-Bowler:** A player who is selected by a vote of the fans, players, and coaching staffs to represent his conference in an all-star game that takes place the week after the Super Bowl. Any player chosen to play in the Pro Bowl is considered among the league's elite. The Pro Bowl is held in Hawaii.

✔ **Restricted free agent:** A player who has completed three accrued seasons and now has an expired contract. Under the terms of the collective bargaining agreement, the club basically controls what he will be paid. Most teams attempt to sign this player to a long-term contract if he's deemed a valuable starter, thus preventing him from being an unrestricted free agent in his fourth season.

✔ **Roster reduction:** Each team is allowed to open training camp with 80 players on its roster. By mid-August, teams have to cut down to 60 players. The next week, each club must cut seven more players, leaving their roster to 53. The weekend before the start of the regular season, teams must announce their active rosters of 45 players. They are allowed to retain eight inactive players.

✔ **Rookie:** A player who's on an NFL roster for the first time. A player who has played in another league, such as the CFL or the Arena League, is still considered a rookie by the NFL.

✔ **Trading period:** Generally it begins in mid-February and ends on the Tuesday following the sixth regular-season game, which is usually in early October.

✔ **Transition player:** This player's club must pay him the average of the prior season's top ten salaries of players at the same position or 120 percent of the player's previous year's salary, whichever is greater. A transition player can seek a contract from another team, but his current team has seven days to match the offer and thus retain his services. A team can have no more than two transition players in the same season, as long as it doesn't also have a designated franchise player.

✔ **Unrestricted free agent:** A player who has completed four or more accrued seasons and now has an expired contract.

✔ **Veteran:** A player who has played at least one season in the NFL.

✔ **Waiver system:** The procedure by which a player's contract or NFL rights are made available by his current team to other teams in the league. During the procedure, the 29 other teams either file a claim to obtain the player or waive the opportunity to do so, thus the term *waiver*. The claiming period is typically ten days during the off-season, but from early July through December, it lasts only 24 hours. If a player is claimed by two or more teams in this period, priority is based on the inverse won-lost standing of the teams. The team with the worst record has priority. If no team selects this player, he's free to sign with any team, including his previous employer. If no one signs him, he is unemployed — technically fired from his profession.

The Draft

The annual NFL draft of college players occurs in late April. The two-day event begins on a Saturday at noon EDT and finishes on Sunday. The draft is held in New York City, generally with some of the top college players in attendance, and is televised by ESPN. If a college player wants to play in the NFL, he usually enters via the draft. In a typical year, more than 2,500 college athletes become eligible for the draft, but only about 240 players are selected in the seven rounds.

Who picks when

The draft consists of seven rounds, and each team is allotted one pick in each round. The team with the worst record in the preceding season selects first. The team with the second worst record selects second, and so on, with the Super Bowl champion picking last in the first round and the Super Bowl loser picking next to last. Teams are allowed 15 minutes to make their selections in the first round and five minutes in rounds thereafter.

If two teams finish with the same record, the tie is broken on the strength of the schedules of both teams. The strength of a team's schedule is based on the total won-lost records of their 16 opponents. For example, in the 1998 draft, Arizona, San Diego, Oakland, and Chicago all finished with 4-12 records, tying for the second worst record in the NFL. Arizona, however, received the second overall selection in the draft because its strength of schedule (124-125-7) ended up being a .498 winning percentage.

Because the league awards extra selections to teams, known as *compensatory picks,* more than 240 players were selected in the last two drafts. Those picks compensate for how many free agents a team may lose during the preceding season.

How picks are made

At the NFL Scouting Combine in Indianapolis in early February, medical doctors and trainers examine prospective players that are hoping to be drafted. These players also submit to weight-lifting and running drills and perform player-specific drills, such as a throwing drill for quarterbacks and a running pattern drill for wide receivers. Players are also tested for illegal drug use and are given intelligence tests. They are measured and weighed and interviewed by countless numbers of coaches, scouts, and club officials. This information-gathering process is so thorough that a casual observer might think the teams are conducting research for some sort of science project.

On draft day, every team has a representative in New York, but the teams' coaching, scouting, and executive staffs remain at the training facilities or team headquarters in their respective cities. Teams usually have one huge room called the "War Room" where staff members meet to discuss potential players and formulate their final decisions prior to announcing selections. Depending on the team, the general manager may consult with the head coach, the director of college scouting, and other club personnel before making a selection.

Usually, the team is in contact with the player on the telephone prior to making the choice in order to inform him of its decision or to ask any last-minute questions regarding health or personal problems. The NFL security department does background checks on all prospective draft candidates and reports its findings to the member clubs when asked.

A player who is not selected has the option of signing a free-agent contract with any team that wants him. These players are the lowest-paid players on the rosters and generally are released during training camp. Teams sign many of these players simply to provide live bodies for the veterans to practice against during training camp. Of course, there's the rare exception of an undrafted, free-agent rookie making the team because he has more ability than a draft choice. It just shows everyone that scouts, general managers, coaches, and other player-personnel department members can make mistakes on their evaluations of all the players eligible for the draft.

Player Salaries

The pay for playing NFL football has risen dramatically in the last ten seasons. In 1988, the average salary of an NFL player was $250,000. It jumped to almost $800,000 in 1997, and that figure eventually may double in 1998 because of the financial impact of the league's new $17.6 billion network television contract, which runs through 2005. The teams are required under the salary cap to share 63 percent of their gross revenues with the players, and the television income is the largest portion (more than 70 percent) of a team's revenue.

Most star quarterbacks averaged $6 million annually in 1997, and that number probably will jump to between $10 million and $12 million a year by the end of the 1998 season. At the bottom of the payroll scale, the minimum salary for a first-year player in 1988 was $60,000, in 1993 it was $100,000, and in 1988 the projected minimum is $144,000, representing a 140 percent increase since 1988.

Early in 1998, defensive linemen who were free to shop their talent to all 30 teams (unrestricted free agents without contracts) realized staggering overall salary packages. Sean Gilbert signed a seven-year deal with the

Carolina Panthers for $46.6 million, and the Minnesota Vikings gave John Randle a $10 million signing bonus — money generally reserved for quarterbacks — to make sure that he didn't jump to the Miami Dolphins. A signing bonus like Randle's is prorated against the team's salary cap over the life of his contract. For example, if he signs for five years, his team is charged $2 million a year against the cap for that $10 million signing bonus.

The only knock on the wage system is the inequity inside the locker room; a definite caste system exists. The way that the free agency system has worked since 1993, 20 percent of players tend to receive 60 percent of a team's payroll, leaving 80 percent of the players with the remaining 40 percent share. To simplify this equation, say a team's total payroll is $40 million for 50 players. In that scenario, the breakdown would be 10 players earning $2.4 million each and the other 40 players earning $400,000 each. That breakdown of salaries create a huge disparity, which is unfortunate considering that football is such a team game. And a great quarterback is nothing without a good offensive line and solid receivers.

The Salary Cap

To understand how an NFL team decides which players to draft, sign in free agency, or outright release, you must understand the salary cap. In 1998, the salary cap was projected to be more than $53 million. The cap is based on players receiving 63 percent of the designated gross revenues of the NFL teams, which include revenue from network television contracts, ticket sales, concessions, parking, and product sales. The designated gross revenues for the 1998 season are projected to be approximately $84.6 million per team.

The salary cap, like free agency, came into existence prior to the 1993 season. It was a negotiated labor settlement between the NFL owners and the NFL Players Association following several antitrust court cases regarding players' rights for movement via free agency. It was designed to put all the NFL teams on equal footing when competing for free agents and signing their number-one draft choices. Teams that don't charge exorbitant ticket prices or whose stadium leases don't provide extra income from luxury suites, parking, and concessions receive funds from the richer teams to supplement their gross revenues in order to make the cap as equitable as possible.

The $53 million cap is the amount of money that each team is allowed to spend on players' base salaries, prorated signing bonuses, and other likely-to-be-earned incentives. (These incentives generally refer to categories that a player most likely will attain in 98 percent of team scenarios, such as reporting to training camp on time and making the roster for a Pro Bowl–caliber player.) For example, if a player signs for five seasons and receives $10 million to sign (his signing bonus), the prorated portion of the bonus is $2 million per season. If that same player's base salary is $1 million, his contract for this particular season counts $3 million toward the salary cap. Pretty simple, right?

Every team is allowed a maximum of 53 active players under its salary cap. If a player is injured and lost for the season, his salary still counts toward the cap. Teams do a lot of juggling during the season as players come and go — clubs rework contracts in order to fit an entire roster under the cap. Each team usually has one executive, called a *capologist,* crunching the salary numbers of the players, making sure that everyone fits under the salary cap.

Although the cap is $53 million, NFL teams actually spend more money than that on their players. In 1998, for example, teams are also required to fund about $6 million in pension and health benefits. And some teams spend more millions in signing bonuses in order to lure top-notch free agents. Teams have been known to give as much as $25 million in one season in signing bonuses alone, which are spread out over a period of years, thus lessening the impact on the salary cap.

HOWIE SAYS

The Larry Bird rule

For fans' sake, I wish that the NFL would institute something like the Larry Bird rule in the NBA, which was instituted when Bird was still a player with the Boston Celtics. Under this rule, the Celtics were allowed to pay Bird whatever he wanted without it impacting their salary cap. If the NFL adopted such a rule, teams would be allowed to sign any of their stars without their salaries counting toward the salary cap. I hate to see teams lose their stars simply because of salary cap restrictions. And what's even more unfortunate is that football fans, from 9-year-olds all the way up to 90-year-olds, are losing the opportunity to watch their favorite player on their team for more than two or three years.

I realize that the adoption of such a rule might push some teams well over the cap limit, but I think that would be all right. I simply don't think it's right to punish a team and its fans because a player can earn an extra million bucks someplace else and that extra million prevents him from signing with his own team because it would push them over the salary cap. Teams should be allowed to protect the players they drafted and helped make stars, especially if both the team and the player can agree to a fair contract.

Big Business and the TV Connection

The best way to explain the popularity of the NFL is to study its network television contract. In 1982, the league received $420 million a year from all three networks and two cable companies to televise games. Beginning in 1998, ESPN is obligated to pay $600 million for one season of Sunday night telecasts. The total obligation of FOX, CBS, ABC, and ESPN for the 1998 season is $2.2 billion. Now you can understand why Super Bowl commercials are priced at $1.3 million per 30 seconds.

For NFL owners, these are grand times. The salary cap is $53 million, and the annual television payments over the next five seasons will average $73 million for each team. And owners benefit from revenue from ticket sales, luxury suites, local radio broadcast rights, concessions, and NFL Properties (the NFL marketing arm for hats, T-shirts, company logos, sponsorships, and so on). Individual club revenue adds another $20 million to many teams' bank accounts.

If you're wondering, *luxury suites* are the glass-enclosed private boxes within a stadium that seat as many as 12 fans and include private bars, rest rooms, couches, and television sets. Most fans have a catered meal or brunch delivered to these suites. Green Bays' Lambeau Field has over 200 luxury boxes, which cost more than $12,000 and are used only for the ten (regular-season and preseason) home games. Some stadiums feature large VIP restaurants and bar lounges for high-roller fans. Some fans have to pay seat licensing fees simply to earn the right to purchase season tickets. These fees are similar to a surtax on each seat and cost fans, on average, between $500 and $2,500 per seat.

Franchise movement

Ever since the NFL lost an antitrust lawsuit in federal court, and thus the ability to prevent the Oakland Raiders from moving to Los Angeles in 1982, six franchises have left their home cities in search of better stadium deals in other cities.

I started with the Raiders in Oakland, and then played most of my career in Los Angeles. In 1995, unsatisfied with the stadium situation in Los Angeles, the Raiders returned to Oakland. That same season, the Rams vacated Orange County, California, for St. Louis, leaving the Los Angeles area without a pro football team. In the 1980s, the Colts left Baltimore for Indianapolis, and the Cardinals left St. Louis for Phoenix, Arizona.

The biggest jolt to the NFL landscape occurred in 1996, when the Cleveland Browns left Ohio for Baltimore and changed their name to the Baltimore Ravens. A new Cleveland Browns franchise will resume play in 1999. The Houston Oilers became the Tennessee Oilers in 1997, settling in Nashville but playing their games in Memphis. In 1998, the Oilers will play their home games at Vanderbilt University in Nashville until a new stadium is completed for the 1999 season.

When the Carolina Panthers and the Jacksonville Jaguars joined the NFL, beginning play in 1995, their entry fee was above $200 million. The new Cleveland expansion team, which is expected to begin play in 1999, will be asked to pay more than double that amount. And if the league ever expands to Los Angeles, the nation's number-two television market, the price probably will be even higher.

Football Around the Globe: The Canadian Football League and NFL Europe

Although speculation occasionally arises that some businesspeople are interested in forming a rival professional football league, the NFL remains uncontested and number one. The NFL also has broadened its interests with committed financial support for two professional leagues, which are national and international in scope but relatively minor when their pool of talent is compared to the NFL's.

Neither the Canadian Football League nor the NFL Europe league plays games during the NFL's critical exposure months of December and January. The CFL — which has teams in Calgary, Edmonton, Hamilton, Montreal, Saskatchewan, Toronto, Vancouver, and Winnipeg — begins play in June and ends in late November with the Grey Cup, its version of the Super Bowl. The CFL begins its 90th season in 1998.

NFL Europe is an offshoot of the World League of American Football, which later became simply the World League. The NFL wanted to globalize American football and in 1991 started a spring league, called the World League of American Football, that had ten charter franchises, seven in the U.S. and three in Europe. This league existed for two seasons, and was restarted as a Europe-only pro league in 1995.

This European league has six teams: Amsterdam; Barcelona; Rhein and Frankfurt in Germany; the England Monarchs, who play their games in London, Bristol, and Birmingham; and the Scottish Claymores, who play most of their games in Edinburgh, Scotland. Twenty-five of the 30 NFL teams supplied a total of 92 players to these six teams for the 1998 season. The season begins in April and is ten weeks long, culminating with the World Bowl in mid-June.

NFL Europe is a marketing tool for the NFL and FOX Sports, which underwrites 49 percent of the league. The league supplies sports programming for FOX Sports and its cable television outlets in the U.S. and Europe.

With NFL games televised in Canada, the Canadian Football League has struggled financially in that nation's major cities. The NFL formed a new alliance with the CFL in 1997 because the stronger American league feared the CFL would cease to exist. Some NFL teams use the CFL to develop players — in some cases, the CFL is like baseball's minor leagues. Plus, the CFL's existence may help to prevent the emergence of a rival major pro football league that could damage the financial stability of the NFL. To help the CFL become more profitable, NFL staff members began working at the CFL's Toronto headquarters to advise the CFL on retail, licensing, and sponsorship efforts. The NFL will also provide promotional support to the CFL that will benefit both the league and the fans.

The NFL/CFL alliance includes a five-year, $3 million advance from NFL Enterprises to help support the game in Canada. According to the NFL, this association is consistent with the league's strategy of developing football into a leading global sport. At one time, the NFL hinted about an expansion into Toronto, but that doesn't seem possible until beyond 2003. Therefore, for now it's important for the NFL to maintain the CFL and also NFL Europe.

Arena Football

Arena football is a fast-paced, offense-oriented indoor sport played with only eight players per team on the field at a time. Six of those eight players must play both offense and defense. The field is 85 feet wide and 66 yards long. The playing field is 50 yards long with the end zones only 8 yards deep. The field is smaller because the games are held in sports arenas that were built for hockey and basketball.

The Arena Football League began its 12th season in 1998 with teams in 14 cities, and wants to build an association with the NFL. Many NFL personnel executives would like to have a working arrangement with the league in order to develop quarterbacks and receivers. The league, which attracted an average of 10,000 fans per game in 1997, averaged almost 92 points a game in 1997. No blitzing is permitted, and defensive teams are allowed to rush the quarterback with only four players. Another oddity is that the rules don't call for any punting, and with all kickoffs and missed field goals, the returner retrieves the ball after it deflects off the netting in an end zone.

The league begins play in May with a 14-game regular season. The top eight teams qualify for the playoffs with single elimination games leading up to the championship game, which is called ArenaBowl. The top team for the last few years has been the Arizona Rattlers, which is coached by Danny White who was a star with the Dallas Cowboys in the 1980s and an All-America quarterback for Arizona State. Arena teams are located in such small cities as Albany, New York; Grand Rapids, Michigan; and Des Moines, Iowa.

Chapter 18

Fantasy Leagues

. . . .

In This Chapter

▶ Understanding how fantasy football works

▶ Putting together a team

▶ Managing and scoring a team

. . . .

Have you ever watched a football game and said to yourself, "Now, if I were an NFL team owner, I'd do some things differently, and my team would make it to the Super Bowl . . ."? Well, you can live out your dream of becoming an NFL team owner by participating in a fantasy football league. These imaginary leagues give you the opportunity to put together your dream team of NFL football players and pit your team against other fantasy football teams from all over the country and around the world. And at the end of the season, you may even win prize money — and more important, bragging rights!

Fantasy football leagues are everywhere, and many different types of leagues exist. I know that a lot of fans are obsessed with these leagues because people ask me for advice all the time. Some of them would rather have me advise them on whom to trade for than ask for my autograph. For example, during the 1997 season when San Francisco 49ers receiver Jerry Rice suffered an injury that forced him to miss much of the season, fans were asking how they could replace him. But there's no way to replace a productive player like Rice, the NFL's all-time leading touchdown scorer and receiver.

In this chapter, I focus on the rules and method of play of one particular type of league: the head-to-head league. I also point out resources for you to use to investigate other types of leagues.

How Fantasy Football Leagues Work

In a head-to-head fantasy football league, you and your fellow owners draft teams of NFL players and compete against each other's teams each week. Your fantasy team roster includes individual offensive players — quarterbacks, running backs, wide receivers, tight ends, and kickers — and defensive or special teams *units,* depending on the particular setup of the league. Throughout the season, you track the performance of the players on your team and tally the points, yardage, and other statistics that they accrue, and you earn points based on those real-life statistics. Table 18-1 lists the common scoring categories.

Table 18-1	Fantasy Football Scoring Categories
Category	*Points Awarded*
Touchdown	6 points
Field goal	3 points
Safety	2 points
Two-point conversion	2 points
Passing yards	1 point per 25 yards
Rushing yards	1 point per 10 yards
Receiving yards	1 point per 10 yards

If your team outscores your opponent's team for the week, you get a win. At the end of the season, you compare your win-loss record against those of the other teams to determine who makes the playoffs — the head-to-head competition of the top teams in the league, leading up to the Fantasy Super Bowl. The last team standing in the playoffs is the Super Bowl champ.

How to Play

Entire volumes have been written on playing fantasy football. I'll skip over most of the intricate details and legalese found in other books and try to give you the basics you need to get started. Refer to a good fantasy football reference like *Cliff Charpentier's Fantasy Football Digest* (Lerner Publications Company) to get detailed coverage of the nuances of fantasy football.

Starting a league

Starting a league is easy. Here's how:

1. **Recruit enough friends, coworkers, or neighbors so that you have eight or ten teams. (Each person fields one team.)**

   Definitely keep to an even number of teams. Scheduling is too difficult with an odd number of teams.

2. **Name your league and have each owner name his or her team.**

   Each owner must submit a team name. (Get creative!)

3. **Select a date for your annual player draft.**

   This is when you choose the players for your team. The weekend before the start of the NFL regular season usually works best.

4. **Agree on an entry fee.**

   This dollar amount can be as high or low as you like. Pool the entry fees together to form the "pot," the cash paid out as prize money to the lucky winners.

That's it! Grab your clipboard and start scouting players as you begin the countdown to the draft.

Taking care of administrative tasks

Your first order of business after forming your league is to appoint an almighty commissioner. The commish arbitrates any and all disputes that crop up (and trust me, controversy rears its ugly head in most leagues).

Once a commissioner is in place, draw up a set of written league rules. (References like *Cliff Charpentier's Fantasy Football Digest* can help you adopt a set of bylaws.) Feel free to customize the so-called standard rules of fantasy football — the goal is to minimize disputes during the season yet keep everything fun. You may even want to hold a predraft party to vote on rules.

Next up is deciding how to track and record the statistics for your league. In most leagues, owners receive reports that show the preceding week's results and summarize season-to-date standings. You can tackle this reporting task in several ways:

✔ **Find a stats service.** The easy, low-maintenance, but most expensive way to track your league. Pay a stats service up front, and they do all the work for you and mail (or e-mail) reports directly to you. If you choose this option, include a portion of the cost in each team's entry fee.

✔ **Buy stats software.** Buy good fantasy football statistics software and download NFL stats from the Internet. You input all your league's teams into the program and then kick back as the program spits out weekly reports and standings. Not as expensive as a stats service, but you do have the one-time cost of the software — split the cost of the software among all the owners. Using software also involves more work: downloading stats, printing and mailing reports, and inputting player and team changes.

Search the Internet and/or the classified ads in fantasy football publications for information about both stats services and software packages.

✔ **Calculate the stats yourself.** The good, old-fashioned (and most time-consuming) way to do your league's stats. All you need to calculate all the team's stats manually are pen and paper, a calculator, and the sports page.

Definitely use a stats service for your inaugural season. Using a service allows you to focus solely on playing the game (the fun stuff) and not worry about all the administrative and stat-keeping junk (the boring stuff). Make sure to find a service that takes care of scheduling as well. Talk to your fellow owners after the first season to see whether they would rather save money and do the stats themselves.

Drafting a team

When draft day arrives, all the owners gather at a central location. The goal for each owner is to draft a team of 15 to 18 players. (Determine the roster limit for each team beforehand; see the section "Filling out your roster" later in this chapter for the breakdown of roster spots.)

How many players to draft at each position is up to you, but here's a safe combination of players to draft: two quarterbacks, four running backs, four wide receivers, two tight ends, two kickers, and two defense/special teams (punt and kickoff return) units.

Each owner selects one player at a time. Generally, the commissioner draws numbers out of a hat to determine the draft order. The owners make their picks in order for the first round. Then they reverse this order for the second round. For example, in an eight-person league, Owners 1 through 8 make the first eight selections in order. Then Owner 8 gets the ninth pick, Owner 7 gets the tenth pick, and so on down to Owner 1, who makes the sixteenth and seventeenth pick, and so on until all owners fill their rosters.

Before the draft, designate two people to record all the player selections. Accurate records can help resolve conflicts that may arise later.

Filling out your roster

Each week, you enter a starting lineup made up of the following players: one quarterback, two running backs, two wide receivers, one tight end, one kicker, and one defense/special teams (punt and kickoff return) unit. You draft an entire team's defense and special teams. If your team's defense or special teams unit scores a touchdown or records a safety, you get points.

The remainder of your players are *reserves.* These players' statistics don't count while the players sit on your reserve squad; instead, reserves serve as backups for your starting lineup. Here's why reserves are important:

- ✔ **To replace poor-performing starters:** If your quarterback, for example, plays poorly, you can replace him in your starting lineup the following week with your backup quarterback.

- ✔ **To replace injured starters:** If your star running back breaks his leg (gasp!), you simply start your backup running back the following week.

- ✔ **To account for bye weeks:** Each NFL team has one *bye week* (a week in which they don't play). Because of bye weeks, you need to insert backup players for your starters whose teams aren't playing that week.

Managing your team after the draft

Fantasy football requires active weekly participation. You can't just kick back after the draft and expect your team to be successful. For starters, each week you must submit your starting lineup. At a minimum, you should

- ✔ **Monitor the schedule:** Don't start a player whose team isn't playing that weekend.

- ✔ **Check out the injury updates:** You obviously don't want to start an injured player.

Consider the following options to try to improve your team over the course of the season:

- ✔ **Free agent acquisitions:** Closely monitor the pool of undrafted players; you may be able to acquire a great player whom no one else drafted.

- ✔ **Trades:** This is the fun stuff. Just like a real wheeling-and-dealing sports team owner, you, too, can put your players up on the trading block and make deals with other owners in your league.

  As a general rule, you must trade equal numbers of players. For example, if you trade two players, you must get two players in return to keep your team whole.

  The rules for free agent acquisitions and trading vary widely. Consult *Cliff Charpentier's Fantasy Football Digest* or fantasy football sites on the Internet to find out more about other leagues' policies regarding free agents.

Figuring your point total and winning

Table 18-2 shows you an abbreviated scoring example. Using this example, you would pit your 64 points against your weekly opponent's total. If you outscore that opponent, you get a win; if he or she outscores you, you lose; if you score the same total, you get a tie. Simple, huh? As the season progresses, you can gauge how well (or how poorly) your team is doing by comparing your win-loss record with the other teams' records.

At the end of the regular fantasy season, the teams with the best records make the playoffs. These high-powered playoff teams vie for the pinnacle of fantasy football — the Fantasy Super Bowl!

Table 18-2	A Scoring Example	
Player	*Scoring Play*	*Points Awarded*
Brett Favre, QB	1 touchdown pass	6
	278 passing yards	11 (1 point per 25 yards passing)
	24 rushing yards	2 (1 point per 10 yards rushing)
Terrell Davis, RB	1 touchdown run	6
	159 yards rushing	15
Keyshawn Johnson, WR	1 touchdown reception	6
	99 receiving yards	9 (1 point per 10 yards receiving)
John Carney, K	1 field goal	3
Chicago Bears, defense/special teams	1 kickoff return touchdown	6
Total		**64**

Of course, financial incentive exists for fielding a strong team (but feel free to eliminate entry fees and play for pride only). Here's one easy way to distribute prize money (dollar amounts will vary based on the number of teams in your league and the entry fee amount):

- Award a small amount ($1 or $2) for each win during the regular season
- Give 20 percent of the pot for the Super Bowl loser
- Give the remainder of the pot to the Super Bowl champ

Where to Find Information about Players

Prior to the draft and throughout the season, you need to stay informed about your players. You can keep up-to-date by reading fantasy football magazines and searching the Internet. If you don't have Internet access, the box scores in your local newspaper provide plenty of good information during the season. *USA Today* publishes complete team and individual statistics, generally on Wednesdays and Thursdays.

Here are some good fantasy football magazines to check out:

- *Fantasy Football Pro Forecast:* Offers valuable tips and insight from the top fantasy experts in the United States, as well as cheat sheets for a variety of unique scoring methods, complete statistics, and a player index for quick and easy access to player information.

- *Fantasy Football Draftbook:* Gives you NFL draft analysis and scoop on the latest trades, player moves, and other late-breaking info.

- *FlashUpdate:* Includes team notes, injury reports and updates, matchup analysis, player and position rankings, and stats.

Fantasy football-related Web sites abound. Here are some sites that offer player profiles, team stats, injury reports, lots of good insider information, and links to even more fantasy sites:

- 1998 Football Fantasy Draft (`www.sportsdrafts.com/`)
- ABC Monday Night Football (`www.abcmnf.com`)
- CNNSI (`www.cnnsi.com/football/`)
- ESPN.sportszone (`www.espn.sportszone.com/nfl/`)
- Fantasy Football (`www.fantasydraft.com`)
- Fantasy Insights (`www.fantasyinsights.com/`)
- FOX Sports (`www.foxsports.com/football`)
- MSNBC Sports - Fantasy Football (`fantasyfootball.msnbc.com/`)
- NFL.COM (`www.nfl.com`)
- Sandlot Shrink (`www.sandlotshrink.com/`)
- Statman Plus, Inc. (`www.statmanplus.com/`)
- The Sporting News (`www.sportingnews.com/nfl/`)
- TFL Report (`www.tflreport.com/tfl003.html`)
- TQStats (`www.tqstats.com`)
- USA Today (`www.usatoday.com/sports/nfl`)

When Joining a National League

If you want to subscribe to and become a member of a national fantasy league, such as an online league, be prepared to select your players based on a monetary amount. In these leagues, every team has a limited but equal amount of imaginary money to spend on players. These leagues require entry fees, but the rewards for winning can amount to thousands of dollars. Plus, these leagues are great ways to test yourself against opponents from many parts of the country and even around the world.

Based on 1997 statistics, players like Green Bay Packers quarterback Brett Favre, Detroit Lions running back Barry Sanders, and Denver Broncos running back Terrell Davis are high-priced selections, ranging from $38 to $40 each. In a $100 league, you could afford to purchase only one of these highly productive superstars and still be able to complete an entire roster.

However, every national fantasy league has a different salary cap system. They also supply standings and overall team records. For the so-called football expert, these leagues may be the best competitive way to test your knowledge of the NFL and its players.

Tips for Fantasy Football Success

Everyone who plays fantasy football will give you a different set of tips, but here are a few that should serve you well in any league:

- ✔ **Check out the prior year's stats.** Make sure that you know who the studs are at each position. Pay special attention to touchdowns scored, because that's the name of the game in fantasy football.

- ✔ **In the early rounds of the draft, take the best player available regardless of position.** For example, if most of the top-notch quarterbacks are taken by the time you reach your turn to pick, snag the best available player, such as a running back or wide receiver. Remember, however, that you must fill in all the necessary positions to field a legal team.

- ✔ **Don't draft a kicker in the early rounds.** There are plenty of decent kickers in the NFL, so use your early draft picks to acquire players at other positions.

- ✔ **Consider a player's opponent for the week when selecting your starting lineup.** If one of your running backs is going up against the best run defense in the league, you may want to start another running back.

Part VI
Staying in the Game

The 5th Wave   By Rich Tennant

In this part . . .

If you're a football player, the game becomes a lot less fun when you get sidelined by an injury or a bad attitude. This part includes two very important chapters: one on the mental game and motivation, and the other on the physical side of things — weight training, conditioning, nutrition, and, most important, injury prevention. Keep yourself or your players in the game by heeding the advice in these chapters!

Chapter 19

The Mental Game and Motivation

....

In This Chapter

▶ Setting goals for the season

▶ Psyching yourself up for a game

▶ Inspiring your team to success

▶ Coaching strategies for various occasions

....

*Y*ou can't control a lot of things in sports, but you *can* control how hard you work. That's what I tell my sons. When you work hard, good things happen — this principle applies to everything you do in life. As a player, you may not be as quick or as fast as you'd like to be, but if you can motivate yourself to work hard, listen to your coaches, and learn, you'll become a better football player.

In this chapter, I get specific about what works and what doesn't when you're mentally preparing for a football game. As an athlete, you must want to play and give it your all, no matter what the odds are or how you're feeling. The ability to play through fear and pain is rather common in football players — especially the great ones.

You Can't Win without Goals

Whether you're a coach or a player, you won't get very far in football if you have no goals — even if your only goal is to win the game you're playing in or coaching today. Motivation and results go hand in hand.

The best way to approach goal-setting as a coach is to focus on it during training camp or prior to the start of the season. While preparing for the upcoming season, sit down with your players individually and formulate together what goals they'd like to attain by the season's end. Of course, you want to win every game, but that goal may be unrealistic. You should set realistic goals — ones that make sense for both the individual player and the team.

I never was an athlete who talked a lot about what I had accomplished on the field, but setting and meeting standards is important for football players. Not every player can be the best at his position, but you should strive to attain some level of consistency. If the running back before you averaged 100 yards a game, then attempt to match that. If your team won the league championship the year before, encourage your team to repeat. Always aim high.

Okay, maybe the running back before you was an All-State player, an all-star. If your skills don't quite match his, you can still set goals for yourself. As a player, your personal goals can be simple ones. For example, you can strive to run a play better and better each time. Take pride in the little things that you accomplish. Or strive not to fumble the ball a single time throughout the season — or, if you're a defensive player, aim for so many tackles or interceptions. Even if the odds seem stacked against you, you must continue to push ahead and not give up. Quitting is the easiest act of all.

Or maybe your team has no returning players, and you can't win. What do you do? As a coach, if you're certain that your team can't possibly finish above .500 because of certain physical limitations, then focus on improving the team's overall performance. Don't allow the players to cheat themselves by slacking off or giving up entirely; encourage them to give a quality effort every time they take the field. Make sure that they take pride in executing the offense and defense the way they practiced it all week.

Setting team goals

Team goals are the best goals to set because they impact the entire team. Yes, some stars do stand out in football, but they don't have great games if their teammates play lousy. For example, even the greatest quarterback in the world won't throw many touchdown passes if his offensive line fails to block for him and he gets clobbered on every down. Because football is such a team-oriented game, goals should focus primarily on the team.

No matter what league your team plays in, your number-one goal should be to make the playoffs, go to a bowl game, or achieve the equivalent at your team's level. In the NFL, teams that make the playoffs stand apart from the rest of the league. Making the playoffs is a status symbol, something the entire team and coaching staff can be proud of accomplishing.

When coaching a perennial loser, a coach should strive to improve the team's overall win-loss record by one or two games. If that goal is still out of reach, strive to improve the scoring on offense and improve the overall defense. The biggest thing is that every day you step on the field as a team or a player, you're working toward getting better, regardless of your record.

The best approach to goal-setting is to set goals that make sense. For example, keep track of how your team performs each and every season and then set next season's goals accordingly, as in these examples:

- If your offense has averaged 15 first downs a game for 5 seasons, make that the goal for this season. Or try to improve that statistic, raising the bar for your offense. When you're playing a team that allowed more than 15 first downs last week, add another 5 first downs to the total; push your offense to reach 20 first downs.

- If your defense has struggled for several seasons, allowing more than 30 points a game, make the goal for this season 25 points — a realistic goal.

- If you play a team twice, your goal for the second time should be not only to duplicate the first game's numbers but also to improve on them by 30 percent. The offense should look to improve in points scored, total yards gained, rushing yards, passing yards, first downs, and turnovers. Your defense should strive to lower the numbers for points allowed, total yards gained, rushing yards, passing yards, and first downs, and should try to create more turnovers.

- When the defense is playing against a great passer or running back, the goal should be to hold that player below his average. If the rusher routinely gains 150 yards, then your goal should be to hold him under 100 yards. If the passer averages 275 yards passing a game, then strive to keep him under 200 yards and not allow him to score any touchdowns. And try to limit his completion percentage to 50 percent or lower.

Win or lose, the defense should attempt to force three turnovers (fumbles or interceptions) per game. Obviously, a shutout is the defense's number-one goal. For your team to win, you also should strive to win the takeaway/giveaway margin (called the *turnover margin*). The Denver Broncos, 1998 NFL champions, had a +10 turnover margin during the 1997–1998 regular season. Some of the NFL's worst teams rank at the bottom of the turnover scale.

Setting individual goals

Individual goals are harder to set because a win for the team should be more important than, say, a defensive player's individual goal of collecting ten tackles, getting two quarterback sacks, and forcing a fumble. Although those numbers are super, if the team loses by 20 points, what do they mean? Nothing (except maybe to that defensive player's parents). Yes, it's true that if every player sets and meets goals, the team should ultimately find success. But the coaching staff needs to emphasize to the players that in their search for individual success they must not lose track of the ultimate goal: a team victory.

Football isn't always about statistics. In football, the opposition may focus on stopping a great player and actually succeed, yet still lose the game because one or more of that player's teammates pick up the slack — the team finds a way to win despite its star player's lack of production. This situation happens all the time because so many players never touch the ball. In fact, more than half the players on the field are unlikely ever to have the ball in their possession. In many instances, a great offensive team is shut down but still wins the game because the team's defense plays impressively or better than they usually do. Or a great passing team is shut down but the offensive linemen work extra hard to get the running game untracked, and the team can win by running instead of passing, its trademark style.

Setting individual goals for the defense is easier than setting them for the offense because the team wins if every defender makes seven to ten tackles a game. Those kinds of numbers are what a linebacker should shoot for. However, a defensive lineman may absorb double-team blocking, do an admirable job containing two offensive linemen, and never be credited with a tackle. But his efforts enable the two teammates around him to have great individual days — one of them is always freed up to make a tackle because no one is blocking him. This defensive lineman's effort is an example of how a good performance doesn't necessarily show up on the stat sheet.

Defensive linemen or linebackers rushing the passer should have quarterback sack goals of one per game. Sixteen sacks in a season generally leads the NFL; any high school player reaching ten sacks over ten games is performing at a high level. A secondary player's goal should focus more on *passes defensed* than on interceptions. A defensive back is credited with a pass defensed when the quarterback throws the ball toward that defensive back and the back either knocks the ball down or makes sure that the receiver doesn't catch it.

When a team has either a great running back or an outstanding quarterback, the best way to set individual goals is to include players in one another's successes. For example, allow the offensive linemen to share in the runner's glory. If you want the runner to gain 200 yards in a specific game, challenge the linemen to make it happen; encourage them to perform at a high level and clear the way for the running back. An offensive lineman receives no greater satisfaction than knowing that he helped pave the way for a great running back. When you set goals in this way, not only does the runner achieve his goals, but many other players achieve their goals as well. Ditto for the quarterback: The linemen's goal should be to make sure that the quarterback isn't hit in the pocket or sacked.

When setting individual goals, the best strategy is to direct the focus toward the team. The quarterback and running back certainly will receive honors after the season ends if they reach their goals, but they can't reach those goals alone. *Team* success should always be the message.

Motivating Yourself

The desire to win should always come from within you, but that's easier said than done. You must motivate yourself in all phases of your life in order to motivate yourself on the football field. You must have an inner drive to succeed, but also be emotionally grounded in order to deal with any potential failure. You must be mature and be fully aware of your limitations.

A great way to motivate yourself is to rely on a teammate, ideally a close friend who is your athletic equal or superior to you, to push you. Create a friendly rivalry and compete with each other in all types of athletic match-ups. You can gauge your achievements by comparing your performance to this other player's performance. For example, when you lift weights together, push yourself to match him or lift more than he does. Do the same when you're running or playing one-on-one basketball for relaxation. Push yourself, but don't be obnoxious about the competition.

If you can't find a friend or teammate to buddy up with, emulate a player on your team or someone you play against. Watch him and try to play and conduct yourself like he does. Having a role model is a great way to make yourself a better player.

Getting into the right frame of mind

It's very important not to dwell on the good or the bad of your prior performance. Dwelling on a bad performance has an obvious negative effect on your upcoming performance. Learn from your mistakes but don't dwell.

Similarly, draw on a good performance, but don't allow it to lead to complacency. When I played in the NFL, I realized how easy it was to become complacent about my efforts on the football field. Granted, playing football is different in the pros because you're paid: Not being mentally prepared and in the right frame of mind can lead to shoddy performances, and poor performances can lead to unemployment. And if you're not ready to play, you can more easily get injured because you're not prepared for every possibility. Failing to get yourself into the right frame of mind or making excuses for your poor performance is not acceptable at any level of football.

Aside from sheer ability, mental toughness is the greatest attribute that any football player can have. Football is like a war; people beat on you. Their goal is to put you on the ground. While you're doing the physical part, you must stay mentally focused on the game and your assignments. You can't screw up and make a mistake. If you can complete your assignments while also absorbing a physical beating, you're mentally tough. An example of mental toughness is a quarterback who stands in the pocket, waits for his receiver to get open, and then throws the ball, knowing that in the next instant he'll be jarred by a tackle.

I talk in the next section about preparing for a big game. But being in the right frame of mind is essential for all games, particularly the ones that you don't think will be very competitive. A player and his teammates must fight through complacency, which often leads to overconfidence and a lack of preparation. A coach may allow his players to have one easy practice before a game that he expects to win by a couple of touchdowns. But players must approach the final practices before a game against a winless team in the same way that they would approach a game against the league champion. Remember, every game is tough. Because football is so physical, you cannot underestimate any team or player. That's when you get hurt; that's when you get beaten.

Preparing for a big game

Whether it's the home opener or the first game of the playoffs, a big game can rattle your nerves and throw off your concentration. These big events offer many more distractions than the run-of-the-mill games do. In the NFL, more reporters are around asking questions, and the commentators are offering more opinions. The same distractions occur in big college games, although college reporters tend to ask fewer negative questions than NFL writers do. If you're a high school player, the hoopla surrounding a big game can be equally as distracting because more of your classmates and their parents are interested in the outcome.

HOWIE SAYS

Dealing with the Super Bowl

Fans often wonder whether the media attention surrounding the Super Bowl is distracting to players. In my experience, as long as a player maintains a normal regimen after he leaves the morning media interviews, he shouldn't find the attention too distracting. His afternoons and evenings are spent practicing, hanging out, and going to team meetings. He's isolated in a heavily secured hotel away from fans. In terms of practicing, he's usually refining his game preparation during Super Bowl week because the team installed the game plan the prior week when they were still at home. By Thursday of Super Bowl week, the official player interviews are finished, leaving plenty of time for the players to return their attention to the big game.

Teams sometimes create their own problems during the week of the Super Bowl by making public comments about the media's questions and the distractions that accompany them. But players and coaches should attempt to enjoy the atmosphere — remember, it's a once-in-a-lifetime thrill — and go with the flow. When you create anxiety, you're doomed as a player. What's the point of complaining or whining about the outside activities associated with the Super Bowl when you have no power to make them go away? Instead, players should approach it as a fun experience but practice hard at the same time. By the weekend, they'll have plenty of time to really zero in on the game.

On any level, you need to keep the big game in the proper perspective. Although it's an important football game, try to prepare for it as you would any other game. You're used to playing in games; you know what your coaches expect of you. To perform at your peak, you must close your mind to outside interference. Just ignore the distractions and plod ahead, performing to the best of your ability. Concentration and confidence lead to success.

Conducting your off-the-field life as normally as possible during the week of a big game is essential. Stick to the same routines. I'm not suggesting that you pretend that nothing unusual is happening; I'm simply suggesting that you enjoy some of the peripheral events while remaining focused on the game at hand.

Visualizing success

When I played, I did a lot of visualization prior to each game. Every night when I went to bed, I would envision myself playing in the upcoming game against the team or the specific players I would be going up against. I remembered the plays that I'd studied on film and plugged myself into what to anticipate and what was expected of me; I envisioned myself on the field doing what I needed to do and achieving success. Through visualization, I felt thoroughly prepared for every game. I knew what to expect from my opponents.

If you're a young player, you may not study film like college and NFL players do, but you can remember how a certain team or type of player performs. What does he like to do? What are his favorite plays? When he blocks you, does he go high or low? Know his traits and trademark style. Try to visualize what he plans to do to you and your team, and think of ways to stop those plans. On weekends, study the players who play your position at the pro level and learn from them. Study how they approach situations that you may face in a game.

As a coach, don't let your players lose sight of the team's goals as the season progresses. Should losses mount or performances fall short of their original goals, reassure your players that they weren't wrong to reach for the top; they must continue to strive for the goals that they set. Communicate to your players that by continuing to work hard, the team can still reach some of those goals.

A Coach's Most Important Job: Motivating His Team

I've always believed that a good football coach has the innate ability to inspire his players. He must be able to get inside the head of a player and bring out his best performance. The coach cannot use the same spiel every week; he has to be different. He has to find some key point that triggers an emotion in a player that inspires him to go out and play to the best of his abilities.

Through the years, I've heard every speech. But each coach motivates in a different way. I know that Jimmy Johnson, who coaches the Miami Dolphins, doesn't coach the same way that Mike Holmgren, coach of the Green Bay Packers, does. Johnson is in control of every facet of his team and keeps a keen eye on his defense. He'll release a player simply to show the entire team that he's the boss.

Holmgren is also emotional, but he doesn't show it on the sidelines as much as Johnson does. He calls the offensive plays and allows his defensive coaching staff a lot of freedom. Johnson has total control of personnel; Holmgren has a lot of input with personnel decisions, but General Manager Ron Wolf has final control. Both coaches portray a sense of authority and control, and the players respect their abilities to have the team fully prepared for every game. When a coach speaks in front of the whole team, whether in a meeting, at the end of practice, on the field, or in the locker room, he must choose his words carefully. Both Holmgren and Johnson also understand that there's a time and place for humor. Laughter can be a splendid release from the tension of an upcoming big game.

Finding the right tone

Being a coach isn't easy. On the youth level, you're dealing with young men *and* their parents. You may get a lot of interference. You must state at the beginning of the season that you will not tolerate any parental criticism of the coaching staff and how they conduct the games. Emphasize to the parents that you only want positive interference and assistance. Throughout the season, you must still communicate with parents, but try to refrain from potentially antagonistic confrontations.

Here are some other tips for being effective as a coach:

- ✔ **Remember that not all communication is verbal.** As a coach, you must be careful of your body language and facial expressions. If you look and act depressed, your players will notice quickly. When speaking to a player, always be positive and honest. When addressing the entire team, always state everything clearly and simply. When correcting a mistake or stressing a particular formation adjustment, say it loudly and always repeat it. And be consistent in your actions and speeches. Don't confuse players by telling them to do things one way one day and then another way the next day.

- ✔ **Try not to use too much sarcasm.** Nothing is worse than telling a player "Way to go!" and then following that praise with a sarcastic remark. You're sending the player a mixed message, and he will disregard your positive reinforcement and focus instead on the negative comment.

- ✔ **Know that having a positive outlook and giving praise when warranted is essential, but that criticism is appropriate sometimes, too.** A player knows when he does something well or plays poorly — so don't beat around the bush. Be direct. Rather than castigating a player in front of the whole team, take the player aside and let him know that he failed in his assignment and must do better next time.

- ✔ **Build character in your players.** You do that by caring for them, showing them that they are more to you than simply bodies that can perform special and sometimes unique tasks on the field. Try injecting some humor into the course of a practice or speech. But if you're not naturally a funny man, you don't have to tell jokes. Be yourself! Also, don't be afraid to laugh at yourself or chuckle when a colleague or player says something funny. Join in the fun, showing your players that you have a softer side to your personality.

- ✔ **Gauge your players' body language.** A football season, including summer training camp, lasts a long time, and on some days, nothing serious needs to be said. It's your job as a coach to know when your team needs a good pep talk or positive reinforcement, or when it's time for you to back off and give your players some space.

- ✔ **Be careful of how you treat your players.** If you have rules, they should be for everyone. As a coach, you never want to lose the respect of your players. If you do, the players won't perform. All the motivational speeches in the world won't motivate a group of players who don't respect their coach.

Coaches must remember that there isn't a wrong way and a right way to handle every situation or predicament. You must go with your instincts. As you grow as a coach, you'll discover what works and what doesn't.

Getting a team in top mental shape

Without question, a coach's primary responsibilities are formulating the design of the offense and defense and calling plays on game day. But a coach is also responsible for making sure that his team has "the edge" — that his players are ready to play both physically and mentally. In order to properly prepare his team to play, a coach must be organized. He must formulate a *game plan* for his team — which outlines how he plans to motivate his team to give the extra effort necessary to compete at the highest level and win.

Before summer practice begins, the coaching staff must prepare playbooks (see Chapter 13) and a practice schedule. Both are necessary to explain to the players what offensive and defensive approaches the team expects to use that season. But the practice format is essential to creating mental toughness. Coaches must make practices feel like real games by putting players in real-game situations.

The best way to create this atmosphere is to begin practice with the bulk of your exercise and running drills. Then, when the team is working on fine-tuning the offense and defense toward the end of the practice, all the players will be tired. You don't want them to be exhausted, but you do want their gas tanks one-quarter full, giving them the sensation of how they may feel in the fourth quarter when the game is on the line.

Doing a few physical drills guarantees that your players will be mentally tough. Here are some examples:

- **Running back drill:** Force running backs to run through two lines of players. These players try to strip the ball from the runner by whacking at his hands and arms, simulating a game situation in which the opposition is hoping to force a fumble.

- **Oklahoma drill:** This three-man drill pits the offense against the defense. The players include a running back, an offensive lineman or fullback, and a defensive lineman or linebacker; try to select players of equal ability. Place two orange cones 5 yards apart and 8 yards away from the running back. The object of the drill is for the back to run between the cones without being tackled by the defensive player. The defensive player, though, must first contend with the offensive blocker one-on-one. When the linemen are in their stances, give the ball to the runner and then blow a whistle, starting the action. The entire team watches the drill, forming a circle around the three participants. This drill points out who the tough guys are, and it also builds camaraderie among the players, who cheer on their teammates.

- **One-on-one drills:** Practice should always include a passing segment in which the quarterback throws to a specific receiver who is being guarded by a defensive back. The defensive back is in competition with the quarterback as well as the receiver. The defensive back focuses on the style of the quarterback: when he's going to throw, how he'll throw it, and with what velocity and arc. All three players visualize and experience what the situation will be like in a game.

✔ **Defensive drills:** Whenever the offense runs plays against the defense, the defense must take charge of the drill. Even when you don't want a lot of hitting in practice for fear of players getting injured, you still must require the defensive players to put a hand, or both hands, on the offensive player with the ball. Never conduct an 11-on-11 drill without some form of contact — you need to simulate a real-game situation.

Motivating with speeches and other techniques

If you ever watch old movies, you may have seen *Knute Rockne — All American,* in which former President Ronald Reagan portrayed Notre Dame player George Gipp, and Pat O'Brien starred as Coach Rockne. In the 1940 film, Gipp dies at a young age while still a player, and at halftime of a losing effort, Rockne beseeches his players to "win one for the Gipper." The players, crying over the death of one of their beloved teammates, run from the locker room yelling and screaming and then go out and win the game. Rockne's speech was fiery and emotionally charged. You couldn't find a dry eye in the house when this movie ran in theaters. That example is obviously an extreme one. But it's customary for coaches to encourage their teams to play for an injured or fallen teammate, to pick up the slack.

To give an inspiring speech, a coach must be in tune with his players. He must know which emotional buttons to push, and he must be genuine. If a coach doesn't get excited easily during the course of a game, then he shouldn't yell and scream in the locker room before a game. Whatever he says should be simple and to the point. Players respect coaches who state the obvious, telling them specifically how they're going to win.

When a team has a long history with a particular rival, the speeches should flow easily. The coach can always recall some past experience, a good story or a particular comment, from which to formulate a speech that emotionally charges the team.

Because so many newspaper stories and broadcast interviews are available, many coaches rely on "bulletin board material" to get their players emotionally interested in a particular game or opponent. Coaches post articles or excerpts from television and radio interviews on the players' bulletin board in the locker room whenever an opponent belittles the team or an individual player. The players read the comments and take the words personally. Coaches always want to make any game or personnel matchup a personal conflict. Being called a name or a shoddy performer evokes strong emotions in a player.

I've known coaches who have fabricated stories (little white lies) to a particular player in order to create a dislike for his opponent. Coaches do so before or during practice by pulling the player aside. "Did you hear what they're saying about you?" is how the line may begin. Who's hurt by it, as long as the team wins? Many players respond to this tactic because they are inspired to disprove the comments while playing the game.

Focusing on the right games

During the course of a long season, a coach must pick his games, his moments, when he wants to fire up his team to play an opponent. Every game has to be played with some emotion, but I think that a coach makes a mistake if he attempts to have his players emotionally high for every game. There will be times during the season when your team simply is good enough to win because they are the better team. Those games, and the ones that you know you'll probably lose, shouldn't have the same emotional focus. Focus on the difficult games, the ones you consider toss-ups (ones that either team is capable of winning), and ask your team for their maximum emotional effort.

However, the players will sense that some games are big games. If the coach is into the game, concentrating more than usual, the players will pick up on that. They will feed off the coach's emotions.

Johnson picked his spot

An example of a coach picking his spot came during the 1996 season, the year Jimmy Johnson returned to coaching. He was coaching the Miami Dolphins, who were playing his former team, the Dallas Cowboys. The media made a huge deal about the game because Cowboys owner Jerry Jones and Johnson, who had coached Dallas to two Super Bowl championships, hadn't parted ways amicably. But Johnson knew that the game was a mismatch. He knew that the Dolphins weren't in control of winning or losing that game. If Dallas played poorly, Miami had a chance to win. If Dallas played well, Miami had no shot.

What did Johnson do? He downplayed the game with his players. He didn't want his players emotionally high for that game because he didn't want them to exert unnecessary energy. He didn't want them sky-high for a game that they couldn't win. (They did lose.) Instead, like any good coach, Johnson wanted his players emotionally high for other games that he believed they had a chance to win.

Chapter 20

Conditioning, Training, and Diet

· ·

In This Chapter

▶ Off-season and preseason conditioning

▶ Strengthening the muscles

▶ Stretching exercises

▶ Choosing pregame and postgame meals

▶ Preventing and dealing with injuries

· ·

*F*ootball is not a sport that's kind to your body. Injuries are part of the game; you will get hurt. But how much you get hurt and how fast you recover are dictated in great part by the type of condition you're in. During my football career, I had three knee operations (I tore both medial collateral ligaments), a shoulder separation, and torn biceps. I also broke an ankle and a foot, tore a calf muscle, and fractured a hand and a wrist. And as I'm writing this chapter, my back is killing me.

I was in good physical condition when I played; being fit saved me from other injuries. But the game, especially on the NFL-level, can be so brutal that sometimes you can't prevent injuries. Knees, for example, weren't built to withstand the force of a 300-pound player crashing on them.

Being in good shape has many advantages. You're less susceptible to injury, and you improve your athletic performance. This chapter shows you how to get — and stay — in shape.

Getting Your Heart into Football Shape

If you've ever watched a football game, you've probably noticed that the field is awfully long — 100 yards to be exact. And if you're not in good cardiovascular shape, those 100 yards can seem like 100 miles when you're running downfield. But never fear: Getting in shape (also known as *conditioning*) isn't complicated. You just have to be dedicated.

This section walks you through the various ways to condition your body at different times of the year. You want to tailor your conditioning program so that you're in shape all year long and in peak shape during the season.

Off-season conditioning

The goal of off-season conditioning is to get a player in shape for training camp. A trainer and a coach can only do so much; they can yell and prod the player into working out, but every player needs to be self-motivated and responsible for his own conditioning. Players need to follow an off-season conditioning program that combines weight training with aerobic exercise. The most common aerobic exercise is running, and a player's level of fitness determines the distance and duration that he runs. The following phases of conditioning are for players who consider themselves in good shape.

Note: Heavier players, guys in the 290 pounds and up range, shouldn't do a lot of strenuous running because it places too much stress on their knees. However, most training rooms are equipped with a computerized harness — called an *unloader* — that the heavier players can use. It functions like a cherry picker, the machine that lifts a car engine from an automobile. The large player puts the trunk of his body in the harness, and a hydraulic lift lifts him just high enough that his feet remain on a treadmill. The purpose of this machine is to lessen a player's weight while he runs on a treadmill for 30 to 45 minutes every other day. The unloader can lessen the weight stress of a 315-pound man by 100 or more pounds.

- **Phase 1 (January and February):** Endurance running — distance training of up to 3 miles. Players should run five days a week.

- **Phase 2 (March and April):** Power running — doing a lot of 440-yard dashes, 330-yard dashes, and finally 220-yard dashes. Players should do a 90-minute workout every other day.

- **Phase 3 (May and June):** Power sprinting. Players should be running only 110-yard sprints and do a 40-minute workout every day.

- **Phase 4 (June and July):** *Ladders,* starting with 110-yard sprints, the longest distance, and finishing with 10-yard sprints, the shortest distance. After sprinting 110 yards, move to 90 yards, then 70 yards, then 50 yards, and finally to 10-yard sprints. Players should do a 40-minute workout every day.

These drills should keep players in shape throughout the year and have them ready for the hard work of training camp.

Preseason conditioning

You may have heard the terms *two-a-days* and *double sessions,* no doubt expressed with contempt. These terms refer to twice-daily practices on the field and the intense period of training and conditioning that takes place immediately prior to the start of the season. These two-a-days occur only in training camp.

The focus of training camp is to prepare a team for the first game of the season. With two-a-day practices, fatigue is going to be a factor. So coaches try to avoid exercises that put large amounts of negative force on their players' already-tired muscles.

In other words, as a player, you shouldn't do any heavy lifting that involves your hamstrings. Those muscles are fatigued enough already. Instead, you want to lift heavy on your quadriceps by concentrating on *closed-chain exercises,* a fancy name for anything that causes your body to come in contact with the ground. Push-ups, squats, or slide boards are examples of closed-chain exercises. They help create an energy process that heals rather than hurts.

Here are some good conditioning drills for the preseason:

- ✔ Doing a 3-mile run in 25 minutes

- ✔ Running 40 to 50 stadium steps up and down for about 30 minutes

- ✔ Doing 15 minutes of speed work (jumping rope, hitting a punching bag, doing fast-paced calisthenics, and so on) and then doing 30 minutes of ladder sprints from 120 yards down to 40 yards (ladder sprints are explained in Phase 4 in the "Off-season conditioning" section, earlier in this chapter)

You should do sprint work on the days that you don't run the stadium steps or a long distance. You should do one of these drills every day of the week. You can take Sunday (or another day) off, if you want to.

Staying in shape during the season

Daily practices help you keep in shape during the season, but doing drills specifically for conditioning is to your advantage as a player and to the advantage of the team as a whole. The team that wins the game is often the one that's in better condition, especially in the early season when the weather is frequently hot and humid.

Here are some drills that you can do at the beginning or the end of practice:

- ✔ **Wind sprints:** Do 8 to 14 reps of 100 yards on Day 1, depending on the time of season, and 6 reps of 100 on Day 3. (You may want to try more reps of a shorter distance, such as 40 yards, too.) Don't run the stadium steps during the season because it's too grueling. That exercise is best left to off-season conditioning.

- ✔ **Jumping rope:** Do 3 reps of a 20-second boxer-like fast skip and 3 reps of a 20-second fast skip in which you raise your knees high.

- ✔ **Low rope drills:** This drill is similar to the one that players used to do with tires, placing a foot inside the middle of ten used tires placed two to a side, five rows deep. The low rope drill consists of six rows of two 18-inch square roped-off openings. The openings are about 10 yards long. With both feet, a player hops forward through the openings. Then he repeats the drill hopping side to side, and then hopping in a zigzag action. Another version of the drill is to put one foot in each opening, landing in opposite openings down the line. Players should complete each rope drill in three to four seconds and do each drill twice.

Your destination during each week of the season is game day, and each day of the week is a step toward that destination. Use this day-by-day schedule to keep your team in peak physical condition for game day:

- ✔ **Day 1** is devoted to recovering from the previous day's game. Take the sorest parts of your body (legs, shoulders, neck) and make them feel better by stretching those muscles — for example, do a light jog or half-speed 50-yard strides. Stretching prevents pulls, relaxes the upper body muscles, and helps break up lactic acid. Day 1 also should be the heaviest running day of the week.

  Some NFL teams increase the number of reps that they run on Day 1 as the season goes on. Teams want their players to build endurance and prepare physically for January, should they reach the playoffs. For example, they may run 8 reps of 100 yards in the first quarter of the season, 10 reps of 100 in the second quarter, 12 reps of 100 in the third quarter, and 14 reps of 100 in the fourth quarter.

- ✔ **Day 2** is traditionally a day of rest, except for injured players, who come in for treatment.

- ✔ **Day 3** is a heavy lifting day, especially for bigger players — offensive and defensive linemen, tight ends, and linebackers — who need the greatest amount of strength. Running usually consists of 6 sets of 100 yards, a routine that does not vary over the course of the season.

- ✔ **Day 4** is a lifting day for the smaller players.

- ✔ **Day 5** can be an optional lifting day for either the larger or the smaller players. Usually half the bigger players lift.

✔ **Day 6** is a day of rest because most trainers adhere to a 48-hour rule. This rule states that a player does not go through a weighted muscle contraction 48 hours prior to game time. They want their players' muscles loose (the body flexible) for the game. Lifting causes the muscles to contract, which can make the players stiff.

✔ **Day 7** is game day.

By tailoring the workout schedule to the day of the week, you help ensure that your players are at their highest energy and strength levels on game day. And they need every ounce of power they can get!

Strengthening Your Muscles

If you're a football player, muscle strength is just as important as aerobic conditioning. After all, you're either dodging or trying to knock down other human beings, some of whom may outweigh you by 100 pounds! Strength training also reduces your risk of injury.

You use nearly every major muscle group when you play football, so making sure that all those muscles are strong certainly is to your advantage. Develop a regular strength training program, lifting every other day so that you give your muscles time to recover. Work to increase the amount of weight and number of repetitions that you can do. You should be able to do 8 to 12 repetitions of each exercise. If you can do more repetitions, increase the weight. If you can't do that many, try lifting less and working your way up.

The rice program

Here's a fun set of exercises that benefit all players, particularly defensive backs and players who handle the ball on offense. Try these exercises if you prefer the "home remedy" approach. First, fill a barrel with 100 pounds of uncooked rice and then do the following drills to improve your wrist and forearm strength. (While doing each of the following exercises, make sure that your wrists are locked.)

✔ Place your open hand in the barrel and, in a circular motion, work your arm in a clockwise and then a counterclockwise motion, 15 times in each direction.

✔ With your palm facing you, place your hand in the barrel and move it back and forth 15 times.

✔ Place your open hand close to you in the barrel, and then push it away 15 times to the other side of the barrel. After every push, remove your hand, drop it into the barrel's edge closest to you, and push again to the opposite side.

✔ Put your hand deep inside the barrel and open and close your hand 30 times.

Top-notch trainers say that each individual is genetically different and that each player should start by choosing a weight that he can lift. Simply find your best weight — the one that really challenges you but doesn't put your body in danger because it's far too heavy for your strength level. What's important is that you lift with the proper technique and go through your numbered sets with a weight that suits you.

Here's a good lifting program that you can follow. You use an Olympic lifting bar for all bar lifts. For the machine lifts, use the specific machines that I list.

✔ **Hang clean:** If you've ever seen Olympic lifters do cleans, you should know that this lift isn't a "clean and jerk." A hang clean is a clean lift off the floor in one fluid motion, accelerating as you pull the weight upward. After you raise the weight, lower it slowly until you rest the weight, with the help of your wrists and hands, on top of your chest.

✔ **Bench press:** Lie on your back and, with assistance, have the bar placed on your chest; then push your arms straight upward, lifting the weight toward the ceiling.

✔ **Incline press:** Instead of lying flat on your back for this exercise, lie at a 60-degree angle. Press the bar outward to work the muscles of your upper chest and back.

✔ **Decline press:** This lift is the opposite of the incline press. You lie at a 60-degree angle downward, working the muscles under your chest and your pectoral muscles from all angles.

✔ **Supine/French curl:** Lie down flat with a bar. With your elbows locked in at the side of your torso and with your forearms in an upward position, bring the bar above your head. The supine curl exercises your triceps.

✔ **Wrist flexion:** While sitting on a bench or a stool, hold the bar in your hands with your palms facing up. Allow the bar to roll in your hand from near your wrist to your fingertips. Then lift the bar above your head. The rolling motion of the bar, rolling through your hands, strengthens your wrists.

✔ **Wrist extension:** While sitting on a bench or a stool, grip the bar in your hands with your palms facing the floor and allow the bar to roll to your fingertips. Then lift the bar above your head.

✔ **Row machine:** This is a back exercise from a freestanding exercise machine. Move your arms forward and then move your elbows outward as you move the weighted pads of the machine outside of your arms.

✔ **Lat pulldown:** The lat pulldown machine helps you do pull-ups. Even though you pull down on the bar, you have the sensation that you're pulling up because the weight is being lowered.

✔ **Preacher curl:** The preacher curl machine looks like a pulpit. You put your elbows in the machine, and your hands are free-falling. Move the weight with your upper arm, working your biceps.

For more information about how to perform these and other weight-lifting exercises, and for more strength training ideas, check out *Weight Training For Dummies* by Liz Neporent and Suzanne Schlosberg (IDG Books Worldwide, Inc.).

Weight Training in the Off-Season

A standard off-season weight training program consists of four lifting days, alternating upper body and legs, heavy and light weights. You should never repeat the same lifting pattern on consecutive days. Daily workouts consist of a total of 16 sets involving one muscle group (primary) in addition to another muscle group (secondary). You can break up these routines by working on another body part — such as forearms — in the middle of this program.

For example, on Day 1, choose your chest and triceps as your primary muscle groups, your back and biceps as your secondary muscle groups, and then work on your forearms in between those groups. On Day 2, choose your shoulders as your primary muscle group, your legs as your secondary group, and break up those sets by working on your forearms. On Day 5, at the end the week, choose your legs as your primary, your shoulders as your secondary, and work on your rotator cuffs in the middle.

The idea is to break up what primary and secondary body parts you're working on by doing another variety of exercises and movements. You can then flip-flop these other exercises through a four- or five-phase program leading up to training camp.

Table 20-1 shows you a sample weight-lifting workout. Again, if you need more basic information, consult *Weight Training For Dummies*.

Table 20-1	**Sample Lifting Program**		
Exercise	*Sets*	*Reps*	*Rest*
Bar – hang cleans	2	12	1:10
Bar – bench press	2	12	1:20
Bar – incline press	2	12	1:10
Bar – decline press	2	12	1:10
Bar – supine – French curls	2	12	1:10
Bar – wrist flexion	2	12	1:00
Bar – wrist extension	2	12	1:00
Rice program	1		1:00

(continued)

Table 20-1 *(continued)*

Exercise	Sets	Reps	Rest
Machine – row – palms facing	1	20	1:00
Machine – lat pulldowns – front	1	20	1:00
Machine – asst. pull-ups – wide grip	1	20	1:00
Machine – preacher curls	1	20	1:00
Pipe – balance – right/left	1	1 minute	1:00

Bulking Up without Steroids

The evils of steroid abuse have been documented, and the risks involved with steroids far outweigh any possible benefits. Instead, young players can put on weight and muscle naturally without using these illegal hormone-enhancing drugs. Medical experts have discovered that extensive use of steroids, which generate almost-synthetic like muscle mass, can cause heart disease, liver failure, and impotency in addition to other medical problems.

Every player needs a good weight training program *and* a good supplement program. Fortunately, some very good protein drinks and engineered foods are available to help you achieve your goal. No player should proceed with a supplement program without discussing all the variables with his team trainer or nutritionist. Allow them to recommend what supplements you need. College and NFL teams include supplements as part of their training-table meal programs. For those of you on high school teams, consult with your family doctor if your parents don't want to rely on a high school trainer or coach.

The whey protein used in today's protein drinks is a better protein — with a higher absorption level — than was used in the past. Players can also take supplements, from protein muscle-builders like *creatine* (the Denver Broncos used this generic drink extensively during their 1997–1998 championship season) to engineered complete foods that provide the protein and nutritional equivalent of five to six meals a day without the high fat content.

The player who needs to put on weight and the player who needs to take it off have a similar goal. Each player has to get to the right ratio of lean muscle mass to body fat. For a small player to get bigger, he needs to eat a lot of extremely dense foods (pasta, bran, bread) or take the equivalent (supplements) and work out. He can bulk up without using steroids.

Stretching

Not only does stretching help you remain injury-free, but it also increases your flexibility, which ultimately makes you a better football player. You can stretch an extra inch to catch that pass or lunge forward another foot to score that touchdown.

Most injuries — hamstring pulls, for example — don't occur because the player isn't trained. They occur because he's fatigued. During training camp, especially, rest is as important as work, and some of the best kind of work is stretching.

Stretching can be called *under-training,* which consists of simple exercises such as lying flat on your back with a towel wrapped around your leg and moving the towel slowly back and forth. That exercise restores the muscle because what you're doing is bringing oxygen into the area, or under-training the muscle. You can also do many exercises directed at the body's core or trunk.

Make sure that you stretch before every practice and game and before you lift weights. Here are some good stretching exercises to do:

- **Shoulder rotation:** Move your shoulders forward and do arm rotations; rotate your arms front and back, six times each way. Your arms should be fully extended and straight while you rotate them.

- **Trunk twist:** Put your hands on your hips, place your feet 24 inches apart, and bend your trunk like Jack LaLanne did 100 years ago. With your head and chest facing forward, bend the trunk of your body five times while your upper body is turned to the left and then repeat the motion, bending five times to the right. Point your feet forward for all these bends.

- **Calf stretch:** Put your right heel back a step and on the ground and put your left foot out in front of you. Keep your right leg straight and bend down with your arms. Hold the stretch for 15 seconds and then repeat with the other leg.

- **90/90 stretch:** Lie on your side and bend your knees into your trunk until you look like a chair. Your knees should be bent so that your upper legs are at a 90-degree angle to your lower legs. Hold your body for 15 seconds, lying on both your right and left sides.

- **Half bow:** Lying on your right side, grasp the foot of your left leg and pull your heel back until it touches your rear end. This exercise stretches your frontal quadriceps. Then turn over and repeat the exercise while lying on your left side. This time you work your right leg. Hold each stretch for 15 seconds.

✔ **Supine hamstring stretch:** Lie down on your back with your knees bent and both feet on the ground, keeping your back flat. Take your right leg and stretch it upward. Bend it and stretch it upward again, very slowly. Hold this bending motion for 15 seconds for each leg.

✔ **Split stretch:** In a seated position, split your legs apart and bend your body down the middle to stretch your abductors, those muscles in the lower part of your stomach. Your hips should be moving during this stretch. You don't want your lower body to be stiff. Do this exercise to the right, left, and middle.

✔ **Groin stretch (also called the butterfly stretch):** In a seated position, put the soles of your feet together and move your legs so that they flap like the wings of a butterfly. Do this stretch for 15 seconds.

✔ **Hip flexor:** In a standing position, move your hips downward to the ground while bending your knees. Keep your chest erect and high during this exercise.

✔ **Trunk rotation:** In a standing position with feet facing forward, twist your upper body as far as you can to the right (and then to the left). Your face and chest should face that same direction at the end of the twist. Repeat this twist six times, clockwise and counterclockwise. Your arms can be at your side, and your hands can be on your hips while doing these twists.

Eating Your Way to Better Football

Looking at the size of some of today's football players, you may think that they eat as much of whatever food they want so that they grow as big as possible. Not true!

The days when a typical training camp meal consisted of three steaks piled on top of a potato with some pasta or a small salad on the side haven't existed since the late 1970s. Today's player is more likely to have a mound of pasta on his plate with plenty of vegetables and fruit and maybe a small piece of meat on the side. The emphasis has switched from protein to complex carbohydrates, and most NFL teams now serve a rice or pasta dish with every meal.

Generally speaking, balance is the key to proper nutrition. Your body needs a wide range of nutrients from a variety of natural sources to maintain itself. Strive to eat numerous vegetables and fruits, an assortment of whole-grain products, and meat and dairy products that have lots of protein. Carbohydrates do provide quick energy, but you need to eat from all four food groups — just like Mom told you!

I'm not giving you top-secret information here. A player knows which foods are good for him and which ones aren't. The trick is getting the player to eat a salad instead of a cheeseburger or an apple instead of that piece of pie.

The most important thing to remember is that even a little bit of a good thing is better than nothing. If you can't eat five servings of fruit a day, eat two. If you don't have any fresh vegetables, eat some frozen ones. And don't beat yourself up if you stray. Just get right back on the program.

Pregame and postgame meals

The meal that you eat the night before a game is more important than the pregame meal, which is the meal you eat the day of the game. The previous night's meal provides the fuel that your body will burn during the game, so it needs to contain the proper amounts of carbohydrates, proteins, and good fats (sauces, milk, butter), not saturated fats.

A good meal to eat the night before a game consists of 60 percent carbohydrates (pasta, rice, and whole grains), 20 percent clean protein (lean meats and fish), and 20 percent good fats (from sauces), with vegetables fitting in there, too.

The pregame meal should not be too heavy or full of fat. It should consist of clean (low-fat) carbohydrates with minimal proteins and minimal fats.

After the game, the top priority is to rehydrate your body — drink as much water as possible while staying away from alcohol, coffee, and herbal-based products that are dehydrating. The postgame meal should consist of similar proportions as the meal the night before the game: approximately 55 percent carbohydrates, 25 percent proteins, and 20 percent good fats.

Water and sports drinks

Hydration is such an important subject that I could devote an entire book to it. Football is obviously a demanding sport, and your body needs to be hydrated to work at peak performance, especially on a hot day when you're losing a lot of fluids.

Plenty of sports drinks are on the market today, from carbonated types that have little or no nutritional value to good old Gatorade, which contains the electrolytes that your body needs. However, Gatorade also contains too much sodium for most trainers' tastes. Other specialty drinks are engineered and used for different and specific things. One example is Cytomax, which secretes a proven *recovery enhancer* directly into your body. Recovery enhancers help your body replenish what was lost during a strenuous workout or game.

Preparing to play in hot or cold weather

Getting acclimated to hot, humid weather can be extremely difficult for a team that doesn't practice in it regularly, just as getting acclimated to the cold can be tough for a team that's used to working out in a warm climate. Unfortunately, no quick and easy way exists to prepare a team for extreme changes in temperatures, just as no miracle, oxygen-rich food exists to ready players for playing at a high altitude.

Basically, the best way that players can prepare for extreme weather conditions is to drink plenty of fluids to keep their bodies hydrated and to take full advantage of equipment that reduces the effects of heat and cold. Simply put, if it's cold, you need to keep your body warm, and if it's hot, you need to make your body cool. For example, use sideline fans and machines that spray a fine mist in hot, humid weather; use caps, creams, gloves, and miniature hand warmers to combat the cold.

Years ago, players wore pantyhose under their pants to keep their legs warm. But today, plenty of cold-weather gear is available, consisting of man-made fibers that are specifically designed to keep your body warm. When you're playing in extreme weather conditions, proper clothing and equipment are more important than what you eat.

 When you're really, really thirsty, though, nothing is better than a cold glass of water — during competition and afterward. Experts recommend that you drink at least eight 8-ounce glasses of water every day, or more if you exercise frequently. Simply remember to drink a lot.

Making Safety a Priority

Nothing ruins a football season more quickly than an injury that sidelines you for several games or the season. Inevitably, when a bunch of large men are trying to knock each other down, people are going to get bumps and bruises. But you can do some things to reduce the risk of serious injury.

Generally speaking, the key to injury prevention is proper training and the development of *proprioceptive strength* — that is, the body's ability to balance with strength or be aware of its balance. Doing different balance techniques fires *proprioceptors,* sensory receptors within your body, which can help prevent an injury when you get hit because your body tightens down the joint before injury occurs.

Think of your body as an electric light. Your brain is the light switch, your nervous system is the wiring, and your muscle is the resulting illumination. Proprioceptors are receivers from the light switch, and every human cell has a receiver.

Proper padding, of course, is also vital to injury prevention. Every player should wear a helmet, a mouthpiece, shoulder pads, knee pads, and so on. Outside of the standard equipment, eye shields are becoming more and more popular as manufacturers continue to make improvements in visibility. Knee braces, which were standard issue for all linemen 15 years ago, have fallen out of favor after studies indicated that players who wore them were suffering just as many knee injuries. As for those nose strips that virtually every NFL wide receiver, running back, and defensive back wears, no scientific proof can support the notion of improved running performance. But they may help prevent snoring.

To help prevent injuries, try to do the following:

- ✔ Warm up before you practice or play.

- ✔ Consider taping your ankles or wearing ankle braces.

- ✔ Use the proper length of cleat. Remember to make adjustments if you're playing on artificial turf and you usually play on grass, or vice versa.

- ✔ Drink plenty of water and eat right.

- ✔ Recognize when you're overly tired and take a break. Fatigue can lead to injury and/or a lack of concentration, and if you're not concentrating while 11 guys are trying to pound you into the ground, bad things can happen!

Playing Hurt versus Playing in Pain

By the time a player gets to the NFL, he probably knows the difference between playing hurt (with a potentially serious injury) and playing in pain (serious bruises or a minor injury that potentially won't worsen while playing). But the distinction is one that every individual must learn for himself after consulting with the team trainer and medical staff.

In the NFL, players are expected to play in pain. Some play hurt, too, like former Los Angeles Rams defensive end Jack Youngblood, who played with a broken fibula in Super Bowl XIV. Youngblood's sacrifice is an extreme example, though, and players (particularly young ones) should always lean to the side of caution.

For minor injuries, the liniments, ice packs, and heating pads being used today aren't that different than the ones that were used 20 years ago, but rehabilitation has become much more aggressive. Team doctors rarely put casts on injured body parts anymore. They use braces instead and start range-of-motion rehab earlier, which reduces muscle atrophy and gets the player back on the field more quickly.

If you do get injured, keep these things in mind:

- ✔ **Give yourself time to heal.** You're no good to your team if you're only working at 80 percent — especially if you re-injure yourself three plays into your first game back.

- ✔ **Take advantage of physical therapy.** Your team's doctor or trainer can help you determine what course of action will help you heal the fastest and the most completely.

Thanks to advances in arthroscopic procedures, injuries that once would have required major surgery and ended a season can be overcome in as little as two weeks with proper rest and rehabilitation.

Football is a tough game, but it's also supposed to be fun — and injuries certainly aren't! Do everything you can to keep yourself healthy and on the roster.

True confessions: How I stay fit

I didn't always eat right when I started playing professional football. But about two-thirds of the way through my career, I became more conscious of what I was eating and the effects those foods had on my physicality, my endurance, and what I got out of my training sessions.

To stay in shape, I do more cardiovascular workouts today than I ever did as a player. I play basketball and do a lot of exercises on the stair climber and treadmill — I try to do as much low-impact aerobic work as I can. Many players today do the same stuff. When I'm getting ready to do a movie, I may lift light weights. I do a lot of repetitions because I want to tone my body.

Part VII
The Part of Tens

The 5th Wave — By Rich Tennant

@RICHTENNANT

MONTANA FOOTBALL

In this part . . .

Every ...*For Dummies* book includes a Part of Tens — a group of chapters, each of which contains ten or so important pieces of information. For this book, I chose to focus on fans in this part. These chapters talk about the players, coaches, and teams that I think exemplify the sport of football and everything that makes it great.

The first thing I did when selecting players for these chapters was to find guys whom I truly respected and whom I knew played every down like it was their last one. Every man on these lists played exactly like that. Reading about them should give you a better understanding of what it takes to play this great game of football.

Chapter 21

The Ten Greatest Defensive Players of All Time

*W*hen naming a top ten at anything, you're bound to exclude a number of players who could easily make someone else's top ten — it's a subjective, personal thing. Everyone has his own top ten defensive players of all time, so here are mine. Some of these selections are predictable, whereas others may raise an eyebrow or two. I also placed some of my contemporary defensive favorites on my Dream Team (see Chapter 23), a compilation of players from both sides of the football, offense and defense.

Doug Atkins

Doug Atkins, a 6'8", 275-pounder from Humboldt, Tennessee, started his athletic career as a basketball player at the University of Tennessee, while also running track. One year, he won the Southeastern Conference high jump title. When the football coach heard of his feats, he asked him to try football and put him at defensive end. Atkins was a natural — he started hurdling offensive linemen like he did high jump bars. He became an All-America at Tennessee and is considered one of the toughest men to ever play football.

Atkins played for 17 years in the NFL, a total of 205 games, mostly for the Chicago Bears and the New Orleans Saints. Eight times with the Bears he was a Pro Bowl selection. He was a terror on the field, refusing to quit. Most teams used two men to block him in order to keep him from destroying their quarterbacks.

Atkins was every bit as funny as he was mean. One of the best anecdotes about Atkins is how he literally (and liberally) interpreted the words of the Bears' tough-guy head coach George Halas. During practice one day, Halas was unhappy with Atkins's practice habits and ordered him to take a lap around the field while wearing his helmet. Atkins took his lap with his helmet on — but that's all he wore. His teammates cracked up, and so did Halas.

Dick Butkus

Dick Butkus, shown in Figure 21-1, was arguably the most intimidating player to ever play defense; I think that players were flat-out frightened of him. He was probably the first defensive player who really caught fans' attention. Kids growing up in the late 1960s wanted to hit and tackle like Butkus, the 6'3", 245-pound middle linebacker of the Chicago Bears.

Butkus was so good that he was All-Pro seven times. He had the speed and agility to make tackles from sideline to sideline and cover the best tight ends on pass plays. The NFL didn't officially begin recording quarterback sacks until 1982, but the Bears say that Butkus had 18 in 1967, a huge number for a middle linebacker. He averaged 12.6 tackles per game — today's pro players think that 10 tackles is a great game. The growling man dominated games, finishing his career with 22 pass interceptions and 25 fumble recoveries.

Besides being a ferocious and violent player, Butkus was an intelligent linebacker. He studied game film and knew what the opposition liked to do on offense. At the snap of the ball, Butkus seemed to fly to wherever the play was headed. He had super instincts, something every player needs to be successful on defense. He played every game as though it were his last, and had he not suffered a serious knee injury in 1970, his career might have lasted a lot longer.

Figure 21-1:
The Bears' Dick Butkus was a fan favorite. Photo credit: UPI/ Corbis- Bettmann.

Kenny Easley

Okay, Ronnie Lott was the best safety, bar none. But this safety, who starred in college at UCLA, across town from USC and Lott, wasn't too far behind. He was the first player in Pac-10 history to be selected all-conference all four years at UCLA, and three times he was an All-America. Easley was a three-sport star at Oscar Smith High School in Chesapeake, Virginia, and was offered college basketball scholarships by ACC and Big Ten colleges.

I realize that Easley played only seven years in the NFL, but he managed 32 interceptions during his career and was named AFC defensive rookie of the year in 1981 after being a first-round draft choice. In 1984, Easley was voted NFL Defensive Player of the Year when he collected ten interceptions, returning two for touchdowns. He was the defensive heart of his team and a huge reason why the Seattle Seahawks finished 12-4 that season, still the finest record in club history.

Easley was 6'3" and 206 pounds, and he hit people like a freight train. He was a wild man on the field, playing with a total disregard for his body. His career was cut short by a serious kidney injury and, believe me, our receivers had mixed feelings. They hated to see Easley retire in the prime of his career, but they sure didn't miss his heavy-handed greeting card when they crossed the middle of the field. As a defensive player, I didn't mind watching him while I rested on the sidelines.

Joe Greene

Most people, especially in Pittsburgh, remember Joe Greene as "Mean Joe Greene" (see Figure 21-2). He was the heart and soul of the great Pittsburgh Steelers defensive teams of the 1970s. Pittsburgh's defensive line was so immovable and suffocating that it earned the nickname "The Steel Curtain." In fact, during a stretch of nine games in 1976, Pittsburgh's defense allowed only 28 points while going 9-0.

However, Pittsburgh fans weren't convinced that Greene — a 6'4", 260-pound defensive tackle from unknown North Texas State — deserved to be the club's first-round draft choice in 1969. The team had suffered through five consecutive losing seasons and had last appeared in a playoff game in 1947. A quarterback or running back made more sense to fans. Going with his own instincts, Chuck Noll, the first-year Pittsburgh coach, ignored some of the scouting reports and built his team, one of the NFL's best ever, around Greene.

The imposing Greene made an immediate impact in the league and was named Defensive Rookie of the Year. He was named All-Pro nine times in the 1970s and was NFL Defensive Player of the Year in 1972 and 1974. In 1972, with the Steelers needing to beat Houston to clinch their first division title ever, Greene had an amazing game — five sacks, a blocked field goal, and a

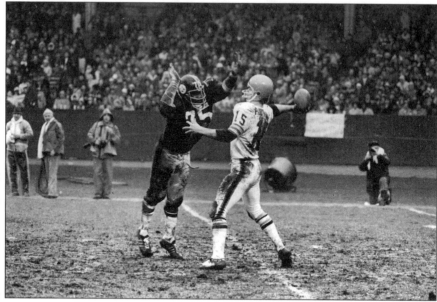

Figure 21-2: "Mean" Joe Greene led the great Pittsburgh Steelers of the 1970s. Photo credit: UPI/Corbis-Bettmann.

fumble recovery — in a 9-3 Pittsburgh win. During Pittsburgh's first Super Bowl–winning season, Greene utilized a new stance, lining up almost sideways between the guard and center. He was able to neutralize those two linemen or shoot a gap from this stance because he had such an unusual combination of speed, quickness, and sheer power. I can't think of a player who was able to duplicate Greene's production from that stance.

Jack Ham and Ted Hendricks

I couldn't separate Jack Ham and Ted Hendricks; they were two of the best outside linebackers I ever saw play. Both had tremendous range and a rare instinct for the game. They saw offensive plays developing before the ball was snapped: They could interpret any running back's stance. And when an offensive player went in motion, it instantly triggered something in their brains.

Ham — a consensus All-America at Penn State, the school known as Linebacker U. — was the only linebacker of the 1970s to be named to eight consecutive Pro Bowls. Ham started 14 games as a rookie and was a Pittsburgh regular until he retired after the 1982 season. He was a big-play performer, much like Hendricks, and was adept at shutting down the short passing game; there were few running backs he couldn't defend.

Besides being extremely quick, Ham was an intelligent player and usually knew his opponents' formations as well as they did. He finished his career with 21 fumble recoveries and 32 interceptions.

Hendricks fell a little short of Ham — 16 fumble recoveries and 26 interceptions — but he was a master when the opposition was pinned near its own goal line. He retired with a record-tying four safeties. Like Ham, Hendricks was a starter on four Super Bowl champion teams. He won three Super Bowls with the Raiders and his first with the Baltimore Colts in Super Bowl V.

Hendricks and Ham opposed each other in the great Steeler-Raider rivalry of the 1970s. Off the field, the iconoclastic Hendricks was the opposite of Ham. Hendricks was a chain smoker and a Good-Time Charlie. Because he was 6'7" and gangly looking, Hendricks was nicknamed "The Mad Stork" coming out of the University of Miami, where he was a three-time All-America. He played in 215 consecutive regular-season games and was selected to eight Pro Bowls.

Mike Haynes

Mike Haynes was probably the best bump-and-run cover cornerback in the history of the game; he could stick with any receiver. His coverage seemed so effortless because of his superior athletic ability and speed. Haynes was unusually tall (6'2") for the cornerback position, yet he was so graceful. I like to call him a "black hole player" — any player he covered seemed to go into a black hole, disappearing from the field.

Haynes finished his 14-year career in 1989 with 46 interceptions, which ranks low on the all-time listing. But in Haynes's case, statistics don't tell the whole story. He was so good that opposing quarterbacks quit throwing in his direction — which is the highest form of compliment for a cornerback. Haynes was a first-round draft choice of the New England Patriots in 1976 and finished his first season with eight interceptions, a 13.5-yard punt return average, and AFC Rookie of the Year honors.

Haynes joined me with the Raiders after seven seasons in New England. With the Raiders, Haynes and Lester Hayes formed one of the finest cornerback tandems in the history of the game. During those years, teams threw toward Hayes because they feared Haynes. And in one season, Hayes had 13 interceptions, one shy of the NFL single-season record. You can't play pass defense without solid cornerbacks, and Haynes simply put on a clinic every game, teaching other cornerbacks how the game should be played.

Ken Houston

How great of a strong safety was Ken Houston? So good that Washington Redskins coach George Allen traded five veteran players to the Houston Oilers for him in 1973. Houston was a defensive back who tackled like a linebacker. For 12 consecutive seasons, between 1968 and 1979, Houston was selected to either the AFL All-Star game or the AFC-NFC Pro Bowl. Without question, Houston was the dominant player at his position in that era.

Houston (6'3", 198 pounds) was a long strider with exceptional quickness and strength. He would sit back from his viewpoint as a safety and attack the line of scrimmage. He had tremendous instincts and owned that proverbial "nose for the ball." With the Oilers, he returned nine interceptions for touchdowns, which still stands as an NFL record. During his career, he intercepted 49 passes and returned them for 898 yards. He also recovered 19 fumbles.

One of the most memorable instances of Houston's signature style of tackling occurred in one of the Redskins' great rivalry games against the Dallas Cowboys in 1973. With seconds remaining, Cowboys running back Walt Garrison caught a short pass and started heading toward the end zone. Houston met him at the 1-yard line, lifted Garrison off his feet (a hit called a *decleater*), and planted him in his tracks. The game ended, and Houston's tackle preserved Washington's victory. Throughout his career, the super-strong Houston repeated this style of bone-chilling tackles.

Sam Huff and Ray Nitschke

Dick Butkus stands alone as the game's best middle linebacker. But Sam Huff and Ray Nitschke (see Figure 21-3 for a photo of Nitschke) stand right behind him in terms of how they tackled running backs from the middle linebacker position. During a 13-year pro career, Huff was a well-known player because his reign of terror emanated from New York City. He appeared on the cover of *Time* magazine when he was 24 and was even the subject of a television special, "The Violent World of Sam Huff." He played in six NFL championship games with the New York Giants before finishing his career with the Washington Redskins.

Both Huff and Nitschke had a nose for the football and were difficult to block from their 4-3 formations. And both seemed to love the violent aspects of the game; losing their helmets after a rousing tackle was a trademark. Both were instinctively tough players who enjoyed football's collisions and brutality.

They were smart players, too. Huff had 30 interceptions; Nitschke had 25. And when Nitschke's team, the Packers, beat Huff's Giants for the 1962 NFL championship, Nitschke was named the game's most valuable player. He was a soft-hearted man who was loved by many thousands of Green Bay Packers fans. He kept a home in Green Bay until his death in early 1998.

Deacon Jones and Merlin Olsen

It's impossible to list one of these great Los Angeles Rams defensive linemen without including the other. David (Deacon) Jones and Merlin Olsen were a dynamic duo for the Rams for ten seasons (1962 to 1971) until Jones was traded to the San Diego Chargers. Olsen joined the Rams as a first-round draft choice in 1962 after an All-American career at Utah State and was a

Figure 21-3:
In the Packers' 1962 NFL Championship win, Ray Nitschke was named game MVP. Photo credit: UPI/ Corbis-Bettmann.

mainstay on the team's defensive line for 15 seasons. Jones entered the NFL as an obscure 14th-round draft choice who had played at South Carolina State and Mississippi Vocational. But regardless of their backgrounds, these two players worked together to wreak havoc on opposing teams. Because of Jones and Olsen, who lined up side by side on the left, the Rams' defensive line (nicknamed "The Fearsome Foursome") was one of the most feared and successful units in the history of pro football.

Olsen, who was 6'5" and 270 pounds, was named to the Pro Bowl team a record 14 consecutive times. He was very agile for a big man, and he clogged the middle of the line, enabling speed rushers like Jones to cause trouble from the outside. Jones, 6'5" and 250 pounds, was light by today's standard for defensive ends, but he used his speed, strength, and quickness to beat offensive tackles who attempted to block him. While he played, Jones coined the term *sack,* which is used today to define the tackling of a quarterback behind the line of scrimmage. Jones claims that he's the all-time sack leader. And it's difficult to argue with him because the NFL didn't begin to include this defensive statistic officially until 1982, or two seasons after Jones was inducted into the Pro Football Hall of Fame. In 1967 and 1968, Jones was chosen as the NFL's best defensive player.

The Rams teams of his era were defense-oriented, and Olsen was their leader. He was team MVP six consecutive seasons and in 1974 was named NFL Player of the Year by the Maxwell Club, an athletic club based in Philadelphia that conducts an annual poll of the national media. In addition to acting on TV dramas such as *Little House on the Prairie,* Olsen was a football analyst on network television for many years after he retired from football.

Jack Lambert

The beauty of Jack Lambert's career is that he came from a small, non-football power (Kent State) and was rather small by NFL standards, only to rise and become a Hall of Famer. At 6'4", 220 pounds, Lambert was Defensive Rookie of the Year with the Pittsburgh Steelers in 1974 after being a second-round draft choice. He was Pittsburgh's defensive captain for eight years, and many people believe that his presence at middle linebacker solidified the Steelers as a great defensive team. (Lambert is one of three Pittsburgh players whom I mention in this chapter.)

Lambert had an 11-year career with the Steelers and starred in their four Super Bowl victories. He was known for his toothless glare and confident demeanor. He was both intimidator and tormentor. Unlike the prototype middle linebacker — the big, huge run-stuffers — Lambert could drop 20 yards deep into pass coverage because he was so quick and fast. He had exceptional range while still possessing the toughness to make rock-solid tackles. No one messed with Jack Lambert, including his teammates.

Lambert was All-Pro seven times and was twice named Defensive Player of the Year. He finished his career with 28 interceptions.

Dick "Night Train" Lane

Dick Lane's story is an improbable one. He played one season of junior college football and a few years on a military team at Ford Ord, California. He was working at an aircraft factory in California, carrying oil-soaked sheet metal, when he showed up in 1952 at the Los Angeles Rams offices looking for work. Coach Joe Stydahar was impressed by his workout and signed him. Lane went on to intercept 14 passes in his 12-game rookie season, a league record that still stands.

Most secondary coverage in those days was man-to-man, and Lane was fast enough to stick with any receiver. Plus he fully understood the passing game because he had been a receiver on his military team. (Lane shifted to cornerback because the Rams already had Tom Fears and Elroy "Crazy Legs" Hirsch, two future Hall of Fame receivers.) Lane also got his nickname via Fears, who was partial to Buddy Morrow music. "Night Train" was one of Morrow's favorite songs, and a teammate put the tag on Lane one night while he sat in Fears's room listening to Morrow's music.

Amazingly, the Rams kept Lane for only two seasons, trading him to the Chicago Cardinals, who later dealt him to the Detroit Lions. His best seasons were with the Lions, where he played the final six seasons of his 14-year career. Lane never won a championship, but he finished with 68 interceptions, third all-time behind Paul Krause of the Minnesota Vikings and Emlen Tunnell, who played 11 of his 14 seasons with the New York Giants.

Bob Lilly

Bob Lilly (see Figure 21-4) was the first-round draft choice of the Dallas Cowboys in 1961 after being a consensus All-America at Texas Christian in nearby Fort Worth. He had such a legendary 14-year career that he earned the nickname "Mr. Cowboy." At 6'5", 262 pounds, Lilly was built like some of today's pass-rushing defensive ends. And he played outside for two seasons before coach Tom Landry moved him to tackle, where his cat-like speed and punishing style forced most opponents to double-team him. Ernie Stautner, his old line coach, remembers some teams putting three blockers in his way.

Lilly was selected to 11 Pro Bowls in his 14 NFL seasons and was so durable that he played in 196 consecutive games. In the early part of Lilly's career, the Cowboys kept winning regular-season games and making title game appearances but couldn't win the championship game. Dallas played in six NFL/NFC championship games in an eight-year period. When the team finally won a title, Super Bowl VI, Lilly sacked Miami quarterback Bob Griese for a record 29-yard loss.

Usually, defensive tackles fall down when they recover fumbles, but Lilly could run. He returned three fumbles for touchdowns and scored again on a 17-yard interception return.

Figure 21-4:
Bob Lilly was a standout tackle for Tom Landry's Dallas Cowboys. Photo credit: UPI/ Corbis-Bettmann.

Gino Marchetti

Big Gino Marchetti was to defensive ends what the Cleveland Browns' Jim Brown was to running backs; he was light-years ahead of his time. Marchetti, shown in Figure 21-5, played the run and the pass equally well — he did it all. And he did it with his hands. When he played (in the 1950s), most defensive linemen used their forearms and shoulders a lot, but not Marchetti. He kept consistent separation with his hands, meaning that he shed blockers instead of battering his way through them by lowering his shoulder or knocking them over with his forearm.

When I first came into the NFL, I studied four or five players, looking for technique and style. I looked at some of Marchetti's old NFL films, and I tried to play the run like he did. His technique and style would have fit in the 1980s or 1990s — he had all the right pass-rush moves, using his hands so well. Marchetti, who was 6'4" and 245 pounds, used his long frame to hound opposing quarterbacks. If the NFL had monitored quarterback sacks when he played, he probably would have ranked ahead of today's great pass-rushers like Reggie White and Bruce Smith.

Marchetti was also a tough guy. In the great 1958 NFL championship game between Marchetti's Baltimore Colts and the New York Giants, Marchetti made a key tackle on Frank Gifford, stopping him short of a first down with three minutes left, forcing the Giants to punt the ball. Marchetti broke his ankle making that tackle. (The Colts rallied to win the game in overtime after Marchetti was carried to the locker room.) The injury forced Marchetti to miss the Pro Bowl game. Had he not missed this game, he could have claimed when he retired that he had made ten consecutive visits to that all-star game — a benchmark for many Hall of Fame players — during his career.

Figure 21-5:
Gino Marchetti was light-years ahead of his time as a defensive end. Photo credit: UPI/ Corbis-Bettmann.

Chapter 22

The Ten Greatest Offensive Players of All Time

* *

In This Chapter

▶ Three quarterbacks whose careers ended in 15 league championships

▶ Runners who combined power with speed and fancy moves

▶ Huge men who dominated defenses, opening up the passing game

▶ Receivers who could play in any era and blocked, too

* *

*W*hen you examine this list of the greatest offensive players of all time, you may wonder why I omitted Jerry Rice, Barry Sanders, and Brett Favre. You can find those players in Chapter 23 on my Dream Team. With a few exceptions, this chapter's main criterion was choosing talented players who were also great champions.

For example, Sammy Baugh played with the Washington Redskins in the 1940s, and some people would argue that he was a better all-around quarterback and player than Otto Graham. Yet Graham achieved something that Baugh never did: He played for ten seasons and led the Cleveland Browns to ten consecutive championship games — a feat that no other quarterback has accomplished.

I doubt that Graham's winning seven championships in ten attempts will ever be matched, considering the parity in the National Football League today. No one has come close to his accomplishment, which makes him a worthy winner in my book. What's great, too, is that Graham was converted to quarterback from tailback, and that his best sport may have been basketball.

Another player who could have made this list but didn't is Bo Jackson, the most gifted physical specimen I ever played with. Bo won the Heisman Trophy at Auburn University as a running back. In the pros, he was a two-sport star, playing football with the Los Angeles Raiders and baseball with the Kansas City Royals, Chicago White Sox, and California Angels. A severe hip injury suffered in a football game ended his career prematurely. What a shame — he had the most incredible, natural, raw physical talent that I've ever seen. I left Bo off because his career was cut too short.

Choosing players for all-time teams is extremely difficult. I ended up with 13 players in this chapter, two over the limit for any offensive team.

Terry Bradshaw

I had to pick Terry Bradshaw or working at FOX Sports would be unbearable; he's like the older brother I never wanted. But kidding aside, Terry was really something in big games. The bigger the game, the better he played. He and Joe Montana of the San Francisco 49ers are the only quarterbacks to have led their teams to four Super Bowl championships. Bradshaw was voted the Super Bowl MVP twice with the Pittsburgh Steelers.

Bradshaw is a great example of a player who refused to quit when his career didn't flourish immediately. Although he was the first player taken in the 1970 college draft, the Steelers didn't immediately turn over the offense and the team to him. But Bradshaw overcame his struggles and his benchings to become one of the all-time greats. For you youngsters, there's a great lesson in Bradshaw's perseverance.

When the Steelers were ready to win, Bradshaw led them to an unprecedented four Super Bowl wins in a six-year period (1974 to 1979). In Pittsburgh's first title run, his touchdown pass to Lynn Swann in the fourth quarter beat the Oakland Raiders in the AFC championship game, and in the Super Bowl that followed, his fourth quarter touchdown pass to Larry Brown clinched the victory over the Minnesota Vikings.

When the NFL liberalized its pass-blocking rules and prevented defensive backs from touching receivers after they ran 5 yards, Bradshaw's throwing talents really blossomed. He had a great arm, and during the 1979 season, the Steelers rode it to the team's fourth championship. In his two championship MVP performances, Bradshaw threw for 627 yards and six touchdowns. Believe me, I know all his stats; I've heard about them enough. If he tells me about the "Immaculate Reception" that robbed my Raiders of a fourth championship one more time, I'll flip!

Jim Brown

Jim Brown, shown in Figure 22-1, was light-years ahead of his time. He also played in an age (1957 to 1965) when the running game was a big part of the offense. Still, with every team geared to stop him, none of their efforts seemed to work. Brown was 6'2", 232 pounds, 10 to 20 pounds heavier than most running backs today and huge for a player in his days. In nine pro seasons, Brown led the NFL in rushing eight times, totaled 12,312 yards, 106 rushing touchdowns, and 756 points. He was Rookie of the Year in 1957 and MVP twice, in 1958 and 1965.

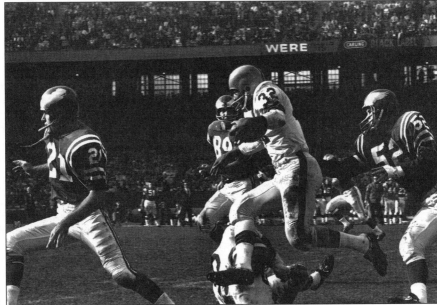

Figure 22-1:
Jim Brown
was a brute
of a running
back who
ran over
opponents.
Photo
credit:
UPI/Corbis-
Bettmann.

What was even more amazing about Jim Brown is that he retired from football at age 30. He decided to become an actor and retired during the shooting of probably his most memorable movie, *The Dirty Dozen*. Had he continued to play, Brown might still hold every rushing record, gained 20,000 yards, and scored 150 touchdowns. To this day, every great runner — from Barry Sanders to Emmitt Smith — is judged by his standards.

Brown, a splendid all-around athlete, dominated his era with a rare combination of power, speed, and size. For such a huge man, his waist was only 32 inches around. He was durable, and his head coach, Paul Brown of the Cleveland Browns, never shied away from using him. At Syracuse University, he lettered in basketball and was an All-American in lacrosse as well as football. He competed in track for one year and finished fifth in the national decathlon championship.

When fans rank their top five players of all-time, Brown should be on everyone's list. Two statistics set him apart: He never missed a game in nine seasons, and his 5.22 yards-per-carry average remains number one.

Dave Casper

I picked Dave Casper as my tight end because he started his college career at Notre Dame as an offensive tackle. Right off, playing that position at that school means that he was a tough, physical player. In 1972, when Casper switched to tight end in his junior season, he instantly became the best blocking tight end in college football. The only way that defenders could stop him was to hold him when he tried to run a pass route. He was simply too big (6'4", 232 pounds), strong, and fast for the average college player.

For such a physical player, Casper had soft hands, an attribute associated with wide receivers and running backs. Most big, tough guys, which Casper was, have hands of stone. He was a very reliable underneath receiver when he joined the Oakland Raiders in 1974. Had Casper played in today's wide-open offenses, he probably would have caught 80 passes a season. In his only Super Bowl appearance, Casper caught four passes, including one for a touchdown. No tight end was more complete than Casper; he could block anyone and also find a crease, that tiniest of open spaces, in any defensive secondary. He was very smart. When I think of the term *wily veteran,* I think of Casper.

Earl Campbell

Earl Campbell ran like an out-of-control bulldozer, but he had Ferrari speed after he broke into the open. Campbell was 5'11", 233 pounds, and people said that his thighs were as big as tree trunks. If he couldn't run around you, he simply ran over you. A Texas native, he was given the gentle label "Tyler Rose," although he simply wreaked havoc on defenses. He won the Heisman Trophy at the University of Texas in 1977 and was an instant superstar when he joined the Houston Oilers the following season.

In his first pro season, Campbell won the rushing title, was named Rookie of the Year, and also was the NFL's Most Valuable Player. The highlight of his rookie season was a Monday night game against the Miami Dolphins in the Astrodome. Campbell rushed for 199 yards and four touchdowns to lead the Oilers (a franchise that has since moved to Tennessee) to a 35-30 victory. The Astrodome in those days was full of wildly supportive fans, waving "Luv Ya Blue!" placards and banners.

Campbell was a repeat winner of the MVP award in 1979, but his best season was in 1980 when he rushed for 1,934 yards, the second-best single-season mark ever behind O.J. Simpson at the time. Campbell made my list because although he was a punishing runner, he missed only 6 games out of 115 due to injuries.

Mike Ditka/John Mackey

Among all the tight ends ever to play, these two went into the Pro Football Hall of Fame, one-two. Fans' first impression of Iron Mike Ditka was his toughness, but he, like Mackey, had exceptional hands. Mackey was faster and more of a breakaway threat than Ditka, but both were head and shoulders above every tight end over a 20-year period. They were powerful blockers and ultimate tough guys. Ditka didn't miss a start for the Chicago Bears in his first 84 games, while Mackey missed only one game in his ten seasons with the Baltimore Colts.

Ditka burst onto the pro scene with 56 catches for 1,076 yards and 12 touchdowns in his rookie season, staggering numbers for a tight end. He was a tremendous two-way player at the University of Pittsburgh, plus he was the regular punter. Ditka caught 75 passes in 1964, a season-high record for tight ends that stood until 1980 and the era of 16 games. Together, these two players caught 758 passes for 11,048 yards and scored 83 touchdowns. Mackey averaged 15.8 yards per catch during his career, and as a rookie in 1963 averaged 30 yards on nine kick returns. He was such a scoring threat that in 1966, he scored six touchdowns covering 50 yards or more.

These two were similar in size, both weighing 224 pounds, but Ditka was an inch taller at 6'3". Both men were fierce competitors on and off the field. Ditka was "Papa Bear" George Halas's personal pick to coach his beloved Chicago Bears. The franchise won its only Super Bowl after the 1985 season with Ditka as head coach. Ditka returned to coaching in 1997 with the New Orleans Saints after spending several years as a television commentator.

Mackey, who was one of quarterback Johnny Unitas's favorite targets, served as president of the NFL Players Association. Many in football believe that his passionate pursuit of player rights as the union leader initially held back his selection to the Hall of Fame.

Otto Graham

Any debate over Otto Graham's selection should cease when you consider that he's the only professional quarterback to lead his team, the Cleveland Browns, to ten consecutive championship games. The Browns won seven of those games, and Graham's teams won more than 83 percent of their games during his career. What's also astounding about Graham is that he played tailback, not quarterback, at Northwestern University. And many people in his town of Waukegan, Illinois, believed that his best sport was basketball.

Browns coach Paul Brown chose Graham in 1946 for his poise, leadership, and ball-handling skills and believed that he would be a great T-formation quarterback, even though he had never played the position. (In the T-formation, the quarterback moved behind the center to take a direct snap, and three players — mostly running backs in the 1930s — were aligned behind him, three across.) In the late 1940s, Graham, who finished his career with a 55.7 completion percentage, was astute at throwing the deep sideline and crossing routes that are prevalent in pro football today. Brown also used receivers in the backfield and put these players in motion, knowing that Graham was smart enough to deal with an evolving offensive strategy. The only knock on Graham and his Browns was that they played in the All-America Football Conference for four years, a league considered inferior to the NFL.

But after Graham and the Browns joined the NFL, their successes continued. In the Browns' 30-28 victory over the Los Angeles Rams in the 1950 championship game, Graham passed for four touchdowns. In the 1954 title game against Detroit, Graham passed for three touchdowns and also ran for three touchdowns. In his final season, Graham led the Browns to another title, this time beating the Rams. In this game, he passed for two touchdowns and ran for two more. Among the old-time quarterbacks, Graham's rating of 86.6 ranks number one (see Chapter 4 to understand the NFL quarterback rating system) and is surpassed by only four modern-day players.

John Hannah

John Hannah was big, mean, athletic, and a steamroller — all perfect ingredients for one of the game's finest all-around offensive linemen. When he came into the NFL in 1973, a first-round draft choice of the New England Patriots, Hannah was the first guard of such size (6'3", 285 pounds) who also could run well; he was a devastating pulling guard.

Some people had doubts about Hannah's ability to adjust to the pro game because he was strictly a zone, straight-ahead blocker while playing in Alabama's wishbone offense, which featured option running by the quarterback, who also pitched wide to running backs. A lineman didn't have to leave his stance and run wide to block, or concentrate on pass-blocking techniques in the wishbone offense. But Hannah had football in his genes (Herb, his father, played pro football with the New York Giants), and he was an adaptable athlete, having won varsity letters in wrestling and track, as well as football, at Alabama.

During his career, the Patriots were a few players and a little luck away from being a championship team. Hannah played in only one Super Bowl (and lost), but he was named All-Pro for ten consecutive seasons (1976 to 1985) and five times was named Offensive Lineman of the Year by the Players Association. In 13 seasons, he missed only 5 of 191 games due to injury.

Don Hutson

Everyone knows that Jerry Rice of the San Francisco 49ers is the best receiver ever, but old-timers will tell you that this Green Bay Packer, Don Hutson, was the best (see Figure 22-2). From 1935 to 1945, Hutson's receptions and receiving totals were almost three times greater than his nearest competitor. Teams didn't throw a lot in those days, but the Packers did because they had "The Alabama Antelope," one of the fastest men in football and among its most graceful. In 1942, Hutson caught 74 passes, more receptions than the combined total of all the players on four different NFL teams that season. He was the consummate deep-ball threat, leading the NFL in touchdown receptions in 9 of his 11 seasons. In his second game as a pro, he caught an 83-yard touchdown from quarterback Arnie Herber. Teams never double- and triple-teamed players until Hutson showed up on the scene.

In college at Alabama, Hutson was an all-around jock. One day, he was playing outfield in a baseball game and left to compete in track. He ran a 9.7-second 100-yard dash, winning the event, before hustling back to his baseball game.

Hutson, a charter inductee into the Pro Football Hall of Fame, was a two-way performer, playing at left end and in the secondary on defense. In his final four seasons, Hutson intercepted 23 passes. His record of 99 touchdown receptions stood for 44 seasons. And he was great until the bitter end, leading the NFL with 47 receptions in his final season.

Figure 22-2: Green Bay Packer Don Hutson was a multi-talented threat on the field. Photo credit: UPI/Corbis-Bettmann.

Before he died, Hutson was asked about modern athletes and whether he could play in today's game. "How many catches would you have today?" the young reporter asked. "Oh, probably about 50," Hutson replied. "Fifty? That's not as many as you had in your prime," the reporter retorted. "Well," Hutson said, smiling, "I am 74, you know."

Hugh McElhenny

People referred to Hugh McElhenny as "The King." On his first play as a pro with the San Francisco 49ers, he ran 60 yards for a touchdown. Some say that McElhenny was the greatest running back to ever catch a screen pass. He was dangerous in the open field, owning the complete repertoire of moves: He could pivot, sidestep, spin, change his pace, and fake you out of your pants. McElhenny likened running in the open field to walking down a dark alley: He instinctively knew what was lurking in every dark corner, where the 11 defenders were hiding to nab him.

More than 60 colleges offered McElhenny a scholarship, and when the University of Washington won his services, the college's football program was immediately investigated for recruiting violations. When McElhenny became a professional in 1952, his teammates laughed, saying that his $7,000 salary meant that he was taking a pay cut.

McElhenny played many of his 13 pro seasons in pain. He needed a steel plate in his shoe and pain-deadening shots in his right foot because of severed tendons that he had suffered as a child. When he retired after the 1964 season, he had played for four different teams and totaled 11,369 all-purpose yards. He was a true game-breaker; he could score from anywhere on the field and via the run, the pass, or the kick return. He averaged 4.9 yards a carry in his first ten seasons, plus he had touchdowns of 94, 86, and 81 yards.

Joe Montana

With the game on the line or a championship to be won, Joe Montana (see Figure 22-3) is the quarterback I want running my team. When I played against Joe Montana — remember, many manic things are happening on the field during a close game — I was always impressed with his ability to remain calm and focused. His composure is merely one characteristic that sets him apart. He was also a tremendously accurate passer — his all-time passing accuracy was 63.2 percent — and once he completed a record 22 consecutive passes.

Montana is one of those great quarterbacks who was raised and played high school ball in a relatively small corner of western Pennsylvania. Joe Namath, Dan Marino, Jim Kelly, and Montana all come from that part of the state, and all figure to be Hall of Famers. Although he appeared thin in build, Montana

Figure 22-3:
49ers quarterback Joe Montana led his team with composure and accuracy. Photo credit: UPI/Corbis-Bettmann.

was a tough quarterback. After major back surgery in 1986, he returned to perform some of his greatest heroics. His most productive seasons were in 1987 and 1989, the latter of which culminated in a 92-yard scoring drive to win Super Bowl XXIII in the final seconds.

Montana was named the Super Bowl MVP a record three times, and in his last two playoff runs to Super Bowl titles, Montana passed for 19 touchdowns without an interception. The beauty of Montana is that he won at every level — high school, Notre Dame, and the NFL — despite some coaches and NFL scouts doubting his abilities. San Francisco Coach Bill Walsh designed an exquisite pass-control offense, and Montana directed it with the passing precision of a surgeon. If he wasn't the best quarterback of all time, he surely was the most instinctive player ever to play this position.

Jim Parker

Jim Parker was the first offensive lineman elected to the Pro Football Hall of Fame. A first-round draft choice from Ohio State, Parker played both ways — offensive and defensive tackle — but Baltimore Colts coach Weeb Ewbank changed all that by starting him at only offensive tackle in 1957. The plan was pretty simple: Parker, all 6'3" and 273 pounds of him, was supposed to protect quarterback Johnny Unitas, one of the greatest passers of all time. In his very first game, Unitas attempted 47 passes and wasn't sacked once. Parker was magnificent at his job.

Parker was the first huge man — who possessed the quickness of a man 60 pounds lighter — to emerge as an outstanding blocker. Until men like Parker arrived, defensive players generally dominated pro football's line of scrimmage; most athletic big men preferred playing defense to offense. Parker's gifts were immeasurable. He was a Pro Bowl player at tackle for four years when Ewbank was forced to shift him to left guard because of injuries to other players. Parker fit perfectly in that role and was named All-Pro at guard for four consecutive seasons. A knee injury ended Parker's career in 1967.

Walter Payton

Mike Ditka, the great Chicago tight end and coach, called Walter Payton the most complete football player he had ever seen. Payton's nickname was "Sweetness," but maybe it should have been "Toughness." He missed only one game in 13 seasons with the Chicago Bears, and that one was a coaching decision by Jack Pardee in Payton's rookie season of 1975.

Excluding his rookie year and his final season, when he no longer was the hub of Chicago's offense, Payton touched the ball an average of 24 times a game for 122 yards, combining rushing and receiving gains. Although Barry Sanders may surpass him some day, Payton holds the all-time rushing total of 16,726 yards.

Players marveled about Payton because he did whatever he needed to do to win, and he stood out because he spent more than half his career on non-playoff teams. In fact, for seven of Payton's seasons, Chicago's record was 17 games below .500. His passion for the game ran deep. He enjoyed blocking and would run a dummy pass route like he was the intended receiver. Heck, he even passed for five touchdowns. In 10 of 13 seasons, Payton rushed for at least 1,200 yards. He needed arthroscopic surgery on both knees after the 1983 season, in which he gained 1,421 yards on those two gimpy knees. Figure 22-4 shows a photo of Payton.

Gale Sayers

If you enjoy watching Detroit Lions running back Barry Sanders, you would have loved Gale Sayers of the Chicago Bears. Sayers was a speedster with shake-and-bake moves, a dazzler in football pads. The only sad thing about Sayers is that two knee injuries shortened his career. Still, in basically a five-season career, he accomplished enough to deserve entry into the Pro Football Hall of Fame on the first ballot. Sayers enjoyed nothing more than returning punts and kicks. In his first preseason game, he raced 93 yards with a kickoff and 77 yards on a punt return, and he also threw a 25-yard touchdown pass with his left (poor) hand.

Figure 22-4:
Walter
Payton,
nicknamed
"Sweetness,"
was a
standout
running
back for the
Chicago
Bears.
Photo
credit:
UPI/Corbis-
Bettmann.

Bears coach George Halas coached more than 40 seasons, and he remarked after Sayers scored six touchdowns on a muddy Wrigley Field against the San Francisco 49ers in 1965 that it was the greatest performance he had ever seen. Sayers gained 336 yards that day, and some people say that he covered more than 130 yards while scoring on an 85-yard punt return in which he zigzagged all over the field.

In basically 12 full games that season, Sayers scored 22 touchdowns and averaged 31.4 yards on kick returns and 14.9 yards per punt return. His 2,272 combined yards by a rookie still ranks second in NFL history. Sayers had only two 1,000-yard rushing seasons, but he did average 5 yards per carry and scored a touchdown 1 out of every 23.7 times he touched the ball.

Art Shell

Art Shell arrived with the Oakland Raiders as a third-round draft choice from tiny Maryland State-Eastern Shore in 1968, a year after Gene Upshaw. However, the two players eventually united to form the best guard/tackle combination in the history of the NFL. Shell, who was 6'5", 295 pounds, became the starting left tackle in 1970 and was named to eight Pro Bowls in the 1970s. He became the Jim Parker of his era. Shell and Upshaw worked as one, dominating their side of the offensive formation on run sweeps.

However, Shell also evolved into a picture-perfect pass-blocker. In Super Bowl XI, Shell virtually buried talented Minnesota defensive end Jim Marshall to help lead the Raiders to victory. Shell was a mammoth man with Gene Kelly's feet. He could *slide-protect* (he had quick feet, which allowed him to shift his body easily in any direction when protecting his quarterback in passing situations) and also hammer defensive linemen with his brutish strength. Shell developed his agility while earning all-state honors in basketball at Bonds-Wilson High in North Charleston, South Carolina.

Shell later became the first African-American to become an NFL head coach and owned a 56-41 record when he lost his Raiders' coaching job in 1994. He opened the door for other African-American coaches like Tony Dungy of the Tampa Bay Buccaneers and Ray Rhodes of the Philadelphia Eagles.

Gene Upshaw

Most fans know Gene Upshaw as the executive director of the NFL Players Association, a title that translates into the leader of the players union, the man debating ownership regarding free agency and essentially more money and benefits for players. The ex-Oakland Raiders guard seemed destined for such a role because he entered the league in 1967, when its popularity was mushrooming, and left in 1981, knowing that pro football had surpassed baseball as America's pastime. Also, he was a Raiders' captain for eight seasons, the same number of years this left guard was named to All-AFC or All-Pro teams.

Upshaw was the first of the really tall (6'5") guards, and he was drafted in the first round to block a specific Oakland opponent: Hall of Fame tackle Buck Buchanan of the arch-rival Kansas City Chiefs. Upshaw had never played guard, but he won the starting job as a rookie and kept it for 15 seasons. Upshaw is the only player to start on championship teams in the old American Football League and in the NFL. The Raiders won the AFL title in 1967 and then Super Bowls XI and XV with Upshaw leading the way. Upshaw was a fierce competitor who was equally adept at run-blocking and pass-blocking. All told, he played in 317 preseason, regular-season, and postseason games with the Raiders, 24 of them playoff games.

Chapter 23
Ten Plus One: A Dream Team

In This Chapter

▶ Three of the greatest quarterbacks of all time

▶ The Minister of Defense and L.T. together

▶ The biggest little running back around

▶ Offensive linemen who gave me a little trouble

▶ The best safety and receiver, both from the 49ers

*Y*ou can't predict the future, but I think that you can tell right away whether a player is capable of greatness. He must be able to play at an extremely high level for a long period of time. He has to be consistent week in and week out. He needs equal amounts of toughness, intelligence, and pride in what he does, and the drive to compete on a weekly — almost daily — basis. And he must have leadership skills. Plus, he has to stay healthy — which has quite a bit to do with being lucky. The players on my Dream Team had all the intangibles: They performed at a high level in the biggest games, when championships were at stake.

During my career, I saw hundreds of players with the ability to be great. But greatness didn't always materialize for them because they became complacent or got sidetracked by the seven deadly sins — greed, sloth, gluttony, and so on — or something else. Staying at the top of the hill is much more difficult than climbing the hill.

Larry Allen

To make any offense function, you need big, strong offensive linemen who can run and dominate at their positions. What is special about the Dallas Cowboys' Larry Allen — who is 6'2", 325 pounds — is that he can play every line position, with the exception of center, at an extremely high level. He played guard much of his career prior to being shifted to left tackle for the 1998 season.

Allen has what line coaches call good feet, meaning that he's very athletic for a big man. He blocks well on the run and has tremendous leverage at the point of attack; he has excellent feet, which allow him to be balanced and maximize his tremendous lower-body strength, coupled with his massive upper body. Powerful defensive linemen can't outmuscle him. Allen has no physical weaknesses, and because he's so committed, he often tries to do too much, like running past the man he was supposed to block in order to block an opponent farther down the field or to block one closer to the area where the ball carrier is headed. This guy will check your will to compete.

Allen is looking at a Hall of Fame career if he continues playing at the same high level that he did in his first four NFL seasons after coming out of tiny Sacramento State. In this free-agency era, I like that both the player (Allen) and the organization (the Cowboys) came to a long-term contractual agreement without a protracted negotiation. Allen wants to remain in Dallas because he views it as an important step toward the Hall of Fame.

Marcus Allen

I picked Marcus Allen to be my short-yardage runner. On my team, when the ball gets inside the opponent's 5-yard line, we're giving it to Marcus Allen. No one was better at finding the end zone than Allen. What's great about Allen is that he did whatever he needed to do to score: He leapt the pile, or he burst outside, or he lowered his head and squeezed through the thinnest of holes. He is what teammates referred to as a money player, which means that he produced when the game's outcome was undecided.

When he retired after the 1997 season, Allen had an all-time best 123 rushing touchdowns, and his 145 total NFL touchdowns rank second only to Jerry Rice. And if you factor in those years that he was benched with the Raiders, you may be talking about the all-time touchdown leader. Allen and I were teammates on the Raiders for 11 seasons, and I've never been around a more consummate professional. He always was prepared to play, and he'd play hurt. Unlike some superstar running backs, Allen didn't mind blocking. In fact, he seemed to actually enjoy it. Allen did all the little things that make a player a champion.

The best statement about Allen's career is that he was the University of Southern California's blocking back — the fullback — when Charles White won the Heisman Trophy in 1979. Two years later, Allen became USC's tailback, and he set 15 NCAA records and won the Heisman himself. When we (the Raiders) won the Super Bowl after the 1983 season, Allen was the MVP of the game, rushing for 191 yards, including a brilliant 74-yard run that was the game's most notable offensive play. Allen was demoted when the Raiders signed Bo Jackson, but he rejuvenated his career with the Kansas City Chiefs.

John Elway, Brett Favre, and Dan Marino

Selecting just one of these great quarterbacks — John Elway, Brett Favre, Dan Marino — to be the Dream Team's starter is impossible. Both Favre and Elway have won a Super Bowl championship whereas Marino's Miami Dolphins lost in their only trip to the championship game. However, all three quarterbacks are winners in my book because they are fearless under pressure, are genuine tough guys, can generate positive yardage out of seemingly impossible predicaments, and can throw the ball as far as necessary. They can handle any inclement weather or perform the necessary last-minute heroics.

Marino holds all the records and was phenomenal at the University of Pittsburgh, where he led the Panthers to a 42-6 record in his four seasons while throwing for 79 touchdowns. Marino has led the NFL in passing yards four different seasons, and in 1984 he set single-season marks of 5,804 yards and 48 touchdowns. Marino has the quickest release of any quarterback ever.

Elway of the Denver Broncos (see Figure 23-1) was the most remarkable athlete I played against because he could be rolling right and stop and throw the ball 50 yards to the opposite side of the field. This former Stanford star is such a great athlete that he could have been a professional baseball athlete, too. Elway impressed me because his receiving corps wasn't loaded with great athletes.

Favre of the Green Bay Packers (see Figure 23-2) may end up being the best quarterback of all-time. You'll have to wait to see, though, because he's played only seven seasons heading into the 1998 season. He's had a remarkable four-year run, throwing for 145 touchdowns in that span while becoming the only three-time winner (1995, 1996, and 1997) of the NFL's Most Valuable Player award. In 1997, he shared the honor with Detroit Lions running back Barry Sanders. After Favre learned the intricacies of Coach Mike Holmgren's West Coast offense, he has become almost untouchable with his ability to spread the ball around. He has developed a fine touch to go with his fastball delivery, and he is fearless in the pocket.

All three quarterbacks embody the leadership qualities essential to the position.

Ronnie Lott

People I respect in football say that Ronnie Lott was the best ever to play safety. The amazing thing about Lott was that he had the ability to play both cornerback, a position that requires quickness and speed, and also safety, where you must be tough and a great tackler. Some of the greatest cornerbacks would never have lined up at safety, which says something about Lott. Coaches said that he hit like a linebacker. Before anyone knew what the phrase post-concussion syndrome means, Ronnie gave and got a number of concussions. He was a torpedo with a homing device. Once, when faced with the option of either missing the playoffs or repairing a badly broken finger, Lott opted to have a third of the finger amputated.

Figure 23-1:
John Elway
of the
Denver
Broncos
is a gifted
athlete.
Photo
credit: UPI/
Corbis-
Bettmann.

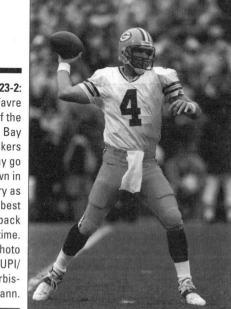

Figure 23-2:
Brett Favre
of the
Green Bay
Packers
may go
down in
history as
the best
quarterback
of all time.
Photo
credit: UPI/
Corbis-
Bettmann.

Lott was an All-America at the University of Southern California. He was a first-round draft choice of the San Francisco 49ers and started at cornerback as a rookie. The 49ers won their first of four Super Bowls that season; the two constant players during that run were Lott and quarterback Joe Montana. Lott was a tremendous leader and had the innate ability to raise the level of play of the people around him. He had toughness in abundance, and he was such a big-play performer. The bigger the game, the better he played. He finished his career with 63 interceptions, and he's often ranked among the top ten players to ever wear a helmet.

Bruce Matthews

Bruce Matthews can play anywhere on the offensive line, which is exactly what he's done since entering the NFL in 1983 as a first-round draft choice of the Houston (now Tennessee) Oilers. Matthews has played all five offensive line positions. Here's his breakdown by position, followed by the number of games started: center 74, right guard 67, left guard 48, right tackle 22, and left tackle 17. He has been named to the Pro Bowl ten times as either a center or guard.

Matthews's family lineage has some football links. His father, Clay, played four seasons of pro football with the San Francisco 49ers in the 1950s. Then Bruce's older brother, Clay, played 19 seasons in the NFL as a linebacker, mostly with the Cleveland Browns. Bruce has played in more than 232 NFL games and has proven to be durable and dependable. He's the ideal Dream Team player because you can plug him into any position along the offensive line.

Anthony Munoz

Only three players have been selected to a record 11 Pro Bowls in their careers. Most casual fans probably have heard of the first two: Jerry Rice and Reggie White. Anthony Munoz, who played 13 seasons with the Cincinnati Bengals, is the third such player to be so honored. Munoz arguably is the most complete offensive tackle ever and is certainly the best of his era (1980–92).

Munoz, who missed only one game in his pro career, was an All-America at the University of Southern California. He possessed a rare combination of strength, size (6'6", 292 pounds), and athleticism. He had such great agility for a large man — he also was a pretty good college baseball pitcher — while possessing a tough-guy attitude when run-blocking. He was a tremendous pass blocker, having the quickness to recover in the rare instances when he was physically beaten. He was a black hole player, meaning that whoever went against him was engulfed in this black hole, disappearing for the remainder of the game.

Munoz was a strong-minded player, too. He missed most of his senior season at USC due to a knee operation, but he returned for the 1980 Rose Bowl game to flatten the Ohio State defenders on his side of the field.

Jerry Rice

Jerry Rice (shown in Figure 23-3) is the greatest wide receiver in the history of the game. In 1997, Rice suffered the first injuries — torn left knee ligaments and a broken left kneecap — of his 13-year career with the San Francisco 49ers. Otherwise, Rice has raced through the NFL gobbling up records and passing defensive backs at an alarming rate. Rice, who played college football at tiny Mississippi Valley State, owns 13 NFL records and has been voted to a record-tying 11 Pro Bowls. He has caught an average of six passes in every one of his NFL starts.

Rice has scored 166 touchdowns and has had 11 1,000-yard receiving seasons and 61 games in which he has caught passes for 100 yards or more. He holds the NFL single-season record with 1,848 receiving yards — set in 1995 when he was 33 — and twice he has been named Player of the Year. He also holds ten Super Bowl receiving records. The beauty of Rice is that he makes everything look extremely easy, but you know that it's not. When he's playing, he has an extra gear for every situation. He has a burst (that is, more speed) to evade being tackled. The competitive fires burn strong in Rice, and most people expect him to continue playing pro football throughout the 1990s. His workout habits are legendary. He has innate ability, but he also has worked as hard as any player in any sport to be the very best.

Figure 23-3: San Francisco's Jerry Rice holds the NFL record for receiving yards. Here, he makes it look easy by zooming past Detroit Lions defenders. Photo credit: UPI/Corbis-Bettmann.

Barry Sanders

How many professional athletes have their finest season in their ninth year? No one but a remarkable athlete like Barry Sanders, shown in Figure 23-4. Sanders actually appeared to be faster and quicker in 1997, the year that he became the third running back to gain 2,000 (actually 2,053) yards in a single season, joining O. J. Simpson and Eric Dickerson. This diminutive player (at 5'8", he's the smallest-looking 200-pounder you'll ever see) has been making fools out of most defensive players since high school. I like to say that he makes the most superb athletes look unathletic when they flat out miss when trying to tackle him.

Sanders is difficult to tackle for several reasons. First, he's a small target, which doesn't leave much room for error. Second, he has super cutback ability, literally stopping and changing direction on a dime. Third, he has powerful thighs. While at Oklahoma State, Sanders took up weightlifting and could squat lift over 600 pounds. Tacklers seemingly bounce off those rock-hard thighs. He set 13 NCAA rushing and scoring records at Oklahoma State en route to the 1988 Heisman Trophy. The yardstick in the NFL is 1,000 yards rushing a season for any good back, and Sanders is the only player in history to hit that number in his first nine seasons while also owning four rushing titles. He has accomplished all these impressive feats while playing on average teams and behind relatively average offensive lines.

Figure 23-4: Barry Sanders evades Redskins' defender Danny Copeland. Photo credit: UPI/ Corbis-Bettmann.

Deion Sanders

In the 1990s, Deion Sanders is the only cornerback who has been capable on a weekly basis of shutting down the opposition's best wide receiver. Sanders proved his impressive credentials in back-to-back Super Bowls, first with the San Francisco 49ers at the end of the 1994 season and then the following season with the Dallas Cowboys. At the time, he was the highest-paid defensive player in the NFL.

Sanders made an immediate impact with the Atlanta Falcons, playing for them for five NFL seasons. But he wanted to win a championship and opted to leave the Falcons for that opportunity. With him playing for the 49ers and the Cowboys, more fans were able to see what a great player he truly is.

Known as "Prime Time" for his athletic exploits, Sanders may be the finest all-around athlete of his generation. For eight seasons, he played both major league baseball and pro football. He is the only player to hit a home run and score a touchdown in the same week. At Florida State, Sanders was a football All-America twice, started in center field at the College World Series, and qualified for the 1988 Olympic Trials as a sprinter. Although he has alienated some fans with his self-promotion antics, Sanders is a superior athlete who can play both ways on the pro level: offensive receiver and cornerback. He also has scored five touchdowns as a kick returner.

Bruce Smith

Bruce Smith is by far the most athletic defensive end in the NFL. The way that he plays with such incredible quickness and dexterity, you know that he must have been a basketball player, too. His Booker T. Washington High School (in Norfolk) team won the Virginia state basketball championship. At 6'4", 275 pounds, Smith has been a nonstop player (he never takes a play off; he's constantly trying) on the Buffalo Bill's defensive line. As a pass rusher, he has an arsenal of moves, making him virtually unstoppable when being single blocked. After the 1997 season, Smith had totaled 154 quarterback sacks, adding an NFL-high 12 in postseason play.

Smith's defensive prowess was the driving force behind Buffalo's four appearances, albeit losing ones, in the Super Bowl between 1990 and 1993. Smith was Buffalo's first-round draft choice in 1985 and earned defensive Rookie of the Year honors. He has had 11 pro seasons of double-digit sacks. As a collegiate, he restored Virginia Tech to prominence, leading his team to a bowl game. In college, Smith had 46 sacks and 25 tackles for losses behind the line of scrimmage. His best season was 1990 when he led the NFL with 19 sacks, only to end the season with a one-point loss to the N. Y. Giants in Super Bowl XXV.

Dwight Stephenson

Some in the media may think that Dwight Stephenson doesn't deserve to be a Hall of Famer because he played only eight seasons in the NFL. But in my opinion, Stephenson was every bit as dominant at his position of center for the Miami Dolphins as Chicago Bears running back Gale Sayers was in his illustrious career. Knee injuries put both men on the sidelines too early, and Sayers basically had a five-year career, playing in only 68 games. Sometimes life isn't fair, but Stephenson deserves all the recognition and accolades.

I played against him, and he was the first center that I knew who could engage a lineman directly over him, put the lineman down, and then shift his attention to other players, such as defensive ends. Stephenson was quick and strong enough to hold off some defenders with a single arm. On his highlight films, he simply embarrasses players with his strength and overall athletic ability.

Lawrence Taylor

Lawrence Taylor ("L.T.") was the best defensive player that I've ever seen. (He's pictured defending John Elway in Figure 23-1.) This N. Y. Giants outside linebacker played in my era (1981–93), and I simply marveled at what he was able to do. You hear about offensive coordinators worrying about the opposition, but teams also had to account for L.T. and form their strategies accordingly. Game plans were devised to avoid him. Joe Gibbs, the great Washington Redskins coach, decided to go with a three tight end offense for the sole purpose of reducing L.T.'s effectiveness. He wanted to frustrate L.T. with as many blockers as he could place on the field.

L.T. was the first of the prototypical big, fast linebackers of today's game. But no one has been able to match his accomplishments and play the way that he did. Today's linebackers may be the same size, bigger or faster, but no one has touched his overall ability to dominate a game. A lot of linebackers read and then react; Taylor simply attacked. At 6'3", 244 pounds, Taylor could dominate a blocker and still have the speed to run down running backs and quarterbacks moving away from him. He was a ten-time-Pro Bowler, an All-America at North Carolina, and was named Atlantic Coast Conference Player of the Year in his senior season. He starred on two Super Bowl championship teams with New York and finished his career with $132^1/_2$ sacks.

Reggie White

Reggie White is the first defensive lineman to weigh 300 pounds and still be able to run a 40-yard dash in 4.6 seconds. When he was at his peak, White had the rare ability to beat offensive linemen around the corner or to steamroll them on his way to the quarterback. He and Bruce Smith may be the best defensive linemen of all-time. In 1982, the NFL officially began keeping records of quarterback sacks, and no player in modern times has done a better job of tackling quarterbacks behind the line of scrimmage (sacks) than White.

At the end of the 1997 season, White had an NFL-record $176^{1}/_{2}$ sacks. And this statistic doesn't include the $23^{1}/_{2}$ sacks that White accumulated in the United States Football League (USFL) in 1984 and 1985. White left the financially strained USFL Memphis Showboats for the Philadelphia Eagles in 1985, playing a total of 31 games that season because the Showboats played in the spring. The Eagles, especially when Buddy Ryan was their coach, had one of the NFL's greatest defenses, and White was its leader. He had 21 sacks in only 12 games in 1987. When free agency began, White received a $9 million signing bonus from the Green Bay Packers. An ordained minister, White's nickname is "The Minister of Defense," and he was named a defensive tackle on the University of Tennessee's all-time team, featuring athletes from all eras.

Kellen Winslow

Kellen Winslow was the best tight end that I ever played against. This San Diego Charger was so big (6'5", 250 pounds) that the safeties couldn't cover him on pass defense, and he was too fast for the linebackers. Winslow was like a wide receiver in a big man's body. He had great hands and was an effective weapon in San Diego's great passing offense of the early 1980s. He had the strength to block, but San Diego's offense was more about throwing the ball; Winslow fit in perfectly because he could settle into an open area in the zone and quarterback Dan Fouts would find him.

Winslow was one of those players who, when the game was on the line, wanted the ball more. In fact, he seemed to get better the more passes he caught. In one of the greatest playoff games ever, Winslow caught 13 passes for 166 yards in a 41-38 overtime victory over the Miami Dolphins. Winslow, who collapsed from dehydration and needed to be helped off the field, blocked Miami's attempt at a field goal with four seconds left to send the game into overtime. Winslow had 319 receptions in a four-year stretch (1980 to 1983), three of which when he was All-Pro, but a knee injury derailed his career in 1984. He missed 17 games over two seasons and was never quite the same offensive force.

Chapter 24

The Ten Greatest Coaches of All Time

*Y*ou may have this same little problem that I do: I don't like choosing sides or picking favorites. With my boys, I know how tough picking a Little League all-star team can be. And now I have to pick the best football coaches of all time.

I went with my gut (and it isn't that considerable, either) in this chapter. I'm not a big history buff, so I didn't consider all the old-timers like Pop Warner and Curly Lambeau. And I skipped over some super college coaches like Ohio State's Woody Hayes and Paul "Bear" Bryant, who actually walked on water in Alabama, I hear. Florida's Steve Spurrier probably is today's college version of Bill Walsh. And who wouldn't want men like Nebraska's Tom Osborne and Penn State's Joe Paterno watching over their sons?

On television, I talk all the time about great coaches, many of them assistants — the men who teach and do the grunt work. Although Terry Bradshaw and I don't always agree, we both root for two young NFL coaches whom we'd both gladly play for if our bodies were capable of making a comeback. They are Bill Cowher of the Pittsburgh Steelers and Tony Dungy of the Tampa Bay Buccaneers. Both of these men exude charisma.

I love Cowher's honesty and enthusiasm. Personality-wise, Dungy is the opposite of Cowher. You see Cowher jumping up and down and running down the Steelers' sideline, butting heads with players and giving them a proud pa–like slap on the backside. When you watch Tony, you never see his demeanor change from one extreme to the other. However, both coaches are proud leaders — you can see that in how their players respond. They are forever trying, refusing to give in to adversity. There is no quit in them. Tony is a person who expects you to act like a man and treats you like a man. Cowher acts like one of his players at times. In the playoffs one year, Cowher made a bad call on fourth down that probably cost his team a victory. Afterwards, he admitted his mistake, saying that he made a bad call. I like stand-up guys!

I spoke with many coaching friends to narrow my list to the following men. Most of them were innovators, and all of them were winners. Everyone speaks of playing hard, win or lose. But I know that a football coach is special when he molds 30 to 50 men into a championship team. All these men are champions. And many of these great coaches are connected to one another. For example, Don Shula worked under Paul Brown. I know that Shula credits Brown for how well organized and prepared he was on game days.

Paul Brown

I loved playing pro football, but I don't know if I could have sat still in a Paul Brown classroom. This man turned football into a science class back in the late 1940s. He even graded every player's performance from game film and sent plays in from the bench. Players were turned off by his classroom approach; however, his revolutionary approach to practice sessions and his demands that players take notes and carry playbooks became commonplace and have remained so for decades, from high school ball to the NFL.

In 1956, Brown wired his quarterback's helmet in order to transmit instructions. More than 40 years later, the NFL allows every team to do so (although those transmitters don't always work).

The Cleveland Browns, who are expected to resume play in the 1999 NFL season, are the only team named after a head coach — that's how talented Paul Brown was. After winning a national championship at Ohio State and coaching Washington High School in Massillon, Ohio, to six consecutive Ohio state championships, Brown was paid the princely sum of $20,000 to coach and build a professional team, called the Cleveland Browns, in 1945. The Browns won four consecutive championships, but the team's success (52-4-2 record) doomed the All-America Football Conference. But when the mighty NFL absorbed the Browns, the team didn't play like second-rate performers. In their first game in the new league, the Browns defeated the NFL champion Philadelphia Eagles. They won three more championships over the next six seasons.

Brown eventually left Cleveland, retiring with a 115-49-5 record. He returned to football in 1968 as the owner and coach of the Cincinnati Bengals, an expansion team. After only three years, the Bengals made the playoffs. Brown died in 1991, and his family continues to have a controlling interest in Cincinnati's NFL franchise.

Joe Gibbs

Although my Raiders beat his Washington Redskins in Super Bowl XVIII, we also lost to Gibbs's team a couple of times during my career. I never thought that its personnel matched up with ours, but Gibbs always had his team ready to play and exploit our weaknesses. From top to bottom, the Redskins were as well-coached as any group I ever faced. His teams always played hard; they were physical as well as daring, and they played together as a team. I know that Gibbs loves NASCAR racing now, but any team looking for a head coach should give him call. He would be great.

Players say that Gibbs was strict but fair. The biggest testament to his abilities is that he won three Super Bowls — and that he won with three different quarterbacks. He didn't need many stars or dominant players to win. He knew how to build on his players' strengths and minimize their weaknesses. Not only was he great with quarterbacks, but he won with big backs (such as John Riggins) and small receivers. His teams were able to play power football (running the ball) one week, and then the next week, he'd open it up and beat you throwing the ball. One of his power football tactics was the three tight end offense. Not only did it help his team's running game, but it also negated the strength of Giants linebacker Lawrence Taylor.

Gibbs, who won 16 of 21 playoff games, was a tireless worker. I heard that he slept in his office two or three nights a week and often worked 20-hour days. I know that a lot of people see Joe as a serious guy, but he can be pretty funny, and I thought he did a great job as an analyst on NBC's pregame show.

George Halas

This coach is my first real old-timer. But I probably wouldn't be writing this book or even have my job at FOX if it weren't for George Halas, the father of pro football. When you think of Chicago, the city of broad shoulders, you immediately think of bigger-than-life men like Mayor Richard Daley, Al Capone, and "Papa Bear" Halas. I can't think of another large American city that has a bigger connection with a football team than Chicago, and it's all due to George Halas.

Legend has it that Halas was cheap with a buck and a strict disciplinarian, but he was also a showman. In 1920, in the Hupmobile showroom of a Canton, Ohio, car dealer, Halas represented one of the NFL's original teams, the Decatur (Illinois) Staleys. (Imagine playing for a team called the Staleys!) A year later, Coach Halas wised up and moved the team to Chicago. The next year, he changed the team's name to the Bears.

Halas realized that the pro game wouldn't survive without stars, so he signed Illinois All-American Red Grange in 1925. At that time, Grange was the most exciting player in college football. The Bears went on a barnstorming tour and played before packed stadiums, showing thousands of fans how great the pro game was. Halas pioneered radio broadcasts of games and also was the first to use a public address system to apprise fans of what was happening on the field: how many yards were gained, who made the tackle, and what the down and distance were.

Halas was associated with the Bears from the team's inception until his death in 1983. He stepped away from coaching three times, and each time a rejuvenated Halas returned to lead Chicago to an NFL championship. He believed in hiring the best assistant coaches, and he didn't mind sharing the credit. Clark Shaughnessy drastically altered the Bears' offense in 1940, and the result was a 73-0 victory over Washington in the NFL title game. The lopsided victory provided national attention for the publicity-starved professional game. Until Don Shula broke his records, Halas was the number one coach with 324 pro football victories.

Jimmy Johnson

Jimmy, like Bill Walsh (discussed later in this chapter), is a super builder and talent evaluator who also happens to be a great football coach. Nothing ever slips by this man. He totally rebuilt the Dallas Cowboys when that great franchise was on the decline back in 1989. He won two Super Bowls with young talent, and then Barry Switzer won another one with players like Troy Aikman, Emmitt Smith, and Michael Irvin. That trio of players is why Dallas remains competitive today, and Johnson drafted each one of them.

Jimmy and I worked together at FOX for two years, and I don't think that I've been around many people who are smarter than he is. I knew that he wanted to coach again, and Miami was the one place he wanted to be. Although he's a native Texan, Jimmy loves the water and weather of Miami. Plus, he came into the national spotlight there, winning a national championship at the University of Miami.

Jimmy has struggled a bit with the Dolphins because the NFL system has changed. He inherited someone else's house, and it came furnished, but because of salary cap restrictions and players' possessive contracts (see Chapter 17 for more details about the pro football draft), Johnson could replace only one or two players at a time. When Jimmy took over in Dallas, he made wholesale changes and rebuilt the Cowboys through the draft; free agency didn't exist in the NFL when he started.

When he left Dallas, the Cowboys were the most talented team in the NFL. Their second-team players could have been starters on other teams — and eventually that's what happened. When free agency began in 1993, Dallas wasn't able to keep all of its players, especially the talented reserves. On a level playing field, I could guarantee you that Jimmy would win another

Super Bowl. But today, another owner's checkbook can beat him to a player he wants. Building a franchise through the college draft takes a lot longer these days. Plus, Jimmy believes that you win with defense (so do I) and by running the football, but Miami's best chance to win lately has been with its quarterback, Dan Marino.

Vince Lombardi

When pro football first started to become popular on television in the 1960s, Vince Lombardi (see Figure 24-1) was in the process of transforming tiny Green Bay, Wisconsin, into the biggest franchise in the NFL. The Packers were as popular as baseball's Yankees; they were a national team. And Lombardi was the game's most recognized coach. Like a story fresh off a movie lot, the Packers appealed to many blue-collar fans because they are owned by the Wisconsin fans and not by some giant corporation.

Lombardi wasn't an innovator; he honed and borrowed from other coaches' methods. He learned the passing game from Sid Gillman while the two were assistant coaches at the U.S. Military Academy. He was a lineman in college, so he knew the blocking techniques as a player. While at Army, the great coach Earl "Red" Blaik showed him what organization and execution mean to a team.

Figure 24-1: Vince Lombardi rides the shoulders of Packer Ray Nitschke after a victory over the Baltimore Colts on December 27, 1965. Photo credit: UPI/ Corbis-Bettmann.

Lombardi was a man of basics, and the Green Bay power sweep was one of his productions. On the power sweep, the two offensive guards would run around end to block, with a fullback leading the way for the halfback carrying the ball. The fans, the opposition, and everyone knew that the play was coming, but the Packers ran it with such precision that few teams were able to stop it consistently.

Over a ten-year period, the Packers won five championships, including the first two Super Bowls. The only championship game that Lombardi lost was his first, 17-13 to the Philadelphia Eagles in 1960.

So much about being a football coach is teaching, and Lombardi was one of the best. "They call it coaching, but it is teaching," Lombardi said of his craft. "You don't just tell them it is so. You show them the reasons why it is so, and then you repeat and repeat it until they are convinced, until they know." Lombardi, like Halas, is one of the game's legendary heroes, and the Super Bowl trophy honors his accomplishments. After trying his hand at management with the Packers, Lombardi returned to coaching with the Washington Redskins in 1969. He led them to their first winning season in 14 years only to die of cancer the following year at age 57. This great man went too soon.

John Madden

John Madden has been the best analyst on television for the last decade, but before he became a TV star and commercial pitchman, he was one of the game's best coaches. His enthusiasm and love of the game were obvious from the very beginning. A knee injury derailed his professional football career; however, he hung around the Philadelphia Eagles for most of the year anyway, learning as much as possible from Eagles quarterback Norm Van Brocklin, a future Hall of Famer.

Madden likes to come across as a lighthearted statesman for the game of football — he loves to garrulously describe the play of the oversized linemen and never seems to take the game too seriously — but he's always been a clever, intuitive leader. Smart like a fox. When you have an opportunity to sit and talk to John, it's like taking an audience with the Dalai Lama; you sit, listen, and learn.

Like a lot of famous coaches, Madden began his coaching career at the very bottom, at a small junior college team in rural California. In a few years, Madden matriculated to San Diego State, studying under Don Coryell, a great passing coach. "John never let his players give up, even if it was in practice," Coryell remembers. "Our practices got heated because John didn't even like to lose a scrimmage." Eventually, Oakland Raiders owner Al Davis hired Madden as an assistant and two years later elevated him to head coach. Madden, only 32, became the youngest head coach in the American Football League.

If you ever watch NFL films on cable television, you may catch a glimpse of Madden during the Raiders' great glory run of the 1970s. A big man, Madden was an emotional coach, much like the Pittsburgh Steelers coach Bill Cowher. He was constantly on the officials, bemoaning terrible calls, waving his arms, and exhorting his players to work harder. Madden coached for only ten years, but he won 100 games faster than any other NFL coach at that time and led the Raiders over Minnesota to win Super Bowl XI. He walked away from the game on top, after the 1978 season, at the age of 42. Many coaches don't earn their first head-coaching position until they are older than that!

Madden never had a strong urge to return to coaching, and deservedly so. He has become an icon in sports television, deciding to remain in the game's fabric by working as a television analyst.

Bill Parcells

Bill Parcells is a throwback coach in many ways. By that, I mean that he could have coached in any era. His greatest strength is his talent to relate to his players and figure out the best approach to utilize their skills and turn them into a winning team. He knows how to push a player's buttons, strike a nerve, and force him to dig deep for something extra, to give a better effort, whatever it takes to win. He's a defensive coach, so his focus has been on that side of the ball, supported by an offense that prefers to run first, pass second. If I were physically able, I'd love to turn back the clock and play for this man. He's a coach who appreciates toughness and personal sacrifice for the good of the team.

A New Jersey guy, Parcells returned to New York City in 1997 to coach the New York Jets. And in typical Parcells fashion, he made an immediate impact. The Jets, who had had eight straight non-winning seasons, finished 9-7 in his first season; the year before, New York had won 1 of 16 games. This is Parcells's third shot at attempting to transform a losing franchise into a Super Bowl contender. His first such accomplishment was with the New York Giants. After one bad season, Parcells enjoyed a remarkable run with the Giants, winning 10, 11, 17, 10, 12, and 16 games between 1984 and 1990. Those teams, led by linebacker Lawrence Taylor and quarterback Phil Simms, won two Super Bowls and three division titles. Parcells was named Coach of the Year in 1986 and 1989.

He worked as a network television commentator for two seasons before returning to coaching with the New England Patriots in 1993. The Patriots were 2-12 in 1992. In his first season, the Patriots won five games, and then an amazing 10 in 1994, when he won his third Coach of the Year honor. The 1996 team went 13-6, losing to the Green Bay Packers in Super Bowl XXXII. Entering the 1998 season, Parcells was the third winningest active coach in the NFL, with a 128-93-1 (.577) record.

Parcells surprised the football world by taking the Patriots to the Super Bowl, knowing that their only chance to win rested with quarterback Drew Bledsoe. Parcells, who would have preferred to control the clock with a running game, proved to everyone that he could win with an offense that went against his basic beliefs and background. However, his finest coaching job was in the Giants' second Super Bowl run. His team was forced to play the end of the 1990 season without Simms, and they neutralized two great offensive teams, the San Francisco 49ers and the Buffalo Bills, with a stifling defense and a ball-control rushing attack. They beat the 49ers by two points and defeated the Bills 20-19 in Super Bowl XXV.

Knute Rockne

I'm sure that many non-football fans have heard of the University of Notre Dame in South Bend, Indiana. Notre Dame is synonymous with college football. And Knute (pronounced *Newt*) Rockne was college football's greatest coach. And what a great name! The sound perfectly suits the image of football: You have to be rock hard and tough to play this game.

"The Rock," as Rockne was affectionately called, guided Notre Dame to three national championships and had an .881 winning percentage — the all-time best winning percentage, college or pro. He won 105 and lost only 12 games. In *Knute Rockne — All American,* a great old movie that you can rent at your local video store, actor Pat O'Brien immortalizes Rockne's famous "Win one for the Gipper" speech. Former President Ronald Reagan, who was a Hollywood star before going into politics, plays the ill-fated George Gipp.

Rockne was a master of the fiery pep talk, a type of speech that even Little League coaches give now and then. When his team was playing badly, he would sarcastically refer to his macho players as girls, which is the last thing tough guys want to hear. But after the game was over and his verbal berating finished, Rockne loved his young players like a father. The players knew that Rockne's rough words weren't personal, even though he scared them at times saying that he might die if they didn't win.

Rockne was an inspirational speaker and traveled the country sharing his thoughts and opinions of life and football. He sold football across the land and made many Americans stand up and take notice. Rockne was the model for much of the motivational locker room rhetoric in Chapter 19.

Rockne was also influential on the field. In 1913, playing end for Notre Dame, he teamed with quarterback Gus Dorais to develop the use of the forward pass in a game against West Point. He was also the first to use *shock troops,* or second-team performers, to wear down the opposition's first string. He believed in playing the best teams every week, which is how Notre Dame became a national team.

Don Shula

I don't know if he is the best coach who ever walked a sideline, but he certainly is the most successful one. Shula retired after the 1995 season and 33 years of coaching in the NFL with more wins (347) than anybody. He also possesses the league's only perfect season: 17-0 in 1972, a season that the Miami Dolphins capped off by winning Super Bowl VII. He was the first head coach to cost his owner a first-round draft choice, the price Miami had to pay Baltimore to hire him away in 1970. The beauty of Shula, NFL executive George Young said, is that "he was best at playing the cards he was dealt." Shula built his offensive and defensive systems around his players, not the other way around, which is more common in the coaching fraternity.

"We take a lot of pride in that," Shula said of his adaptability. "My philosophy was to get the most out of the talent you have, then design your system to best take advantage of that talent. I'd rather not tell a player, 'Hey, this is my system and demand they either do it this way, or I'll find someone else.'"

Shula had tremendous success with three different styles of offenses: He played power football with Larry Csonka in the early 1970s, a more balanced scheme with the Colts back in the 1960s, and at the end of his career he pretty much turned the offense over to Dan Marino's big arm and allowed him to throw as much as he wanted. Players win championships, and Shula was fortunate to have quarterbacks such as Johnny Unitas, Earl Morrall, Bob Griese, and Marino guiding his teams. (Unitas and Griese are already in the Hall of Fame, and Marino will be, considering that he owns virtually every passing record in pro football.)

I don't fully comprehend the backroom politics that are prevalent in the NFL, but I know that Shula was respected by his peers and upper management. He was always at the forefront of advocating better rules, and he always supported instant replay, which the fans see at home, but the officials don't use at the moment. (The replay system is used to rectify an improperly made call on the field.)

Shula had to be great; he coached 11 of the players in the Pro Football Hall of Fame, ranging from the 1960s to the 1980s. And that number will grow as more players become eligible for the honor.

Bill Walsh

They don't call this man "The Genius" for nothing. He built the San Francisco 49ers out of the ashes (they were a 2-14 team when he took over) and transformed them into the dominant franchise of the 1980s. To this day, his imprint on the team remains visible. In Chapter 4, you can read about the West Coast offense. Well, Walsh created the West Coast offense, and as many as nine NFL teams, including successful teams like the Green Bay Packers and Denver Broncos, use a version of it.

In Walsh's third season, the 49ers won their first of his three Super Bowls. His first offensive team had an incredible lack of talent, but he designed a system that truly worked for them. The 49ers, unlike the Raiders, worked on throwing short, possession-type passes. To them, a 5-yard gain was a 5-yard gain, whether it was a pass or a run play. Walsh didn't care; he simply wanted to maintain possession and keep the ball moving.

In the process of devising this offensive system, Walsh developed one of the game's best quarterbacks, Joe Montana. Now, Montana didn't have the greatest arm, nor was he the biggest guy. But he was one of the toughest and definitely one of the greatest quarterbacks under pressure, maybe the best decision-maker pro football has ever seen. Walsh deserves a lot of credit for Montana and for designing a passing offense that was an extension of the running game.

Although Walsh was a huge factor in developing quarterbacks like Dan Fouts, Montana, and Steve Young, he's also a great judge of talent at other positions. His drafts built the 49ers into champions, and I know that he had to watch only five plays by Charles Haley in college to know that Haley would be a great pass-rusher in the NFL. Jerry Rice, probably the best receiver who has ever played, was another Walsh selection.

Although many players benefited from his offensive system, Walsh was often quick to release or trade veteran players that he thought were expendable or were running out of time. This policy caused some animosity in the locker room, but Walsh believed that teams needed a constant infusion of young talent. He always seemed to be ahead of the curve, allowing an experienced veteran to depart while grooming a faster, quicker rookie for the role. Walsh was criticized for being cold and calculating, but I know that he had a soft spot for many of his players and simply was dealing with the extremely high expectations of pro football owners.

Walsh is another coach connected to Paul Brown's tree. He coached under Brown in Cincinnati, but when he wasn't named Brown's successor, he moved on, thus becoming available to the 49ers, whose owner, Eddie DeBartolo, Jr., studied Walsh while Walsh was coaching at Stanford University.

Chapter 25

The Ten Best Teams of All Time

In This Chapter

▶ Halas, Lombardi, and Rockne coached greatness

▶ Two teams with two Heisman winners each

▶ Miami's perfect season

▶ Walsh and Johnson built dominance

▶ Rooney was one lucky owner

1've found that nothing in life after football matches the intensity, the pressure, and the feeling of accomplishment of participating in and then winning the Super Bowl. You feel like you're the best on the face of the earth. Often, a championship stamps the winning team as exceptional. The sad part is that, oddly enough, the team who loses a Super Bowl would be better off as the league's 14th best team, rather than the second best, because fans never let you forget that you lost.

The 1990–1993 Buffalo Bills come to mind. They played in four consecutive Super Bowls, a feat that no other team has accomplished. But because they lost all four games, some people label them losers. Not me, though. They almost made this list.

Still, I had to judge the teams listed in this chapter by their championships and their historical importance to football, both college and professional. Forty or fifty years ago, college football ranked above the NFL in popularity, and in summer, a group of college all-stars played the defending NFL champions in an exhibition game. The college kids even beat the Green Bay Packers, the Chicago Bears, and the Cleveland Browns in a few of these games. Of course, those games meant more to the collegians, who would soon enter NFL training camps as rookies. They wanted to prove their worth and show the pros that they weren't pushovers.

These all-time best teams (listed in alphabetical order) had exceptional talent and ability on both sides of the ball, but they also had qualities like character and determination. And they had coaches, such as Vince Lombardi and Don Shula, who were great leaders.

Chicago Bears (1940–43)

The Chicago Bears went 41-6-1 in the four seasons between 1940 and 1943, winning three NFL (world) championships during that time. George Halas, the team's founder and Chicago's coach for 40 seasons, participated in only two of these title runs because he joined the Navy midway through the 1942 season (the Bears were 6-0 when he left). In 1963, the National Academy of Sports Editors voted Chicago's 1940 team, which defeated the Washington Redskins 73-0 for the world championship, the greatest professional team of all time. Believe me, these teams, which were long on grit, dedication, and toughness, would hold their own against today's superstars.

When the NFL began in 1920, the Bears were just another team. But Halas built them into a winner and developed stars like Red Grange and Bronko Nagurski. He helped put excitement into pro football; in 1942, a crowd of 101,100 came to Soldier Field — still home to today's Bears — to watch the Bears beat the college all-stars 21-0. At the time, this game was bigger than most professional rivalries because college football was more popular than the pro game with most football fans.

These teams had six Hall of Fame performers in guard Danny Fortmann, quarterback Sid Luckman, running back George McAfee, defensive tackle George Musso, tackle Joe Stydahar, and center/linebacker Clyde "Bulldog" Turner. All six played both offense and defense (which is almost unheard of in pro football today), and Luckman led or tied for the lead in NFL passing in four of his nine seasons.

Cleveland Browns (1946–55)

Selecting a single team from this ten-year period of the Browns is impossible, but the accomplishments of this franchise are unparalleled during that period — or, for that matter, in any ten-year span of professional football. The Browns played in ten straight championship games and won seven. Hall of Fame coach Paul Brown, who had an eye for talent, preparation, and strategy, built this juggernaut.

Now, some old-timers may disparage this team's overall success because four of those championships came in the now-defunct All-American Football Conference, which some NFL people believe was an inferior league. But in their first season in the NFL, the Browns won 10 of 12 regular-season games and beat the Los Angeles Rams in their first NFL championship game.

The Browns won all four AAFC championship games by an average of 18 points, and in their last 38 AAFC regular-season games, they had a 34-1-3 record. Cleveland's dominance continued in the NFL, where they won five consecutive conference titles and two more NFL championships. Cleveland crushed the Detroit Lions by 46 points in 1954 and the Rams by 24 in 1955. In this ten-year period, the Cleveland Browns won more than 83 percent of their games.

Besides having the game's most innovative coach in Paul Brown, the Browns had four Hall of Fame offensive linemen (Frank Gatski, Mike McCormack, Bill Willis, and Lou Groza) and one of the game's finest all-around quarterbacks in Otto Graham. Groza was also a placekicker, scoring 1,608 points in 21 seasons, and was named Player of the Year in 1954. The Browns were loaded on offense with Graham directing the show. Marion Motley, another Hall of Famer, was a devastating runner and blocker — I think he was the best fullback until Larry Csonka came along and played for the Dolphins. Dub Jones, Mac Speedie, and Dante Lavelli may have been the finest collection of receivers ever on one team. The Browns had everything!

Dallas Cowboys (1992–95)

For the most part, Jimmy Johnson built this team, although he was the head coach only for its back-to-back Super Bowl victories in 1993 and 1994. San Francisco kept the Cowboys from making a third straight Super Bowl appearance, but new head coach Barry Switzer led them back to the dance after the 1995 season to win Super Bowl XXX. In this four-year period, Dallas dominated the NFL by winning 59 of 75 games — a .787 winning percentage.

If free agency hadn't come into effect after the 1993 season, Dallas may have ruled the NFL for many more years, because it had not only superstars but also one of the deepest rosters in the league, comparable to the great Pittsburgh teams of the 1970s. Its second-team players actually became starters on other teams. For example, Dallas had a record 11 Pro-Bowlers in both the 1993 and the 1994 seasons, four of whom — Russell Maryland, Ken Norton, Thomas Everett, and Mark Stepnoski — ended up playing elsewhere after that due to free agency.

Jimmy Johnson built the offense around quarterback Troy Aikman, running back Emmitt Smith, and wide receiver Michael Irvin. This trio accounted for much of the action, with Smith leading the way with 10,160 yards rushing and 108 touchdowns in his first seven seasons. Aikman is rugged and strong-armed and one of the most efficient quarterbacks in history, plus he owns an 11-2 record in playoff games. Irvin averaged 1,419 yards per season in receiving over a five-year period. The offensive line, led by Larry Allen, Nate Newton, and Eric Williams, remains a powerful entity, while the defensive secondary continues to be one of the best with Deion Sanders, Kevin Smith, and Darren Woodson. Leon Lett ranks as one of the best defensive tackles in the game today.

Green Bay Packers (1965–67)

This team won three consecutive NFL championships and then defeated the American Football League's representatives (Kansas City and Oakland) in the first two Super Bowls, following the 1966 and 1967 regular seasons. The NFL and AFL merged into one league in 1970, making Super Bowl V the first game that actually could be called the NFL championship. What was impressive about these Packer teams was their transformation under head coach Vince Lombardi. Before Lombardi arrived in 1959, the Packers were a 1-10-1 football team. In only one season, Lombardi had these so-called losers competing for the NFL title, and when they won their first championship, 14 of the 22 starters had been with the club during that dismal 1958 season.

Lombardi was characterized as a taskmaster, but most of his players loved him. He was known for his inspirational speeches, and his fighting spirit infected his players so much that they achieved more than seemed realistic at the time. Of course, this team was also blessed with talent. Quarterback Bart Starr flawlessly directed the offense and owned three NFL passing titles. The starting backfield included Hall of Famers Jim Taylor and Paul Hornung, who set an NFL scoring record of 176 points in 1960. The defense was led by a group of Hall of Famers: tackle Henry Jordan, middle linebacker Ray Nitschke, defensive end Willie Davis, and safeties Herb Adderley and Willie Wood. The offensive line was spearheaded by guard Jerry Kramer and tackle Forrest Gregg, a Hall of Famer who also coached his former team for four seasons in the mid-1980s.

Green Bay thoroughly dominated the 1960s and put this tiny Wisconsin town on the national map. After Lombardi's death from cancer on September 3, 1970, the NFL named the Super Bowl trophy in his honor.

Miami Dolphins (1970–74)

Most observers would say that Pittsburgh, Oakland, and Dallas actually fielded better teams in the 1970s. But never mention that in the presence of ex-Miami Dolphins coach Don Shula. Shula, pro football's all-time winningest coach (347-173-6 in 33 seasons), believes that his team deserves to be called the very best of all time.

The 1972 Dolphins are the only unbeaten, untied team in NFL history. Shula's team finished a perfect 17-0-0 when it beat Washington 14-7 in Super Bowl VII. In the perfect season, the Dolphins won three playoff games by an average margin of 5.7 points, not an overpowering number. They repeated as champions in 1973, finishing 15-2, but then they went eight seasons without winning another playoff game.

The only knock on Shula's perfect team was that it was loaded with *good* players, not the *superstar* talent that the Pittsburgh Steelers had in the 1970s, the San Francisco 49ers had in the 1980s, and the Dallas Cowboys had in the early 1990s. Quarterback Bob Griese was hardly the best player in the NFL at his position in this era, considering that Joe Namath was the quarterback of the New York Jets and Roger Staubach was leading the Dallas Cowboys during the 1970s. However, Griese was an accurate passer and superb field general. The backfield featured three runners, all with different and complementary styles: Larry Csonka was a bruising fullback; halfback Jim Kiick was a multipurpose back and blocker; and Mercury Morris ran like his name — an all-out speedster. Now the defense was filled with no-name performers, which is why they were called the "No-Name Defense." Nick Buoniconti, Manny Fernandez, and Jake Scott led this unit, with Scott earning Super Bowl MVP honors for intercepting two passes in Super Bowl VII.

Notre Dame (1946 and 1947)

Even Notre Dame fans can't choose between these two postwar teams that went unbeaten. Both were named national champions. However, the '46 team did play a scoreless tie against Army, which featured two Heisman Trophy–winning running backs in Doc Blanchard and Glenn Davis.

Frank Leahy, whose difficult practices are a part of Notre Dame lore, built this powerhouse that produced an amazing 43 players who eventually played pro football in either the NFL or the All-America Football Conference. In fact, second-team quarterback George Ratterman left after the '46 season to start for the Buffalo Bills rather than play behind All-America Johnny Lujack. Many of the players were veterans of World War II, and some of the second-string players could have been stars at other colleges. Nine players on the '47 Irish team were All-America at some point in their careers. Both Lujack, who was also a superb defensive back, and Leon Hart won the Heisman Trophy. Hart, an end, remains the only lineman to ever win the trophy.

Just consider these rankings of the '46 team: ranked number one nationally in offense and defense, third in pass defense, first in rushing defense, and first in rushing offense. In a nine-game season, the team allowed only four touchdowns, no extra points, and no field goals. The '47 team finished second in total offense but ranked in the top ten in seven other categories.

Both teams featured end Bill Fischer and tackle George Connor, each of whom won the Outland Trophy, emblematic of the best lineman in college football. Connor, who was all-NFL at three positions (offensive tackle, defensive tackle, and linebacker) during his career with the Chicago Bears, was one of the finest interior defensive lineman in the history of Notre Dame. Other stars were Marty Wendell, a linebacker and guard, and Jim Martin, who played end and eventually became an All-America tackle.

Oakland/Los Angeles Raiders (1980–85)

I played for the Raiders and, believe me, I thought we'd be winning or playing in the Super Bowl every year. Before I arrived in Oakland, quarterback Jim Plunkett led the Raiders to victory over the Philadelphia Eagles after the 1980 season. When I joined the team the following year, most of that talent remained. At the end of my third pro season in 1983, we won Super Bowl XVIII, whipping the Washington Redskins 38-9. We won 23 regular-season games over the next two seasons but somehow failed to win another playoff game. The Raiders had to be satisfied with winning two championships during this period, and Plunkett led us both times. Plunkett, a former Heisman Trophy winner at Stanford, was typical of the castoffs from other teams who eventually displayed their skills for the Raiders. Owner Al Davis had an eye for talent, and he always took a chance on a player who'd been a first-round draft choice.

This period signaled the end of the glory years for the Raiders, who did have the best winning percentage in sports for more than 20 years. Our team was highly talented on defense: We had Hall of Fame linebacker Ted Hendricks, the late Lyle Alzado as a pass rusher, Rod Martin and Matt Millen at linebacker, and the best cornerback tandem, Mike Haynes and Lester Hayes, in the league. The offense was loaded, too, with Marcus Allen, who was MVP of Super Bowl XVIII, tight end Todd Christensen, and receiver Cliff Branch. We could stretch a defense with our great offensive speed at the wide receiver position and had the best punter in the league in Ray Guy. I made some great friends on these teams, like nose tackle Bill Pickel, who went to his share of Pro Bowls, and I don't know a tougher, more physical safety than Vann McElroy. Tom Flores, our coach, was especially adept at offensive game plans. We knew who to attack and when.

Pittsburgh Steelers (1974–79)

You could say that this dynasty was built on some of Pittsburgh owner Art Rooney's Irish luck. He wanted to hire Penn State coach Joe Paterno, but Joe said no. Rooney settled for Chuck Noll, who had been an offensive line coach with the Baltimore Colts.

After the 1969 season, a coin flip decided the number-one draft choice. The Chicago Bears called heads; the coin landed tails. The Steelers then drafted a strong-armed quarterback from Louisiana Tech named Terry Bradshaw. With Noll calling the shots and orchestrating the draft and Bradshaw running one of the game's most balanced offenses, the Rooneys made two very fortunate employment decisions. And the rest is history, as they say. Pittsburgh won 80 of 103 total games and four Super Bowls over a six-year reign — a championship hardware collection unmatched in the NFL annals.

Rooney was a beloved owner, and his son, Art Rooney, Jr., headed a scouting department that scoured all the small colleges, including many all-black schools. Key starters like John Stallworth, L. C. Greenwood, and Ernie Holmes came from such schools, and none of them was drafted higher than the fourth round. In 1974, the Steelers' draft included Lynn Swann, Jack Lambert, Stallworth, and Mike Webster — two Hall of Famers (Lambert and Webster) and two (Swann and Stallworth) who have been nominated numerous times only to come up short on the final ballot. Franco Harris and Rocky Bleier, a Vietnam hero, were the running backs, while Bradshaw was spectacular in the Super Bowls. In 1976, the Pittsburgh defense, led by "Mean" Joe Greene and Jack Ham, shut out five teams and allowed four others only 28 points in a nine-game stretch. This team had coaching, charisma, and talent.

San Francisco 49ers (1984–89)

San Francisco was the first club since the Pittsburgh Steelers to win back-to-back Super Bowls, and, all told, this franchise has five NFL championships. From 1984 to 1989, San Francisco was 81-25-1 (.757 winning percentage) and won three Super Bowl championships. This team was built by the resident genius Bill Walsh, who turned the 1989 edition over to George Seifert, who mopped up with a 17-2 record in his first year as a head coach. These 1980s San Francisco teams had two of the greatest offensive players of all time — quarterback Joe Montana (see Figure 25-1) and wide receiver Jerry Rice. Also, running back Roger Craig was one of the sport's best multipurpose performers. In 1985, Craig scored 24 touchdowns and led the team with 1,050 yards rushing and 1,016 yards receiving.

Figure 25-1: Joe Montana led the great 49ers teams of the 1980s. Photo credit: UPI/Corbis-Bettmann.

Montana and Rice could shred any defense, and under Walsh's system, the 49ers played a ball-control offense. They mixed the run and pass to keep opponents guessing and were experts at managing the clock; they wore down opposing defenses by keeping their offense on the field and racking up a lot of points. San Francisco also developed into a fine defensive team, led by safety Ronnie Lott. In Super Bowl XIX, they controlled Miami's high-flying Dan Marino, who had thrown 48 touchdown passes that season. In the latter years, Charles Haley developed into one of the game's most dominant defensive ends, while Lott continued to play at a high level.

Eddie DeBartolo, Jr., was a free-spending owner, and guys wanted to play for this first-class organization during this period. The organization continues today as one of the NFL's finest.

Washington Redskins (1982–91)

I know that my Raider team beat them in Super Bowl XVIII, but that's the only time coach Joe Gibbs and his Redskins (122-49 in this era) lost a championship showdown. The Redskins may not have been as talented across the board as other championship teams, but they were tough, smart, and well coached. In the three Super Bowls that this team won, they outscored the opposition 106-51 and totaled 1,419 yards of offense to the opposition's 786. Translation: The Redskins of this era believed in total dominance. The Redskins of this era were unique because they won with three different starting quarterbacks. Joe Theisman beat Miami in Super Bowl XVII, Doug Williams blitzed Denver in Super Bowl XXII, and Mark Rypien took care of Buffalo in Super Bowl XXVI.

What really set this team apart was its ability to compete in all facets of the game. Beginning with their offensive line, the Redskins were intent on winning every physical battle. The Redskins relished wearing out the opposition, beating them down and finally driving the stake through the opposing team's heart with a long pass completion or some gadget play that Gibbs pulled from his bag of tricks. During this period, the Redskins could hammer a team with running backs like John Riggins, Timmy Smith, and Gerald Riggs. In the first Super Bowl win, Riggins broke open the game with a 43-yard run on fourth down, while Smith ran for a Super Bowl record 204 yards on 22 carries, or 78 more yards than he gained during the regular season.

With such a devastating running attack, the Redskins effectively used play-action passes to keep the opposition off balance. In 1989, Art Monk, Gary Clark, and Ricky Sanders all had 1,000-yard receiving seasons. The defense, which was ably coordinated by Richie Petitbon, had dominant players on the line in tackle Dave Butz and ends Charles Mann and Dexter Manley. And the secondary was led by the incomparable Darrell Green. For the first two Super Bowls, placekicker Mark Moseley decided many a game, finishing his career with 300 field goals. Finally, the last major ingredient of the Redskins' success was Gibbs's coaching staff; it was one of the finest in the NFL, with everyone a Gibbs loyalist.

Appendix
Football Speak

audible: What a quarterback does when he changes the play at the line of scrimmage by calling out prescribed signals to his teammates.

backfield: The group of offensive players — the running backs and quarterback — who line up behind the line of scrimmage.

blitz: A defensive strategy in which a linebacker or defensive back vacates his customary position or responsibility in order to pressure the quarterback. The object of a blitz is to tackle the quarterback behind the line of scrimmage (also known as a *sack*) or force the quarterback to hurry his pass, thus disrupting the offensive play. A blitz generally involves more than four defensive players rushing the quarterback.

bomb: A long pass play in which the passer throws the ball to a receiver between 35 and 40 yards past the line of scrimmage.

bump and run: A technique used by defensive backs to slow down receivers. The defender bumps the receiver at the start of the play and attempts to keep his hands on him legally for 5 yards before running downfield with him.

carry: The act of running with the ball. In statistical charts, a runner's rushing attempts are listed as carries.

center: The offensive player who hikes (or *snaps*) the ball to the quarterback at the start of each play. The term *center* comes from the fact that this player is flanked on either side by a guard and a tackle; he's the middleman (or center) in a contingent of five offensive linemen or blockers. He handles the ball on every play and also snaps the ball to the punter and holder.

completion: A forward pass that's caught in-bounds by an eligible receiver.

cornerback: A defensive player who lines up on one of the wide parts of the field, generally opposite an offensive receiver. He's generally isolated on the "corner" edge of the defensive alignment.

count: The numbers that a quarterback shouts loudly while waiting for the ball to be snapped. The quarterback informs his teammates in the huddle that the ball will be snapped on a certain count.

counter: A running play designed to go against (counter) the intended pursuit of the defense.

defensive back: A member of the defensive secondary. Defensive backs form the line of defense whose job is to prevent receivers from making catches and then making lots of yards after the catch. Safeties, cornerbacks, and nickel backs are considered to be defensive backs.

defensive end: A defensive player who lines up at an end of the defensive line. His job is to contain any run plays to his side and prevent the quarterback from getting outside of him. On passing plays, he rushes the quarterback.

defensive line: The defensive players who play opposite the offensive linemen. The defensive line is made up of *ends, tackles, nose tackles,* and *under tackles.* Defensive linemen disrupt the offense's blocking assignments and are responsible for clogging certain gaps along the line of scrimmage when they are not in position to make the tackle themselves.

defensive tackle: A defensive player who lines up on the interior of the defensive line. His job is to stop the run at the line, or to shoot through the offensive line and make a tackle in the backfield. If he can't make a play, he needs to prevent the opponent's center and guards from running out and blocking the linebackers.

double foul: A situation in which each team commits a foul during the same down.

double-team: To play two defenders against one offensive player in order to prevent him from making a big play. Usually, it's receivers who are double-teamed.

down: A period of action that starts when the ball is put into play and ends when the ball is ruled dead (meaning that the play is over). The offense gets four downs — first, second, third, and fourth — to advance the ball 10 yards. If it fails to do so, it must surrender the ball to the opponent, usually by punting on fourth down.

down lineman: A defensive lineman.

draft: The selecting of mostly collegiate players for entrance into the National Football League. The draft occurs on a weekend in late April. The NFL team with the preceding season's worst record selects first, and the Super Bowl champion selects last. Each team is awarded one selection per round, and there are seven rounds.

draw: A disguised run, which means that it initially looks like a pass play. The offensive linemen retreat back like they're going to pass-protect for the quarterback. The quarterback drops back and, instead of setting up to pass, turns and hands the ball to a running back. The goal of every draw play is for the defensive linemen to come charging after the quarterback, only to be pushed aside by the offensive linemen at the last instant. To fool the defense with this run, a team must have an above-average passing game.

end zone: A 10-yard-long area at both ends of the field — the promised land for a football player. A player in possession of the football scores a touchdown when he crosses the plane of the goal line and enters the end zone. If you're tackled in your own end zone while in possession of the football, the defensive team gets a safety.

extra point: A kick, worth one point, that's typically attempted after every touchdown. The ball is placed on the 2-yard line in the NFL, or the 3-yard line in college or high school, and generally is kicked from inside the 10-yard line. It must sail between the uprights and above the crossbar of the goalpost to be considered good. Also known as the *point after touchdown,* or *PAT.*

fair catch: When the player returning a punt waves his extended arm from side to side over his head. After signaling for a fair catch, a player cannot run with the ball, and those attempting to tackle him can't touch him. However, a player can signal for a fair catch and then allow the ball to sail over his head, hoping that it bounces into the end zone for a touchback. If the returner drops the ball, it's a fumble and can be recovered by anyone. The ball is placed where the player catches the ball. If it rolls into the end zone, the ball is placed on the 20-yard line.

field goal: A kick, worth three points, that can be attempted from anywhere on the field but usually is attempted within 40 yards of the goalpost. Most kickers stand 7 to 8 yards behind the line of scrimmage when striking the ball, which is held by a teammate. Like an extra point, the kick must sail above the crossbar and between the uprights of the goalpost to be considered good. On missed field goals from inside the 20-yard line, the defense takes over at the 20-yard line. On misses outside the 20, the defense takes possession from the spot of the kick.

first down: A team begins every possession of the ball with a first down. The offense must gain 10 yards or more (in four downs) to be awarded another first down. Teams want to earn lots of first downs because doing so means that they are moving the ball toward the opponent's end zone. See also "down."

flanker: A player who catches passes, also known in more general terms as a *wide receiver*. In an offensive formation, he usually lines up outside the tight end, off the line of scrimmage.

flat: The area of the field between the hash marks and the sideline and in close proximity to the line of scrimmage. A pass, generally to a running back, in this particular spot is described as a *flat pass*.

formation: A predetermined setup (or alignment) that the offense or defense uses.

foul: Any violation of a playing rule.

franchise player: In the NFL's current collective bargaining agreement, a player who is designated by his team and must be paid the average salary of the top five players at his position. Football reporters often use this term to describe a superstar player who is invaluable to his team. Detroit Lions running back Barry Sanders, for example, wasn't designated as his team's franchise player, but his unbelievable talent warrants the comment that he's a franchise player — translation, the franchise would be worth nothing without him.

free agency: An opening signing period, usually beginning in mid-February, during which an NFL team can sign any unrestricted player who is without a contract. Teams traditionally bid against one another through an agent for a particular player's services. An unrestricted free agent player is totally unencumbered if he has completed four seasons in the NFL. A restricted free agent player is one who has completed three NFL seasons. Any team signing him would owe some draft-choice compensation to his previous club.

free kick: See "kick."

free safety: A defensive player who lines up the deepest in the secondary. A free safety is the equivalent of baseball's center fielder; he defends the deep middle of the field and seldom has man-to-man responsibilities. A coach wants this player free to read the quarterback and take the proper angle to break up or intercept any forward pass thrown over the middle or deep to the sidelines.

fullback: An offensive player who lines up in the offensive backfield and generally is responsible for blocking for the running back and also pass-blocking to protect the quarterback. Fullbacks are generally bigger than running backs, their counterparts in the backfield. Fullbacks also serve as short-yardage runners.

fumble: When any offensive player loses possession of the football during a play. The ball can simply drop from his hands or accidentally pop free by the force of a tackle. Either the offense (if they're lucky) or the defense (if they're not) can recover the fumble.

gap: The open space between players along the line of scrimmage when they are aligned. For example, there is a wide gap between the offensive guard and tackle.

goalpost: The poles (which are bright gold in the NFL) constructed in a U-shape at the rear of each end zone through which teams score field goals and extra points. The post that holds the U is 10 feet tall and placed approximately 80 feet from any sideline. The *crossbar* (the horizontal bar), which is 18 feet, 6 inches in length, sits atop the post. The two *uprights* (the vertical bars that define the left and right sides of the goalpost) extend 30 feet above the crossbar and are 3 to 4 inches in diameter. A 4-inch x 42-inch ribbon is attached to the top of each upright, giving kickers a sense of the wind.

guard: A member of the offensive line. There are two guards on every play, and they line up on either side of the offensive center. The guards protect the quarterback from an inside pass; they block defenders immediately over them and also swing out (known as *pulling*) and run toward either end, looking to block any defender when the ball carrier runs wide.

halfback: An offensive player who lines up in the backfield and generally is responsible for carrying the ball on run plays. Also known as a *running back* or *tailback*.

hang time: The seconds in which a punted ball remains in the air. If the punt travels 50 yards and is in the air for more than four seconds, that's very good hang time.

handoff: The act of giving the ball to another player. Handoffs usually occur between the quarterback and a running back.

hash marks: The two rows of lines near the center of the field that signify 1 yard on the field. On a professional field, the hash marks are 4 inches wide and located 70 feet, 9 inches from the sidelines. On college and high school fields, they're located 60 feet from the sidelines. Before every play, the ball is marked between or on the hash marks, depending on where the ball carrier was tackled on the preceding play.

hole number: The offensive coaching staff gives a number to each gap or space between the five offensive linemen and the tight end. The players, particularly the running backs, then know which hole they should attempt to run through.

holder: The player who catches the snap from the center and places it down for the placekicker to kick it. A holder is used on field goal and extra point attempts.

huddle: When the 11 players on the field come together to discuss strategy between plays. On offense, the quarterback relays the plays in the huddle, which can be in the form of a semicircle or with teammates lined up in two rows of five facing the quarterback. On defense, the captain, generally a linebacker or secondary player, relays the coach's instructions for the proper alignment and how to defend the expected play.

hurry-up offense: An offensive strategy that's designed to gain as much yardage as possible and then stop the clock. It's generally used in the final two minutes of a half when time is running out on the offense. The offense breaks the huddle quicker and runs to line up in the proper formation, hoping to get off as many plays as possible. Offenses tend to pass in the hurry-up, and receivers are instructed to try to get out-of-bounds, thus stopping the clock.

I formation: An offensive formation that looks like an I because the two running backs line up directly behind the quarterback.

incompletion: A forward pass that falls to the ground because no receiver could catch it, or a pass that a receiver dropped or caught out-of-bounds. After an incompletion, the clock stops and the ball is returned to the same line of scrimmage.

interception: A pass that is caught, and thus stolen from the offense, by a defensive player.

key: Either a specific player or a shift in a particular offensive formation that serves as a clue to a defensive player. From studying a team's tendencies, he immediately knows which play they will attempt to run and to what direction.

kick: A play that occurs after a team is awarded a safety. This term is sometimes used to refer to a placekicker's attempt to kick a field goal or extra point. Also known as a *free kick.*

kickoff: A free kick that puts the ball into play at the start of the first and third periods and after every touchdown and field goal.

lateral: A sideways pass thrown from one offensive player to another. A lateral is not considered a forward pass, so players can lateral to one another beyond the line of scrimmage.

line of scrimmage: The imaginary boundary between the two teams prior to the snap of the ball. The offense's and defense's scrimmage lines are defined by the tip of the ball closest to them and stretch from sideline to sideline. The term implies a play from scrimmage, and the defensive team usually lines up less than a yard away from where the ball is placed.

linebacker: A defensive player who lines up behind the defensive linemen and generally is regarded as one of the team's best tacklers. Depending on the formation, most teams employ either three or four linebackers on every play. Linebackers often have the dual role of defending the run and the pass.

man-to-man coverage: Pass coverage in which every potential offensive receiver is assigned to a particular defender. Each defensive player must stick to his receiver like glue and make sure that he does not catch a pass thrown in his direction.

motion: When an offensive receiver or running back begins to move laterally behind the line of scrimmage — once his teammates have assumed a ready stance and are considered set — he is *in motion.* This motion cannot be forward, and only one player is allowed to move at a time.

neutral zone: The area between the two lines of scrimmage, stretching from sideline to sideline. The width of this area is defined by length of the football. The offensive and defensive teams must remain behind their scrimmage lines.

Other than the center, no player can be in the neutral zone prior to the snap; otherwise, an encroachment or violation of the neutral zone penalty is called.

nickel back: An extra defensive back who is used in some defensive formations. He's referred to as a *nickel back* because he becomes the fifth defensive back on the field.

nose tackle: The defensive player who lines up directly across from the center, or "nose to nose" with him. His job is to defend the middle of the offense against a running play. This position is also called a *nose guard.*

offensive line: The human wall of five men who block for and protect the quarterback and ball carriers. Every line has a center (who snaps the ball), two guards, and two tackles. Teams that run a lot may employ a blocking tight end, too, who also is considered part of the offensive line.

offensive pass interference: A penalty in which, in the judgment of the official, the intended receiver significantly hinders a defensive player's opportunity to catch a forward pass. The offensive player is usually guilty when a pass is thrown inaccurately and he anticipates that the ball will be intercepted. Occasionally, neither the offensive nor the defensive player has gained position and both players, virtually simultaneously, make contact in attempting to catch the ball. This incidental contact is not viewed as a penalty.

officials: The men in the striped shirts (the slang term is *zebras*) who officiate the game and call the penalties. Their decisions are final.

offside: A player is offside when any part of his body is beyond his line of scrimmage or the free kick line when the ball is snapped.

off-tackle: The oldest run around — a byproduct of the old single wing offense of 90 years ago. The off-tackle is a strongside run, meaning that the running back heads toward the end of the line where the tight end, the extra blocker, lines up. The runner wants to take advantage of the hole supplied by the tackle, the tight end, and his running mate, the fullback. He can take the ball either outside the tackle or around the tight end. He hopes that the fullback will block the outside linebacker, giving him room to run.

option: When a quarterback has the choice — the *option* — to either pass or run. The option pass is more common in high school and college football, where quarterbacks may be excellent runners and coaches don't mind them running.

pass interference: A judgment call made by an official who sees a defensive player make contact with the intended receiver before the ball arrives, thus restricting his opportunity to catch the forward pass. The penalty awards the offensive team the ball at the spot of the foul with an automatic first down. See also "offensive pass interference."

PAT: See "extra point."

pigskin: A slang term for the football, which is actually made of leather, not pigskin.

pitch: The act of the quarterback tossing the ball to a running back who is moving laterally away from him toward either end of the line of scrimmage.

placekicker: The player who kicks the ball on kickoffs, extra point attempts, and field goal attempts. Unlike a punter, a place-kicker either uses a tee or kicks the ball while it's being held by a teammate.

play-action pass: A pass play that begins with the quarterback faking a handoff to a running back while he's dropping back to pass. The quarterback hopes that the defense falls for the fake and doesn't rush him.

pocket: An area that extends from a point 2 yards outside of either offensive tackle and includes the tight end if he drops off the line of scrimmage to pass-protect. The pocket extends longitudinally behind the line back to the offensive team's own end line.

point after touchdown: See "extra point."

possession: When a player maintains control of the ball while clearly touching both feet, or any other part of his body other than his hand(s), to the ground in-bounds. A team is also considered in possession of the ball whenever it has the ball on offense. A team's possession ends when it scores, turns over the ball, or punts the ball, or when a half of the game ends.

post: A forward pass that the quarterback throws down the center of the field as the intended receiver attempts to line up with the goalpost.

punt: A kick made when a player (the *punter*) drops the ball and kicks it while it falls toward his foot. A punt is usually made on fourth down. The farther it flies from the line of scrimmage, the better.

punter: The lone player who stands 10 to 12 yards behind the line of scrimmage, catches the long snap from the center, and then kicks the ball after dropping it toward his foot. Occasionally, the same player punts and kicks.

quarterback: The offensive player who receives the ball from the center at the start of each play. Usually, the quarterback is the leader of his team. He informs his teammates in the huddle of the play that will be run and then hands the ball to a running back or throws to a receiver after the ball is snapped to him.

receiver: See "wide receiver."

red zone: The unofficial area from the 20-yard line to the opponent's goal line. Games are won and lost depending on how teams perform in this area; offenses want to score touchdowns, and defenses strive to prevent them from doing so. Holding an opponent to a field goal in this area is considered a moral victory by the defense.

redshirt: A player who skips a year of eligibility due to injury or academic trouble. For example, a *redshirt freshman* is a player who is in his second year of school but is playing his first season of football. Players have four years of eligibility and five years in which to use them, so they can be redshirted only once.

return: To catch the ball after a punt or kickoff and run it back toward your own end zone.

reverse: A play in which the running back receives a handoff from the quarterback and then runs laterally behind the line of scrimmage before handing off to a receiver or flanker running toward him. The offensive line blocks as if the direction of the play is designed for the running back. This play works only if the receiver is a fast and tricky runner and the interior defensive players and linebacker fall for the running back's initial fake.

route: The prescribed direction and exact distance, coupled with specific physical movements, that a receiver follows when he runs from the line of scrimmage for a forward pass. Every receiver has a route that he must run on a particular play.

running back: An offensive player who runs with the football. Running backs also are referred to as *tailbacks, halfbacks, fullbacks,* and *wingbacks,* depending on their exact responsibilities.

sack: To tackle the quarterback behind the line of scrimmage, resulting in a loss of down and yardage. A pass-rusher registering a sack is like a gunslinger registering a notch in his pistol.

safety: A two-point score by the defense that occurs when one of its players tackles an opponent in possession of the ball in his own end zone.

salary cap: The maximum amount of money that a team can spend on player salaries in a given year under a formula that includes base salaries, prorated portions of signing bonuses, and likely-to-be-earned incentives. The salary cap figure is a league-wide number that every team must use. The cap number is 63 percent of designated gross revenue of league-wide income, the bulk of it from network television contracts and stadium ticket sales.

scheme: A slang term used to describe offensive and defensive formations and the overall strategy for using such a formation.

screen pass: A forward pass in which at least two offensive linemen run wide to a specific side of the field and then turn and block upfield for a running back who takes a short pass from the quarterback. A screen pass is effective against defenses who rush the quarterback and play man-to-man coverage in the secondary.

secondary: The four defensive players who line up behind the linebackers and wide on the corners of the field opposite the receivers and basically defend the pass. These defensive players are called *defensive backs,* who are separated into *safeties, cornerbacks,* and, occasionally, *nickel backs.*

shotgun: A passing formation in which the quarterback stands 5 to 7 yards behind the center before the snap. This setup enables the quarterback to scan the defense while standing back from the line of scrimmage.

sidelines: The sides of the field along its long part, where players, coaches, trainers, and the media stand. These areas are not part of the actual playing field; they are considered out-of-bounds.

single-wing formation: An offensive formation devised by legendary coach Pop Warner in 1906 after rules outlawed helping the ball carrier advance the ball by pulling or pushing him. The object was to concentrate great blocking power at the point of attack, which meant that three backfield teammates might block for the player carrying the ball. These days, this formation is never seen in the NFL and is rare even on the youth and high school levels.

slant: A run play in which the runner slants his angle forward after receiving the ball rather than running straight toward the line of scrimmage. This play is used to take advantage of defenses that overpursue, or when an offensive lineman believes that pushing the defensive linemen to one side will be more effective.

snap: The action in which the ball is thrown by the center to the quarterback, to the holder on a kick attempt, or to the punter. With arms extended in front of him, the center grips the ball on the ground and hurtles the ball backward between his legs. Some centers keep their faces pointed forward, and others turn and glance between their legs to make sure of the direction of the snap. After the snap occurs, the ball is officially in play. On most snaps, the quarterback is directly behind the center, placing his hands under that player's behind in order to receive the ball more accurately.

special teams: The 22 players who are on the field during kicks and punts. These units have "special" players who return punts and kicks, and also players who are experts at covering kicks and punts. Most teams have "special" units to block field goal and extra point attempts as well as punts.

spiral: The tight spin on the ball in flight after the quarterback releases it. The term *tight spiral* is often used to describe a solidly thrown football.

split end: A player who catches passes, also known in more general terms as a *wide receiver*. In an offensive formation, the split end usually lines up on the line of scrimmage.

stance: The position that any player assumes prior to the snap of the ball and after he is aligned.

strong safety: A defensive player who generally lines up deep in the secondary, but often aligns close to the line of scrimmage. In most defenses, this player lines up over the tight end and is responsible for both playing the pass and supporting the run. A strong safety usually is bigger and more physical than a free safety and should be a great open-field tackler. See also "free safety."

strong side: The side of the offensive formation where the tight end aligns. With a right-handed quarterback, the strong side is generally to his right side.

stunt: A maneuver by two defensive linemen in which they alter their course to the quarterback, hoping to confuse the offensive linemen and maximize their strengths. In most stunts, one defensive lineman sacrifices himself in hopes of his teammate either going unblocked or gaining a physical advantage in his pursuit.

substitution: The act of a player running onto the playing field, replacing another player. This player is called a *substitute*.

subway alumni: First used to describe the many New York City fans who followed Notre Dame football. The term has since evolved into a description of followers of any college team who didn't attend or graduate from that institution.

sweep: A fairly common run in every team's playbook. It begins with two or more offensive linemen leaving their stances and running toward the outside of the line of scrimmage. The ball carrier takes a handoff from the quarterback and runs parallel to the line of scrimmage, waiting for his blockers to lead the way around the end. This run is designed to attack the defensive end, outside linebacker, and cornerback on a specific side. Most teams that have a right-handed quarterback run the sweep toward the left defensive end. The sweep often begins with the other running back faking a handoff and running in the opposite direction of where the sweep is headed.

tackle: To use your hands and arms to bring down an offensive player who has the ball. *Tackle* also refers to a position on both the defensive and offensive lines. Offensive tackles are outside blockers on the line of scrimmage, whereas on defense the tackles are in the inside position, generally opposite the offensive guards.

takeaway: How a defense describes any possession in which it forces a fumble and recovers the ball or registers an interception. Any turnover that the defense collects is called a takeaway.

tailback: An offensive player whose primary role is to carry the ball. Also known as a *running back* or *halfback*.

tight end: An offensive player who serves as a big receiver and also a blocker. Unlike a wide receiver, this player lines up beside the offensive tackle either to the right or to the left of the quarterback. The side of the field on which the tight end lines up is known as the *strong side*.

touchback: A situation in which the ball is ruled dead on or behind a team's own goal line, provided that the impetus came from an opponent and provided that it is not a touchdown or a missed field goal. After a touchback, the ball is spotted on the offense's 20-yard line.

touchdown: A situation in which any part of the ball, while legally in the possession of a player who is in-bounds, goes on or beyond the plane of the opponent's goal line. A touchdown is worth six points.

trenches: Where the big guys in football butt heads. Think of trench warfare from World War I, with the big guys digging in with their cleats and lowering their heads before crashing into one another.

turnover: A loss of the ball via a fumble or interception.

two-minute warning: The signal that two minutes remain in the half.

veer: A quick-hitting run in which the ball is handed to either running back, whose routes are determined by the slant or charge of the defensive linemen. The term *veer* comes from the back veering away from the defense.

weak side: The side of the offense opposite the side on which the tight end lines up.

wide receiver: An offensive player who uses his speed and quickness to elude defenders and catch the football, but who is not expected to perform dirty deeds like blocking and tackling. One of football's glamour positions. Teams use as many as two to four receivers on every play — more if you count running backs and tight ends who are also eligible to catch a forward pass. Wide receivers also are known as *pass catchers*.

zone coverage: Coverage in which the secondary and linebackers drop away from the line of scrimmage into specific areas when defending a pass play. *Zone* means that the players are defending areas, not specific offensive players.

Index

● ●

● ●

● Z ●

IDG BOOKS WORLDWIDE
BOOK REGISTRATION

We want to hear from you!

Visit **http://my2cents.dummies.com** to register this book and tell us how you liked it!

- Get entered in our monthly prize giveaway.

- Give us feedback about this book — tell us what you like best, what you like least, or maybe what you'd like to ask the author and us to change!

- Let us know any other *...For Dummies*® topics that interest you.

Your feedback helps us determine what books to publish, tells us what coverage to add as we revise our books, and lets us know whether we're meeting your needs as a *...For Dummies* reader. You're our most valuable resource, and what you have to say is important to us!

Not on the Web yet? It's easy to get started with *Dummies 101*®: *The Internet For Windows*® *95* or *The Internet For Dummies*, 5th Edition, at local retailers everywhere.

Or let us know what you think by sending us a letter at the following address:

...For Dummies Book Registration
Dummies Press
7260 Shadeland Station, Suite 100
Indianapolis, IN 46256-3945
Fax 317-596-5498

BUSINESS AND
**GENERAL
REFERENCE
BOOK SERIES
FROM IDG**

**COMPUTER
BOOK SERIES
FROM IDG**

Register This Book and Win!